The Asbury Journal

VOLUME 75 • 2020

Spring & Fall

First Fruits Press
Wilmore, Kentucky
c2020

ISSN 1090-5642
The Asbury Journal

ISBN 9781648170249
Volume 75 • 2020
Includes Number 1 (Spring) and Number 2 (Fall)

Digital version at http://place.asburyseminary.edu/asburyjournal/

For all other uses, contact: First Fruits Press

The Asbury Journal

Wilmore, Ky. : First Fruits Press, c2020.
23 cm.
Semiannual
"The Asbury Journal publishes scholarly essays and book reviews written from a Wesleyan perspective."
Reprint. Previously published: Wilmore, Ky. : Asbury Theological Seminary,
c2020. ISSN 2375-6330
ISBN 9781648170249 (v. 75)
1. Theology -- Periodicals. 2. Methodist Church -- Periodicals. I. Title.
II. Asbury Theological Seminary.
BX8001.A785

First Fruits Press
The Academic Open Press of Asbury Theological Seminary
204 N. Lexington Ave., Wilmore, KY 40390
859-858-2236
first.fruits@asburyseminary.edu
asbury.to/firstfruits

The Asbury Journal

SPRING 2020

VOL.75 . NO.1

The Asbury Journal

EDITOR
Robert Danielson

EDITORIAL BOARD
Kenneth J. Collins
Professor of Historical Theology and Wesley Studies
J. Steven O'Malley
Professor of Methodist Holiness History

EDITORIAL ADVISORY PANEL
William Abraham, *Perkins School of Theology*
David Bundy, *New York Theological Seminary*
Ted Campbell, *Perkins School of Theology*
Hyungkeun Choi, *Seoul Theological University*
Richard Heitzenrater, *Duke University Divinity School*
Scott Kisker, *Wesley Theological Seminary*
Sarah Lancaster, *Methodist Theological School of Ohio*
Gareth Lloyd, *University of Manchester*
Randy Maddox, *Duke University Divinity School*
Nantachai Medjuhon, *Muang Thai Church, Bangkok, Thailand*
Stanley Nwoji, *Pastor, Lagos, Nigeria*
Paul Numrich, *Theological Consortium of Greater Columbus*
Dana Robert, *Boston University*
Howard Snyder, *Manchester Wesley Research Centre*
L. Wesley de Souza, *Candler School of Theology*
Leonard Sweet, *Drew University School of Theology*
Amos Yong, *Regent University*
Hwa Yung, *United Methodist Church, Kuala Lampur, Malaysia*

All inquiries regarding subscriptions, back issues, permissions to reprint, manuscripts for submission, and books for review should be addressed to:

The Asbury Journal
Asbury Theological Seminary
204 N. Lexington Avenue, Wilmore, KY 40390
FAX: 859-858-2375
http://place.asburyseminary.edu/asburyjournal/
© Copyright 2020 by Asbury Theological Seminary

ISSN 1090-5642

The Asbury Journal

VOLUME 75:1

Spring 2020

TABLE OF CONTENTS

Features

The Asbury *Journal*

Timothy C. Tennent
President and Publisher

Douglas Mathews
Provost

The Asbury Journal is a continuation of the Asbury Seminarian (1945-1985, vol. 1-40) and The Asbury Theological Journal (1986-2005, vol. 41-60). Articles in The Asbury Journal are indexed in The Christian Periodical Index and Religion Index One: Periodicals (RIO); book reviews are indexed in Index to Book Reviews in Religion (IBRR). Both RIO and IBRR are published by the American Theological Library Association, 5600 South Woodlawn Avenue, Chicago, IL 60637, and are available online through BRS Information Technologies and DIALOG Information Services. Articles starting with volume 43 are abstracted in Religious and Theological Abstracts and New Testament Abstracts. Volumes in microform of the Asbury Seminarian (vols. 1-40) and the Asbury Theological Journal (vols. 41-60) are available from University Microfilms International, 300 North Zeeb Road, Ann Arbor, Michigan 48106.

The Asbury Journal publishes scholarly essays and book reviews written from a Wesleyan perspective. The Journal's authors and audience reflect the global reality of the Christian church, the holistic nature of Wesleyan thought, and the importance of both theory and practice in addressing the current issues of the day. Authors include Wesleyan scholars, scholars of Wesleyanism/Methodism, and scholars writing on issues of theological and theological education importance.

ISSN 1090-5642

Published in April and October

Articles and reviews may be copied for personal or classroom use. Permission to otherwise reprint essays and reviews must be granted permission by the editor and the author.

The Asbury Journal 75/1: 6-7
© 2020 Asbury Theological Seminary
DOI: 10.7252/Journal.01.2020S.01

From the Editor

I write the introduction to this issue of The Asbury Journal in the middle of a global pandemic, the likes of which has not been experienced by most of those alive today. Classes at Asbury Theological Seminary have shifted online, people are under stay-at-home orders, and churches have been unable to meet for over a month. How do we as the Church respond to such a situation? With churches closed during Easter, we had to think about what it meant to be part of the Body of the resurrected Christ in isolation from each other. It was an odd time, and even though we may be beginning to emerge from it, we can expect the ramifications of this time to reverberate through academia within the Church for the next few years at least. This makes it a perfect time to also look back at history and sideways across cultures to gain some perspective about different issues the Church has faced in the past.

Winfield Bevins sets the stage for this volume by raising the reality of church planting accomplished in England during the height of the Victorian era. We don't often think of that period as a time of rapid church growth in the period of industrialization and rising poverty, but it was. Philip Hardt brings before us the challenges of Methodism at its height in New York City, as it set out to dominate the issue of Catholic schools and the teaching of the Bible in the city, while Samuel Rogal goes back even further to the personal challenges Methodism's founder John Wesley faced in his own tumultuous marriage. Kim Okesson reveals the passion well-known mystery writer Dorothy Sayers brought as a woman and Christian theologian who sought to bring Christ to the masses through her unique insights into communication. Robert Danielson uncovers the challenges faced by a holiness missionary couple in India, who faced a famine and totally changed the way they understood their mission.

As we move from the history of the Church in the West to a more global perspective on cultural crises, Dwight Mutonono examines the cultural challenge of Christians kneeling before leaders in Zimbabwe and Yohan Yong seeks to understand how a common phrase used in the Philippines can either create powerlessness among people, or be transformed to empower them. Finally, in the From the Archives essay, we explore the relationship between an Asbury administrator and academic and Iva Durham Vennard, one of the great holiness women educators, who has often been forgotten by history, but who struggled to raise others, especially women, to reach the world for Christ. Without friends like John Haywood Paul, this might have been an impossible challenge in her day, but together they worked to overcome all kinds of educational barriers.

This issue should remind us that crisis and challenges are not new situations in the Church. Rather, every generation of Christians must direct their attention to new issues both cultural and physical. The Corona Virus epidemic is just one of another continuous stream of trials in a long history of difficulties. The Church will always face challenges, some external and some internal, some personal and some decidedly public, some rooted in our identity, gender, or culture, and some rooted in the unavoidable realities we must rise to face. The commonality is that through the love of God, the good news of Jesus Christ, and the power of the Holy Spirit we can get through such trials. As the Apostle Paul wrote from prison, "...for I have learned in whatever situation I am to be content. I know how to be brought low, and I know how to abound. In any and every circumstance, I have learned the secret of facing plenty and hunger, abundance and need. I can do all things through him who strengthens me" (Philippians 4:11-13 ESV). As a people, our security is in the person of Jesus Christ, our Lord and Savior, not in the situations or calamities that surround us. While everything around us may seem to be crumbling and falling apart, we have the ability to stand contented and without fear, knowing God is the one who holds the future. We can even face Covid-19 and be more than conquerors (Romans 8:37).

Robert Danielson Ph.D.

The Asbury Journal 75/1: 8-22
© 2020 Asbury Theological Seminary
DOI: 10.7252/Journal.01.2020S.02

Winfield Bevins

Victorian Church Planting: A Contemporary Inquiry into a Nineteenth Century Movement

Abstract:

When people think of Victorian England, church planting isn't the first thing that comes to mind. However, there was a significant movement that swept across the country in the mid to late 19th century that resulted in the planting of thousands of new churches that was well documented. The purpose of this article is to demonstrate that there was a church planting movement in England that helped transform the nation in the 19th century. It will examine the causes, characteristics, and trajectory of this movement, while offering a contemporary application of lessons for church planting today.

Keywords: Church planting, 19th century, England, Church of England, Victorian era

Winfield Bevins is the Director of Church Planting at Asbury Theological Seminary, Wilmore, KY. He is the author of several books and is currently pursuing a Ph.D. at the University of Aberdeen, Scotland.

A few years ago, Bishop Stephen Cottrell was having a conversation with a priest who was boasting about his churches 150th anniversary. Cottrell replied to him by saying, "So you're running a church plant?" He goes onto to remind him that, "Every church was planted at some point. Every church owed its existence to the dedicated ministry of a particular group of Christians at a particular time who were seeking to respond to the needs and challenges of their day by establishing some new expression of Christian life."[1]

I had a similar realization on a recent visit to England while teaching on the topic of "church planting in the 21st century." As I looked around London, where hundreds of church buildings were built in the early to mid 19th century, I began to think to myself, "Isn't it ironic that I am teaching on church planting in the 21st century in historic church buildings that had been planted over a hundred years ago." Surely, there is nothing new under the sun. While church planting may be receiving more publicity now than in years past, it is not a passing fad. As a result, I began to do my own personal research on church planting in 19th century in England and what I found was nothing short of inspiring.

Let's be honest, when you hear or think of Victorian England, church planting isn't the first thing that comes to mind. However, as we shall see there was a significant movement that swept across the country in the mid to late 19th century that resulted in the planting of thousands of new churches that was well documented. The purpose of this article is to demonstrate that there was a church planting movement in England that helped transform the nation in the 19th century. It will examine the causes, characteristics, and trajectory of this movement, while offering a contemporary application of lessons for church planting today.

19th Century England

The 19th century, also referred to as the Victorian Era, ushered in an era of unprecedented prosperity to England as well as major cultural change and upheaval. There was vast population growth in major cities like London that was the result of migration from other countries and rising birth rates. There was also tremendous economic development that resulted from the Industrial Revolution. This contributed to increased poverty, pollution, and child labor in factories where children as young as six years old worked hard hours for little or no pay. As towns and cities grew rapidly around factories, problems such as urban crime, poverty, alcohol abuse, prostitution, and high infant mortality increased. It is estimated that nearly 160 babies per 1000 under one-year-old would die each year in England.[2] All of this led to a national concern about the spiritual and moral welfare of England and its future.

The Victorian church responded to the national changes by founding hundreds of religious organizations including church schools, mission, and welfare organizations. Church planting, or church-extension as it was commonly called, was but one solution that the Church of England used to address the growing changes and challenges of the 19th century context. Archbishops of Canterbury William Howley, Charles Longly and Archibald Tate were all supportive and actively involved in the work of church planting in the Church of England in the 1800s.[3] In 1836, Charles James Blomfield, the Bishop of London, issued "Proposals for the creation of a fund to be applied to the building and endowment of additional churches in the metropolis," making provision for new churches and schools to meet the needs of the rapidly increasing population of London with the goal of "expatiating over the whole metropolis by building fifty churches at once."[4] Blomfield aimed to have a church for every 3,000 people and believed that once a church was built that it would have a larger impact on the surrounding community. By the time of his retirement in 1856, 200 new churches were built in the diocese.[5]

On the national front, K. D. M. Snell's social history of England offers a statistical analysis of the establishment of new ecclesiastical parishes in the nineteenth century. Between 1835 and 1896 there were nearly 7,500 new ecclesiastical parishes formed; with two boom years of 1844 (193 parishes) and 1866 (113 parishes). A fifth of all Anglican churches had been built after 1801. In the second half of the century, Snell estimates that at times during the season from 1835 to 1875 new churches were being completed at a staggering rate of one every four days.[6] The number of Church of England churches and chapels increased from under 12,000 in 1831 to well over 17,000 in 1901, with a net increase of nearly 50% over 70 years. It is also important to take into consideration that alongside the construction of entirely new churches, there was extensive rebuilding, extension, and restoration of existing structures.[7]

This wasn't just a top down phenomenon, coming from bishops and the highest levels of leadership in the Church of England, but included a grassroots movement of young emerging leaders. Along with the growing need for church planting, the national context of change and development produced young energetic clergy who were mission minded and open to the work of pioneering new churches not that different from modern day church planters. According to Francis Orr-Ewing,

> A new breed of cleric built on the growing energy of nineteenth-century Britain, harnessed the spiritual vitality of an increasingly confident laity, and took advantage of the increasing flexibility within the structures of the Church of England. Together this led to an unprecedented time of commissioning and building new churches, establishing parishes and forming new ministries and mission organizations.[8]

It is also important to note that churches didn't just build themselves; it required massive amounts of money to be raised for building new churches. As early as 1818, Parliament voted to spend £1 million to help build new churches in areas of population growth, which resulted in a number of new churches in London that included All Souls' Langham Place, Holy Trinity Marylebone Road, St Mary's Bryanston Square, and Christ Church Cosway Street.[9] According to Prof. John Wolffe's calculations, the Victorian Church of England raised something between £3 and £5 billion comparable to 21st century standards just for building new churches, a striking achievement by any standards or time period.[10]

Church planting during this time period was the result of important collaborations between the government, bishops, church planters, as well as donors and key lay people. It could be said "it takes a village to plant a church." One example is Charles James Blomfield, the Bishop of London who we discussed earlier, who helped raise millions of pounds for church planting for churches to reach the growing masses in places like King's Cross, Euston, Paddington, and Bethnal Green. Blomfield worked closely with the Prime Minister, Robert Peel, to raise funds for new churches. Peel passed an Act of Parliament by which over the next sixty years very large numbers of parishes were planted and churches built as the populations of the parishes increased including: 19 in Marylebone, 21 in Paddington, 28 in Kensington, 37 in Islington, 22 in Hackney, and 30 in St Pancras.[11] This could only have been possible with deep collaborative relationships and Kingdom partnerships between clergy, lay people in church, and people in the marketplace working together for the sake of Christ.

Contemporary Lessons for Today

The previous section reveals phenomenal statistical growth related to church planting in Victorian England, which are significant by any measure or standards. This article is not about triumphalism of the past; the Victorian Church was not without its faults or errors. Many have criticized the Victorian church for issues related to colonization and the import of British imperialism. However, this is not the purpose of my paper. There are many sociological and cultural factors that contributed to this movement of church planting, so for the limited scope of this paper I will focus on the lessons that we can learn from this movement in history for the church today.[12]

We find ourselves in another major cultural transition that is no less significant than the industrial revolution. In the United States alone, there are around 180 million who have no connection to a local church, making it one of the fastest growing mission fields in the Western Hemisphere.[13] It is estimated that 660,000 to 700,000 people leave the traditional church every year.[14] In accordance with this trend, the Pew Research Center has noted that nearly one third of young adults now say they have no religious affiliation. This young-adult group is often called the "nones" because they are disavowing association with any organized form of religion, which makes them North America's second largest religious group.[15] In England, Church membership has declined from 10.6 million in 1930 to 5.5 Million in 2010; from about 30% to 11.2%. If current trends continue, membership is forecast to decline to 2.53 million (4.3% of the population) by 2025. The avowedly non-religious – sometimes known as the "nones" – now make up 48.6% of the British population.[16] These are sobering statistics, indicating that massive cultural shifts are on the horizon for today's church. What lessons and insights can we learn from the Victorian church planting movement for today's church that is facing an increasingly global, multicultural, and secularized world?

Anglican's Missionary Heritage

First, traditional churches can and do plant new churches. This case study of church planting in the 19th century reminds us that Anglicanism is an ancient faith tradition that has a rich missionary heritage. Rather than being anti-mission, there is something within the very DNA of the Anglican tradition – rooted in the sacraments – that prepares and compels believers to join in the mission of God. It could be argued that the history of Anglicanism is the history of missions and that mission and church planting is at the very heart of our Anglican heritage.[17] Many great missionary thought leaders have come out of the Anglican tradition, such as John Wesley, William Wilberforce, Henry Venn, Rolland Allen, and Leslie Newbigin, to name a few.

Anglicans can claim Celtic missionaries like Patrick (387–493), who brought the gospel to Ireland, baptized thousands of people, ordained hundreds of ministers, and helped plant hundreds of churches throughout the British Isles. Christianity continued to spread throughout the British Isles like wildfire under the gifted leadership of men such as Columba (521–597). Using their influence, Columba and other Christian leaders established monastic communities in Iona, as did Aidan in Lindisfarne. The churches and monasteries of this movement became some of the most influential missionary centers in all of Europe. Missionaries went out from Ireland to spread the gospel throughout the world. These Irish monasteries helped preserve the Christian faith during the dark ages.

Anglicans can claim a Benedictine monk named Augustine who was sent by Pope Gregory to evangelize the Anglo-Saxons. Due to his influence, many consider Augustine the "Apostle to the English." He eventually arrived in Kent (the southeast corner of England) in 597 with a team of monks. Augustine became the first archbishop of Canterbury and established a center for Christianity in Britain. From that time onward, Canterbury became a hub for sending out missionary bishops across England and beyond.

Anglicanism constituted a missionary faith in the 17th and 18th centuries and expanded rapidly through mission organizations of the Church of England such as the Society for Promoting Christian Knowledge (SPCK, founded in 1698), the Society for the Propagation of the Gospel in Foreign Parts (SPG, founded in 1701), and the Church Missionary Society (CMS, founded in 1799). These Anglican mission organizations helped spread the gospel throughout the world and sowed the seeds for what is now the worldwide Anglican Communion.

Anglicans can claim the Wesleyan revival, which was an Anglican renewal movement that started in the Church of England and quickly grew into a worldwide missionary movement. Starting from only a handful of people, Methodism established hundreds of societies in England and the United States. By the time of John Wesley's death in 1791, the Methodists had become a global church movement with more than 70,000 members in England and more than 40,000 in the new United States and other mission stations around the world.[18] Even though the Church of England could not contain it, the Wesleyan revival stands out as an Anglican renewal movement.[19]

Anglicans can claim the Anglo-Catholic revival of the 19th century that sought to recover the Catholic thought and practice of the Church of England. Centered at the University of Oxford, the proponents of the Oxford Movement believed that the Anglican Church was by history a truly "catholic" church. In time, the ideas of the Oxford movement spread throughout England and into other provinces planting dozens of new Anglo-Catholic expressions of church. The contributions of the Oxford movement can still be seen in Anglican churches around the world today in a variety of ways including: the use of liturgy and ritual in church worship, the central place of the Eucharist in worship, the use of vestments, the importance of ordained ministry, the establishment of Anglican monastic communities for men and for women, and a strong emphasis on the importance of educated clergy.

Finally, the extensive growth of the global Anglican Communion is a testament to the enduring missionary spirit of Anglicanism. Although it started in England, Anglicanism has become one of the world's most multicultural and multiethnic churches. Philip Jenkins reminds us, "By 2050, the global total of Anglicans will be approaching 150 million, of whom only a tiny minority will be White Europeans."[20] Located on every continent, Anglicans speak many languages and hail from different races and cultures. Anglicanism has grown into a worldwide family of churches, which has more than 80 million followers in 161 countries making it the third largest body of Christians in the world. In fact, to be an Anglican is to be a part of a global missionary movement. For instance, there are now more Anglicans worshipping in Nigeria than in England, Canada, and the United States combined.[21] The explosive growth of global Anglicanism has created many new realities that can only be understood through the lenses of mission and church planting.

Diversity of Styles of Church Planting

Secondly, the Victorian church planting movement was diverse and included both evangelical and Anglo-Catholic church plants. At first, these may seem like opposing extremes, but in many ways these different streams are symbiotic and belong together. Former Archbishop Michael Ramsey once said, "For the Anglican Church is committed not to a vague position wherein the Evangelical and the Catholic views are alternatives, but to the scriptural faith wherein both elements are of one."[22] Both the evangelical and Anglo-Catholic streams of Anglicanism were spiritual renewal movements that gave birth to new churches.

Consider the following examples of 19th century church plants. Evangelical church planter Thomas Gaster, was a CMS missionary who served in India and then planted in All Saint Peckham, London in 1867. The church began with about 20 people meeting in the Gaster's sitting room to over 600 adults in the congregation with a children's service for 800 children on Sunday afternoons.[23] An example of an Anglo-Catholic church planter was Richard Temple West who planted St. Mary Magdalene, Paddington in 1865. The first church service register from July 1866, shows three Sunday masses and a daily Mass, with 75-100 Sunday communicants, increasing to about 150 in 1867. From the start, West and his members reached out to the local community and eventually established a convalescent home for the poor in Weymouth Street, off Harrow Road. The church continued to grow under West's leadership and by 1886 the congregation had grown to over 1,000. These are but two great examples of evangelical and Anglo-Catholic church plants in the 19th century.[24]

The different streams of Anglicanism remind us that not everyone looks, acts, or thinks alike. Anglican churches come in all shapes and sizes and are very diverse; ranging from Anglo-Catholics who are more high church, employing a more ceremonial and expanded liturgy, to evangelical Anglicans who are typically more low church, employing fewer ceremonial practices. Regardless of worship styles and preferences, I believe both expressions are vital and can reach people whom the other cannot. We need both working together on mission. Archbishop Justin Welby recently said,

> The real issue of the Christian faith, is not whether we worship in a traditional or radically different way but whether we worship God with commitment and passion that opens our lives to His power to change and renew us. Knowing Him is neither traditional or modern-but it is essential. Why does it have to be one or the other? They're both doing immensely valuable work, and different people are encountering God in each service.[25]

Victorian church planters responded by planting new churches that attempted to meet the pressing needs of their day in innovative new ways, which parallel the current Fresh Expressions movement in a number of ways. Many of the Victorian church plants started in homes, bars, schools, and engaged their local communities in fresh new ways. Many of the planters went into the highways and hedges to go where the church was not, or had not been, such as the slums of the East End of London.[26] Stories abound of the slum priests who ministered to the poorest of the poor and those displaced in society. These were both evangelicals and Anglo-Catholics ministering among the urban poor and the places that needed them most. Many of them utilized nontraditional methods to reach people in their local context.

One story was Reverend Arthur Osborne Montgomery Jay (1858–1945) who had been selected by the bishop of London as Vicar of Holy Trinity, Shoreditch, in late 1886 to reach the outcasts of the Old Nichol district. This district was one of England's worst slums. Nichol was described by one person as "a district of almost solid poverty and low life, in which the houses were as broken down and deplorable as their unfortunate inhabitants."[27] When Jay entered the parish there was no church building; instead services were held in the loft of a stable, which smelt of manure. Jay's first service on New Year's Eve only had 14 people. However, within ten years he had raised enough money to build a church, social club, lodging house, and gymnasium. Jay became controversial for two things: being a high-churchman and for having a boxing ring where many pugilists got their start. By the late 1880s, Jay and others had come to realize that one of the best ways to engage poor men was through boxing. To combat his critics, Jay once preached a sermon at Holy Trinity, called "May a Christian Box?" Some of the boxers who got their start in Jay's gym were Jack the Bender, Lord Dunfunkus, Old Squash, Tommy Irishman, Scrapper, and Donkey. Jay's story shows us that that there is no place where the church cannot go to reach people for Christ.

Ancient Faith, Fresh Mission

Let me end this article with a question that is probably already in your mind. "Is spiritual renewal possible for traditional churches or mainline denominations that are stagnant or in decline?" The answer is yes. One of the most exciting examples that I know of renewal is happening, ironically within the Church of England, the very church that we have been discussing. In the midst of rapid decline in national church attendance, there is a multiplication movement brewing in the Church of England that is bringing renewal to churches and communities across England. In 2015, the former Bishop of London, Richard Chartres, delivered a lecture entitled "New Fire in London" in which he talked about the growth within the Diocese of London through church planting. He shared the following commitment to mission, "We are pledged to establish 100 new worshipping communities in the Diocese in the next five years."[28] To help accomplish this vision, Ric Thorpe was consecrated as bishop of Islington with a special focus on church planting in London. Ric Thorpe oversees London's church growth strategy to plant 100 churches in London by 2020 and 200 city-center church-plants around the country by 2030. Ric's passion is to plant churches in London and across England. "I'm energized by spending time with people who feel God's call to go somewhere else and do something new," Ric said. "Just to spend time with them and to help them articulate the plans that God has for them and to work out what they need to do to go to the next level, and to help them think through what might be next on the horizon." [29]

Ironically, many of the churches that are being planted are in older church buildings that were originally planted in the Victorian era. One example of the churches that Ric helped plant is on the East End of London at St Peter's Anglican Church in Bethnal Green, which sits just off Warner Place, between Old Bethnal Green and Hackney Road. The church spire stands tall amidst the surrounding housing. St Peter's has been a place of worship since 1841 and was on the brink of closing its doors just a few years ago. Members cried out, "We don't want St Peter's to close after we've died."[30] In 2010, the Rev. Adam Atkinson was appointed to lead the church into a new season. Along with others, Adam helped restart the church with the mantra, "Honour the past, navigate change in the present, and build for the future." He began not with change, but with prayer, conversations, and building new relationships. As a result, the old members began to become open to new ideas. In a few years, St Peter's has grown from 20 to over a 100, being highlighted on BBC London News as a model of church renewal and community transformation.

St Peter's Bethnal Green describes themselves as a "cross-tradition" Anglican church, so they worship God in many styles, encountering God through the scriptures, the sacraments, and the Spirit. "We're designed to worship and it matters who we give our worship to." As a church, they have traditional liturgy, follow the church year, observe the sacraments, and use traditional vestments in liturgy. They offer both a high-church as well as an informal style, which helps them reach a wide variety of people including young adults and families. While on the surface they may appear traditional, they are also very non traditional in their outreach to the community. They are engaging their local community with various outreach ministries including: a food bank, employment training program, a credit union, and they have given start-up space to two local businesses. They are even making plans to transform the underground crypt of the church into a recording studio to provide young people with another potential escape from gang violence, which is rampant in Hackney Road. Atkinson is engaged with the larger faith community and helps open the church to the wider community, particularly Bangladeshis. Atkinson has also become friends with the head of East London Mosque.[31] Like Jay, the 19th century priest who built a boxing ring to reach people in his local context, Adam is also using innovation and tradition to reach his local context in fresh new ways.

Today, we stand at another major crossroads of cultural change where the church must once again proclaim the faith afresh for a new generation.[32] We are not called to go where the church is, but to follow the example of these Victorian church planters and find the places where the church is not working for the sake of the gospel through church planting. The Church of England recognizes that one size doesn't fit all, when it comes to church planting and fresh expressions.[33] In 2003, the former Archbishop of Canterbury, Rowan Williams, called for a "mixed economy" of church that would include both traditional and fresh expressions of church to meet the new challenges of a post-Christian and post-modern context. In his own words, "We have begun to recognize that there are many ways in which the reality of 'church' can exist... These may be found particularly in the development of a mixed economy of Church life"[34] This article reminds us that even an ancient faith with historic roots are over a 1,500 year-old period of time can find fresh new ways to plant new churches for a new generation.

End Notes

[1] Stephen Croft, Ian Mobsby, and Stephanie Spellers, editors. *Ancient Faith, Future Mission: Fresh Expressions in the Sacramental Tradition.* (New York: Seabury Books, 2010), 56.

[2] For some resources on the social and religious history of 19th century England see Robert Currie, Alan Gilbert, and Lee Horsley. *Churches and Church-Goers: Patterns of Church Growth in the British Isles since 1700.* (Oxford: Clarendon Press, 1977); K. D. M. Snell, *Parish and Belonging: Community, Identity and Welfare in England and Wales, 1700–1950* (Cambridge, 2006); P. C. Hammond, *The Parson and the Victorian Parish* (London, 1977); B. Heeney, *A Different Kind of Gentleman; Parish Clergy as Professional Men in Early and Mid-Victorian England* (Springfield, 1976); S. J. D. Green, *Religion in the Age of Decline, Organisation and Experience in Industrial Yorkshire, 1870-1920* (Cambridge, 1996).

[3] Archbishops of Canterbury William Howley, Charles Longly and Archibald Tate were all supportive and actively involved in the work of church planting in the Church of England in 1800s. P.G. Maxwell-Stuart, *The Archbishops of Canterbury.* (Gloucester: Tempus, 2006), 238-245.

[4] Warwick William Wroth, "Charles James Blomfield (1786-1857)" from an article published in 1885. http://www.historyhome.co.uk/people/blomfield.htm

[5] See Malcom Johnson, *Bustling Intermeddler: The Life and Work of Charles James Blomfield* (Gracewing, 2001).

[6] K. D. M. Snell, *Parish and Belonging: Community, Identity and Welfare in England and Wales, 1700–1950* (Cambridge, 2006), 409-414). See also J. Wolffe, 'What can the Twenty-First Century Church of England Learn from the Victorians?' *Ecclesiology*, 9 (2013), 205–222, who offers an alternative to the 7,423 numbered by Snell in the 60 years before 1896: "Between 1831 and 1901 it has been estimated that there was a net increase of 5,485 in the total number of Church of England churches, while many of the 12,000 or so churches already standing in 1831 were subjected to extensive restoration and reordering or even complete rebuilding." p. 206, citing A. D. Gilbert, *Religion and Society in Industrial England: Church, Chapel and Social Change 1740-1914* (London, 1976), 28.

[7] Wolffe, "What can the Twenty-First Century Church Learn from the Victorians?" project/projects/What_can_we_learn_from_the_Victorian_Church.pdf

[8] Francis Orr-Ewing. *Rev. Thomas Joseph Gaster: An Urban Missionary in Historical and Theological Context.* PhD dissertation. P. 7.

[9] Cited in a paper by Dr. William M. Jacob, "Church Planting in Victorian England." All Saints' Margaret Street, November 4, 2018. Dr. Jacob is Visiting Research Fellow, King's College London.

[10] John Wolffe, "What can the Twenty-First Century Church Learn from the Victorians?" Hooker Lecture, Exeter Cathedral and Marjon University College, Plymouth. (2010), 7-8. https://www.open.ac.uk/ Arts/building-on-historyproject/projects/What_can_we_learn_from_the_ Victorian_Church.pdf

[11] Cited in a paper by Dr. William M. Jacob, "Church Planting in Victorian England." All Saints' Margaret Street, November 4, 2018.

[12] For some resources on the social and religious history of 19th century England see Robert Currie, Alan Gilbert, and Lee Horsley. *Churches and Church-Goers: Patterns of Church Growth in the British Isles since 1700.* (Oxford: Clarendon Press, 1977); K. D. M. Snell, *Parish and Belonging: Community, Identity and Welfare in England and Wales, 1700– 1950* (Cambridge, 2006); P. C. Hammond, *The Parson and the Victorian Parish* (London, 1977); B. Heeney, *A Different Kind of Gentleman; Parish Clergy as Professional Men in Early and Mid- Victorian England* (Springfield, 1976); S. J. D. Green, *Religion in the Age of Decline, Organisation and Experience in Industrial Yorkshire, 1870-1920* (Cambridge, 1996).

[13] George G. Hunter III, *The Recovery of a Contagious Methodist Movement* (Nashville, TN: Abingdon Press, 2011), 28.

[14] Phil Zuckerman, *Living the Secular Life: New Answers to Old Questions* (New York: Penguin Books, 2015), 60.

[15] For an in-depth study on the spirituality of youth and young adults, see Christian Smith and Melinda Lundquist Denton, *Soul Searching: The Religious Lives and Spiritual Lives of American Teenagers* (Oxford: Oxford University Press, 2005) and Christian Smith and Patricia Snell, *Souls in Transition: The Religious and Spiritual Lives of Emerging Adults* (Oxford: Oxford University Press, 2009). Their findings showed that the majority of youth adhere to a vague understanding of religion, which the authors call "Moralistic Therapeutic Deism" (or "MTD"). For statistics on the over all state of youth involvement in religion among North Americans, the Pew Research Center has observed that about one third of older Millennials— adults currently in their late 20s or early 30s—now say that they have no religion, which is up 9 percent among this age range from 2007. Nearly one quarter of Generation X now say that they have no particular religion, or they describe themselves as "atheists" or "agnostics." See http://www. pewforum.org/2015/05/12/americas-changing-religious-landscape/.

[16] UK Census report on the state of religion in Great Brittan. https://faithsurvey.co.uk/uk-christianity.html.

[17] Bede records the early missionary expansion of the Church of England in *The Ecclesiastical History of the English People* (Oxford, OUP, 2008). Stephen Neil discusses the missionary expansion of Anglican Church in *Anglicanism*. (Baltimore, MD: Penguin Books, 1958). See also the recent statement by the House of

Bishops of the Church of England on Mission and Church Planting. "Planting new churches is a long-established and effective means of establishing the presence of a Christian community to witness to the gospel in new places, and of enabling that witness to be shared with more people in all places. It is integral to how the Church of England has shown its commitment to apostolicity and sought to express its catholicity (see paragraph 1 above). All our churches were once planted. There have been previous periods in Church history of intensive planting of churches: notably for the Church of England in mediaeval times, Queen Anne's 50 New Churches, the Victorian era, and the interwar period." http://www.centreforchurchplanting. org/stories/house-of-bishops/.

[18] See Winfield Bevins, *Marks of a Movement: What the Church Can Learn from the Wesleyan Revival.* (Grand Rapids, MI: Zondervan, 2019). See also Ryan Danker, *Wesley and the Anglicans.* (Downers Grove, IL: IVP Academics, 2017).

[19] Michael Ramsey, *The Anglican Spirit.* (New York: Seabury Classics, 2004), 30.

[20] Phillip Jenkins, *The Next Christendom: The Coming of Global Christianity.* (New York: Oxford Press, 2002), 59.

[21] Timothy Tennent, *Invitation to World Missions: A Trinitarian Missiology for the Twenty-first Century* (Grand Rapids, MI: Kregel, 2010), 31.

[22] Michael Ramsey, *The Gospel and the Catholic Church: Recapturing a Biblical Understanding of the Church as the Body of Christ* (Peabody, MA: Hendrickson Publishers, 2009), 178–79.

[23] For an excellent introduction see Francis Orr-Ewing. *Rev. Thomas Joseph Gaster: An Urban Missionary in Historical and Theological Context.*

[24] The *Religious Census of London,* reprinted from the *British Weekly,* Hodder and Stoughton, London, 1888, p. 32. I am indebted to Dr. William M. Jacob's presentation "Church Planting in Victorian England" for introducing me to the work of West and his work at St. Mary Magdalene.

[25] Justin Welby cited in Andrew Atherstone, *Archbishop Justin Welby: The Road to Canterbury.* (London: Darton, Longman, and Todd, 2013), 48.

[26] See D. B. McIlhiney, *A Gentleman in every Slum: Church of England Missions in East London. 1837-1914.* (Eugene, OR: Wipf & Stock Pub., 1988).

[27] Charles Booth cited in Sara Wise, "Inside the skin of a slum." *Church Times*, December 2018 https://www.churchtimes.co.uk/articles/2008/4-july/news/uk/inside-the-skin-of-a-slum.Sara Wise also wrote *The Blackest Streets: The Life and Death of a Victorian Slum* (Metropolitan Books, 2010).

[28] Richard Chartres, "New Fire in London," Lambeth Lecture, 30 September 2015. http://www.archbishopofcanterbury.org/articles.php/5621/bishop-of-london-delivers-lambeth-lecture-on-church-growth-in-the-capital.

[29] This is taken from an online interview Ric Thorpe gave with Asbury Seminary. See it in full here https://asburyseminary.edu/voices/26615.

[30] Some of this section is from their church website http://www.lovebethnalgreen.com/a-congregation-revived.

[31] See John Bingham, "Vicars should grow beards to reach out to Muslims, bishop suggests." *The Telegraph*. Wednesday 27 February 2019. https://www.telegraph.co.uk/news/religion/12115434/Vicars-should-grow-beards-to-reach-out-to-Muslims-bishop-suggests.html

[32] The phrase "fresh expressions" comes from the preface to the Declaration of Assent, which Church of England ministers make at their ordination to affirm, "which faith the Church is called upon to proclaim afresh in each generation." The term "fresh expressions" echoes these words and suggests, "something new or enlivened is happening, but also suggests connection to history and the developing story of God's work in the Church." Cited in Archbishop's Council on Mission and Public Affairs, *Mission-Shaped Church: Church Planting and Fresh Expressions in a Changing Context.* New York, Seabury Books. 2009), 34.

[33] According to Travis Collins, a fresh expression is "a form of church for our changing culture, established primarily for the benefit of people who are not yet members of any church." Travis Collins, *Fresh Expressions of Church.* (Franklin, TN, Seedbed Publishing. 2015), 5. The key points of emphases within this definition are the ideas of "changing culture" and reaching those not involved in existing churches. The Fresh Expressions movement began in England a little over a decade ago and has resulted in the birth of more than 3,000 new communities alongside existing churches in the United Kingdom. For more information on Fresh Expressions of Church see Winfield Bevins, "Innovative Fresh Expressions of Church." *Innovative Church Planting: Engaging the Marketplace with Entrepreneurial Church Planting,* Glossa House, LLC, and Digit Oral Publishing Services, LLC, 2018.

[34] Archbishop's Council on Mission and Public Affairs, *Mission-Shaped Church: Church Planting and Fresh Expressions in a Changing Context.* New York, Seabury Books. 2009, 26.

The Asbury Journal 75/1: 23-45
© 2020 Asbury Theological Seminary
DOI: 10.7252/Journal.01.2020S.03

Philip F. Hardt
Methodist Political Involvement in the School Bible Issue: the Council, The Christian Advocate and Journal, the Mayor, and the Superintendent of Schools

Abstract:

During the early 1840s in New York City, prominent members of the Methodist Episcopal Church, both lay and clergy, used four political avenues to oppose Roman Catholic efforts to both secure public funds for their own parish schools and also eliminate the daily reading of the King James Bible. These avenues included participation before the Common Council, "political" editorials in the Christian Advocate and Journal, the election of a strongly pro-Bible Methodist mayor, and appointment of a similarly-minded Methodist superintendent of schools. The questions of what caused the Methodists to take such a strong stand and why some compromise could not be achieved are also addressed.

Keywords: Bishop John Hughes, James Harper, David Reese, nativism, New York City schools

Philip F. Hardt is pastor of Glendale Maspeth UMC in Glendale, NY. He received a Ph.D. in Historical Theology (American period) from Fordham University in 1998. His dissertation was published as The Soul of Methodism.

Introduction

Those who are used to Methodism's 20th and early 21st century record of generally taking politically liberal positions will be shocked to learn that the Methodist Episcopal Church (hereafter, MEC) of the mid-19th century could easily be described as the "religious right" of its time. Indeed, it may come as a surprise to 21st century Methodist sensibilities nurtured in the ecumenical movement to know that, in the 1840s, many Methodists in New York City (hereafter, NYC) used the existing political process to strenuously oppose Catholic efforts to change the Protestant-oriented school system. Moreover, these overtly political efforts contrast with the standard Methodist narrative of exponential growth during the first half of the 19th century through evangelistic preaching, camp meetings, tract distribution, book publishing, and missions. Indeed, some well-known NYC Methodists, such as Phoebe Palmer, generally avoided all political involvement so as to focus on spiritual concerns. Yet, during the first part of the 1840s, as Irish Catholic immigration surged in NYC, many Methodist pastors and laity had absolutely no hesitation in leading the political support for the increasingly controversial practice of reading the King James Bible (hereafter, KJB) in the "common schools." This article will show how many NYC Methodists politically supported the Bible issue through their intervention at the Common Council (hereafter, CC), their own editorials in the Christian Advocate and Journal (hereafter, CAJ) editorials, the election of a pro-Bible Methodist mayor, and the appointment of a Methodist superintendent of schools.

Before showing how NYC Methodists practically led the attack, it is necessary to provide the social, political, and religious context for the controversy.

Socio-Cultural Context: Catholic Resistance to Protestant-Oriented "Common Schools"

Denominational "free schools" or "charity schools," as they were sometimes called, and the Public School Society (hereafter, PSS), a multi-denominational voluntary organization, provided the earliest free education for children in NYC. The Methodist "charity school" had been established in the 1790s and the PSS in 1805 as a way to educate any child who could not afford the expensive private schools. A board of trustees and a president governed the PSS and, by 1840, it administered one hundred schools. Denominational schools had ceased to exist in 1824 when the Common

Council voted to stop giving public funds to religious schools. Although the PSS was not sectarian, it did provide moral and religious instruction of a more general type through daily Bible reading, hymns, prayers, and a book of religious exercises based on a question and answer format. This approach, however, was challenged in 1840 as Irish Catholic immigration steadily increased. Due to the Protestant orientation of the common schools, many Irish Catholic parents kept their children either at home or had them attend the eight overcrowded parish schools. Concerned about this problem, Governor William Seward made the education of children a top priority in his annual message to legislators in January 1840 (Bourne 1870: 636-644).

The Political Context

Although this issue began as a strictly local issue, it soon involved three relatively new national political parties: the Democrats, the Whigs, and the American Republican Party (hereafter, ARP). Formed in the 1820s, the Democrats appealed to the working class, welcomed immigrants into their party, and ultimately supported the Catholic cause for change. The Whigs, who began a decade later, had a constituency of businessmen such as manufacturers, shopkeepers, merchants, and ship owners. It also included many conservative Protestant evangelicals since its platform favored such moral issues as temperance and strict observance of the Sabbath. Moreover, its anti-Catholic and anti-immigration positions led it to oppose any change in the Protestant-oriented common schools. The third national party, the ARP, originated in New York City in 1842 with an even stronger anti-Catholic and anti-immigration platform. Unsurprisingly, it also gave vehement support to retaining the KJB in the schools (Reichley 1992: 89-108).

The Intersection of Religion and Politics

From 1840 to 1845, five leading Methodists played critical roles in the "Bible in the Schools" controversy: Dr. Thomas Bond, Rev. George Peck, Rev. Nathan Bangs, James Harper, and Dr. David Reese. In 1840, Bond, Peck, and Bangs, working as a committee, submitted a "remonstrance" to the CC challenging the Catholic petition asking for public funds for their own schools. Bond was a medical doctor from Baltimore and local preacher who had been appointed as editor of the CAJ in 1840. Peck was the new editor of the Methodist Quarterly Review (hereafter MQR). Bangs had served as the first editor of the CAJ from 1828 to 1832 and editor of the MQR beginning in 1832 (Simpson 1878: 86, 116, 698). The fourth key Methodist was James Harper who was born in Newton, Long Island, in 1795 to devout Methodist parents. At age sixteen, he was apprenticed to Abraham Paul, a printer in Manhattan, who was a fellow Methodist. Six years later, he and his brother John started their own printing company, which became Harper and Brothers in 1833. In early 1844, the ARP nominated him as their mayoral candidate due to his strong support for the retention of Bible reading in the schools, which had become a hotly contested issue since 1840. Due to his sterling reputation as a businessman and a devout Christian, he was elected mayor with strong Whig support in April, 1844. During his one-year term, he reformed the police department, improved municipal services, and hired people based on their ability and not on party affiliation (Caliendo 2010: 256-259, 399-401). Finally, Dr. David Reese played a key role in the administration of the public schools. Reese had graduated from medical school and practiced medicine in Baltimore before arriving in NYC in 1820. Reese was a local preacher, a manager of the Missionary Society of the MEC, and president of the Young Men's Missionary Society (1830-1838). In 1844, he was appointed as the superintendent of schools for the city and county of New York where he championed the reading of the KJB in the common schools.

Review of the Literature

Since the public school issue occurred in NYC and had national implications for both the states and the Catholic Church (which eventually formed its own parochial school system), it has generated a significant amount of scholarship with most of it coming from the Catholic authors. This scholarship can be grouped into four main categories. First, primary source materials include the petitions and remonstrances in the published documents of the Board of Aldermen, William Bourne's magisterial History of the Public School Society of the City of New York (1870), and Bishop Hughes' correspondence and addresses. Second, contemporary accounts of the issue can be found in both the religious and secular press of the time and William L. Stone's History of New York City (1868). Third, three biographies (by Catholic authors) of Bishop Hughes present the issue through his perspective. These include Life of the Most Reverend John Hughes (1866) by John Hassard, the bishop's secretary; Dagger John (1977) by Richard Shaw; and Dagger John and the Making of Irish America by

Richard Loughery (2018). Finally, Vincent Lannie's Public Money and Parochial Education (1968) and Gotham, by Edward Burrows and Mike Wallace (1999) provide extremely helpful overviews. To sum up, the primary source materials are abundant and accessible and the Roman Catholic position is thoroughly presented since Bishop Hughes was such a pivotal figure in the development of the Catholic Church in America who also left an extensive amount of letters and other materials. Yet, no scholarly work has yet described the Methodist opposition and attempted an analysis of their efforts.

Methodist Political Involvement (1): The Common Council (1840)
    The first way that Methodists engaged in the political process was their three-pronged campaign over eight months in 1840 to persuade the CC to reject repeated Catholic requests for public funds for their own schools and the elimination of both the KJB and Protestant-oriented textbooks. Spurred on by intense frustration with the anti-Catholic bias of the "common schools" and encouraged by a sympathetic governor (Seward), the Roman Catholic leadership sent a petition to the CC in March, 1840, for assistance who then referred it to the Committee on Arts and Sciences and Schools (Lannie 1968: 32). Alarmed at the Catholic petition and Irish Catholic immigration in general, several denominations sent remonstrances (i.e, counter-petitions) to the council including one by the Methodists, which was "signed by Gilbert Coutant and one thousand and seventy-six others" (Board of Assistants 1840: 378). The Methodist remonstrance noted that in 1824 the CC had ended the policy of giving public funds to denominational schools. Although the Methodists had argued against that new law, it had, along with all the other denominations, accepted the council's decision. The remonstrance further stated its approval of the PSS's administration of the schools and warned the council that giving public funds to Catholic schools would, "in their estimation, be a perversion of the Public School Funds" (Board of Assistants 1840: 378-80). A month later, the committee on the schools urged the rejection of the Catholic petition based on two reasons: the 1824 law and state and federal constitutions that barred public funds for religious groups in an attempt to keep the church and state separate. Unsurprisingly, the council voted sixteen to one to reject it (Lannie 1968: 32-34, 44-48).
    The return, however, of their relatively new bishop, John Hughes, both energized and united the disorganized body of Catholics. Hughes

had been on a fundraising tour of Europe and upon arrival decided that a second more comprehensive petition should be submitted to the CC. During the summer of 1840, Hughes called a series of meetings in which he exhorted his people to stay united and demand their political and civil rights from the council. He also gave a public address explaining the Catholic position to New Yorkers and personally helped draft the second petition. In response, the PSS sent its own remonstrance while "the pastors and churches of the city's MEC formed a committee of three to prepare a further remonstrance against the Catholic claim." (Lannie 1968: 51-70). The Methodist remonstrance was also comprehensive and covered three main areas: the traditional argument against public funds for religious schools; the fear that the Roman Catholic Church would ultimately gain political control and join church and state together as in Europe; and scathing criticism of Hughes for refusing to consider "a book of extracts from the Bible" to be used in place of the KJB. On the second point, the Methodists were not alone as several new nativist political parties were also warning about the threat of Catholic domination (Bourne 1870: 199-201).

Since the CC felt this issue was so important, it held two days of hearings on October 29 and 30, 1840. As in the previous encounter, the three main issues were public funds for religious schools, the KJB, and the anti-Catholic textbooks. After addressing the question of public funds, Bishop Hughes presented two objections to the use of the KJB. First, he felt that the non-denominational approach to the Bible was too generalized since it aimed to be acceptable to all students. Moreover, he believed that the daily reading of the Bible without "note or comment" was dangerous for Catholic students since it lacked the Church's interpretation and teaching. He also feared that this approach might lead some Catholic students to become Protestants or even "infidels" (Bourne, 1870: 288). In contrast, Dr. Bond, speaking for the Methodists, argued that reading a chapter of the Bible each day was designed only to teach the "purest morals in which all agree" (Bourne 1870: 270-271). Similarly, Nathan Bangs asserted that the Bible readings included only "general doctrines" that all Christians believed such as belief in "one Savior, the Holy Spirit, forgiveness of sins, regeneration of the heart by the Holy Spirit, justification by faith, and a future day of judgment" (Bourne 1870: 275).

More importantly, Bishop Hughes objected to the Protestant principle of "private interpretation" which he said had led to the formation of numerous Protestant churches. Moreover, Hughes reiterated that

"Catholics do not believe that God has vouchsafed the promise of the Holy Spirit to every individual, but that he has given His Spirit to teach the Church collectively, and to guide the Church, and therefore we do not receive as the Bible, except what the Church guarantees" (Bourne 1870: 290). In contrast, Dr. Bond pointed out that the PSS was willing to use a book of extracts from the Bible that some Catholic bishops in Ireland had proposed for use in their country although some other Catholic bishops had asked for the pope's approval before consenting to use it. Bond noted that Bishop Hughes had not responded to that offer and speculated that he was waiting for the pope's approval, too, and unable to make the decision himself. Bond felt that since this was an American issue, Bishop Hughes should be able to decide for himself and not depend on a "foreign power" (Bourne 1870: 263-4).

Catholic (Partial) Victory at the State Level

Predictably, three months after the hearing, in January 1841, the CC voted sixteen to one to reject the Catholic petition. Undeterred, and with the open support of Governor Seward, Bishop Hughes and the Catholic leadership sent a third petition to the state legislature. The PSS, too, sent a remonstrance defending their position. Once again, the petition was referred to a committee for study who also sought the opinion of John Spencer, the state superintendent of schools. Spencer also supported some kind of school reform in NYC. Due to its controversial nature, the bill was tabled until the following January (1842).

During the spring of 1842, the committee finally sent its recommendation to the state assembly who passed a version of it and sent it to the senate where it narrowly passed by a vote of thirteen to twelve. The law, however, did not permit public funds for Catholic schools and still permitted the reading of the KJB. At the same time, it put NYC under the statewide "district school system" thereby ending the monopoly of the PSS. Now, each NYC "ward," or election district, would be treated as a separate "town" in which it would elect two commissioners and one inspector who would supervise its schools. In addition, the commissioners from every ward (seventeen in all) would form a citywide Board of Education (Burrows and Wallace 1999: 631).

Although seriously weakened, the Protestant establishment continued to fight to at least keep the KJB in the schools. It did this on two fronts. The first way was through the municipal elections. Even though commissioners were now elected in each ward, "Protestant die-hards quickly won control of the new Board of Education and ruled that classroom reading from the KJB was not precluded by the ban on sectarianism" (Burrows and Wallace 1999: 631). Secondly, the formation of the ARP in 1842 in NYC reinforced the efforts of the Board of Education since along with its anti-immigration and anti-Catholic positions, its platform sought "to prevent the exclusion of the Bible from the use of schools" (1844: 8). Similarly, the ARP's "Address of the General Executive Committee to the People of the United States" stated: "We believe the Holy Bible, without sectarian note or comment, to be a most proper and necessary book, as well as for our children as ourselves, and we are determined that they shall not be deprived of it, either in or out of school" (1845: 10). While the school issue was being debated in the state legislature and before the formation of the ARP, the Methodist weekly newspaper, the CAJ, published two politically tinged editorials condemning not only the Catholic political efforts but the Catholic Church itself.

Methodist Political Involvement (2): The *Christian Advocate and Journal* (1841)

The second way in which Methodists entered in the political arena was through two strongly worded anti-Catholic editorials. Since Dr. Bond was the editor and had been deeply involved in the earlier CC effort, it seems quite probable that he also wrote these strongly worded editorials. The first editorial, "The Romanists and Common Council of NY," was published in the CAJ on February 3, 1841 just a few weeks after the CC had rejected the second Catholic petition. It began with praise for the CC for rejecting what it called "the most preposterous and absurd application" and condemnation for what it saw as Bishop Hughes' political activism. For example, it referred to him as an "American agitator" and an "American O'Connell" referring to a nationalist politician in Ireland. Next, it warned that Catholics would try to get a majority of CC members elected at the next municipal election (in April) who would be favorable to their cause. The editorial lamented that it might be possible since many Protestants seemed uninterested or indifferent due to the high number of "nominal Protestants" and "infidels." Therefore, it urged readers to vote only for those candidates who signed a "pledge" stating that they would support the PSS. More importantly, it argued that if NYC allowed public funds for Catholic schools, it would embolden Catholics in the other two large cities of Baltimore and

Philadelphia. Finally, after pointing out the danger of Protestant students attending Catholic colleges (a fairly common occurrence at this time), it concluded: "We are not sorry that the bishop has opened our eyes to our own folly in committing the education of our children to our enemies – enemies not only of our faith but of our civil institutions."

The second editorial in the CAJ, "Romanism in NY," appeared on November 10, 1841, just two months before the state legislature was to take up the Catholic petition again. This editorial went into even greater depth as to why Catholics should not get public money. The first reason was that the Catholics were asking for too much money. Based on the Irish population being twenty percent, Bishop Hughes had asked for thirty thousand dollars. This amount, however, was not fair since the Catholics, who were generally poorer, paid less in taxes and, therefore, should get less. Second, the editorial voiced concern about those Protestant minority children who would have to attend a majority Catholic school based on the neighborhood population. It warned that Protestant children "...might be inveigled or seduced by Jesuitical artifice, the superstitious dogmas and practices of Popery." Moreover, these children would be taught that they were heretics, "cursed by God and the church," and subject to punishment and even burning at the stake if the Catholics ever acquired total political control. Third, the editorial believed that Catholic and Protestant children should go to school together so that they could mix with each other so thereby becoming "useful citizens" through these "social associations." Moreover, Catholic students who attended the common schools could begin to think for themselves instead of relying on the pope's pronouncements. Finally, the editorial repeated the familiar concern that a Catholic political majority in America would most likely lead to the kind of persecution that had occurred in Europe. This is illustrated in the editorial's final sentence that "under their debasing superstition, they are as ready now as ever a Romanist populace were, before or since the Reformation, to shed the blood of Christian martyrs."

At the same time, not all Methodists believed that the church should involve itself in local politics, even if it was about the Bible. This is illustrated in the period leading up to the municipal elections in April 1842, about five months after the second editorial. Although the state legislature was poised to pass the bill placing NYC schools under the control of the state's "district school system," Protestant supporters of the PSS sought to elect candidates would both repeal the new law, if possible, and retain the

KJB in the schools. An April 5, 1842 article in the New York Evening Post, a Democrat paper, entitled, "Politics in the Churches," described what it considered some questionable political activity that had occurred in three Methodist churches: Forsyth Street, Mulberry Street, and Greene Street. According to the article, notices had been read from the pulpits of these churches inviting members to a meeting to discuss "important business." These notices had come from members who supported the Whigs. At the subsequent meetings "a circular was read requesting that five persons be appointed a committee, to meet in convention this evening, at Constitution Hall, and there to make arrangements for the charter election of next week, with a view to prevent the choice of any candidate for the CC who is supposed to be in favor of a change in the Common School System." In addition, at one of the meetings, a member who was a Whig called for some Democrats to serve on this committee so as to divide the Democrats who usually supported the school changes. The article noted that the purpose of this convention was to elect a Whig majority to the CC; it also condemned the churches' political efforts as "a worse example of the profane union of church government with politics, than any we have had yet." At the same time, it praised the Methodists in those churches who "when they learned the objective of the meeting, they disapproved of it and withdrew. They hold that the church should not thrust herself into ward meetings nor distribute votes at the polls." Despite this minority view, exactly two years later, in April 1844, the Methodists took control of the highest municipal office with the stated intention of retaining the Bible in the schools.

Methodist Political Involvement (3): A Pro-Bible Methodist Mayor (1844-1845)

The third way that Methodists entered the political arena was through the election of James Harper, a dedicated Methodist and publisher, who was an uncompromising supporter of the KJB. To be sure, Harper was a total political newcomer as he had never sought office before but felt public service was a duty he could not shirk if asked. As the April 1844, municipal elections drew near, the ARP nominating committee met with him and offered him the nomination. He had much to commend himself to their party. His credentials included membership in the "Order of United Americans," successful businessman, evangelical Christian, and rigid moralist who opposed drinking, gambling, and prostitution. Moreover, these qualities would strongly appeal to the ARP's constituency of merchants, ship makers, tradesmen, and shopkeepers who were dissatisfied with both Democrats and Whigs. The election results validated their choice as Harper outpolled the LocoFoco candidate (a more radical working class party) by twenty-four thousand six hundred six to twenty thousand seven hundred twenty six. The Whig candidate received slightly more than five thousand votes. A man of his word, in his short victory speech Harper vowed to carry out his responsibilities as mayor "in conformity with the principles of our party" (Harper Papers; Burrows and Wallace 1999: 632; Caliendo 2010: 399).

During the mayor's one year tenure, it does not seem likely that Mayor Harper and Bishop Hughes had any direct personal contact although the bishop attempted at least twice to communicate his concerns to the mayor. The first instance occurred in early May 1844, just after Mayor Harper had been elected but before he began his term. During this time, riots had occurred in Philadelphia between nativists and Irish Catholic immigrants. Several people on both sides had been killed and two Catholic churches had been destroyed. A nativist delegation from Philadelphia was planning to come to NYC to join forces with the nativists in Manhattan and parade through part of the city trying to provoke a riot with the Irish Catholics. Before the day of the planned rally, Bishop Hughes called upon the outgoing mayor, Robert Morris, a Democrat. Bishop Hughes warned him of the potential for violence and advised him to call out the militia. In addition, he gave Mayor Morris the following advice: "Moreover, I should send to Mr. Harper, the mayor-elect who has been chosen by the votes of this party (i.e., the APR). I should remind him that these men are his supporters; I should warn him that if they carry out their design, there will be a riot; and I should urge him to use his influence in preventing this public reception of the (Philadelphia) delegates." It is unknown if Morris contacted Harper, but the leaders called off the rally and violence was averted (Hassard, 278).

The second interaction occurred just a few weeks later when Bishop Hughes sent a long letter (it was later published in pamphlet form) addressed to Mayor Harper but published (!) in The Courier and Enquirer on May 20, 1844. The letter, which was entitled, "On the Moral Causes That Have Produced the Evil Spirit of the Times," attempted to do three things: vindicate his involvement in the school issue, attack the editors of two pro-Protestant papers, and put Mayor Harper "on notice" or even rebuke or warn him because of his association with the ARP. To be sure, Bishop Hughes viewed the ARP basically as an outgrowth of the intense anti-Catholic feeling since the controversial Carroll Hall meeting on October 29, 1841, which he blamed on the combination of two factors: sermons and editorials. In his letter, Hughes asserted that many preachers "had entertained their congregations with political sermons on the school question for months before – so also for months after. Whatever might be the text from the Bible, the abuse of the Catholic religion, under the nickname of popery, together with all the slang, and all the calumnies furnished by the New York Herald, the Commercial Advertiser, the Journal of Commerce, and other papers of that stamp, was sure to make up the body of the sermon." Hughes believed that these repeated assaults had "birthed" the ARP in 1842. Again, he asserted: "By this process the minds of the people were excited, their passions inflamed, their credulity imposed upon, and their confidence perverted. Then came the new party. It is impossible that the training of the pulpits should not have predisposed a large number of persons to join in the movement, which they had been taught to believe as a duty of their religion…Sir, I think I shall be able to prove to you, that these slanders, originating in Bennett's Herald, the Commercial Advertiser, the New York Sun…repeated, embellished and evangelized from many of the pulpits of the City…forming the staple of political excitement, in the association which placed you in the honorable chair you enjoy."

Although Mayor Harper did not respond publicly to Bishop Hughes' measured warning about his party, at least two newspapers rose to his defense. For example, the May 22, 1844 edition of the Journal of Commerce chided Bishop Hughes both for deriding the aims and energy of the new party and also for failing to even offer him congratulations on his victory. In a gently sarcastic admonishment, the paper stated: "Considering that the letter was addressed to the Mayor, some little forbearance might have been expected toward the great movement, which overturning everything in its way, has just placed his Honor in the chair. Gentlemanly courtesy, to say nothing of all the Christian graces, of which the bishop is so conscious, requires this."

James Gordon Bennett also took Bishop Hughes to task in his usual "go for the jugular" way. His immediate response listed three reasons. First, Bennett blamed Hughes for the ARP since he had first injected himself into politics at the Carroll Hall meeting. Bennett mentioned that his editorial the day after the meeting (in 1841) had labeled Hughes a "political agitator" and asserted that this action "has been, not the sole, but one of the chiefest of the causes which have produced the origin of the ARP, and the introduction of religious animosities into politics." Moreover, Bennett feared that Hughes' involvement would lead to two new political parties along religious lines. Second, Bennett felt that, although the ARP had initially been too extremist, it had settled down considerably in the past two years. In the May 22, 1844 edition of the Herald, he assured readers that "the violent, proscriptive, and intolerant declarations of the 'Native Americans' are no longer poured forth in this city. The true...ground of the party is now discerned and occupied by its intelligent and influential members. And the excellent message of Mayor Harper assumes this ground and no other. The achievement of city reform – a just and righteous administration of the laws – fidelity in all respects to the Constitution – these are the great principles on which the new CC declare they intend to act." Finally, Bennett believed that although Harper ran on the ARP ticket, he was a principled man who would not deliberately harm the Catholic population. For example, he related the story of how Mayor Harper had received anonymous letters asking him as a "nativist" and a Protestant to fire one of his female employees who was Catholic. Instead, he promoted her.

In sum, it is not known if the bishop and the mayor had any direct personal contact during his one-year term. The mayor was extremely busy with his mayoral duties and also with his publishing business in his spare moments. He did, however, take one action of immense importance to the school Bible cause: the appointment of Dr. David Reese, a fellow Methodist and close friend of Harper's, to the position of superintendent of schools for the city and county of NYC on September 10, 1844.

Methodist Political Involvement (4): A Methodist Superintendent of Schools (1844-1845)

The final Methodist political intervention occurred during the energetic tenure of Dr. Reese. In just four short months, Reese made a strong case not only to the Board of Education but also to the general public for required Bible reading which had begun to lapse in certain ward schools since the state had begun to intervene. To his credit, Reese took an even-handed approach to the controversial issue. For example, he encouraged the use of the Douay Bible in schools where Catholics were a majority and, unlike other Protestant critics, did not accuse Bishop Hughes of trying to exclude the Bible from the schools (Hassard 1866: 280-281). Before describing his efforts, it is necessary to relate what had occurred from April 1842, to September 1844, when Reese was appointed.

Although the state law had been passed in May 1842, protests and counter protests had followed. For example, on April 11, 1842, in an apparent defensive measure, the Protestant-majority Board of Education had passed a resolution stating, "no school in which any religious or sectarian doctrine or tenet was taught should receive any portion of the school moneys to be distributed by this act." It was aimed at perceived Catholic efforts to get public funds but Bishop Hughes interpreted it as referring to Bible reading since, in his opinion, reading the "Bible was teaching a sectarian doctrine and therefore" he "demanded that the schools in which it was read should not be included" in the funding. In response, Colonel William L. Stone, a Presbyterian, a longtime member of the School Commission and current superintendent of schools, opposed Hughes' interpretation and the two of them carried on a "public discussion," probably in the press, for some time. Agreeing with Stone, the Board of Education amended its earlier resolution on November 13, 1844, stating that "the Bible, without note or comment, is not a sectarian book, and that the reading of a portion of the Scriptures without note or comment, at the opening of the schools, is not inculcating or practicing any religious or sectarian doctrine or tenet of any particular Christian or other religious sect." It was into this turbulent and uncertain new situation that Reese made his argument for reading the Bible in the schools and also urged political action to ensure it (Stone 1868: 507-509).

First, Reese published a pamphlet in October just before the November state elections based on his visitation of the seventeen wards entitled, "To the Board of Education for the City and County of New York – Bible or No Bible! That is the Question." First, he noted the decline of Bible reading in the city's schools. He cited the example of the two commissioners in the Catholic-majority fourteenth ward who had issued a resolution on April 6, 1843 that the Catholic Douay Bible and the KJB were to be read on alternate days. Yet, a month later, they verbally told the teachers that the Bible was "sectarian" and that Bible reading was to stop. Reese also noted that the second resolution was never recorded in the minute book while the first was contained in the minute book. Five other wards – the first, fourth, sixth (another Catholic-majority ward), eleventh, and twelfth – had followed their example. Reese condemned this action as not only in defiance of his authority but also a gross misinterpretation of the existing state law that permitted Bible reading. He called on the Board of Education to condemn this action and "recommend the use of the Holy Scriptures, without note or comment, in all the schools of the city and the county" since the Protestant founders of the schools and current parents of the students both wanted the scriptures used. In addition, he reminded them that they had petitioned the state legislature that ward commissioners "shall not be authorized to exclude the Holy Scriptures, without note or comment, or any selections (i.e., textbooks) therefrom, from any one of the schools." Finally, in a more political vein, he urged his hearers to elect only persons who supported the Bible reading in the schools (1845: 1-6).

Reese's second effort to shore up political support for the Bible issue occurred in his Christmas afternoon address at the Broadway Tabernacle entitled, "Address on Behalf of the Bible in the Schools," with Mayor Harper in attendance. First, he again summed up the current situation: Bible reading occurred in three quarters of all schools but not in four wards which included a student population of two to three thousand. He attributed the absence to two factors: Roman Catholic parents who opposed the KJB and anti-Bible parents who saw the Bible as just an ordinary book. Again, he faulted the Board of Education for lacking the resolve to force these schools to include Bible reading. Another concern was that these four ward commissioners had persuaded the Board of Education to still grant them funds to run their schools. Moreover, these ward commissioners had criticized Reese for being "politically motivated." In response, Reese mentioned that the law permitted "moral and literary" training since the aim of the public schools was not only to educate its youth but also to unify the country. Indeed, Reese argued that the non-sectarian use of the Bible facilitated this since it taught universal morals rather than sectarian doctrine. At the same time, Reese acknowledged that the recent education laws had transferred power from the superintendent to the seventeen ward commissioners making his job more difficult. Nevertheless, he planned to enforce the existing law or cut off their funding. He was ultimately unsuccessful since the Board of Education ruled that he did not have the authority to make Bible reading compulsory (1845: 1-8). Despite his valiant efforts, a new state law (and successful lawsuits) eventually forbade all Bible reading further secularizing the city's schools.

The Puzzle of Methodist Leadership

Although several other clergy from different denominations spoke at the CC's hearing in 1840 and also gave addresses in support of the KJB in their own churches, it is abundantly clear that the Methodists were uniquely positioned to take the undisputed leading role. In the four years, from 1840 to 1844, highly accomplished pastoral and professional Methodists and their church members strove mightily in what eventually turned out to be a losing cause. But, the question remains: Why did the Methodists and not one of the other longer-established denominations take the lead?

Three answers seem possible. The first answer is its sheer size. For example, by the 1840s, the MEC in NYC may have been the largest or one of the largest "newer" denominations. From just three churches in 1800, it had grown to thirteen churches in two circuits. Second, the MEC still retained a high degree of evangelical fervor, which manifested itself in the emphasis on personal conversion, class meetings, and revival meetings. This evangelical fervor would have naturally supported Bible reading in the schools as a way of reinforcing what was taught in the home (often through family prayer) and in their churches. This is illustrated in the 1841 CAJ editorials which lamented the lack of support for the Bible issue from "timid Protestants," "nominal Protestants," and "religious indifferentism." To be sure, the other denominations such as the Episcopal Church had their "evangelical wing" but the Methodists always seemed to be at "fever pitch" when it came to presenting and defending the message of the Gospel. Moreover, some of the older Protestant churches had begun to "liberalize" which led them to focus more on social reform issues such as abolitionism.

Finally, and most importantly, NYC was headquarters for practically all of the national Methodist institutions such as the Mission Society, the Tract Society, and the formidable Book Concern. The location of the Book Concern was especially significant since its highly educated and articulate editors of both the CAJ and the MQR were stationed in Manhattan. This significance was apparent when the MEC appointed two current editors, Dr. Bond and Rev. Peck, and a former editor, Nathan Bangs, to the committee to draft the remonstrance to the Common Council in the fall of 1840. To be sure, these men brought impressive credentials to the debate. For example, Dr. Bond was not only an eminent physician who had been offered a medical professorship, but was also well read in both the English and classical authors. On the pastoral side, he was a local preacher, an author of two apologetic works, and past editor of The Itinerant, a Baltimore church periodical which supported traditional Methodist doctrine and polity. Reverend George Peck also had a distinguished background: presiding elder on two separate occasions, author of several theological treatises including "Scriptural Doctrine of Christian Perfection," and principal of the Oneida (New York) Conference Seminary. Finally, Nathan Bangs had been a missionary to Canada, presiding elder, General Conference delegate, and the previous editor of both the CAJ and the MQR. These were seasoned veterans who had preached, defended, and articulated the faith. Since the most controversial national issues such as African colonization, abolition, and the administration of public schools were often fought first in NYC, the Methodists had their top spokesmen, both lay and clergy, securely in place (Simpson 1878: 85-86, 226, 698).

The Inability to Compromise

In addition to the puzzling question of the Methodists' fervent and unrelenting political pressure, another question comes to mind: "How is it that a compromise on the issues could not be reached?" Why couldn't both sides yield somewhat so that both Catholic and PSS-MEC concerns be accommodated? Since we are so used to living in an "ecumenical age" after the Second Vatican Council, we have to ponder more deeply the radically different realities, hopes and fears of 1840s NYC. Four factors seem to explain this complete intransigence, deep mistrust, and mutual hostility.

First, the question of public funds for a denominational school seemed to the Protestant majority a long-settled issue. The PSS and others argued that if one denomination received school funds that it would open the door to all denominations receiving funds. Moreover, state and federal constitutions had explicitly sought to keep the church and the state separate. In contrast, Bishop Hughes believed it was only fair that Catholics who were taxed should receive some benefit from it. Today, that would be analogous to a "tax voucher" for parents who send their children to a private or religious school which some states now see as reasonable. To be sure, in our 21st century pluralistic society, tax vouchers, although a reasonable compromise, are still resisted by a majority of states revealing an enduring antipathy to supporting private or religious schools with public funds. Of course, American public schools today do not have the overt anti-Catholic and pro-Protestant textbooks and condescending attitudes of the teachers. Sadly, no such compromise on funding could be achieved in the 1840s as the persistent Catholic political efforts only led to mob behavior on both sides and extremely vicious attacks on Bishop Hughes in the press. Although Bishop Hughes hoped that American democratic principles and processes would overcome deep-seated prejudices, it was clearly the wrong time and place. Similarly, in his analysis of the public funding issue, Vincent Lannie has written, "...regardless of the defects of the PSS and the validity of certain Catholic charges, the Catholic position seemed sectarian, unconstitutional, and un-American to the majority of the citizens of that day" (1968: 101).

Secondly, Bishop Hughes was unwilling to compromise on the Bible and textbook issues, which could have at least provided a temporary solution while the state government worked out the details. Predictably, this refusal both frustrated and angered the PSS and its supporters. This refusal to compromise was illustrated at the 1840 hearing. Thomas Sedgwick, one of the two PSS lawyers to speak, suggested that the schools use a book of extracts from the Bible that had recently been approved for use in Ireland although some dissenting bishops had asked for the pope's approval before using it. The following day, at the second hearing, Dr. Bond suggested that Bishop Hughes' silence so far was due to his dependence on what the "foreign power" (i.e., the pope) would say. Although it is not clear how the pope eventually ruled, if he did so at all, Bishop Hughes refused to even consider that suggestion.

Bishop Hughes also rejected the sensible offer of the PSS to revise their textbooks to eliminate any anti-Catholic bias. Bishop Hughes had apparently indicated a willingness to consider their proposal but after they sent him a number of problematic books, he refused to even review them to the consternation of the PSS. In an address, he gave his reasoning: "As if we have nothing to do but to mark out a passage and it will disappear! Are we to take the odium of erasing passages which you hold to be true? And have you any right to make such an offer? If we spend the necessary time in reviewing the books to discover offensive passages, you give us no pledge that you will even then remove the objectionable matter. After all our troubles, you may remove it or not as you see fit" (Hassard 1866: 238). This is all the more surprising since, at one point, Catholic representatives had indicated their own willingness to make concessions such as allowing the PSS to examine their potential teachers, allowing state officials to inspect their schools and textbooks, teaching Catholic doctrine only after school hours, and avoiding criticism of other denominations. In sum, while reasonable people on both sides were willing to put aside their differences, Bishop Hughes apparently only wanted one thing: separate "Catholic public schools" (Hassard 1866: 238-239; Lannie 1968: 112-117).

The third factor that doomed compromise was the depth of mistrust, hostility, and bitterness that many Protestants, including the Methodists, felt toward the Catholic Church despite Bishop Hughes' assurances to the contrary. For example, at the October 1840, hearing, Dr. Bond sharply criticized the Catholic Church for its persecution of Protestants in Europe. In addition, his speech was filled with sarcasm and accusations. Similarly, Hassard noted, "the remonstrance of the Methodists was expressed with a great deal of temper and bristled with sharp epithets" (1866: 235). Put on the defensive at the hearing, Bishop Hughes tried to be conciliatory but also lapsed into sarcasm as well. Later, in an address at a mass meeting of Catholics, he expressed his frustration that the Protestant speakers had ignored the funding issue in order to disparage the Catholic Church. In his address, he said, "No, but the Reverend Dr. Spring, and the Reverend Dr. Bond, and the Reverend Dr. Bangs and company came with an old volume of antiquated theology and exclaimed, 'What monstrous people these papists are!' The CC heard them and instead of examining the facts in which the rights of their constituents are involved, entered on the consideration of abstract theological reasoning" (Hassard, 1866: 239). Richard Shaw, however, blamed both sides for the inability to compromise. Referring also to the October 1840, hearing, he wrote: "The frustrating element of the whole debate was that neither side seemed capable of understanding the limits of their own prejudice or of properly addressing the prejudice of the other...What the arguments did present was a potpourri of the religious antagonisms between native and new-immigrant America" (1977: 147).

Finally, the nativist parties included Bible reading in the public schools as one of their major issues along with anti-immigration, which ensured an even deeper polarization. As Irish Catholic immigration increased, nativists feared they would be more loyal to the pope than to American political institutions. In addition, they feared that a future Catholic majority would persecute Protestants as had happened in Europe. Although Bishop Hughes had raised some good points regarding the civil rights of Catholics, he was facing an avalanche of nativist opposition of which the school issue was just one issue among many. Given the tense political climate of the 1840s, moderating some of his school positions might have won him some Protestant friends instead of earning their enduring hatred.

Conclusion

To sum up, after the PSS itself, the MEC in NYC involved itself in a spectacularly overt political way to fight a Catholic-Democrat political alliance which sought to change the way common schools were administered and, in particular, to eliminate the daily reading of the KJB. This deeper insight of Methodist involvement in one of the great national issues of the day has great significance since it adds more support to the hypothesis that early American Methodism, with its fervent evangelical approach still intact, tended to take politically conservative positions. Some of these included support for nativist political parties, anti-immigration policies (especially against Irish Catholic immigration), African colonization, and opposition to abolition, which was seen as too extreme and divisive. Thus, a majority of early American Methodism, including its leadership and periodicals, can deservedly be seen as the "conservative evangelicals" and the "religious right" of its time.

Yet, more research into Methodism's social, cultural, and political role needs to be done. One possibility is an examination of Methodist involvement in the school issue in Philadelphia and Baltimore, the other two large cities of the time. Both cities struggled with the issue and the Baltimore conference issued a resolution supporting school Bible reading. Another area to explore would be the political affiliations of Methodists in NYC and elsewhere. It would be helpful to know what percentage were members of the various parties such as the Whig, Democrat, LocoFoco, Abolition, and American Republican Party and if that caused division in the local churches (mainly but not only between the business and working classes) and in the conference which often dealt with these "political" issues. The 1830s and 1840s were a particularly volatile period in American history and many riots over various matters occurred in NYC and other major cities. These in-depth studies will provide a more comprehensive and much-needed understanding of Methodism's socio-political impact on the early American republic.

A Chronology of the Bible Issue

1805   Free School Society (later, Public School Society) organizes free schools for the poor

1824   Public funds for denominational "free schools" ended

1840   PSS administers one hundred "common schools" in New York City

March 12, 1840   Roman Catholic Church petitions CC for funds for eight Catholic schools

April 27, 1840   Board of Aldermen reject Catholic petition by sixteen to one vote

Sept. 1840   Bishop Hughes sends second petition to CC for funds

Oct. 29-30, 1840	Common Council holds two day open hearing on petition
January 1841	Governor Seward again calls for NYC school reform
Jan. 11, 1841	CC rejects second Catholic petition for school funds (15-1)
February 1841	Bishop Hughes sends petition for funds to state legislature
April 1841	Spencer recommends elected education commissioners for each ward in NYC
Nov. 3, 1841	Democrats in NYC win state assembly and senate seats
January 1842	State assembly takes up education issue
April 1842	School reform bill passes. NYC placed under state's "district school system"
April 12, 1842	Nativists attack Irish neighborhood and St. Patrick's after municipal elections
April 1844	James Harper, a Methodist, elected mayor of NYC (one year term)
Sept. 10, 1844	Harper appointed Dr. David M. Reese as Superintendent of Schools
Oct. 1844	Dr. Reese's pamphlet, "Bible or No Bible! That is the Question," is published
Dec. 25, 1844	Dr. Reese's gives "Address in Behalf of the Bible in the Schools"
April 1845	Democrat candidate defeats James Harper in mayoral election
1853	Public School Society ceases existence

Works Cited

ARP

    1844   "The Crisis! An Appeal to our Countrymen on the Subject of Foreign Influence in the United States." New York: 201 Broadway.

    1845   "Address of the ARP of the City of New York to the People of the United States." New York: J. F. Trow and Company.

Board of Assistant Aldermen

    1840   *Journal and Documents of the Board of Assistants, of the City of New York.* Vol. 15. New York, NY: Printed by Order of the Board.

Bourne, William

    1870   *History of the Public School Society of the City of New York.* New York, NY: William Wood and Company.

Browne, Joseph H.

    1844   Papers. "John Hughes Biographical Materials." Box 8. Columbia University Rare Book and Manuscripts Library.

Burrows, Edward and Mike Wallace

    1999   *Gotham.* New York, NY: Oxford University Press.

Caliendo, Ralph

    2010   *Part One: The Mayors of New York before 1898.* Xlibris Corporation.

Harper, James

    1844-45   Papers. New York Historical Society.

Hassard, John

    1866   *Life of the Most Reverend John Hughes.* New York, NY: Appleton and Company.

Lannie, Vincent P.

    1968   *Public Money and Parochial Education.* Cleveland, OH: Case Western Reserve University Press.

Reese, David

    1845   "Bible or No Bible! That Is the Question." New York.

    1845   "Address in Behalf of the Bible in the Schools." New York: J. F. Trow & Co.

Reichley, James

    1992   *The Life of the Parties.* New York, NY: Free Press.

Simpson, Matthew
    1878   *Cyclopaedia of Methodism*. Philadelphia, PA: L. H. Everts.

Stone, William L.
    1868   *The History of New York City*. New York, NY: E. Cleave.

The Asbury Journal 75/1: 46-70
© 2020 Asbury Theological Seminary
DOI: 10.7252/Journal.01.2020S.04

Samuel J. Rogal
John and Molly: A Methodist Mismarriage

Abstract:

While not much is known about Mary (Molly) Goldhawk Vazeille, the wife of John Wesley, her story has been interpreted in many ways, and often incorrectly over time. This article explores the historical evidence of her life as a wealthy widow with children who married the founder of Methodism later in life. This contentious relationship is often little understood because of the lack of solid documentation and the multiple interpretations often overlaying the story, which were added by writers with other agendas. It does seem clear that John's brother Charles was especially unhappy with this marriage in the beginning, and the subsequent events in the relationship led to divisions between the couple that have been open to numerous interpretations.

Keywords: Mary (Molly) Goldhawk Vazeille, John Wesley, Charles Wesley, Methodism, marriage

Samuel J. Rogal has served in the faculty and administration of Waynesburg College, Iowa State University, SUNY College at Oswego, Mary Holmes College, and Illinois State University before retiring from the chair of the Division of Humanities and Fine arts at Illinois Valley Community College in 1998. He has been a lifelong scholar of the Wesleys, their hymnody, and 18th century British literature.

Perhaps the lowest point, both literally and figuratively, within the long life of John Wesley (1703-1791) occurred on Monday or Tuesday, February 18 or 19, 1751. A week earlier, Sunday, February 10, on his way, on foot, to preach to the Methodist congregation at Snowsfields chapel, the forty-eight-year-old Wesley proceeded to cross London Bridge, where he suffered a hard fall on the ice, "the bone of my ankle lighting on the top of a stone." Several unidentified persons helped him to the chapel, where he managed to endure through the delivery of a sermon, after which a surgeon bound his leg and "made a shift,"[1] enabling him to stumble to the Methodist chapel in West Street, Seven Dials, where he preached again. From there he took a coach to the home of his friend and financial adviser, Ebenezer Blackwell (1711-1782) in Change Alley, then by chair to the Foundery, Upper Moorfields. However, the sprain and the pain worsened, forcing him into a week of rest, prayer, writing,[2] and conversation at the Threadneedle Street[3] home of forty-one-year-old widowed Mrs. Mary (Molly) Goldhawk Vazeille (1710-1781). Whatever the substance of the conversation, the two of them united in marriage a week later, with Wesley struggling down the aisle on his knees—that fact supported by the Methodist leader noting in his journal for Monday, March 4, 1751, that "Being tolerably able to ride, though not to walk, I set out for Bristol."[4] The exact aisle proves a matter for debate: Luke Tyerman[5] and Nehemiah Curnock[6] determined that the ceremony went forth at the church of the Rev. Charles Manning,[7] a mutual friend of the couple, at Hayes, Middlesex, while John Telford[8] opted for Wandsworth, a section of London where Mrs. Vazeille owned a country house. Although the groom soon would recover, the marriage would remain in a predominately crippled state until, three decades later, the bride passed on to the higher world.

Molly Vazeille Wesley, of Huguenot descent and a resident of London, had been, at some point prior to her marriage to the Methodist leader, a member of a Methodist society in that city. Her union to Anthony[9] Vazeille the elder (?-1747), an affluent London merchant, also of Huguenot descent, had produced four children: Anthony Vazeille the younger (1740?-1754?) appeared to have died prior to his mother's passing in 1781, since her will provided that his younger brother, Noah Vazeille (1746?-?), then residing in Stratford, Essex, receive the house in Threadneedle Street. A third son, not identified by name, died in 1754, while a daughter, Jane (Jeanne) Vazeille Matthews Smith (1736-1820), had married, first, John Matthews (?-1764) of London, and they produced two children—John Matthew the younger and Jane Matthews the younger (1760?-?), the daughter having been baptized by John Wesley in 1760). Jane Matthews Smith then married William Smith (1736-1824), a native of Corbridge, Northumberland, and eventually a steward of the Newcastle-upon-Tyne Methodist circuit—the marriage resulting in the births of Jane Smith (1770-1849) and Mary Smith (1769-1795).[10] In addition to children, Mary Goldhawk Vazeille brought to her second marriage the sum of £10,000 (according to John Telford) settled upon her and her children by way of the departed Anthony Vazeille the elder, that yielded £300 yearly from the Three per Cents—money invested in British government securities and yielding 3% per year. However, later editors of Charles Wesley's correspondence reduced that total sum to £3000.[11]

At this point, before the discussion of this "mismarriage" can go forward, one must be aware of the problems concerning the evidence available. First, there exists nothing in the way of primary sources from Molly Wesley, herself, which, of course, prevents her from offering any defense of her actions. One must remain content to view her through the eyes and minds of others. Secondly, the same holds true for her son, Noah Vazeille, who plays a minor role in the drama. Thirdly, the published editions of John Wesley's journals, as thorough as they might appear, represent extracts— volumes issued years after the actual events and edited by Wesley for publication, but revealing omissions of and gaps in matters that he did not wish to share with his readers. Indeed, the entries for February 18-20, 1751 of those published journals contain no references to the marriage, while entries for February 21-23 simply do not exist. John Telford, who edited eight volumes of John Wesley's correspondence, did not have access to, or chose not to include, all of the letters, while the most recent and thoroughly improved edition of those letters, currently crawling its way to finish line, extends (as of this writing) only to1765. Finally, Charles Wesley plays no small part in the affair, but the fairly recent two-volume publication of his manuscript journal, which he never intended for others' consumption, comes to an abrupt halt after November 1756, and even that collection has serious gaps. The first volume of the most recent edition of his correspondence extends from 1728 to 1756, and (again as of this writing) demonstrates no evidence of a second birth in the near future. One should approach the Wesleys' biographers with caution, and certainly need not bother consulting nineteenth-century editions of the works by either brother.

In any event, Mary Goldhawk Vazeille's introduction to the Wesleys came by way of the brothers' friend, Edward (Ned) Perronet (1721-1792), a native of Sandridge, Kent—the Perronet family themselves of Huguenot descent. The cryptic journal comment by Charles Wesley, entered for Thursday, July 20, 1749, seemingly establishing the tone for the entire affair: "At Ned Perronet's met Ms. Vazeille, a woman of sorrowful spirit."[12] That same summer, the family of Marmaduke Gwynne the elder (1694?-1769), Charles Wesley's father-in-law, beset with financial problems, removed from Garth, Brecknockshire, Wales, to a house in Brand Lane, Ludlow. Sarah Gwynne Wesley, in February 1750 traveled to Ludlow to be with her family. One suspects that Mrs. Vazeille had intensified her Methodist interests and activities during the fall and winter of 1749-1750, both in London and Bristol, for on Tuesday, May 15, 1750, Charles Wesley "set out [from Bristol] with Mrs. Vazeille, &c., for Ludlow, and the next day saluted our friends there. During our nine days' stay, they showed her [Mary Vazeille] all the civility and love that they could show, and she seemed equally pleased with them." From Ludlow, the group, including Mrs. Vazeille, made their way to Oxford, then on to London, and on Saturday, June 2, 1750, Charles and Sarah Gwynne Wesley "took up our quarters for eight or nine days at Mrs. Vazeille's house in Threadneedle Street.[13] Thus, for the remainder of the year, Mrs. Vazeille found herself upon a number of occasions a welcome member of Charles Wesley's Methodist circle.

The question now arises as to when John Wesley entered upon the stage. Unfortunately, specificity does not always have a part in this drama, and one must be prepared to engage in speculation. John Wesley might easily have met Mrs. Vazeille upon one of six occasions, either at London or Bristol, prior to his journey to Ireland in June 1750: July 20, August 1, 1749, at Bristol; August 1-28, 1749, London; October 28- November 8, 1749, Bristol; November 10, 1749- January 29, 1750, London; February 3-27, 1750, London; March 2-20, 1750, Bristol. Thus, his initial letter to her from Dublin, Ireland, dated June 19, 1750 and addressed to her home in Threadneedle Street, could not be considered an initial step upon virgin ground, epistolary or otherwise. Further, the tone and the substance of that letter suggest strongly that the two had met and had exchanged words— conversations that had absolutely nothing to do with the romantic throbbings of the heart. What wended its way through the primitive eighteenth-century British postal system proved nothing less than an epistolary homily:

My Dear Sister

I am glad to hear that you have been with my brother at Ludlow. Sally Perrin[14] sent me a little account of what passed there, and of her proposal to you of taking a longer journey together, if the way should be made plain. I believe riding, so far as your strength will allow, will much confirm your bodily health. And the conversing with those in various parts who know and love God will greatly strengthen your soul. Perhaps, too, he who sendeth by whom he will send[15] may make you useful to some of them. If it be so, I trust it will humble you to the dust: you will so much the more be vile in your own eyes,[16] and cry out, 'Not unto me, O Lord, but unto thy name give the praise!'[17] O let us work for our Lord while the day is: the night cometh, when no man can work.[18] I have gone through calms and storms,[19] rough weather and smooth, since I came into Ireland. But all is good while he walks with us[20] who has all power in heaven and earth.[21] I hope you have some time daily for meditation, reading, and prayer. My dear sister, peace be with your spirit! Next month I hope to be in Bristol...[22]

—which, most likely, will provide an opportunity for another meeting. Indeed, John Wesley arrived in Bristol on Tuesday, July 28, 1750, remaining there until Monday, the 30th of July.

If there exist portraits of Mary Goldhawk Vazeille before or after her marriage to John Wesley, few have been blessed to locate and gaze upon them. Among the fortunate, Mrs. G. Elsie Harrison, among the corps in the between-the-wars parade of biographers of John Wesley,[23] described, after her own fashion, one of those portraits:

At the Methodist Mission House [London] today [c1937-1938] there hangs a picture of the lady. She [the portrait] is discreetly disposed of behind a door in the room which gives the pre-eminence to large representations in colour of John Wesley escaping from the fire [at Epworth rectory, Lincolnshire] and escaping to heaven from his death-bed. Her station is not far removed from Threadneedle Street, which she might glimpse over the head of the modern Methodists as they administer Wesley's World Parish[24] in that great Committee Room. There is a certain dash about her carriage and a look in her eye as of Mona Lisa's enigmatic glance,[25] but the prevailing face is the face of a shrew.[26]

Unfortunately, after reading those lines, one still has not a clear vision of Mrs. Vazeille's physical qualities. Consultation with additional biographers of John Wesley requires one to consider the idiosyncrasies and agendas of each, and then to tread carefully through the observations that will follow. According to Henry Moore (1751-1844), Methodist itinerant preacher and one of the three of John Wesley's literary executors, Mrs. Vazeille, whom he likely knew and observed, "appeared to be truly pious, and was very agreeable in her person and manners. She conformed to every company, whether of the rich or of the poor; and had a remarkable facility and propriety in addressing them concerning their true interests."[27] Richard Watson (1781-1833), formerly president of the Wesleyan Methodist Conference, an historian of Wesleyan Methodism, and a defender of John Wesley, portrayed Mrs. Vazeille as "a woman of cultivated understanding, as her remaining letters testify;[28] and that she appeared to Mr. Wesley to possess every other qualification, which promised to increase both his usefulness and happiness, we may conclude from his having made choice of her as his companion."[29] Thomas Jackson (1783-1873), Methodist itinerant preacher and eventually chair of Divinity at the Theological College, Richmond, Surrey, cast a dark shadow over the character of Mrs. Vazeille, claiming that, "Neither in understanding nor in education was she worthy of the eminent man to whom she was united; and her temper was intolerably bad. During the lifetime of her first husband, she appears to have enjoyed every indulgence; and, judging from some of his letters to her, which have been preserved,[30] he paid an entire deference to her will. Her habits and spirits were ill adapted to the privations and inconveniences which were incident to her new mode of life, as the travelling companion of Mr. John Wesley."[31]

In reviewing the entire affair, Rev. John Hampson the younger (1753-1819), rector of St. John's Church, Sunderland, Durham, and not always a friendly biographer of John Wesley, nonetheless sought a middle ground when he declared, at the outset that,

> The connection was unfortunate. There never was a more preposterous union. It is pretty certain that no love lighted their torches on this occasion; and it is as much to be presumed, that neither did Plutus[32] preside at the solemnity. Mrs. Wesley's property was too inconsiderable, to warrant the supposition that it was a match of interest. Besides, had she been ever so rich, it was nothing to him; for every shilling of her fortune remained at her own disposal; and neither the years, nor the temper of the parties could give any reason to suppose them violently enamoured. That this lady accepted his proposals, seems much less surprising

than that he should have made them. It is probable, his situation at the head of a sect,[33] and the authority it conferred, was not without its charms in the eyes of an ambitious female. But we much wonder, that Mr. Wesley should have appeared so little acquainted with himself and with human nature. He certainly did not possess the conjugal virtues. He had no taste for the tranquility of domestic retirement: while his situation, as an itinerant, left him little leisure for those attentions which are absolutely necessary for the married life.[34]

Two to five years later, John Whitehead (1740-1804), Methodist itinerant preacher turned Quaker and physician, then returned to Methodism, underscored Hampson's observations:

Mr. Wesley's constant habit of travelling, the number of persons who came to visit him wherever he was, and his extensive correspondence, were circumstances unfavourable to that social intercourse, mutual openness and confidence, which form the basis of mutual happiness in the married state. These circumstances, indeed, would not have been so very unfavourable, had he married a woman who could have entered into his views, and have accommodated herself to his situation. But this was not the case. Had he searched the whole kingdom, he would hardly have found a woman more unsuitable in these respects, than she whom he married.[35]

"In no respect was she a helpmeet for him," complained John Wesley's principal nineteenth-century biographer, Luke Tyerman (1820-1889). "At home she was suspicious, jealous, fretful, taunting, twittering, and often violent. Abroad, when itinerating with him, it too generally happened, that nought could please her."[36] Tyerman also found, in his subject's unfortunate marriage, an opportunity for an adult Sunday school lesson, the subject—marriage: "Was there ever a marriage like John Wesley's?" he asked the class.

It was one of the greatest blunders he ever made. A man who attains to the age of forty-eight, without marrying, ought to remain a bachelor for life, inasmuch as he has, almost of necessity, formed habits, and has acquired angularities[37] and excrescences,[38] which will never harmonize with the relationships and the duties of the married state. Besides, if there ever was a man whose mission was so great and so peculiar as to render it inexpedient for him to become a benedict,[39] Wesley was such a man. His marriage was ill advised as well as ill assorted.[40] On both sides, it was, to a culpable extent, hasty, and was contracted without proper and sufficient thought. Young people entering into hurried marriages deserve and incur censure; and if so, what shall be said of Wesley and his wife? They married in haste and had leisure to repent. Their act was, in a high degree, an act of folly; and, properly enough, to the end of life, both of them were made to suffer a serious penalty. It is far from pleasant to pursue the subject; but perhaps it is needful. In a world of danger like this, we must look at beacons, as well as beauties.[41]

In the century following, the agendas of Methodists clerics' reactions to the marriage had given way to the dreams and fantasies of writers who found the distinct line between fiction and biography extremely difficult to locate. For one example, the prolific historical novelist and writer of children's fiction, Gabrielle Margaret Vere Campbell (1886-1952), publishing as "Margaret Bowen,"[42] tried her hand at biography in 1938 and produced a *Life of John Wesley*. Bowen obviously had read Henry Moore and at least had skimmed the pages of Samuel Richardson's epistolary novel *Pamela, or Virtue Rewarded* (1740-1741), and someone, perhaps, had schooled her on the details of eighteenth-century widow's garb. Further, as with a number of psychologists and social historians who have admired John Wesley, Bowen joined with her nineteenth-century predecessors in expressing her displeasure at John Wesley having failed to secure for himself the hand of Grace Norman Murray (1716-1803), the woman he *should have married*, chose, on the rebound, as it were, to settle for Mrs. Vazeille. Thus, Bowen adorned her pages with this overly dramatic image of John Wesley's mate:

> She was middle-aged, seemed of a quiet disposition, meek and pious; she was neither well-educated nor intelligent and had less than the usual share of feminine tact and duplicity; though she was 'able to accommodate to any company in which she found herself.' Molly Vazeille was like Pamela,[43] a servant who had married her master, but she had not the virtues of that fictitious heroine; her husband had pampered her and she had been put to no test of character. She was well off and pious, because a widow could be little else without causing a scandal, and Molly was orthodox with the orthodoxy of the stupid female who thinks her dignity is one with respectability. She had joined the Methodists, as so many women did, for the pleasure of cosy tea-drinkings

with fellow-sinners, and that delightful meddling with other people's businesses which is so delicious to her type when glossed over with religion. John [Wesley] stayed at her house, found her cosy deferential, ardent in good works, a not unworthy successor to his other diaphanous[44] loves. How familiar was that widow's garb worn by his mother[45], Lady Huntingdon,[46] and Grace Murray![47] Mary's bland features looked out from a high pleated cap; she was modestly swathed to the neck in crape, with black robes and sad-coloured shawls. In this attire, suggestive both of the grave and of the angelic garments of the heavenly hosts, women surely looked their best. John [Wesley], who dreaded fine ladies and painted *belles*, found these meek, drab widows the acme of feminine perfection.[48]

Mrs. G. Elsie Harrison's "study" of John Wesley—another fictional recreation under the guise of biography and published in the same year as Mrs. Bowen's effort—emphasizes the women in John Wesley's life.[49] She presented a different portrait of Mary Goldhawk Vazeille—a woman possessed of a keen degree of perception and fully capable of engineering the machinery of villainy, of manipulating Charles Wesley, and of seizing the advantages to be gained from John Wesley's inherent human weaknesses. "Molly Vazeille was ever in the habit of calling a spade a spade," claimed Mrs. Harrison, never one to avoid a cliché. "She had once reigned in Threadneedle Street as a banker's wife,[50] and she was at home in that region of hard currency, of obvious cash and clear-cut values. With the clearest of clear eyes, she saw those early Methodists just as they were and not at all as they fondly[51] hoped they were in the recesses of their own minds." Mrs. Harrison, perhaps more upset at Charles Wesley and his outspoken opposition to his brother's marriage than had been Mrs. Vazeille, harps long and loud as she filters the younger Wesley through the eyes and mind of her *character*, Mrs. Vazeille. In contrast to John Wesley's hard work and self-sacrifice on the Methodist itinerancy, she sketches Charles Wesley within the context of "the fat, rounded face of the complacent and well-fed. . . The Methodists must still see the haloes on their saints, but it is more likely that the picture of Charles Wesley is as clear as Molly Vazeille saw him." Insofar as concerns John Wesley and the constant bickering that came with their marriage, Mrs. Harrison maintained, simply, that "Mrs. Vazeille saw John Wesley as a man and a husband and not at all as God's messenger of salvation."[52]

Actually, biographical and critical perspectives have not undergone radical changes over the more than eight decades following the publications of Mrs. Bowen and Mrs. Harrison. Writing in 1990, Professor Henry Abelove strained his imagination to view the diminutive John Wesley through a gay stereopticon, focusing upon the notion that "with Wesley, religion retained its libidinous and even sexual component." Nonetheless, through whatever the instrument, Abelove cast no new light upon Mrs. Vazeille. generating the currents of his arguments from the usual antiquated fuses: Hampson, Moore, and Jackson, with a generic spark or two from such surveys as Lawrence Stone's *The Family, Sex, and Marriage in England, 1500-1800* (1972). Thus, in the language of the 1990's, Professor Abelove could only inform his readers, as writers before him had conveyed to their readers, that prior to the marriage, Mrs. Vazeille had been on the fringes of the Methodist movement, "Now she observed close up the love that his followers felt for him, and like many others, she could account for a love so deep only on the supposition that Wesley was misbehaving sexually. She grew fretful and jealous, opened his mail, spied on him, forbade him to meet his women followers in private, beat him, and, eventually after seven years of marriage, left him."[53]

A year later, a more reasonable and more informed critical eye appeared to have placed the entire matter into proper context. W. Reginald Ward, an *emeritus* professor of modern history and one of the editors of John Wesley's journals, contended that

> On the surface, Mrs. Vazeille looked to be a suitable candidate for J[ohn]W[esley]'s hand. She was past the age at which she might be accused of evoking a juvenile passion in the great man; she was comfortably provided for, and, by arranging for her property to be settled upon her and her children, JW avoided the reproach of marrying for money encountered by George Whitefield; she had no connection with the gossips of Bristol or Newcastle; and JW repeatedly assured Henry Moore "that it was agreed between him and Mrs. Wesley, previous to their marriage, that he should not preach one sermon less on that account. 'If I thought I should,' said he, 'my dear, as well as I love you, I would never see your face once more.'" (Moore, *Wesley*, 2:173) This was a rash undertaking on the part of a woman who, unlike Grace Murray, had no first-hand experience of the rigours of itinerant life, and one which casts a curious light on JW's commitment to the union. In any case, the marriage began under the worst possible auspices.[54]

Unfortunately, this survey of contemporary and later reactions to the "mismarriage" will come to its end with a statement relative to "beauty," set upon a page of a biography published in the bicentennial year of John Wesley's birth. Rev. Ralph Waller, a Methodist minister described as "a leading authority on the Wesleys," simply and cryptically, and without documentation, described Mary Goldhawk Vazielle as "an attractive woman."[55] Obviously, the well-intentioned Reverend might easily fall into line among those of his predecessors who had, as he, taken their eyes away from Luke Tyerman's "beacon."

If biographers and historians agree, at beast, to interpret the marriage between a Mary Vazeille and John Wesley as social tragedy, they should, as quickly and easily, identify the preliminaries to that union as something akin to stage-like humor. By at least January 1751, if not before, John Wesley most probably had reached a decision to marry. Now, in the natural ways of a well-ordered world, two approaches to reaching such a decision appear most expedient:

> (1) man meets woman, they love each other, they marry;
>
> (2) man or woman determines to marry, he or she consults a catalogue of available potential candidates with whom to unite, selects a mate, proposes marriage, and they marry.

However, English Methodists of the eighteenth century, led and encouraged by John Wesley, complicated the process considerably, particularly as concerned its preachers, by establishing rules. Initially, the preacher had to consult the leadership of the society within his circuit, then with the London Methodist society, and, at some point, seek permission of his intended's parents. In John Wesley's case, he, as a Methodist preacher, also needed to send a letter to all of his preachers and to all of the Methodist societies, stating his reasons for the marriage and asking them for their prayers. Two years earlier, such a bureaucratic labyrinth had delayed, and then presented Charles Wesley with the opportunity to destroy John Wesley's prospect of marriage to Grace Murray. Therefore, the Methodist leader, on January 26, 1751, while at Oxford, circumvented his own process and wrote to his friend Vincent Perronet of Shoreham, Kent, concerning his marital intentions. Returning to London, Wesley noted in his journal for Saturday, February 2, 1751, "Having received a full answer from Mr. Perronet, I was clearly convinced that I ought to marry. For many years I remained single because I believed I could be more useful in a single than in a married state. And I praise God, who enabled me so to do. I now as fully believed that in my present circumstances I might be more useful in a married state, into which, upon this clear conviction, and by the advice of my friends, I entered a few days after."[56] Note that the journal extract entry failed to mention the name of Wesley's intended bride—a strange but not entirely surprising omission. The published journal *Extract* did not reach the press until 1756, at which time relations between John Wesley and his wife had not yet reached the uncomfortable stage.

In any event, on that same Saturday of February 2, 1751, John Wesley sent for Charles Wesley, informing him that,

> ...*he was resolved to marry!* I [Charles Wesley] was thunderstruck, and could only answer he had given me the first blow, and his marriage would come like the *coup de grace.* Trusty Ned [Edward] Perronet followed, and told me the person was Mrs. Vazeille! One of whom I never had the least suspicion. I refused his [Edward Perronet's] company to the chapel and returned to mourn with my faithful [wife] Sally [Sarah Gwynne Wesley]. Groaned all the day, and several following ones, under my own and the people's burden.[57] I could eat no pleasant food, nor preach, nor rest, either by night or by day.[58]

Edward Perronet, in all probability, had received his information from his father, Vincent Perronet, that in the letter to the elder Perronet in late January 1751, John Wesley had mentioned the name of Mrs. Vazeille as his intended wife. It also means, without the same degree of probability that Mrs. Vazeille had agreed to marry John Wesley prior to his seeking advice from Vincent Perronet. No matter who had mentioned what to whom, nor when, the effect of the news upon Charles Wesley proved considerable, particularly in view of having succeeded in having thwarted his brother's efforts at matrimony at Newcastle-upon-Tyne in 1749. Further, he found his already expressed burden intensified by an excessive cough and a severe sore throat, his wife accompanying him with her own expressions of sympathy. On Wednesday, February 6, 1751, John Wesley "met with the single men [of the London Methodist society] and showed them on how many accounts it was good for those who had received that gift God to 'remain single for the kingdom of heaven's sake,'[59] unless where a particular case might be an exception to the general rule"[60]—the general rule being his own.

For more than an entire month, even before the marriage actually occurred, Charles Wesley could not free himself from the reality of his brother's marriage to Mrs. Vazeille, fearing that it would impose severe limitations on the Methodist leader's activities and reduce his stature and effectiveness as the leader of the Methodist organization. For example, on Sunday, February 3, 1751, he "Gave the Sacrament, but without power or life. No comfort in it, no singing between, no prayer after it." Two weeks later, on Sunday, February 17, he "Dragged myself to the [Methodist] chapel, and spoke in those words, 'Thy sun shall no more go down,' etc.[61] The whole congregation seemed infected by my sorrow. Both under the word, and at the Sacrament, we wept and made supplication.[62] It was a blessed mourning to us all. At the Foundery heard my brother's lamentable apology[63] [for his forthcoming marriage], which made us all hide our faces. Several days afterwards I was one of the last that heard of his marriage." Following administration of the Sacrament on Sunday, February 24, Ebenezer Blackwell "fell upon me in a manner peculiar to himself, beating, driving, dragging me to my dear sister." That action on the part of Ebenezer Blackwell might have been an attempt by the Wesleys' friend to reconcile Charles Wesley to his brother's marriage and, at least, to recognize his new sister-in-law. However, Charles Wesley's journal entry for that day ends abruptly, followed by a gap of four days. On Friday, March 1, a Miss Hardy, a London resident and undoubtedly a member of the London Methodist society meeting at the Foundery, related to Charles Wesley "my brother's apology that 'in Oxford he had an independent fellowship, was usually honoured, etc., but left all[64] for the people's sake, returned to London, took up his cross,[65] and married; that at Oxford he had no more thought of a woman than any other animal upon earth, but married to break down the prejudice between the world and him!' His easily won lady sat by. He said, 'I am not more sure than God sent his Son into the world,[66] than it was his will I should marry.'" By Saturday, March 9, Charles Wesley evidenced signs of improvement, stating that he "Felt great emotion in the word, both morning and evening," and on Thursday, March 14, he "Saw the necessity of reconciliation with my brother, and resolved to save the trouble of umpires."[67] Finally, and mercifully, on Saturday, March 16, 1751, Charles Wesley "Called on my sister; kissed and assured her I was perfectly reconciled to her, and to my brother."[68]

A principal problem underlying this marriage began to appear almost immediately following its outset, the source being none other than John Wesley himself. On Tuesday, March 19, 1751, he left Bristol for London, having been "desired by many to spend a few days there before I entered upon my northern journey." Thus, he arrived at London on Thursday the 21st and remained until Wednesday the 27th. "I cannot understand," he opined, "how a Methodist preacher can answer it to God to preach one sermon or to travel one day less in a married than in a single state. In this respect surely 'it remaineth that they who have wives be as though they had none.'"[69] Arriving on that same day at Tetsworth, Oxfordshire, approximately forty miles from London, Wesley attempted to compensate for the separation of time and distance between his wife and him. "My dear Molly, do I write too soon? Have not you, above all the people in the world, a right to hear from me as soon as possibly I can? You have surely a right to every proof of love I can give, and to all the little help which is in my power. For you have given me even your own self." However, John Wesley, at age forty-eight, cannot play extended chords upon the linguistic strings of romance. He quickly falls back upon what he knows best—the sound and the sense of Holy Scripture. "O how can we praise God enough for making us help meet for each other![70] I am utterly astonished at his goodness. Let not only our lips but our lives show forth his praise!"[71] For the remainder of this letter—three of its four paragraphs—Wesley directs his wife to matters of Methodist business that he has left to his wife's charge. The epistle might just as well have been directed to a Methodist itinerant preacher or to a Methodist society elder. How would it have been received by a woman recently married to a man who had spent, during the five weeks or so of their union, more time on the back of his horse than in their marriage bed?

One cannot cite often enough those qualities that dominated the marriage of Molly Vazeille to John Wesley: misunderstanding, jealousy, and outright incompatibility.[72] For example, on Wednesday, January 13, 1771, at London, John Wesley noted, "For what cause I know not to this day, [Mary Wesley][73] set out for Newcastle [to stay with her daughter, Mrs. Jane Vazeille Smith], proposing 'never to return.' *Non eam reliqui, nn dimisi; non revocabo* [I did not desert her; I did not put her away; I will not recall her.]" However, more than a year later, according to Wesley's journal entry for Tuesday, June 30, 1772, Mrs. Wesley had returned to her husband, residing with him in their residences at Bristol and London, and even traveling with him.[74] Then followed six more years of haggling and bickering before Mary Wesley departed from her husband a third time (the second instance in

1775), apparently without informing him in advance of her plans. Thus, he wrote to her one last time, from Bristol on October 2, 1778:[75]

> As it is doubtful, considering your age [68] and mine [75], whether we may meet any more in this world, I think it right to tell you my mind once for all without anger or bitterness. . . .Ever since (and, indeed, long before) you have made my faults the constant mater of your conversation. Now, suppose an husband has many faults, is it the art of a prudent wife to publish or conceal them? You have published my (real or supposed) faults,[76] not to one or two intimates only (though perhaps that would have been too much), but to all Bristol, to all London, to all England, to all Ireland. Yea, you did whatever in you lay to publish it to all the world, thereby designing to put a sword into my enemies' hands. . . .If you were to live a thousand years, you could not undo the mischief that you have done. And till you have done all you can towards it, I bid you farewell.[77]

Interestingly enough, Molly Wesley might not always have acted alone in the display of her "mischief." Late in the game, Noah Vazeille, her youngest child, at some point prior to his mother's death in 1781, assumed residence in Stratford, Essex. Should readers wish to embrace all or parts of Elsie Harrison's soap-opera dramatics within her biography of John Wesley, Noah Vazeille rises as one of the villains of the piece, a devious associate of his equally devious mother. Unfortunately, in scoring the few pages of information about the children of Anthony and Mary Vazielle, one must consider what one discovers and sift it critically through an especially fine strainer. Mrs. Harrison, however, tended to rely upon a process of threading the few crumbs of such facts through her highly charged imagination and projecting before her readers such scenarios as this:

> The whole of the Miss Sophy episode[78] was conned over[79] by Mrs. John Wesley in the company of her son, Noah Vazeille. Together they decided it would make fine printed matter for the papers, and looked for more incriminating manuscripts in the fastness of his [John Wesley's] private desk. The bureau in Wesley's room was broken open and his papers stolen, and there, as one glorious find, the whole of that long treatise on Grace Murray came to light.[80] Noah Vazeille took possession on the instant and carried it in triumph[81] away from the Foundery[82] Later he gave it to a friend, and later still it found its way into the British Museum. It is from that old manuscript with its corrections in the well-known

hand of [John] Wesley that the evidence comes from the friendship of this man and this woman with the background of Alexander [Murray, Grace Murray's husband] the sea captain and wonders of the Grace of God in that unemotional museum collection of England's treasures this strange document holds its place. It is right that it should be there with Diana's Temple and the relics of primitive man, for it is eloquent of the ageless love of man and woman and of their unconquerable faith in the love of God.[83]

After wiping away her own tears of sheer emotion, Mrs. Harrison provided her readers with yet another snippet of Noah Vazeille's chicanery, reporting that Molly Wesley "died in 1781 and was buried without Noah Vazeille informing Wesley of the event."[84] True. John Wesley's journal extract entry for Friday, October 12, 1781, reads, "I came to London and was informed that my wife died on Monday [October 8th]. This evening she was buried, though I was not informed of it until a day or two after."[85] Perhaps Noah Vazeille never extended any effort to inform his stepfather of Mary Wesley's death, but he certainly would not have been the only person aware of that event. Nonetheless, Mrs. Harrison proved herself not content to let the dog sleep. "There is a suggestion," she wrote, "of a blow given and received even at the very last by that angular woman [Molly Wesley]. . . . Well the plotters knew that the leaders of the Methodists ought to have been at his wife's funeral, for was he not known as the apostle of holiness?"[86] The "suggestion," of course, places Noah Vazeille among the plotters. The only problem, insofar as concerns Mrs. Harrison's story, points to the fact that no plot really existed.

Turning to the issue of John Wesley's manuscript account of his relationship with Grace Murray, Mrs. Harrison proved correct, but only on her own terms. Another among her bothersome biographical practices concerns her ignoring the specificity of such mundane items as names and dates. Not wishing to impede the swelling tide of her readers' tears, she clings to generalities—"Later he [Noah Vazeille] gave it [John Wesley's manuscript] to a friend, and later still it found its way into the safe keeping of the British Museum."[87] According to the editors of the *Dictionary of National Biography (DNB)*, Noah Vazeille retained Wesley's autograph account until some time prior to 1788, for in that year it proved to have been in possession of a friend of his, one Naphtaly Hart, who retained it until bequeathing it to the British Museum in 1829.[88] Umphrey Lee (eventually president of Southern Methodist University), who printed a transcript of the manuscript in his 1928 biography (republished in 1954) of John Wesley, differed from the *DNB* account: "The one who gave the manuscript to the museum in 1788," declared Lee, "certified to the fact that Noah Vazeille of Stratford, Essex, had been the original owner, and to the fact that some verses appended to the book are in the handwriting of John Wesley himself."[89] Mrs. Harrison, proclaiming to the last the villainy of Noah Vazeille, maintained that in Grace Murray's last years, she "wanted to get the story of her life which Mr. Wesley had written down from her mouth, but Noah Vazeille had been at his thieving work and that old manuscript found its way into the British Museum instead."[90]

The details of the "mismarriage," upon the vehicles of fact, anecdote, and pure fiction finally ground its way to its obvious and only conclusion. John Wesley provided no evidence of his concern as to when or where his wife would be laid to her final rest. *The Gentleman's Magazine* for October 1781 (51:49), however, most conveniently provided all interested parties with the information: "Died Mrs. M. Wesley, aged 71, wife of Mr. John Wesley, the celebrated Methodist, Oct. 8, 1781," with burial in Camberwell[91] churchyard. Thus, in death, she remained firmly affixed to John Wesley and to Methodism. The inscription on her stone described her, simply and generically, as "a woman of exemplary piety, a tender parent, and a sincere friend." Mary Vazeille Wesley bequeathed to her son, Anthony Vazeille, her money—the sum of which had been reduced from the original £10,000, left to her by her first husband, to £5000. To John Wesley she left a ring!

What came of all of this? From one perspective, not much. Mary Goldhawk Vazeille Wesley managed a leading role in a single scene within the long dramatic narrative of John Wesley's life and work. Their eventual separation deposited her into the deepest bowels of historical oblivion. John Wesley—married, separated, and widowed--continued to lead Methodism as a principal participant in the eighteenth-century evangelical movement; he continued to travel, to preach, to write, to edit, and to educate. He sought to ease poverty, to advance his views on politics, on war, on revolution. He held fast to his determination "to live and to die in the Church of England." Nineteenth-century biographers of John Wesley managed to enlarge their volumes by a chapter, while later biographers and historians of eighteenth-century Methodism extended their works anywhere from a paragraph to a single sentence. From a more significant perspective, perhaps, the "mismarriage" of Mary Goldhawk Vazeille to John Wesley would provide a significant essay by a broadly educated sociologist or psychologist in a large anthology of "mismarriages" between the notables of world history. If nothing else, it would satisfy the insatiable appetites of those who feast upon the failures of others.

End Notes

[1] "Shift" here equals "an expedient device necessitated by circumstances."

[2] The writing consisted of work on the eleven-page *A Short Hebrew Grammar* (1751) and the eighty-two pages of thirty-five Biblical *Lessons for Children, Part IV*, which would not reach the press until 1754.

[3] Threadneedle Street initially recorded in 1598 as Three-Needle Street, then as Thred-Needle-Street in 1616, as Thridneedle Street in 1656, and Threed Needle Street in 1666. Possibly named from the "three needles" that appear in the arms of the Needlemakers' Company, or, more likely, from the thread and needle in the arms of the Merchant Taylors' Company, particularly because the Merchant Taylors' Hall has stood on this street since the fourteenth century. See A.D. Mills, *A Dictionary of London Place Names* (Oxford: Oxford University Press, 2001): 227.

[4] See W. Reginald Ward and Richard P. Heitzenrater (eds.), *The Works of John Wesley. Journal and Diary III (2743-1754)* (Nashville: Abingdon Press, 1991), 20:378-379.

[5] Luke Tyerman, *The Life and Times of the Rev. John Wesley, M.A. Founder of the Methodists* (New York: Harper and Brothers, 1872), 2:101.

[6] Nehemiah Curnock (ed.), *The Journal of the Rev. John Wesley, A.M.* (London: Charles H. Kelly, 1909-1916): 3:515.

[7] Charles Manning (1714-1799), B.A. Gonville and Caius College, Cambridge (B.A, 1736); vicar of Hayes, Middlesex (1738-1756); sympathetic to the Wesleys and the Methodist cause; John Wesley preached in Manning's church on at least fifteen occasions. See Ward and Hetzenrater, *Journal and Diaries III*, in *Works*, 20: 263, 321, 487.

[8] John Telford, *The Life of John Wesley* (London: Hodder and Stoughton, 1886): 253.

[9] Professor Ward identified him as "Anthony" Vazeille—Ward and Heitzenrater, *Journal and Diaries III*, in *Works*, 20:484; John Telford labeled him "Ambrose" Vazeille—John Telford (ed.). *The Letters of John Wesley, A.M.* (London: The Epworth Press, 1931), 3:63.

[10] Ward and Heitzenrater, *Works*, 5:369.

[11] Telford, *Letters*, 3:63; Kenneth G.C. Newport and Gareth Lloyd (eds.), *The Letters of Charles Wesley. Volume I, 1728-1756* (Oxford: Oxford University Press, 2013): 449.

[12] S.T. Kimbrough, Jr., and Kenneth G.C. Newport (eds.), *The Manuscript Journal of the Reverend Charles Wesley, M.A.* (Nashville: Kingswood Books/Abingdon Press, 2007-2008), 2:578.

[13] Kimbrough and Newport, *Manuscript Journal*, 2:594.

[14] Sarah (Sally) Perrin (fl. 1735-1780), initially a resident of Bradford, in the West Riding of Yorkshire, and a Quaker evangelical, moved to Bristol, Gloucestershire, where she eventually became John Wesley's housekeeper. She married John Jones, one of John Wesley's preachers, corresponded consistently with Charles Wesley, and became a leader within Methodist women's bands and prayer meetings.

[15] Exodus 4:13—"And he [Moses] said, O my Lord, send, I pray thee, by the hand of him whom thou will send." (KJV)

[16] Psalms 15:4—"In whose eyes a vile person is contemned; but he honoureth them that fear the Lord. He that sweareth to his own hurt, and changest not." (KJV)

[17] Psalms 115:1—"Not unto us, O Lord, not unto us, but unto thy name give the praise: for thy loving mercy, and for thy truths sake." (BCP) "Not unto us, Lord, not unto us, but unto thy name give glory, for thy mercy and for thy truth's sake." (KJV)

[18] John 9:4—"I [Jesus Christ] must work the works of him that sent me, while it is day: the night cometh, when no man can work." (KJV)

[19] Luke 8:24—"And they [Jesus Christ's disciples] came to him [Jesus Christ], and awoke him, saying, Master, Master, we perish, then he rose and rebuked the wind and the raging of the water: and they ceased, and there was a calm." (KJV)

[20] Galatians 5:25—"If we live in the Spirit, let us also walk in the Spirit." (KJV) Philippians 3:16-17—"Nevertheless, whereto we have already attained, let us walk by the same rule, let us mind the same thing. Brethren, be followers together of me [Paul], and mark them which walk so as ye have us an example." (KJV)

[21] Matthew 28:18—"And Jesus came and spake unto them [the disciples], saying, All power is given unto me in heaven and in earth." (KJV)

[22] Frank Baker (ed.), *The Works of John Wesley. Volume 26. Letters II, 1740-1755)* (Oxford: Clarendon Press, 1982): 429-430.

[23] *Son to Susanna. The Private Life of John Wesley* (Nashville: Cokesbury Press, 1938), by G. Elsie Harrison, daughter of Dr. J. S. Simon,

principal of Didsbury College, and the wife of Rev. Archibald Walter Harrison (1882-1946), Methodist minister and educator.

²⁴ "I look upon *all the world as my parish*: thus far I mean, that in whatever part of it I am, I judge it meet, right, and my bounden duty, to declare unto all that are willing to hear the glad tidings of salvation." John Wesley, Monday, June 11, 1739 (Ward and Heitzenrater, *Journal ad Diaries II*, in *Works*, 19:67). See, also, in the Book of Common Prayer (BCP, 1662 edition), "Communion," Exhortation 3: "To him [Jesus Christ] therefore with the Father, and the holy Ghost, let us give (as we are most bounden) continual thanks, submitting our selves to his body will and pleasure, and studying to serve him in trust holiness and righteousness all the dayes [*sic*] of our life. Amen." (Brian Cummings [ed.]. *The Book of Common Prayer. The Texts of 1549, 1559, and 1662* [Oxford: Oxford University Press, 2011], 398-399)

²⁵ *Mona Lisa*, the portrait by the Florentine painter, sculptor, architect, engineer, and scientist, Leonardo da Vinci (1452-1519), in the Louvre, Paris, France (stolen in August 1911, recovered in December 1913); reportedly represents "La Gioconda," the wife of the Florentine Francesco del Giocondo.

²⁶ Harrison, *Son to Susanna*, 318-321.

²⁷ Henry Moore, *The Life of the Rev. John Wesley* (London: Kershaw, 1824-1825), 2:172.

²⁸ According to one source, "only three letters of hers [Molly Vazeille Wesley] survived the Methodist shredders." Stephen Tompkins, *John Wesley, a Biography* (Oxford, England: Lion Publishing, 2003; rpt. Grand Rapids, Michigan: William B. Eerdmans Publishing Company, 2003): 137.

²⁹ Richard Watson, *The Life of John Wesley, A.M.* (London: Wesleyan Conference Office, 1831), cited in Tyerman, *Life of John Wesley,,* 2:102.

³⁰ Who knows where those letters might be preserved?

³¹ Thomas Jackson, *The Life of the Rev. Charles Wesley, M.A., Some Time Student of Christ Church, Oxford. Comprising a Review of His Poetry; Sketches of the Rise and Progress of Methodism; with Notices of Contemporary Characters*, 2 vols. (London: John Mason, 1841; American edition, New York: G. Lane and P.P. Sandford, 1842), 2:568.

³² Plutus, in Greek mythology, the personification of wealth; a son of Iasion and Demeter, and intimately associated with Irene, goddess of peace; she often represented in art as holding the infant Plutus; supposedly blinded by Zeus so that he might not bestow his favors exclusively on good men, but should distribute his gifts without regard to merit; by a number of accounts, however, Plutus received a cure and thus gave wealth only to those whom he could perceive as being honest.

[33] Technically, eighteenth-century Methodism under John Wesley cannot be termed a "sect," for Wesley never separated his loosely entwined religious organization from the Church of England, nor himself from the priesthood of that Church. Hampson, and a large majority of his clerical colleagues, assumed a contrary view, even though he had embraced Methodism prior to his episcopal ordination.

[34] John Hampson the younger, *Memoirs of the Late Rev. John Wesley, A.M., with a Review of His Life and Writings and a History of Methodism from Its Commencement in 1739 to the Present Time 1791* (Sunderland, Durham: James Graham, 1791), 2:124.

[35] John Whitehead, *The Life of the Rev. John Wesley, M.A., Collected from His Private Papers and Printed Works; and Written at the Request of His Executors. To Which Is Prefixed, Some Account of His Ancestors and Relations; with the Life of the Rev. Charles Wesley, M.A. Collected from His Private Journal, and Never Before Published* (London: S. Couchman, 1793-1796), 2:263. Dr. Whitehead attended the dying John Wesley, his patient refusing to allow any other physician to come to his bedside.

[36] Tyerman, *Life of John Wesley*, 2:114-115.

[37] "Angularities" here means relating to one's manner and acquired habits, particularly stiffness, formality, and lack of accommodation.

[38] "Excrescences" here means natural outgrowths or appendages.

[39] "Benedict" here means a newly married man; a confirmed bachelor who marries.

[40] "Assorted" here means suited, matched.

[41] Tyerman, *Life of John Wesley*, 2:106.

[42] "Marjorie Bowen" being but one (yet the best known) of her several pseudonyms.

[43] Suggesting comparisons and contrasts between Molly Vazeille and Samuel Richardson's Pamela Andrews suggests one's total ignorance of both.

[44] "Diaphanous" here means permitting light and vision to pass through; perfectly transparent or translucent; vague or insubstantial.

[45] Susanna Annesley Wesley (1669-1742).

[46] Selina Shirley Hastings, Countess of Huntingdon (1707-1791), patroness of George Whitefield and the Calvinist Methodists.

[47] Grace Norman Murray Bennet (1716-1803), John Wesley's second serious love, who, also for the second time, hesitated in a direct

proposal of marriage and thus lost (through a concerted effort by brother Charles Wesley) the game to a rival.

[48] Marjorie Bowen, *Wrestling Jacob. A Study of the Life of John Wesley and Some Members of the Family* (London: The Religious Book Club, 1938): 299-303.

[49] Henry D. Rack referred to Mrs. Harrison's "overblown style and cavalier treatment of facts" (*Reasonable Enthusiast: John Wesley and the Rise of Methodism*, 3rd ed. [London: Epworth Press, 2002]:x), while Richard P. Heitzenrater (*The Elusive Mr. Wesley*, 2nd ed. [Nashville: Abingdon Press, 2003]:382-383) considered that in Mrs. Harrison's *Sons to Susanna*, the writer "manipulated historical facts rather loosely to fit her own psychological preconceptions in her somewhat sensationalist view of Wesley's relationship with his parents. It seems the psychohistorians have always been better psychologists than historians. . . ."

[50] Scholars generally have agreed upon Anthony Vazeille's occupation as a merchant (and an affluent one at that), not a banker.

[51] "Fondly" here means foolishly.

[52] G. Elsie Harrison, *Son to Susanna*, 318-321.

[53] Henry Abelove, *The Evangelist of Desire: John Wesley and the Methodists* (Stanford, California: Stanford University Press, 1990): 36-37.

[54] Ward and Heitzenrater, *Journal and Diaries III*, in *Works*, 20:378.

[55] Ralph Waller, *John Wesley: A Personal Portrait* (New York: Continuum, 2003): 100.

[56] Ward and Heitzenrater, *Journal and Diaries III*, in *Works*, 20:378.

[57] Numbers 11:11—"And Moses sad unto the Lord, Wherefore hast thou afflicted thy servant? And wherefore have I not found favour in thy sight, that thou layest the burden of all the people upon me?" (KJV) See, also, Numbers 11:17.

[58] Kimbrough and Newport, *Manuscript Journal*, 2:602.

[59] Matthew 19:12—"For there are some eunuchs, which were so born from their mother's womb: and there are some eunuchs, which were made eunuchs of men: and there be eunuchs, which have made themselves eunuchs for the kingdom of heaven's sake. He that is able to receive it, let him receive it." (KJV)

[60] Ward and Heitzenrater, *Journal and Diary III*, in *Works*, 20:378.

[61] Isaiah 60:20—"Thy sun shall no more go down; neither shall thy moon withdraw itself: for the Lord shall be thine everlasting light, and the days of thy mourning shall be ended." (KJV)

[62] 1 Samuel 13:12—"Therefore said I [Samuel], the Philistines will come down now upon me to Gilgal, and I have not made supplication unto the Lord: I forced myself therefore, and offered a burnt offering." (KJV)

[63] "Apology" here means a justification and/or explanation.

[64] Once the holder of a university fellowship either at Oxford or Cambridge entered into marriage, he had to resign that office. John Wesley's resignation letter (in Latin) "To the Rector and Fellows of Lincoln College, Oxford" dates June 1, 1751. See Baker, *Letters II*, in *Works*, 26:462.

[65] Matthew 16:24—"Then said Jesus unto his disciples, If any man will come after me, let him deny himself, and take up his cross, and follow me." (KJV)

[66] John 3:17—"For God sent not his Son into the world to condemn the world; but that the world through him might be saved."(KJV)

[67] "Umpire" here the word has not changed in meaning since its introduction into the English language in the middle of the fifteenth century. It continues to refer to one, in government or law, for instance, who serves as a mediator between or among contending parties. In the United States, one rarely sees the word outside of the gates of a sporting arena. The English poet William Cowper found room for the word early in his lengthy poem, "Tirocinium; or, a Review of Schools (1785)—

> For her [the soul] the Judgment, umpire in the strife
> That Grace and Nature have to wage through life,
> Quick-sighted arbiter of good and ill,
> Appointed sage preceptor of the Will. . . . (29-32)

[68] Kimbrough and Newport, *Manuscript Journal*, 2:602-604.

[69] Ward and Heitzenrater, *Journal and Diaries III*, in *Works*, 20:380. See, also, 1 Corinthians 7:29—"But this I [Paul] say, brethren, the time is short: it remaineth, that both they that have wives be as though they had none;. . ." (KJV)

[70] Genesis 2:18—"And the Lord God said, It is not good that the man should be alone; I shall make him a help meet for him." (KJV)

[71] Baker, *Letters II*, in *Works*, 20:453-454

[72] One might raise the question as to why the couple simply did not seek divorce early in the marriage and be done with it. The answer is even simpler: until 1857, a divorce in England could be obtained only through a private Act of Parliament—although in Scotland divorce proved easier to secure. In 1857, the English Divorce Court eased access to divorce, granting separation to men who could prove their wives' adultery, and to women on grounds of their husbands' adultery, as well as to husbands' cruelty. The Court also assessed a cost. In 1968, an Act significantly liberalized the divorce laws.

73 Wesley omitted his wife's name from the published extract (1777) of this entry.

74 Ward and Heitzenrater, *Journal and Diaries V,* in *Works,* 22:262, 339.

75 In a brief article, "John Wesley's Ordination of Dr. [Thomas] Coke As Bishop for America," *Methodist Recorder,* December 8, 1898, 4, the London publisher, Rev. Charles H. Kelly, referred to a letter by John Wesley that sold at a London auction on November 4, 1898 for £12.10s. "Is this a part of that letter?" inquired John Telford.

76 A number of those private papers appeared in *The Gospel Magazine,* edited by one of John Wesley's antagonists, Rev. Augustus Montague Toplady (1740-1778), of whom Wesley once pronounced, "I do not fight with chimney-sweepers." See Telford, *Letters,* 5:192; Arnold Lunn, *John Wesley* (New York: The Dial Press, 1929): 276.

77 Telford, *Letters,* 6:273-274, 321-322.

78 John Wesley's abortive love affair with the teenage Sophia Christiana Hopkey in Savannah, Georgia, during his equally abortive mission there in 1735-1737.

79 "Conned over" here means studied, learned, inspected, investigated, examined. The editors of the *Oxford Universal Dictionary* cite a most apt statement from Jonathan Swift—"Conning old topics like a parrot," while William Shakespeare's lines from *Julius Caesar* fit as well: "All his faults observ'd,/Set in a notebook, learn'd and conn'd by rote." (4:3:95-96).

80 See J. Augustin Leger, *John Wesley's Last Love* (London: J.M. Dent and Sons, 1910): 1-2, 66, 83, 97, 136, 139, 143, 188.

81 The reason for Noah Vazeille's state of "triumph" has never come to light. Again, one becomes hard pressed to distinguish between reality and Mrs. Harrison's imagination.

82 More than likely from West Street Chapel, London, where John Wesley had established his residence.

83 Harrison, *Son to Susanna,* 329-330.

84 Harrison, *Son to Susanna,* 331.

85 Ward and Heitzenrater, *Journal and Diaries VI,* in *Works,* 23:225.

86 Harrison, *Son to Susanna,* 331-332.

87 Harrison, *Son to Susanna,* 329.

88 "Wesley, John," in *Dictionary of National Biography (DNB).*

[89] Umphrey Lee, *The Lord's Horseman: John Wesley the Man* (New York and London: The Century Company, 1928): 267.

[90] Harrison, *Son to Susanna, 355.*

[91] Camberwell, London, south of Walworth, east of Brixton, west of Peckham, and north of Herne Hill—currently within the London borough of Southwark; in the eighteenth century, a village surrounded by fields and known for its flowers and fruit trees; the parish church, in Church Street, dedicated to St. Giles, patron saint of cripples and mendicants, destroyed by fire in 1841. "In the churchyard," announced either Weinreb or Hibbert, "now [c. 1983] cleared as a public open space, are buried John Wesley's shrewish wife, Mary, who died in 1781; Miss Lucy Warner, who was 32 ins. high and ran a local school; and James Blake, who sailed the world with Captain [James] Cook." See Ben Weinreb and Christopher Hibbert (eds.), *The London Encyclopaedia* (London: Macmillan, 1983; rpt. Bethesda, Maryland: Adler and Adler, Publishers, Inc., 1986): 114.

The Asbury Journal 75/1: 71-87
© 2020 Asbury Theological Seminary
DOI: 10.7252/Journal.01.2020S.05

Kim Okesson
Dorothy Sayers, Communication and Theology: A Lifetime of Influence in British Society

Abstract:

This paper examines the writings of Dorothy Sayers through the lens of transportation theory and feminist communication theory. Dorothy Sayers's early childhood and educational years are considered in light of their impact on her work as an adult. Her role as a writer and a lay theologian is discussed. The role of women in England during the first part of the twentieth century is considered. Attention is given to Sayers's writings across multiple literature genres and the strength this brings to her communication of theological truth.

Keywords: transportation theory, feminist communication theory, England, women, theology, creeds

Kim Okesson is the Director of Admissions and an adjunct professor in the School of Communication Arts at Asbury University, Wilmore, Kentucky. Kim is in her final year of coursework as a PhD student at Regent University, studying communication.

Introduction

Dorothy Sayers, an author, theologian, and playwright, moved in the same intellectual circles as C.S. Lewis and J. R. Tolkien. She was not one of the original 'Inklings' but she was already a successful author by the time she engaged in philosophical discussions and debates with that influential group and enjoyed their friendship (Carpenter 1979: 189). She was a gifted communicator and knew the power of narrative to teach spiritual truth. She wrote sixteen novels in her lifetime and twenty-four non-fiction books.

Sayers was known for her ability to wordsmith and was "the author of plays, letters, essays, lectures, and a highly regarded translation of Dante's *Divine Comedy*" (Cart 2018: 12). The gospel themes evident in her work include "conscience, sin and grace, covetousness, pride, despair and hope, and much more (Cart 2018: 12). She made important contributions to the church and society through her writing, yet few, according to Simmons (2005) have explored it in depth. Simmons (2005: 17) attributes this to the huge volume of her writing and the massive variety in her writing. Her writings include poems, short stories, plays for radio and the stage, children's books, novels, letters, literary reviews, essays (theological, political, creative commentary) and translations (most notable her translation of Dante) (Simmons 2005: 18).

Her impact as a female scholar during her lifetime, as a peer of male scholars still viewed as giants today, is significant. She not only had a place at the table, but she led the way for many women who would make their careers in the academy and in scholarship, years after her death. "By almost any measurement, Dorothy Leigh Sayers was one of the giants of the first half of the 20th Century. As a scholar, writer, and a public speaker, she excelled" (Tischler 1980: 1). She was masterful at indirect communication. As she sought to display the gospel in her writings, she wrote almost as much fiction as she did non-fiction. Similar to G.K. Chesterton, she wrote mysteries. Unquestionably, Dorothy Sayers contributed to both our understanding of theology and communication. The aim of this paper is to illustrate how Dorothy Sayers was a national leader in England and used her profound communication skills to influence British society both inside and outside the church, through her effective communication of the gospel to a nation that believed it was Christian.

Biographical Background

Dorothy Sayers was an only child, born in Oxford in 1893. Her father, Henry Sayers, was a chaplain and her mother, Helen Mary Sayers was the headmaster at Christ Church Choir School (Reynolds 1993: 1). Dorothy was taught at home, but her lessons were alternately taught by governesses, her father, and her mother (Reynolds 1993: 13). Her father taught her Latin and started her lessons when she was only six. Her parents were known for their love of theater and took her to London annually to see a production. She also was encouraged to play-act and Sayers regularly identified herself with her favorite characters in books (Reynolds 1993: 8). As she grew, she also produced plays, made costumes, props, and programs as well as authored long narrative poems, which she illustrated (Reynolds 1993: 22). An artist of her caliber, from a young age, naturally turned her everyday life experiences into art (Tischler 1980: 8).

Before she became a teenager, her parents predicted her attendance at university and chose Oxford as the best university for her (Reynolds 1993:27). They planned her high school years accordingly, choosing an elite boarding school for her preparation. She did eventually enroll at Oxford, even though at the time Oxford only admitted female students but did not confer degrees on them. In 1920, when Dorothy Sayers was 27, Oxford University "had consented to regularize the position concerning degrees for women. Up until then they had been eligible for the title to a degree that were not official graduates" (Reynolds 1993: 97). Dorothy Sayers was one of the first female graduates of Oxford University: she was awarded with B.A. and M.A degrees.

After her graduation, Dorothy Sayers went on to a lifetime of writing. Although her writings included both fiction and nonfiction there was nothing frivolous about her personality or her publications. Simmons (2005: 9) describes her as both a participant and an observer in society, which afforded her a unique perspective. She was a writer, not a formal academic, although she had advanced degrees. She was not a member of the clergy, although she wrote theologically and spoke to gatherings of clergy. She was a lay person in the church, yet she was not an average lay person; she was a creative intellectual who was masterful at communication. Sayers was a very intentional author; she sought to communicate foundational truths about God and humanity, in all of her works.

Theoretical Framework

In this paper, Dorothy Sayers' works are analyzed through the lens of two communication theories: feminist communication theory and transportation theory. Feminist communication theory has three primary characteristics. First, it is political. "Feminist communication theory assumes that the world we know is unjust and requires change" (Rako & Wackwitz 2004: 6). This theory focuses on those who have been marginalized because of gender and exists out of the need to make that marginalization stop. According to Rako and Wackwitz (2004: 6), the very nature of it being political makes it personal, as well as encouraging and producing "multiple understandings and reimagining of our world."

Secondly, feminist communication theory is explanatory. It validates experience and speaks through experience. This allows it to, "help groups and individuals make sense of their everyday lives and meanings that shape our very identities and experiences" (Rako & Wackwitz 2004: 6). Thirdly, it is polyvocal; the voices that contribute to this theory are varied, as individuals and in ideals. It speaks to and from the margins. "It allows for the exploration of individual stories, complex relationships, personal interpretations, and multiple realities" (Rako & Wackwitz 2004: 6).

Feminist communication theory gives voice. It allows women to speak, gives the respect to be heard, and access to areas previously or consistently denied to women. There are communicative forums throughout society which have historically, and some currently, which deny women voice. This denial is evident in interpersonal, group, organizational, and mediated communication. Allowing the voice of any marginalized group to come out of the margins is a primary focus for feminist theory (Littlejohn, Foss, & Oetzel 2017: 449).

Transportation theory was developed by Melanie Green and Timothy Brock to explain the effect of one being, "transported into the narrative world" (Littlejohn, Foss, & Oetzel 2017: 167). The idea of transportation in communication is when one becomes "so enmeshed in the story you are experiencing that you are swept away from your world and into the world of the story" (Littlejohn, Foss, & Oetzel 2017: 167). When a person experiences this, they commonly lose track of time, space, and can commonly picture themselves in the story. Interestingly, transportation frequently results in a person being unaware of events happening around him or her and experience strong emotions, both positive and negative (Littlejohn, Foss, & Oetzel 2017: 167).

Transportation theory depends on narrative, however fiction and non-fiction can be equally effective and the medium is not restricted to stories in print. Plays, musicals, films, story festivals, television shows, etc. can all result in transportation of the listener, reader, or observer. Essential to transportation theory is the result of the reader or viewer making a change in his or her real life, based on what he or she experiences while transported into the narrative world. According to Green and Brock (2000: 703), literature written for the popular audience, detective or romance novels, may be criticized by scholars as not being the highest class of literature, yet have proven to be particularly effective in transporting the reader. Both transportation theory and feminist communication theory are evident throughout Dorothy Sayers's writings. Her writings were also thoroughly theological, despite her protests that she was "just" a writer.

Writings and Theology

Sayers was a contemporary of Lewis and she was prolific in her writing, yet she is much less studied, and in particular rarely called a theologian (Simmons 2005: 12). Few have examined her important contribution to the church in this regard (Simmons 2005: 17). "Her vocation as a writer was a vital part of what equipped her to be an especially effective lay theologian" (Simmons 2005: 19). Her skills in communication were a gift to the church and she sought to use them to bring the church into right relationship with the God it claimed to worship.

Dorothy Sayers was not an ordained member of the clergy; she was considered an intellectual member of the laity in the church. She was regularly invited to write letters and plays to help explain Christianity and make it accessible to the common person. James Beitler (2019: 62) praises Sayers for her ability to illustrate and teach hard truths realistically through drama, which had a profound impact on the church. In 1940, Sayers had taken the clergy of England to task over their lack of ability to teach the creeds, and in some instances their lack of teaching the creeds at all, in a way that people understood them to be relevant to their everyday lives. According to Sayers, the clergy failed to view Christianity rhetorically and by doing so, made no effort to communicate to the audience in a way the audience could understand (Beitler 2019: 62). Her exasperation was expressed in her statement, "They've got the most terrific story in the world and they don't tell it" (Beitler 2109: 62). Beitler (2019: 65) brilliantly states, " . . . the stage was at one and the same time Sayers's workplace and her pulpit." Sayers stewarded her gifts and talents to use art to communicate spiritual truth.

Transportation of the audience was a goal for Sayers as she wrote. According to Beitler (2019: 68), her work showcases Quintilian's concept of *energeia*. Energeia is the realistic depiction of an event, done with such excellence, persuasion, and emotion, the event seems real to the audience (Beitler 2019: 68). Sayers was an author and playwright who gave much time and attention to the poetics of space. For example, in her greatest mystery novel, *The Nine Tailors,* she hired an architect to draw the parish church, so she could realistically set scenes in the space through her writing. Through her dramatic works Sayers sought to connect with her audience in ways the traditional teaching in the church could not.

The central question Fred Craddock (1978), author of *Overhearing the Gospel: Preaching and Teaching the Faith to Persons who have Heard it All Before,* asked was how does one person communicate the Christian faith to another? This question was one that Dorothy Sayers asked as well, as she saw the church in England not communicating the gospel or the doctrines of the church effectively. She spent much of her career writing and speaking towards that end. Craddock stated that many an author and rhetor has had to face the truth about the Truth, "is being available does not mean it will be appropriated" (Craddock 1978: 15). "There is no lack of information in a Christian land; something else is lacking, and this is a something which the one man cannot directly communicate to the other" (Craddock 1978: 9). Even though Sayers wrote broadly and across numerous genres, she was singularly focused and committed to honoring people and the message by seeking understandable avenues of communication.

Dorothy Sayers knew her stories were theological, even though she did not attend a seminary or have an official position in the Church of England. This idea is supported by C.S. Song (2011) in his book, *In the Beginning were Songs, not Texts: Story Theology.* All people, all over the world, from all time were and are storytellers. Song (2011: 18) states, "A story worthy of its name grips you in the depths of your heart and mind, forces you to look deeply into yourself and into human nature, and compels you to examine relations between you and other human beings, between human beings and the world, nature and creation, and relations between human beings and God. If this is what story does, it is profoundly theological." Hauerwaus and Jones (1997: 5) argue the value of narrative by defining it as an invaluable conceptual category for understanding methods of argument, "displaying the content of Christian convictions," and articulating personal identity.

Sayers believed that creative work was of the highest order. "She discovered that the statements in the creeds concerning God the Creator were an exact description of the human mind when engaged in an act of creative imagination" (Reynolds 1993: 311). All of humanity bears the image of God, therefore all creating is in the image of the divine act of creating (Harrison 2004: 253). The doctrine of the Trinity, the three in one, represented for her the creative process as a three-fold work (Reynolds 1993: 310). This three-fold work of human creation includes idea, power, and energy (Harrison 2004: 253). Idea, power, and energy are all part of the same creative conceptualization process; they are one, like the Father, Son, and Holy Spirit (Beitler 2019: 83). "Idea," analogous to the Father, is the creative concept that starts in the mind of the artist. "Energy," analogous to the Son, is the process of making the conceptual material. "Power," analogous to the Spirit, is the effect this materialized concept has on the audience.

Sayers' work was all the more valuable to the church in England as she understood the myths, concerns, and questions of the society around her. She knew British culture. The process of understanding a culture or an audience involves knowing the myths present in the society. Song (2011: 18) speaks to the importance of theology being the matrix in a story, thus myths give the rhetor insight into what a community believes about the big issues of life: birth, death, creation, good, evil, right, and wrong. Through understanding the myths in a culture, the rhetor or author can craft stories with the same concerns or values, which then also communicate ultimate Truth.

Writing Genres and Theology

Dorothy Sayers' writing in advertising, detective fiction, translation, and play-writing are the genres through which her theological voice was heard the strongest. Each of these four genres had a particular characteristic or set of characteristics which illustrated her gift for "speaking" theologically through text.

Advertising.

Her early career was in advertising. A successful advertiser must know and understand the culture he or she is selling to and must also have a writing ability which is succinct, yet meaningful. Sayers was notable for her economy of words (Simmons 2005: 46). There were three ways her experience in advertising helped her write theologically. First, Dorothy Sayers was trained to identify unclear writing (Simmons 2005: 47). If an advertisement in the newspaper left the public wondering what it meant, the advertisement was useless. Similarly, clergy who spoke and wrote using lofty theological sentiment or antiquated language, left the public wondering what it all meant, rendering the message useless. Sayers could not tolerate this kind of ambiguous and ineffective communication. Secondly, advertisers were attentive to the details of the ordinariness of life, how people thought, and what was tolerable. Sayers wrote, *Creed or Chaos* to address the very common misunderstandings people in England had about Christianity. "In this, she took the traditional teaching of the church and put them into dialogue with the understandings and misunderstandings the average person has about Christianity" (Simmons 2005: 48). Lastly, her experience in advertising improved her own clarity of writing and the impact of her religious works (Simmons 2005: 48).

Detective Fiction.

Detective fiction was a common genre in the early 20th century. Interestingly, the skill Sayers developed in writing detective stories aided her in communicating the gospel. In a detective story, the author must map out a story with enough logical sequence so the plot is believable for the reader. Her play, *The Man Born to be King,* was an incredible artistic labor as she translated it from the original Greek and created her own synthesis of the four Gospels. She then wrote the play in such a way as to make the story coherent (Simmons 2005: 49). This play showcased her writing capacity and ability. She wrote one coherent story, to be performed as twelve radio segments with each segment capable of standing on its own, in and of itself.

Authors of detective fiction also craft arguments. The clues along the way must lead to a logical conclusion. This is evident in Sayers' *Creed or Chaos?* In this essay, "she anticipated the responses of the uninstructed person to the various doctrinal assertions of the Christian faith" (Simmons 2005: 50). It also requires research. Crafting this type of argument or plot requires research on the part of the author to create realistic settings both architecturally and geographically, lifelike relationships between characters, historical accuracy, and attention to details of language and dialect. Sayers studied campanology, the art of bell-ringing, for two years before she wrote her novel, *The Nine Tailors.* The story of *The Nine Tailors* opens with a nine-hour pealing of the bells. Additionally in the plot, a lost and then discovered document, which must be decoded for the mystery to be solved, required the main character to have knowledge of bell ringing and bell towers.

Finally, good detective fiction allows the author to present the same story or the same situation from the perspective of many different people. This grants the author the opportunity to gift the story both a richness and a depth (Simmons 2005: 51). Sayers was concerned with what was being proclaimed from the pulpit in the church as well as what the person in the pew heard. This dual perspective allowed her the unique position of "explaining theology from the inside out" (Simmons 2005: 51). This is evident in her novel, *The Documents in the Case,* in which the case is told from multiple perspectives. Lastly, her creativity and artistic ability in writing detective fiction employed her imagination. She created people and places, conversations and concerns, destiny and dynasties, all from within her own mind. She lived in this creative space and had no tolerance for people and institutions of influence who had a platform for proclamation yet were utterly lacking in imaginative ability to communicate with their audience (Simmons 2005: 52).

Translations and Plays.

Similarly, her work in translation helped her hone skills which were useful for communicating theologically. Translation work from antiquated language to modern language assists the public to hear a timeless message in a new light. The Church of England still used the King James Version, which although it had beautiful Shakespearean style English, was largely unrelatable to the average person in the twentieth century. When she translated the Gospels to write *The Man Born to be King,* she used modern language, which shocked and impressed her audiences (Simmons 2005: 53), the effect she hoped it would have. As traditional language had lost its meaning, her goal was to have people hear doctrine and theological truths for the first time in a way they could understand and perceive as relevant to their lives (Simmons 2005: 65).

As a playwright, Dorothy Sayers brought history and theology to life. She was convinced that a play would have more impact on society than volumes of theological texts (Simmons 2005: 56). Sayers was persuaded that the majority of the people in the church "are exceedingly surprised to discover that the creeds contain any statements that bear a practical and comprehensible meaning" (Sayers 1978: 41). She believed the incarnation was the most wondrous part of Christianity, yet tragically the incarnation was also one of the least understood doctrines in England. Determined to address this, Sayers allowed the dogma to "speak for itself" by putting it on stage (Simmons 2005: 55). She was passionate about her plays. She read the story of Jesus' life through the lens of great drama and it thrilled her soul (Simmons 2005: 56).

In *The Dogma is the Drama*, she chastised the church for making scripture boring: stating, "Somehow or other, and with the best intentions, we have shown the world the typical Christian in the likeness of a crashing and rather ill-natured bore – and this in the name of the One who assuredly never bored a soul in those thirty-three years during which he passed through the world like a flame" (Simmons 2005: 67). In response to hearing one of her plays on the BBC, one listener stated, "We quickly felt the wild, unruly, unfriendly atmosphere of the inn and as the play progressed and as we followed each sidelight on the environment of the little family the whole scene became amazingly vivid . . . None of us realized before how much we had just accepted the story without properly visualizing it" (Beitler 2019: 82). Audience members who attended her play, *The Man Born to be King*, responded to it with statements that included: *enthralling, deeply moving, made it come alive, better than dry as dust sermons, real humanity, the scene and people came alive, it took me back through all the ages to the cave at Bethlehem* (Beitler 2019: 82).

Women and Feminism

Dorothy Sayers was a strong, out-spoken advocate for women. She had lively debates with C.S. Lewis as to the ordination of women in the Church of England, after he initiated a dialogue with her about her thoughts on the issue in 1948 (Simmons 2005: 145). Through her life, she modeled the impact a woman could have stewarding her gifts with excellence for the building up of society and the church.

Dorothy authored, *Are Women Human?* In this text she rebuked the common rhetoric of human rights and human issues consistently attributed to men, while women's rights were another category altogether. At this point in history, men's choices defined human choices (Simmons 2005: 148). Women were still denied opportunity to vote and were denied access to certain careers. Although Sayers had earned her degree from Oxford and had the distinction of being one of the very first to be granted her degree, she had to wait ten years after completing her coursework before Oxford determined it was acceptable to confer degrees on women

(Tischler 1980: 61). Her graduation was an unforgettable, life-changing moment for all that it symbolized, both for her intellectual achievement but also for what the "delay said about the life of womankind" (Tischler 1980: 21). For forty years prior to Sayers enrolling at Oxford, women had been fighting for equality in opportunity, education, degrees, and professional life (Tischler 1980: 15). Women were prohibited from many professions and marriage was considered the highest goal for all women. To Sayers, this was a profound waste of human potential and resource (Tischler 1980: 61).

Sayers used her fiction writing to illuminate the tragedy of the wasted lives of women. In *Unnatural Death,* she illustrated the "right kind of feminism" as her characters were strong women, devoted to their faith, capable in their work and fulfilled (Tischler 1980: 62). Sayers insisted that work was given to humanity by their Creator, not just to men, or just to women. Conversely, God gave each person gifts and abilities; those gifted for the work, should do that particular work. Gender, according to Sayers, was not a qualification for work. "The purpose of work must be found in the value of its product, which must be of the quality that it glorifies God. As creators, people must make themselves subservient to the work for which they are best suited, in order to bring into being that which they were created to create" (Harrison 2004: 240). Humans were made to work; Her perspective was that work is not something one must do to live, but rather what one lives to do (Harrison 2004: 257). Work was not discriminatory based on gender; work was God-given (Fletcher 2013: xvii).

Sayers did not see a distinction between men and women for work or any other aspect of life . Again, from her book *Are Women Human?,* she had strong words for the "imbeciles" who asked her to speak about the topic of detective fiction, "from a woman's perspective" (Nordlinger 2015: 28). Her response to such a question was , "Go away and don't be silly. You might as well ask what is the female angle on an equilateral triangle" (Nordlinger 2015: 28). Her goal for all women was for them to think of themselves as human, equal, not inferior or superior, to all other humans (Norlinger 2015: 28). *Gaudy Nights,* one of her detective novels, also illustrates this belief. In this novel, Sayers placed the main character, a woman, in a university as a leader and an intellectual, who used her intellectual skills to solve the crime (Tischler 1980: 62). This was the first novel, in the genre of detective fiction, to highlight a woman (Johnson 2015: 23).

Communication Theories

Through the above overview of themes in Sayers' writing as well as her own commitment to writing well, it is evident that transportation theory is supported by her endeavors. She painstakingly spent her career writing and creating so as to connect with her audience or readers, to open their eyes to what seemed unknowable, yet was able to be known. In her plays, she desired complete transportation, such that the experience would be all-encompassing for those in the audience yet also create real, persistent life change. This is the very definition of transportation theory. It is noted that Sayers' fiction works displayed a keen sense of space and time. The year, season, day of the week, phase of the moon, the history, the people, local customs, language, and even dialects are all evident and appropriate throughout her fiction works. "Her novels, for all their activity, are firmly rooted in immediate reality" (Tischler 1980: 36). Whether she was writing a fiction novel or a play for BBC radio, her goal remained consistent, engage and educate the general population through realistic writing.

Similarly, Dorothy Sayers was a champion of people, all people, at a time in history when women were fighting for equal rights on many levels. The reality of World War II substantially changed the role of women in society, which caused many to realize, for the first time, that women could fulfill roles outside of the home. Feminism communication theory radiates from her writings. From the time her father took great care and attention to teach her from a young age, she knew the inherent value of women. She also personally experienced the marginalization of women in her college years and professional life. According to Tischler (1980: 15), at the time Sayers was in university, no woman could attend Oxford without confronting dominant masculinity. She was confounded by the societal dance of "role by gender" and used her fiction and nonfiction writing to champion humanity, the image of God in all humanity, and the ability of all of humanity to contribute to society through meaningful, God-given work.

The Craft of Writing

If Dorothy Sayers were alive today, most certainly she would be spoken of as one who had a calling on her life to write and create. She worshiped God through her work, and as a result, could not do her work half-heartedly, sloppily, lazily, or for her own glory. Sayers, raised by her clergy father, understood the role of the church in society as well as the profound truth of the creeds of the church. She knew the church had a primary role in educating the masses about Jesus. Through her active participation in the church as a lay person, she also knew the church was failing at the sacred task of bringing Jesus to the people. Dorothy Sayers was an author who lived in a society where many people claimed to be Christian, yet in her interactions with them she knew they did not understand what they claimed to believe. This resulted in the church and Christianity being the object of "bad press" (Sayers 2004: 1). Those who attended church were complaining of dull drama (Sayers 2004: 1).

In her book, *The Whimsical Christian: 18 essays,* she makes the profound call to the church to "Let us, in heaven's name, drag out the living drama from under the dreadful accumulation of slipshod thinking and trashy sentiment heaped upon it, and set in on an open stage to startle the world into some sort of vigorous reaction" (Sayers 1978: 27). It was in this setting she made her famous statement, "it is the dogma that is the drama" (Sayers 1978: 27). The dogma was indeed the drama for Dorothy Sayers and she would not allow the ineffectiveness of the church to dissuade her from honing her own skill to communicate the divine message. One avenue of honing her skill was her formation of the "Mutual Admiration Society" (Tischler 1980: 19). This was a group of like-minded women she initially met at Oxford. They became lifelong friends. They met together to share ideas, collaborate on writing, and support each other as female intellectuals in a male-dominated society (Tischler 1980: 19).

She held herself to high standards, as is evident in her relentless research which informed the background of her work. She also held others to high standards. When asked to speak to clergy or to answer letters about theological questions, she was direct and frank about how the church was not communicating well and needed to view theology rhetorically, as something which must be communicated in ways the reader or listener understood (Beitler 2019: 62). Work was definitively worshipful for Sayers. She bore witness to her Creator through her work, her commitment to being faithful to her calling as an artist, and her devotion to her vocation (Beitler 2019: 62). Sayers' commitment to excellence in her writing is evident through the fact that her mystery novels have never gone out of print (Armstrong 2005).

Lord Peter, one of Sayers' main characters in detective fiction, was a keen observer of human behavior. Sayers developed his character as one who was convinced "people act out of their deepest religious, philosophic, and emotional commitments" (Tischler 1980: 45). Sayers, of course, held this belief herself. Through her observation of people's behaviors, she was able to discern the worldview of her community, her readers, and her audiences. According to Sayers, the creative mind was the one most able to tell the story of God, as it was astute in both intellect and in understanding humanity" (Sayers 2004: 273). She was keenly aware England claimed to be Christian, yet the observable behavior revealed a complete lack of real understanding of what people claimed to embrace. Human behavior reveals the fundamental beliefs and values held by the individual or the community. Therefore, she took the mantle of properly communicating the gospel, the creeds, the life of Christ, and the mystery of God, in her writing. As she grew in her writing ability, she became adept at using the mode of communication and the literature genre which would best communicate her message to the masses. "Sayers the lay theologian modeled the ability and the desire to bring her faith to bear on 'week-days' as well as Sundays" (Simmons 2005: 158). She accomplished this through addressing doctrine in addition to topics such as hobbies, work, and economics (Simmons 2005: 158). She was motivated and thrilled by ideas, therefore at the core of her being she could not tolerate a church that produced wrong thinking or fuzzy logic (Tischler 1980: 10).

Transportation theory posits that to the degree a person is "absorbed into a story or transported into a narrative world, they may show effects of the story on their real-world beliefs" (Green & Brock 2000: 701). Sayers used her understanding of the real world to expertly author believable stories that transported people. She sought change in the real world, in both belief and behavior, which motivated her to write with excellence. Her detective fiction novels have been compared to Conan Doyle and found superior. She maintained the chronology of her stories for twenty years, during which time she wrote eleven novels, twenty-one short stories, and an eleven-part weekly series in a periodical (Tischler 1980: 36).

Feminist communication theory gives voice to the marginalized, particularly women. Sayers had a powerful voice during her lifetime and used it to speak for herself and on behalf of others who were marginalized. Importantly, her perspective on feminism was based in her theological understanding of humanity. She did not exalt women above men, nor base her argument on a particular characteristic of women. Rather, she argued for women based on the work of the Creator in endowing all of humanity with his image. Therefore, there is no space for any human to be marginalized. She used her novels and her nonfiction texts to illustrate the full humanity of women, which challenged society on many levels in the early and mid-twentieth century.

Conclusion

Most of the authors who have written on Sayers mention the lack of scholarship surrounding her life and work. Simmons' (2005) book, *Creed Without Chaos: Exploring Theology in the Writings of Dorothy L. Sayers,* is one of the first to present research on Sayers as a theologian. This is a definite area in which more research is needed. It is evident Sayers' writings effuse theology. Her life was theologically informed, as was her thinking and writing. She may have been overlooked because she was female scholar or it may be that Simmons was correct in attributing it to the vast variety and volume of her work. There seems to be enough theological material in her fiction work alone, however, that a lifetime of study could be done to reach the depths of her theological themes and instruction.

Dorothy Sayers "had a unique combination of talents: a keen theological sense coupled with tremendous writing skill and a concern for how ordinary people understood Christianity. In an increasingly complex and fragmented world, we need these gifts more than ever"(Simmons 2005: 12). Although Dorothy Sayers wrote in the twentieth century, tempting one to discount her work as irrelevant for a modern audience, her mastery of transportation in teaching Christian doctrine is as important today as when she originally wrote. Her passion for the reality of the *imago dei* and the life-altering ramifications of this reality for all of humanity is a relevant example of God's perspective and intentions for humanity, even in the 21st century. Christian communication scholars can learn a tremendous amount from the example of her life and writings. Her commitment to excellence, her love of doctrine, her incredible attention to detail, her expansive knowledge of her culture and society, her insatiable appetite for learning, and her humility in continually working to become a better writer, and therefore a more effective communicator, are all characteristics which made her an effective and influential communicator and are qualities worth emulating for any communications scholar.

Works Cited

Armstrong, C.
    2005   "Dorothy Sayers: 'The dogma is the drama' an interview with Barbara Reynolds." *Christianity Today.* Retrieved from https://www.christianitytoday.com/ct/2005/decemberweb-only/52.0a.html

Beitler III, J.E.
    2019   *Seasoned Speech: Rhetoric in the Life of the Church.* Downers Grove, IL: InterVarsity Press Academic.

Craddock, F. B.
    2002   *Overhearing the gospel: Preaching and Teaching the Faith to Persons Who Have Heard it all Before.* Nashville, TN: Abingdon Press.

Fletcher, C.M.
    2013   *The Artist and the Trinity: Dorothy Sayers' Theology of Work.* Eugene, OR: Pickwick Publications.

Green, M.C., & Brock, T.C.
    2000   "The role of transportation in the persuasiveness of public narratives." *Journal of Personality and Social Psychology,* 79(5): 701-721.

Harrison, W.H.
    2004   "Loving the creation, loving the Creator; Dorothy L. Sayers's Theology of Work." *AnglicanTheological Review,* 86(2): 239-257.

Hauerwas, S. & Jones, G.L.
    1997   *Why Narrative? Readings in Narrative Theology.* Eugene, OR: Wipf and Stock.

Johnson, D. E.
    2015   "Dorothy L. Sayers and Virginia Woolf: Perspectives on the woman intellectual in the late 1930s." *Virginia Wolf Miscellany,* 87: 23-25.

Littlejohn, S.W., Foss, K.A., & Oetzel, J.G.
    2017   *Theories of Human Communication.* (11th ed.). Long Grove, IL: Waveland Press.

Nordlinger, J.
    2015   "Sing it, Dorothy." *National Review,* 67(6): 27-28.

Rako, L. & Wackwitz, L.
    2004   *Feminist Communication Theory: Selections in Context.* Los Angeles, CA: Sage.

Reynolds, B.
    1993   *Dorothy Sayers: Her Life and Soul, a Biography.* New, York, NY: St. Martin's Press.

Sayers, D.L.
    2004   *Letters to a Diminished Church: Passionate Arguments for the Relevance of Christian Doctrine.* Nashville, TN: Thomas Nelson.

    1978   *The Whimsical Christian: 18 Essays.* New York, NY: MacMillan Press

Simmons, L. K.
    2005   *Creed Without Chaos: Exploring Theology in the Writings of Dorothy L. Sayers.* Grand Rapids, MI: Baker Academic.

Song, C. S.
    2011   *In the Beginning were Stories, not Texts: Story Theology.* Eugene, OR: Cascade Books.

Tischler, N.M.
    1980   *Dorothy L. Sayers: A Pilgrim Soul.* Atlanta, GA: John Knox Press.

Wehr, K.
    2016   "Dorothy L. Sayers' use of the four gospels in the Man Born to be King." *Journal of Inkling Studies,* (6)2: 3-62.

The Asbury Journal 75/1: 88-106
© 2020 Asbury Theological Seminary
DOI: 10.7252/Journal.01.2020S.06

Robert A. Danielson
"When We are Going to Preach the Word, Jesus will Meet Us:"
Ernest and Phebe Ward and Pandita Ramabai

Abstract:

In the 19th century, holiness missions spread to various parts of the world, including India. Ernest and Phebe Ward were part of that movement. They went as faith missionaries, but were also recognized as the first missionaries of the Free Methodist Church. In the course of their mission work in Central India, their traditional radical form of holiness mission was transformed into orphanage work by a severe famine. Through their holiness connections and orphanage work, they became associated with the Pentecost Bands and with Albert Norton, a close partner with Pandita Ramabai. This paper raises the potential importance of these connections in terms of the influence of holiness connections on Ramabai and the Mukti Revival of 1905, which led to the growth of Pentecostalism in India.

Keywords: Ernest Ward, Phebe Ward, Pandita Ramabai, Free Methodist, missions, India

Robert A. Danielson is the Scholarly Communications Librarian as Asbury Theological Seminary in Wilmore, Kentucky. He is a missiologist with a Ph.D. in Intercultural Studies and teaches in the E.S.J. School of World Missions and Evangelism at Asbury Theological Seminary as an affiliate faculty.

Introduction

In January of 1881, Ernest Freemont Ward and his wife Phebe arrived in Bombay (Mumbai), India as the first missionaries of the Free Methodist Church.[1] With a radical view of Wesleyan-Holiness teachings, the Wards set off to evangelize Hindus and Muslims in Central India. By 1892, they were in Raj Nandgaon. In 1897 a major famine struck the area forcing the Wards to reevaluate their missionary goals and establish an orphanage to handle the crisis of abandoned children. In December 1897, a small band of Free Methodist workers arrived in Raj Nandgaon to form the first Pentecost Band in India. Bringing the same passion for Wesleyan-Holiness teaching, they too became involved in the orphanage, adding a school and chapel to the mission work.

In 1898, about 600 miles away near Bombay, Pandita Ramabai was establishing her own missionary school and orphanage in Kedgaon-the well-known Mukti Mission.[2] While her primary goal was to support child widows, the massive famine also expanded her mission to include female famine victims. In Pentecostal studies, Pandita Ramabai is known for a 1905 revival (including the speaking in tongues), which predated the Azusa Revival by two years (when the Pentecostal Movement is traditionally accepted as being established).[3]

This paper explores primary source documents from E. F. and Phebe Ward and highlights records of interactions between Pandita Ramabai and these Free Methodist missionaries, as well as potential influences their Wesleyan-Holiness teachings and mission work may have had on this early outbreak of Pentecostalism in India.

The Wards Go to India

In 1878, Ernest Freemont Ward, the son of an abstractor of titles in Illinois, had a sanctification experience in a Free Methodist camp meeting and his ensuing passion for holiness led him to join the Free Methodist Church the following year. In October of 1880, Ward was made both a deacon and an elder at the same conference in Freeport, Illinois and he also married Phebe Cox, a teacher three years his senior. On November 15, 1880, using money Phebe had saved, the couple left for India. As an account of Free Methodist missions, written in the mid-1930's notes, "Ernest F. Ward announced to the conference that he and his wife were called to India and were going soon. They did not offer themselves to the organized Board that already existed. They did not ask for support. They did want the authorization and prayers of the church."[4] By January of 1881 they arrived in Bombay, and eventually they become recognized as the Free Methodist Church's first foreign missionaries.

However, Ward did not just step into a vacuum. He was encouraged to go to India (and even to marry Phebe!)[5] by Albert Benjamin Norton, a missionary sent out in 1872 by the Foreign Mission Board of the Methodist Episcopal Church in response to an urgent need by Rev. William Taylor.[6] Norton becomes a very important person in Ramabai's story and the history of the Mukti Revival.[7] Norton was close to Ramabai and was asked by her to establish a boy's orphanage in Dhond (Daund) as a complement to the Mukti mission's focus on girl orphans or widows. It is Norton who early on reports on the Mukti Revival in one of the first issues of the *Apostolic Faith*, the official paper of the Azusa Revival.[8] A group of Pentecostal missionaries join his work in December of 1908,[9] and Norton reports on his own experience of the baptism of the Holy Spirit and speaking in tongues on March 5, 1909.[10]

There is also evidence of early contact between the Wards and Pandita Ramabai. During their early years in Ellichpur (Achalpur), the Wards had taken in an Anglo-Indian girl, named her Theodosia and raised her with their daughters. Since they were self supporting, the Wards sold their house in Ellichpur to pay the costs of their first furlough in 1892. Because they could not afford to take Theodosia with them, Phebe had to find a place for her. Ethel Ward writes,

> Mrs. Ward took a hurried trip to Poona (Pune) too before they sailed. She went to a fine Children's Home orphanage there where she left her adopted girl, Theodosia. The separation was keenly felt by both of the sisters, but funds did not permit their taking her to America, and later the way opened for her to finish high school and take a medical course in North India. Later Dr. Scudder found her and chose her to help in their big Mission Hospital in Vellore, South India, where she worked many years with this famous Dr. Scudder. On this trip to Poona, Mrs. Ward visited Pandita Ramabai's Widows' Home and saw Mrs. Sorabji[11] and daughter. She was much impressed with these fine women, the noblest of India's daughters, splendid types of womanhood.[12]

For the most part, the early ministry of the Wards focused on evangelistic preaching in the bazaars, selling literature and tracts, and working to save souls. This was at the core of most holiness missions. In line with this approach, the Wards, while in Bombay waiting to sail for their first furlough in 1892, met two young women who had arrived from America as representatives of the Pentecost Bands, a holiness-based evangelistic group loosely connected to the Free Methodist Church. These two young ladies were Laura Douglas and Bessie Sherman.[13] Along with the Wards they held some tent meetings and established the first Free Methodist society in India in Byculla, Bombay.[14] It is not clear if the Wards joined the Pentecost Bands at this time or after their return to the U.S., but they are listed in *The Pentecost Herald*, the main paper for the Pentecost Bands, in 1894 with Ernest Ward as the leader of Band no. 12 and Phebe Ward as the leader of Band no. 22 with Bessie Sherman as the Assistant Leader.[15]

The Famine of 1897 and Mission Changes Direction

After their first furlough in 1892, the Wards returned to India to a new location- Raj Nandgaon in present day Chhattisgarh state on the border with Maharashtra state. Ward's journals show a missionary passionate for saving souls and the holiness teachings of the Free Methodist Church, but in 1897 a major famine struck the area and the Wards begin to help by burying the dead and taking in abandoned children, creating an orphanage out of necessity. Much of this activity is recorded in the Wards' book, *Echoes from Bharatkhand*.[16] The situation was getting desperate and overwhelming the physical and emotional resources of the Wards as independent self-supporting missionaries. In one account Phebe Ward sends a letter in September of 1897 (before the arrival of the Pentecost Band) in which she is clearly exhausted,

> I love the way of the cross this morning, by which I am crucified to the world and the world unto me. I presume you have heard of Bro. Ward's and Louisa's serious illness with cholera. God loosened our hands by the singular providence and let me get a breathing spell, from where I was living at high pressure speed. The change was much needed; I might say imperative. Bro. Ward is improving now but it has been a veritable fight with death. A less stronger man would probably have succumbed, Louisa too though not so ill, has had a long pull. Blood poisoning set in which has kept her from getting on her feet... Some of our loveliest ones (orphans) have gone to heaven. I have sat and watched them leave us, when it seemed as if this famine was a giant fiend, stealing away our jewels. I can never describe the awfulness of this famine! I have grown old

in eight months and can wear Bessie Sherman's clothes easily, I am so thin. We shall be glad to hear the out coming party have left America.[17]

It is interesting that this letter is published right next to the first mention of Pandita Ramabai in *The Pentecost Herald*, an account written by Alfred S. Dyer, the editor of *The Bombay Guardian*.

The Pentecost Bands, which had split from the Free Methodist Church in 1895 over issues of denominational authority and their radical holiness stance, answered the need by sending a group of workers led by Frank Hotle, along with his wife Della and daughter Eliza, William McCready, and Elizabeth Tucker. This group arrived in Bombay November 28, 1897, where they proceeded to set up an orphanage in Nagpur and gather orphans locally.[18] In the Pentecost Band's account for May 25, 1898,[19] it notes,

> Bro. Ward came today to get his daughter Louisa, who has been here for a two weeks change. We were all very glad to see him and we had a real breaking through time at prayers. Bro. Ward feels his heart is with us and that the Lord would be pleased to have him cast his lot among us. We told him to pray much about it, and if he still felt his place was in the bands, we would gladly welcome him.

In the account for May 27th, 1898 (two days later), the Pentecost Band's account notes, "Bro. Ward returned home today; but before going he gave us his name to be sent to the *Pentecost Herald* to be enrolled among the workers." The Wards position in regards to the Free Methodist Church is unclear at this time. In Burritt's history of Free Methodist missions it lists the Wards as beginning their service in 1880 and records them in the list of Free Methodist Missionaries from 1885-1895, however they are missing from the list from 1895-1905, and then reappear on the list from 1905-1915 as beginning their service in 1906.[20] Since the Pentecost Bands withdrew from the Free Methodist Church in 1895, Ward's move to the Pentecost Bands in 1898 may have been seen as a move away from the Free Methodist Church. However, since the Wards were always self-supporting and independent, their denominational affiliation may have always been a bit flexible.

On June 21, 1898 (less than a month after Ward joins the Pentecost Band in India), the decision is made to combine the orphanages at Nagpur and Raj Nandgaon. The account records,

After prayerful and careful consideration, we decided that it would be profitable and pleasing to God for the two orphanages at Nagpur and Raj Nandgaon to be united as our forces thus concentrated would enable us to more properly adjust matters so as to lessen or more fully equalize the burdens of each worker. The decision seems to be met with the favor of God as the railroad company gave us free pass for over fifty children and we took them from Nagpur to Raj Nandgaon today. Our family of children number up to one hundred and eight now.

The Wards may have remembered this event differently. Ethel Ward wrote,

Then they (the Wards) learned that a party of four missionaries from the Pentecost Band work had begun a Mission in Nagpur which was nearer than others. "Let us invite them," said Mr. Ward, and his wife consented. So the letter of invitation was written. "Yes, we can come," was the reply, "and it is surely an answer to our prayer because we have had to pay such a high rent here that we have been contemplating moving elsewhere."[21]

Raj Nandgaon and The Pentecost Bands

After joining the Pentecost Bands and formally following under the leadership of Frank Hotle, some problems began to emerge. The initial problem most likely came with Ernest Ward being a 16-year veteran missionary in India, fluent in the language and culture of the people, who had done all of the hard work to build the mission at Raj Nandgaon putting himself under the leadership of Frank Hotle, a newly arrived missionary with no knowledge of the language or the culture, and with no sweat-equity in the mission. Hotle decided that Ernest and Phebe needed to be sent back to the U.S. on furlough, but they would leave their five-year-old daughter behind in India. Ethel Ward related this event as follows,

Adjustment! That was the great problem now. That has ever been the perpetual problem on every mission field. Hundreds of years before, the prophet Amos knew this and wrote, "Can two walk together except they be agreed?" And here were six to "walk together." Mrs. Elizabeth Tucker and Mr. Wm. McCready were two of

the band from Nagpur but Mr. and Mrs. H____ *were*
the "leaders" and they "determined" (Acts 15:37) that
it would be best for the Wards to take a furlough to
America now and leave Louise in India to save expense
and insure the Wards returning to Raj Nandgaon again.
The rest "agreed," so it came the decision was that they
should go on furlough.[22]

If Ethel Ward presents the family's views accurately, it can be seen
that there was a great deal of frustration with the Hotles for this decision
(since Ethel chooses to not even use the Hotle name in her book and refers
to them as "leaders" in quotation marks). While articles in *The Pentecost
Herald* and accounts in the journals of the Pentecost Bands are silent on this
relationship, and Ward and Hotle seemed to continue working together,
the strain of being forced to leave a five-year-old child for over a year in
a place which has just experienced massive famine and death must have
been immense.

In September of 1898 the Wards returned to the United States
without five-year-old Louise. They were able to reunite with their daughters
Ethel and Bessie who had been left at the "Reaper's Home" in Virginia during
their previous furlough in 1892. The Wards set out to speak at churches
and camp meetings, raise funds, write articles for *The Pentecost Herald*,
and promote the work in India. Because Pandita Ramabai was involved in
dealing with orphans from the same famine in the same region of India, it
is not surprising that her name begins to be mentioned in connection with
the Wards' speaking. It is interesting to note that in an article about one of
the Wards' speaking engagements by Fannie Birdsall, she concludes with
a brief plug to "Send 5 cents for the illustrated sketch of the life of Pandita
Ramabi (sic)."[23]

Even while the Wards are in the United States, Frank Hotle makes
a special trip to Kedgaon in April of 1899 to visit Pandita Ramabai and
visit her work. [24] The main goal here was to get ideas for similar work the
Pentecost Bands hoped to start with child widows in a new mission station
in Gondia.

Connections with Pandita Ramabai

While Raj Nandgaon is roughly 600 miles (almost 1,000
km) inland from Kedgaon, the site of Pandita Ramabai's Mukti Mission,
missionaries had to frequently travel near Kedgaon on their way to Bombay

to both travel home and to pick up other missionaries coming back to India. This allowed for more interaction between the areas than distance might normally account for.

The leadership tensions in the Pentecost Bands continued to grow, culminating in a situation at the Harvest Home camp meeting in 1901.[25] Phebe notes in her diary on October 7, 1901,

> Harvest Home camp meeting began Sept. 25, Wed. About Sat. morn. Ernest objected to some teaching of the Bands in the holiness meeting. His manner displeased the workers and upon holding to his position, he was forbidden to take part in the meetings. He fainted away while standing in the eve. meeting which was construed by the workers to be the judgment of God. I could not quite see it as he was able to attend the meetings the next day. If Bro. Hotle had not previously forbidden him to speak it would have looked more reasonable to me... I was much distressed about things as I truly loved the Bands and felt that God was with them. But when Bro. Ward withdrew from the Bands, I felt God wanted me to stand by him. I can see things in the Bands that I know is not of God, such as forcing workers to take convictions from leaders as from God, and there was a relief in my heart when we left Raj Nandgaon. I was much tossed about during the trial, sometimes thinking I could not get through to heaven without the severe dealing of the Bands with me.[26] But when I think of things that have happened in dealing with different workers and the severe and harsh treatment used, I cannot but contrast it with the spirit of Jesus and it makes me more sure that this sudden and extraordinary move is from God. For Ernest did not think of severing his connections with the Bands when he went to H.H.

While the Wards are no longer listed as members of the Pentecost Bands in India in the *Pentecost Herald* after February of 1902, their daughter Ethel remains with the Bands until the end of 1904, and this becomes a matter of great concern for the Wards. Forced to leave the mission they had founded, the Wards were taken in by their old friend Albert Norton, who ran the Dhond boy's orphanage, which was a partner mission to Ramabai's Mukti Mission in Kedgaon.

From December of 1901 to April of 1902 the Ward's worked with Norton and had contact with Ramabai's work. Ernest took Methodist missionary C.B. Ward to visit Ramabai in February of 1902, and from an account in her diary from Friday, March 28, 1902 we know Phebe and her daughters Bessie and Louisa visited Pandita Ramabai along with Bessie Sherman's father C.W. Sherman well before the 1905 Mukti revival. Part of her account notes:

> Bro. Sherman, Bessie, Louisa and I started at 4:15AM for Kedgaon. Found a S.A. officer, Mr. Lewis, bound for the same place, so we all went together. Ramabai's *tonga*[27] waiting there when we arrived. Only a short ride, and we were in the grounds of the famous Mukti Mission. Everything looked so substantial, from the fine rooms we were ushered in to the great fat bullocks that took us in. Trees and plants everywhere…
>
> The church is a large building seating three thousand. It is a long building with two rounding sides capable of holding a large number. They have school in this building. She (*referring to Maribai, the head nurse*) took me to the small room where they had their first school room- they have prayers there every morning at four with the teachers. At 9:00 AM they had a special service for Good Friday. It was a sight to see that large body of girls and young women in the immense building. The floor is of wood- narrow boards. The pulpit a raised wooden platform, with a seat running around its four sides, which serves for a step for the platform. Bro. Sherman preached in English about the resurrection morning. Bro. Gadre interpreted into Marathi. I was struck with this thought, that those women when they went with the message, Jesus met them. When we are going to preach the Word, Jesus will meet us.[28]

Despite the close connections with both Norton and Ramabai, both missions did not seem significantly instilled with the holiness teachings for Ernest Ward. He writes to Phebe on April 7, 1902 about the possibility of working with either Norton or Ramabai,

> I have very little hope of a permanent affiliation with this work (*he is writing from the Nortons' work in Dhond*). Both sides of the house are neither in harmony with our teaching nor our practice on thorough holiness lines if we are at all aggressive, and until they radically change will continue to head us off in our work among the orphans. I think it should be exactly the same at Khedgaon if they had invited us there and I don't see why Bro. Sherman has any hope in that direction. I don't see a bit for true holiness with the advisors P.R. (*assumed to stand for Pandita Ramabai*) has about her now (or) P. herself, unless she shows a desire to shake loose of

everybody unspiritual who have a controlling voice at home or abroad.

The Wards go on to Sanjan to join up with the work of Sherman's Vanguard mission, until they ultimately return to the Free Methodist Church and its work in Yeotmal in June of 1904. Their daughter Ethel leaves the Pentecost Bands at this time and joins them in their work for the Free Methodist Church.

The Wards and the Radical Holiness Movement

Within the context of understanding the Wards' mission, it is important to address their theological position as part of the radical side of the Holiness Movement. As Howard Snyder points out, the Free Methodist Church in part defined itself as a "radical" holiness group, "Though maintaining some irenic contact with the broader Holiness Movement, its leaders and writers often warned against too low a standard of holiness: an experience that did not go deep enough, was not sufficiently world-denying, and compromised particularly with the amusements and ostentations of the age."[29] The Wards were aligned with this way of thinking. This can be seen in part from Ernest Ward's rapid acceptance of the Pentecost Bands' ideas in India, even after the Pentecost Bands had split from the Free Methodist Church. In addition, Ward entertained a number of radical holiness figures in India. Both William Godbey[30] and E.E. Shelhamer[31] visited with E.F. Ward in their various trips around the world. It is also exhibited in his involvement with the formation of a Holiness organization in India as well as his involvement in helping establish the Harvest Home Camp Meetings in India as part of the Pentecost Bands work.

Despite this close relationship in terms of a radical approach to holiness, the Wards seemed to move back into a more formal relationship with the Free Methodist mission effort by 1906. Ethel Ward writes,

> The Wards truly felt like pilgrims and strangers going from pillar to post with no settled abiding place, but they never forgot their church home- the Free Methodist Church... But now the Pentecost Bands which Rev. Dake had started as the young people's organization in the church, as well as the Vanguard Mission were both independent organizations outside the church. Hence it was with great joy that they received word from the Yeotmal District (the Free Methodist Mission), "Come home. We need you. Four of our missionaries have gone

> on furlough and we have an empty bungalow for you to occupy."[32]

It seems that the Wards did leave the umbrella of the Free Methodist Church to formally align themselves with the Pentecost Bands in 1898 for a short period, but then returned in 1904.

The Mukti Revival and the Free Methodist Mission in India

It is natural at this point to wonder if the Wards had a close relationship to Pandita Ramabai, as I am suggesting, then where is the evidence of the influence of the Mukti Revival on Free Methodist missions in India? Such evidence clearly exists. First, it must be remembered that Ernest and Phebe Ward seem to have broken with the Pentecost Bands about 1902, and were in Yeotmal by the time of the Mukti Revival in June of 1905. According to Helen Dyer's account of the Mukti Revival, it began in late June 1905 and quickly spread to other areas of Pune including Soonderbai Powar's Zenana Training Home and the Methodist Boy's School in Pune, then the Boy's Christian Home in Dhond (run by Albert Norton), then,

> Longing for Revival, the Free Methodist Mission at Yeotmal, Berar, was in the right attitude for blessing. Schools were closed in order that missionaries, teachers, and pupils might wait on the Lord. This was the last week in August 1905. On the Saturday night of this week of prayer the answer came. The meetings were over, but twenty were still "tarrying" when at 10:30 p.m. the Holy Spirit came like a shock of electricity; some shouted the praises of God, some danced, some ran, and some fell to the ground, under the power of God. All present were Christians with one exception, and she was converted. The others were all baptized with the Holy Spirit. Then the work spread to the unconverted in the orphanages. There was true conviction of sin, which resulted in confession followed by forgiveness and great joy.[33]

Only after the revival in Yeotmal does Dyer note the revival was then taken to Bombay and other areas. Burritt also notes in passing, "During the cool season of 1905 there was a mighty outpouring of the Spirit on our district (Yeotmal) as well as other parts of India. The revival that followed will ever be remembered by those who were privileged to witness it. The results still abide."[34]

While such evidence is not conclusive, the early days of the Mukti Revival seem to indicate a spread through networks of people close to Ramabai and the Mukti Mission. The fact that this revival spread to Yeotmal and the Free Methodist Mission, while Ernest and Phebe Ward are there, just one month after the revival starts, indicates some level of relationship, even if that connection is primarily through Albert Norton of the Boy's Christian Home in Dhond and the five months the Wards lived and worked there in 1902. How the Wards may have personally impacted Ramabai with their holiness views can probably never be determined.

Concluding Thoughts

The common Pentecostal narrative of the origin of Pentecostalism tends to emphasize speaking in tongues (or *glossolalia*), the particular sign of the Pentecostal experience of the Baptism of the Holy Spirit, which began in Charles Parham's Bible School in Topeka, Kansas on January 1, 1901. One of his students, William Seymour, led revival meetings on Azusa Street in Los Angeles in April of 1906. These revivals led to an explosion of people taking the Pentecostal message throughout the world. Two prominent stories from outside of the United States tend to create problems for this narrative. One is a Pentecostal revival in the Methodist Episcopal Church in Valparaiso, Chile under the direction of Rev. Willis C. Hoover in 1902 (four years before Azusa Street). The other is the Pentecostal revival in the Mukti Mission at Kedgaon, outside of Bombay (present day Mumbai) led by its founder Sarasvati Ramabai (more commonly known by her title, Pandita Ramabai) in June of 1905 (one year before Azusa Street).

Often in these narratives, even in some academic circles, the role of the Wesleyan-Holiness Movement is overlooked, minimalized, or simply missing from the narrative. This paper seeks to add new insight into the Wesleyan-Holiness influences on the Mukti Revival and Pandita Ramabai by examining primary source materials from the papers of the first Free Methodist missionaries, Ernest F. Ward and his wife Phebe, as well as documents from the first Pentecost Band in India, which joined with Ward in his work. Previous narratives of the Mukti Revival have linked it to the influence of the Welsh Revival under Evan Roberts from 1904-1905, which influenced similar revivals in India from 1905-1906. To my knowledge, linking the Mukti Revival with the influence of Ward and the Pentecost Bands in India has not been suggested before.[35]

In his article, *Inventing Pentecostalism: Pandita Ramabai and the Mukti Revival from a Post-Colonial Perspective*, Suarsana raises important questions about Pentecostalism's claim to incorporate the history of Pandita Ramabai and the Mukti Mission into the global history of Pentecostalism.[36] The revival at the Mukti Mission among child widows in India began in 1905 with claims of speaking in tongues one full year before the Azusa Street Revival from which Pentecostalism normally records its founding. Suarsana notes the inclusion of Ramabai's mission in Pentecostal history is more of a colonial rewriting of history than actual fact. Minnie Abrams (who worked with Pandita Ramabai) wrote personal narratives making herself a central figure in this revival[37], while Helen Dyer (a personal friend of Ramabai's) wrote from the "Higher Life" and Keswick Movement's Holiness perspective crediting the influence of the Welsh Revival carried by Welsh missionaries to the Khasi Hills.[38] Both perspectives tend to neglect the voice of Pandita Ramabai herself in the process. Pentecostalism and the Holiness Movement have both tried to claim the Mukti Revival by controlling the historical narrative. Suarsana's argument is persuasive and encourages scholars to take a closer look at the story of Pandita Ramabai and the Mukti Revival, as well as the outside connections that may have impacted its development.

This paper is not an answer to the problem of understanding what actually occurred in 1905 in the Mukti Mission in Kedgaon, India (Maharashtra state). If anything, this paper will add more fuel to the fire by adding a new potential list of characters to the story. It is hoped that more information gathered from primary sources about the Holiness mission work in the area will add to understanding the influences that may have played a role in the 1905 Mukti Revival. One voice left missing from this conversation is that of the missions of the Free Methodist Church, and two influential sources that may have played contributing roles to understanding this revival, both the Wards and the Pentecost Bands.

End Notes

[1] Much of the material relating to the lives of Ernest and Phebe Ward come from the Ward family papers held by the Archives and Special Collections of B.L. Fisher Library at Asbury Theological Seminary, Wilmore, KY and microfilm of the Papers of Ernest F. Ward held by the Marston Memorial Historical Center and Free Methodist Archives in Indianapolis, IN.

[2] There are many good works on the life and work of Pandita Ramabai, for one good general overview of the history involved, cf. Allan Anderson, "Pandita Ramabai, the Mukti Revival and Global Pentecostalism," in *Transformation* (2006) 23(1):37-48.

[3] For a more in depth view of the development of Pentecostalism in India, cf. Stanley M. Burgess, "Pentecostalism in India: An Overview." *Asian Journal of Pentecostal Studies* (2001) 4(1): 85-98.

[4] Carrie T. Burritt, *The Story of Fifty Years*. Winona Lake, IN: Light and Life Press. Page 67. First Fruits Reprint retrieved at: https://place. asburyseminary.edu/freemethodistbooks/13/.

[5] Cf. *Ordered Steps or the Wards of India* by Ethel Ellen Ward, Winona Lake, IN: Light and Life Press, 1951: 23, 25, 103-4.

[6] William Taylor, *Four Years' Campaign in India* (1880) New York: Philips and Hunt: 238-239.

[7] See also "Albert B. Norton and the Mukti Revival: From Faith Missions to Pentecostal Advocate" by Robert A. Danielson, *Pneuma* 42 (1):1-20 (2020).

[8] *The Apostolic Faith* (Los Angeles, Cal.), vol. 1, no. 7 (April 1907), p. 2.

[9] "Our Missionaries Have Reached India," by R. E. Massey and "Jesus is Victor" by Mary Courtney, *The Bridegroom's Messenger* 2(30): 3 (Jan. 15, 1909).

[10] "Rain in the Time of the Latter Rain- A Testimony," by Albert Norton, *The Bridegroom's Messenger* 2(39): 3 (June 1, 1909).

[11] Cornelia Sorabji (1866-1954) was the first female graduate from Bombay University, the first female advocate in India, and the first woman to practice law in India and she was also a social reformer and friend of Pandita Ramabai. She was a major advocate of education for women and helped establish several girls' school in Pune.

[12] *Ordered Steps or the Wards of India* by Ethel Ellen Ward, Winona Lake, IN: Light and Life Press, 1951: 69-71.

[13] Bessie Sherman was the daughter of holiness leader C.W. Sherman of the Vanguard Mission of St. Louis, MO, and she would be a friend and supporter of the Wards, especially Phebe during their time in India.

[14] *Ordered Steps or the Wards of India* by Ethel Ellen Ward, Winona Lake, IN: Light and Life Press, 1951: 69-71.

[15] *The Pentecost Herald*, vol 1, no. 2, May 1894, p. 4.

[16] Published in 1908, Chicago, IL by the Free Methodist Publishing House.

[17] The Pentecost Herald, vol. 4, no. 16, (whole no. 71), November 15, 1897, p. 3.

[18] The trip of this group is reported quite extensively in The Pentecost Herald, vol. 4, no. 14 p. 2 (October 15, 1897), vol. 4, no. 15 p. 3 (November 1, 1897), vol. 4, no. 17 (December 1, 1897), vol. 4, no. 18 (December 15, 1897), and vol. 4, no. 20 p. 6 (January 15,1898).

[19] All references and quotations from the Pentecost Bands of India come from the Records of Pentecost Bands in India, microfilm at Asbury Theological Seminary, ARC1010 1989-006 reel 1. This microfilm contains the records of three bands: Band #1 at Raj Nandgaon (1897-1905), Band #2 at Gondia (1899-1905), and Band #3 at Dondi Lohara (1899-1949). The originals are kept at the Marsden Memorial Historical Center in Indianapolis, IN. The quotes used in this paper are from the records of Band #1 unless otherwise specified.

[20] Carrie T. Burritt, The Story of Fifty Years. Winona Lake, IN: Light and Life Press. Page 67-71.

[21] Ethel Ellen Ward, Ordered Steps, or the Wards of India, 1951, Winona Lake, IN: Light and Life Press, p. 93.

[22] Ward, Ordered Steps, pp. 94-95.

[23] The Pentecost Herald, vol. 5, no. 16, (whole no. 95), November 15, 1898, p. 8.

[24] The Pentecost Herald, vol. 6, no. 6, (whole no. 109), June 15, 1899, p. 6.

[25] Harvest Home Camp Meetings were a part of the Pentecost Bands ministry brought over from the United States. These annual camp meetings focused on holiness teaching to encourage the Pentecost Band workers.

[26] In her letter to Ernest in April 22, 1902, reflecting back on their experience, Phebe writes of even more extreme events emanating from the Hotles' leadership,

> You know that Bro. Hotle wanted me out of the way so they could run things as they pleased and they thought they saw in me a formidable foe. You remember the day you and he locked me up as he thrust me in that little room, he said "Your power in Raj N- is broken," because I insisted on knowing the state of my own soul. He told Sr. Vail I had to be taken to America to get me out of the way. How sad! Instead of utilizing the God given power in me- they would not have it when it ran

counter to their opinions. That was the secret of your being taken from Khairagarh. They could not handle you so well there.

[27] Or *tanga*, is a light carriage used in India, Pakistan, and Bangladesh, which is traditionally pulled by a horse and has two-wheels.

[28] While this is from Phebe Ward's journal held in the Ward Family Papers at the Archives and Special Collections of the B.L. Fisher Library, Asbury Theological Seminary, Wilmore, KY. The full extended quote has also been published in Robert Danielson, "From the Archives: Ernest F. Ward: The First Free Methodist Foreign Missionary," *The Asbury Journal* (2015) Vol. 70:1, p. 172 - 180. Available at: https://place.asburyseminary.edu/asburyjournal/vol70/iss1/11.

[29] Howard A. Snyder, "Radical Holiness Evangelism: Vivian Dake and the Pentecost Bands," In *The Radical Holiness Movement in the Christian Tradition: A Festschrift for Larry D. Smith*, edited by William Kostlevy and Wallace Thornton, Jr. 2016 Lexington, KY: Emeth Press, p. 70.

[30] William Godbey, *Around the World, Garden of Eden, Latter Day Prophecies and Missions*, (1907) Cincinnati, OH: God's Revivalist Office, p. 437, 474, records visiting the Free Methodist Mission in Yeotmal.

[31] There is a photograph in the E.E. Shelhamer Papers in the Archives and Special Collections of B.L. Fisher Library of Asbury Theological Seminary, Wilmore, KY that shows Ernest and Phebe Ward and other missionaries in India, which was taken of E.E. Shelhamer's trip. This gives evidence to their meeting, which would not be unusual given some of the early connections both share with the Pentecost Bands.

[32] Ethel Ellen Ward, *Ordered Steps or the Wards of India*, Winona Lake, IN: Light and Life Press, 1951: 107-8.

[33] Helen S. Dyer, *Revival in India: "Years of the Right Hand of the Most High."* (1907) London: Morgan and Scott, page 61.

[34] Carrie T. Burritt, *The Story of Fifty Years*. Winona Lake, IN: Light and Life Press. Page 71.

[35] This is not to suggest that the Wards and the Pentecost Bands in India were primary drivers of the revival, or to suggest that they were the only influences. Stanley M. Burgess' 2001 article "Pentecostalism in India: An Overview" in the *Asian Journal of Pentecostal Studies* 4(1): 85-98 demonstrates that there are plenty of contenders for Pentecostal influence in India, both before and after the Mukti Revival. The goal here is to simply introduce the Free Methodists as serious additional potential influences in the region prior to the Mukti Revival.

[36] Yan Suarsana, "Inventing Pentecostalism: Pandita Ramabai and the Mukti Revival from a Post-Colonial Perspective," in *PentecoStudies* (2014) 13(2): 173-196.

[37] Minnie Abrams, *The Baptism of the Holy Ghost and Fire: Matt: 3:11* (1906) Kedgaon, India: Mukti Mission Press, and "How the Recent Revival was Brought About in India: The Power of Intercession," in *The Latter Rain Evangel* (July 1909) 1(10): 6-13.

[38] Helen S. Dyer, *Revival in India: "Years of the Right Hand of the Most High."* (1907) London: Morgan and Scott.

Works Cited

Abrams, Minnie
1906   *The Baptism of the Holy Ghost and Fire: Matt: 3:11.* Kedgaon, India: Mukti Mission Press.

1909   "How the Recent Revival was Brought About in India: The Power of Intercession." *The Latter Rain Evangel* (July) 1(10): 6-13.

Anderson, Allan
2006   "Pandita Ramabai, the Mukti Revival and Global Pentecostalism." *Transformation* 23(1):37-48.

Burgess, Stanley M.
2001   "Pentecostalism in India: An Overview." *Asian Journal of Pentecostal Studies* 4(1): 85-98.

Burritt, Carrie T.
ca1935   *The Story of Fifty Years*. Winona Lake, IN: Light and Life Press. First Fruits Reprint retrieved at: https://place.asburyseminary.edu/freemethodistbooks/13/.

Courtney, Mary
1909   "Jesus is Victor." *The Bridegroom's Messenger* 2(30): 3.

Danielson, Robert
2015   "From the Archives: Ernest F. Ward: The First Free Methodist Foreign Missionary." *The Asbury Journal* 70(1):172-180.

2020   "Albert B. Norton and the Mukti Revival: From Faith Missions to Pentecostal Advocate." *Pneuma* 42 (1): 1-20.

Dyer, Helen S.
1907   *Revival in India: "Years of the Right Hand of the Most High."* London: Morgan and Scott.

Godbey, William
1907   *Around the World, Garden of Eden, Latter Day Prophecies and Missions.* Cincinnati, OH: God's

Revivalist Office. First Fruits Reprint retrieved at: https://place.asburyseminary.edu/godbey/12/.

Massey, R.E.
1909 "Our Missionaries Have Reached India." *The Bridegroom's Messenger* 2(30): 3.

Norton, Albert
1909 "Rain in the Time of the Latter Rain- A Testimony." *The Bridegroom's Messenger* 2(39): 3.

1907 *The Apostolic Faith* (Los Angeles, Cal.) 1(7): 2.

Pentecost Bands of India
1897-1949 *Records of Pentecost Bands in India*. Microfilm at Asbury Theological Seminary, ARC1010 1989-006 reel 1. This microfilm contains the records of three bands: Band #1 at Raj Nandgaon (1897-1905), Band #2 at Gondia (1899-1905), and Band #3 at Dondi Lohara (1899-1949). The originals are kept at the Marsden Memorial Historical Center in Indianapolis, IN.

The Pentecost Herald
1894 1(2): 4 (May).

1897 4(16): 3, (whole no. 71), (November 15).

4(14): 2, (October 15).

4(15): 3, (November 1).

4(17): 1 (December 1).

4(18): 1 (December 15).

1898 4(20): 6 (January 15).

5(16): 8, (whole no. 95), (November 15).

1899 6(6): 6, (whole no. 109), (June 15).

Snyder, Howard A.
2016 "Radical Holiness Evangelism: Vivian Dake and the Pentecost Bands," In *The Radical Holiness Movement in the Christian Tradition: A Festschrift for Larry D. Smith*, edited by William Kostlevy and Wallace Thornton, Jr. Lexington, KY: Emeth Press.

Taylor, William
1880 *Four Years' Campaign in India*. New York, NY: Philips and Hunt.

Ward, Ethel Ellen
    1951   *Ordered Steps or the Wards of India*, Winona Lake, IN: Light and Life Press. First Fruits Reprint retrieved at: https://place.asburyseminary.edu/firstfruitsheritage material/173/

Ward, Ernest and Phebe
    1908   *Echoes from Bharatkhand.* Chicago, IL by the Free Methodist Publishing House.

Suarsana, Yan
    2014   "Inventing Pentecostalism: Pandita Ramabai and the Mukti Revival from a Post-Colonial Perspective." *PentecoStudies* (2014) 13(2): 173-196.

The Asbury Journal 75/1: 107-126
© 2020 Asbury Theological Seminary
DOI: 10.7252/Journal.01.2020S.07

Dwight S.M. Mutonono
The Leadership Implications of Kneeling in Zimbabwean Culture

Abstract:
This paper considers the implications of public officials and church members kneeling to their leaders as a cultural expression of honor. Zimbabweans, like many Africans, kneel or crouch when interacting with people in authority. In traditional culture children are socialized to kneel to elders, and this becomes a deeply ingrained part of their way of life. While the practice of kneeling, even in private, is not as prevalent as it used to be, recently high-level Zimbabwean public officials have been recorded kneeling before authority figures. They justify their behavior based on culture. Church members do the same to their leaders and similarly justify their conduct as cultural behavior. This paper analyses and critiques this conduct, considering cultural changes to assess the leadership implications of continuing this practice in modern day Zimbabwe.

While the continued private practice of the culture is the prerogative of individual Zimbabweans and cannot be legislated against, the public expression of kneeling is now counter-productive. It is not achieving the original intentions of honoring the behavior's recipient. Because of abuse and possible interpretive misunderstandings, it should be stopped. Recommended ways of transforming the culture are given.

Keywords: leadership, honor, kneeling, Africa, Church

Dwight Mutonono is from Harare, Zimbabwe. He has a Masters in Leadership and Management from Africa Leadership and Management Academy (ALMA) in Zimbabwe, a Doctor of Ministry in Transformational Leadership for the Global City from Bakke Graduate University in Seattle, Washington, and is working on a Ph.D. in Intercultural Studies at Asbury Theological Seminary.

Introduction

A strong part of Zimbabwean culture and socialization is the honoring of elders or those in power. The visible expression of this is to kneel in the presence of such people. The phenomenon of high officials, such as ministers of state or Supreme Court judges, publicly kneeling to their superiors in the social hierarchy is disconcerting, as is the same practice being done within the church.

This paper will analyze the possible effects of the phenomenon of kneeling before elders in the context of public leadership spheres and worship in the church. First, as a background to the issue being analyzed, specific instances of the occurrence of this phenomenon will be presented. The main content of the paper is divided into three parts: the cultural background and rationalization of the practice, the modernized Western view of the practice, and a discussion on what is an appropriate way to honor elders publicly. The implications of public kneeling will be considered before concluding with recommendations regarding the practice for the Zimbabwean context.

Cultural Background and Rationalization for Kneeling

A 2017 newspaper article named several government ministers and senior officials who have publicly knelt before former President Robert Mugabe and his wife Grace. The ministers and officials named in the article, and in some instances recorded and shown on television doing so are: Patrick Chinamasa, the late John Nkomo, Martin Dinha, Ignatius Chombo, Didymus Mutasa and Rita Makarau.[1]

Rita Makarau, a Supreme Court judge, was the chairperson of the Zimbabwe Electoral Commission at the time that she was pictured kneeling before then President Mugabe. When asked, she defended her actions, saying,

> "I have been brought up to say that when you are speaking to someone older than you kneel down. That's who I have been brought up [sic] and it was difficult for me to change just like that when he called me to his side," Makarau said, adding that she also finds herself kneeling when conducting her duties as a Supreme Court Judge.
> "I find myself kneeling to the chief justice if I have to speak to him. I can't get rid of that upbringing like I said. Even at work I find myself kneeling, maybe I need to go for training (to get rid of it)."[2]

The last sentence in Makarau's quoted words seems to indicate that kneeling is something she does reflexively, perhaps without even consciously knowing that she is doing it. This would be something deeply ingrained in her psyche and culture. In her view, stopping it would probably require training of some kind to change the behavior.

The phenomenon of kneeling in public is not limited to the political sphere. I have seen it on numerous occasions in religious gatherings. Women often kneel when serving food to their leaders, and as a pastor I have been a recipient of this kind of treatment. Though I have felt some discomfort, refusing the treatment might cause unnecessary offense and distract people's attention from the worship event. I have also felt inadequately prepared for the inevitable questions about why I am reciprocating a respectful action with a public insult if I try to change the behavior. I have seen the extremes of this when visiting a fellow pastor's office. The office culture, which they had established, is that the personal assistant does not speak to the pastor standing, she must be on her knees. Congregants of some mega-churches have publicly knelt to some of their prophets in places like airports or out in the streets. Gunda and Machingura relate one such instance, "Those who managed to evade the human wall made by Prophet Angel's bodyguards would kneel on the tarmac before greeting him."[3] It is important to attempt to better understand the cultural background that results in such public behavior.

Zimbabwe has a number of different ethnic groups. These include the Shona, Ndebele, Tonga, Korekore, Ndau, Venda and Kalanga and other smaller groups. The cultures, in as far as the phenomenon of kneeling is concerned, are culturally similar within Zimbabwe, and though a Shona or Ndebele or other ethnic group might be mentioned in various sections of this paper, the ethnic group should be read as representative of Zimbabwean culture in general. This practice of kneeling in the presence of elders is deeply ingrained in all of Zimbabwean culture, and it is taught from childhood. Nicolson, in his review of Michael Gelfand's *African Background: The Traditional Culture of the Shona-Speaking People* says,

> Within the family, respect for seniority and for the ancestral spirits are overriding concerns. Respect is shown by submission and the customs of avoidance, handclapping, kneeling or sitting at the appropriate times. In the kinship system as a whole, and in particular in the three types of procedure—the use of a third party (mediation), the giving of presents (reciprocation) and

the payment of money or possessions (compensation)—
Professor Gelfand shows how the concern for maintaining
protocol is almost obsessive. This perhaps explains the
well-known Shona characteristic, avoidance of hasty
decisions. He suggests that the slower tempo of life is
deliberate and designed to prevent falling into error.[4]

Kneeling is therefore part of a broader scheme of showing respect
for seniority and ancestral spirits. When the prophet is understood as a
mediator between this world and the spirit world (replacing the position of
the spirit medium or diviner in the African religious scheme),[5] then kneeling
in his or her presence is understandable. This is also the case, of course in
the instance of kneeling before Presidents and the like as alluded to in the
introduction.

The practice of kneeling is deeply ingrained, particularly among
women who are supposed to kneel for men. Men would generally crouch
in the presence of elders, but women kneel in the presence of men. My
wife does not kneel when she gives food that she has cooked to me, but
many of my friends who are culturally modernized in many other respects
will have their wife kneeling as she gives them food. Omoregie describes
the practice at the *kurova guva* (to beat the grave) also known as *kugadzira
mudzimu* (to prepare the spirit)[6] ceremony, a practice that also happens in
burial rituals,

When the *varoora* [daughters in law] walk on their knees
as they approach the grave, it is a sign of their respect
both to the deceased and all members of the family. It
can therefore be said that this action is symptomatic of
their "inner feelings and attitudes" (of respect). This links
well with what happens in everyday Shona life. When
a young girl talks to an elder, she kneels down while
young men crouch as a sign of respect.[7]

Children are socialized to kneel or crouch in the presence of
elders. In a traditional Zimbabwean home, this is normal and expected.
Not kneeling is showing deep disrespect to the elder. Given this context
and background, the behavior described in the background section of this
paper is perhaps more understandable. However, we are also living in
a globalized environment in which the dominant culture is shaped by
ideas from modernity and the ubiquitous attitude of Western superiority,
that has prevailed since the time Africa was colonized, Christianized,

and encountered the Western world. Hiebert describes such prevailing attitudes this way,

> Roughly from 1800 to 1950 most Protestant missionaries in India, and later in Africa, rejected the beliefs and practices of the people they served as "pagan". ...*tabula rasa* the missionary doctrine that there is nothing in the non-Christian culture on which the Christian missionary can build and, therefore, every aspect of the traditional non-Christian culture had to be destroyed before Christianity could be built up... To become Christian one had to accept not only Christianity but also Western cultural ways. ... One reason was the emergence of colonialism with its belief in the superiority of Western cultures. ...Colonialism proved to the West its cultural superiority. Western civilization had triumphed. It was the task, therefore, of the West to bring the benefits of this civilization to the world... Christianity, civilization and, later, commerce (the three Cs) went hand in hand. Western civilization was spreading around the world, and it was assumed that people would become both Christian and "modern."[8]

The attitude of Western superiority and tutelage of the uncivilized is still with us, and in instances like those being described in this paper can result in condescending narratives about African backwardness. Nevertheless, it is vital to focus on how some of these attitudes play out in the public arena.

Kneeling as Seen from the Widespread Western Modernity Perspective

Zimbabweans who are more modernized in their thinking, or are still traditional but non-conformist, will find the public kneeling displays by high officials abhorrent. I once had a discussion on this topic with a Masters level class in Harare and the exchanges became so heated and explosive I had to control the class. Some will tenaciously hold on to this part of their culture and nothing will change that position, even after shifting from their traditional cultural practices in many other respects. Culture changes to suit and adapt the new needs and values that come from mixing with other cultures. Some practices in any given culture, which were practiced a hundred years ago, are no longer compatible with today's norms and values and therefore get dropped in time, others survive even though their usefulness is questionable. In addition, it is important to note that Zimbabwe went through a colonization that was far more than a cultural exchange between equal parties.

As the quote above from Hiebert shows, many Christian missionaries and colonial powers saw nothing of value that could be built on in indigenous Zimbabwean cultures; the existing culture was to be destroyed and English culture would replace it. Cultural imperialism occurs when one party is stronger than the other and the stronger party coerces the weaker one to adopt its culture. In the public sphere this is especially true. Zimbabwe adopted Western ways of governance and protocol wholesale. Their structures are exactly the same as in the United Kingdom. However, in instances like showing honor and respect, the subdued Zimbabwean cultural instincts sometimes pop up and are judged according to expectations of the imposed colonial structures that they are at variance with.

The British Broadcasting Corporation had this perspective on the respectful behavior of Zimbabwean leaders towards past President Mugabe,

> As in much of Africa, respecting your elders is ingrained in Zimbabwe's culture. And 93-year-old Robert Mugabe, a liberation fighter who became the country's leader at independence in 1980, is seen as the father of the nation. It explains the respectful tone used by opposition leader and bitter rival Morgan Tsvangirai when calling for President Mugabe's resignation. He said Mr [sic] Mugabe should step down "in line with the national expectation and sentiment, taking full regard of his legacy and contribution to Zimbabwe pre and post-independence."[9]

The respect shown to Mugabe even while he was being removed by a coup was fascinating. It was a very polite and respectful coup. Mugabe was publicly deferred to throughout. The army that removed him refused to say at any point that they were removing him, instead they were dealing with some criminal elements surrounding the president. The actual words that were used to describe the military intervention, as they called it, are,

> Fellow Zimbabweans, following the address we made on 13 November 2017, which we believe our main broadcaster, ZBC and *The Herald*, were directed not to publicise [sic], the situation in our country has moved to another level.
> Firstly, we wish to assure the nation that His Excellency, The President, of the Republic of Zimbabwe, and Commander in Chief of the Zimbabwe Defense Forces, Cde R.G. Mugabe and his family are safe and sound and their security is guaranteed.

> We are only targeting criminals around him who are committing crimes that are causing social and economic suffering in the country in order to bring them to justice. As soon as we have accomplished our mission we expect that the situation will return to normalcy.[10]

The world will find the respectful behavior of Zimbabweans in public spheres to be counterproductive and unexpected. Opposition leaders are expected to be confrontational and candid, not respectful and deferring. Ministers of state should show respect, but this should be done in a manner that does not make the president unquestionable or look monarchical. How can a person who is submissive to the extent of publicly kneeling before a president then be able to differ with him? As for Supreme Court justices kneeling to a president, that would be scandalous and threatens the whole governance of political institutions, specifically separation of powers, in the country. This behavior is misaligned to the expected Western norms of a functional democracy.

When it comes to kneeling before a church leader, most Western churches would throw their hands up in horror at the thought of someone kneeling before them in a worship service or at a church related activity. While the idea of respecting elders and leaders is generally universally acceptable; the Zimbabwean tradition of kneeling, especially publicly to show respect needs closer critique, which is what this paper is attempting to do. The Zimbabwean Church needs to engage in the process of self-theologizing and contextualizing.[11] To lead the way in terms of handling culture, the Church needs to think clearly about how the Bible affects culture.

> To recognize that theologies are done by humans in their contexts means that we must study human contexts deeply to know how they shape our thinking, and to seek the biblical message not through the eyes of our culture, but as it was understood by those who recorded it. We need to study human cultures to build understanding among them and to communicate the gospel in them in ways that transform them in the light of God's truth, beauty and righteousness.[12]

To contextualize the idea of kneeling as a sign of respect, it is important that it be examined under the overarching question of how Zimbabweans today should show respect to leaders and elders.

What Appropriate Ways Can Zimbabweans Find to Honor Elders and Leaders?

Here I need to first describe the cultural factors underpinning the practice of public kneeling before leaders. After understanding these factors, the possible ways in which the same meaning intended by the outward action can be explored. I will then consider the meanings that the outward act of public kneeling has, first for the participants, then second for the various observers, before discussing the most appropriate ways to show honor in today's context.

Cultural Factors Behind the Act of Kneeling

There are cultural factors at play in the observable action of kneeling in Zimbabwean culture. Anthropology helps to better understand what brings about such a phenomenon as that being discussed in this paper. Robbins talks about what he calls "the cultural construction of identity and social hierarchy."[13] Social hierarchy and/or gender identity are at play when people feel the need, even instinctively, to kneel in the presence of certain leaders.

Americans can move from one status to another and one relationship to another with different people, but in their minds remain essentially the same person.[14] This is not the case with the Japanese, for example, who change the way they refer to themselves depending on the speaker's relationship to the listener. This influences how Japanese advertise on television. It is rude for Japanese, depending on who is speaking, to give an imperative like "drink coke!" "Japanese advertisers have a problem with *keigo* because actors should not give imperative commands (e.g., "drink Coke") for fear of offending people. They solve the problem by using low-status people who are nonthreatening (such as clowns, coquettish women, or children) to issue the commands."[15] Robbins goes on to describe how traditional societies are organized,

> In traditional societies, kinship is the central organizing principle—the main determinant of a person's social identity. Anthropologists working with traditional societies are often "adopted" by a family. This act, although also a signal of acceptance, serves the practical purpose of assigning an outsider a social identity through which others can approach him or her. To have no kinship label or designation in such societies is to have no meaningful place in the social landscape.[16]

Zimbabwe is a typical traditional society as described by Robbins. Most Zimbabweans in influential leadership positions grew up in a rural traditional environment, or are one generation from the rural-urban migration; that is, if they were not born in the rural areas, their parents were. Whether in church or society, leaders are referred to by kinship terms, such as fathers or mothers in Zimbabwe today. The conduct in the presence of these "fathers" and "mothers" is parallel to the cultural prescriptions regarding how one treats kin. Kneeling in the presence of a father or mother is appropriate, and as far as cultural expectations go, expected. Therefore, similar behaviors are expanded beyond the traditional kin group to other political and religious leaders.

Former president, Mugabe was referred to as the "father" of the nation. His wife, Grace when she entered politics as the leader of the ruling party women's league, a position from which she attempted to eventually become the president after Mugabe, which resulted in the coup that removed Mugabe, took on the title "mother" (amai) of the nation. She was generally referred to as "Dr. Amai" in that period. What is notable is how she perceived that position and her role, even before publically angling for the presidency.

> ... Muchemeyi said: "Grace told an executive meeting that she is "already the President" and would not want to be appointed VP, as it was a lower post.
> "The First Lady said I'm the wife of the President, I'm the president already ... I plan and do everything with the President, what more do I want, for now the position of the women boss is enough."
> Last year, Grace said Vice-President Emmerson Mnangagwa and Phelekezela Mphoko took instructions from her.[17]

In Grace Mugabe's mind, based on the traditional society's kingship related stratification as described by Robbins, she was a "mother." The next step in that process of thinking is to see the rest of the nation as her children, which is exactly what she did, placing herself above the Vice-Presidents in that stratification. She would expect people to kneel before her; publicly making high officials do that, and referring to them publicly as her children.

The *emic* and *etic* approaches that were first developed by linguist Kenneth Pike and used by anthropologist Marvin Harris are useful analysis tools to interpret the effects of Grace Mugabe's thinking and conduct. They distinguish between meanings understood by actors (the people themselves, and in this case, Grace Mugabe) calling them *emic*, and *etic* which is what independent observers interpret as really happening.[18] In her mind, as she went about her business, she was a mother to the nation and expected people to culturally treat her as that with all the protocols that go with it. Some probably did reciprocate in the expected manner and from the heart complied with cultural procedures like kneeling before her. However, though people publicly complied with culturally expected norms, the political events that transpired, culminating in the coup and the public utterances of these same people after the coup, reveals that perhaps outwardly people were kneeling, but inwardly they were not. If not at the level of the participants, then certainly in the eyes of observers, like the media, the interpretation (*etic*) of the meanings associated with the act of kneeling was not the same as Grace Mugabe's. In this sense, we must consider the meanings associated with the outward action of kneeling, especially in public spaces today.

Meanings Associated with Kneeling

A 2011 newspaper article recorded then Minister of Mines and Mining Development, Obert Mpofu responding to a question concerning the way he signed one of his letters to President Mugabe. He had signed it by describing himself as Mugabe's ever-obedient son,

> "President Mugabe is my father, he is my father and the signing off as 'your ever obedient son' was not a mistake. When I go to see him I refer to him as baba (father)," Mpofu said amid laughter from journalists. "I don't drink (alcohol) and any decision I take is sober. I do things knowing they are good. I regard President Mugabe as my father," he said. Mpofu (60) said he also referred to his seniors and bosses as his fathers...[19]

While the newspaper article accused Mpofu of "bootlicking," his expressed motivation in doing what he did is that he genuinely regarded Mugabe as his father. So, if he was to kneel for Mugabe, it would be an outward expression of a heartfelt respect that a son gives to a father. Robert Strauss says,

> In 1936, Ralph Linton introduced the terms *form*, *function*, and *meaning* to the field of cultural anthropology

in his book, *The Study of Man*. Years later, anthropologist Charles H. Kraft ...rekindled interest in these concepts as he addressed communicating across cultures. He argued that the form/meaning distinction, if not the most important skill in cross-cultural communication, is one of the most important skills...

How are these terms conceptually defined?
- *Form* refers to any cultural element – a material object, word, idea, pattern, or ritual.
- *Function* is the intended purpose of that form in a society.
- *Meaning* is what the forms convey denotatively and connotatively... the associations which any society attaches to it.[20]

Using this framework to analyze kneeling, it can be established that when done according to the cultural construct, the practice of kneeling (*form*) has an intended purpose of conveying respect (*meaning*). Zimbabwean journalists as shown so far in this paper are now questioning the practice at two levels. First, is the form still conveying the same meaning it did originally? While kneeling might be a show of respect in the heart of the one who does it , and the recipient of the action understands it that way; when done in public, the meanings that others associate with that act might be very different to what is going on in the hearts of the people who are directly involved. The world and even some Zimbabweans have very different understandings of what is happening. The contexts in which this is being done give very different meanings to the form than might be intended, thus the outcry from more modernized Zimbabweans, Zimbabwean journalists, and media from other parts of the world. The imported Western structures of governance that Zimbabwe has adopted interpret the kneeling of public officials to a President or other high office as dysfunctional governance systems. They see values like the need for accountability, impartiality, and justice, which drive the establishment of the structures that Zimbabwe adopted, at risk. How can a person who is showing such public displays of subservience possibly ask the tough questions to those in authority as their jobs expect of them?

Second, the journalists are questioning whether the form is still really aligned to the meaning in the hearts of those who ostensibly show respect in public, whether through kneeling or other outward forms of honoring. The second question is behind a critique of *The Herald*, a newspaper that is widely regarded as a Zimbabwean government mouthpiece,

> In August, the paper ran a typically fawning portrait of Grace under the headline "A Loving Mother of the Nation."
> "Loving mother, compassionate philanthropist, astute businesswoman, perceptive politician, remarkable patriot, these are all adjectives that can be used to describe the First Lady Dr [sic] Grace Mugabe," *The Herald* gushed.
> Less than three months later and in the wake of a coup that threatens Mugabe's presidency and has seen both he and Grace expelled from ZANU-PF, her *Herald* portrayal was starkly different.
> "Grace Mugabe lacked grooming and true motherhood as shown by her foul language," the paper quoted the ZANU-PF's youth wing as saying.
> "We take exception to the vulgar language which had become part of Mrs [sic] Mugabe's vocabulary," it quoted a Youth League cadre as saying.
> Zimbabweans, many of whom are devoutly religious and culturally conservative, often take offense at profanities.
> The piece featured an unflattering picture of an unsmiling Grace - a sharp departure from the "loving mother" portrayal that included photos of her smiling and holding infants.[21]

The accusation is therefore that kneeling and other forms of ostensibly honoring leaders like writing glowing newspaper articles, or calling them mother or father, is nothing more than selfish and insincere attempts by those doing it to curry favor from the leaders. They do not really respect the leaders; they are duplicitous flatterers, sycophants or "bootlickers" as the newspaper quoted above describes it. The observed behavior not only of *The Herald*, but also those around the first family in the period just preceding the coup and just after was revealing. For some of them in the previous week were literally and publicly singing the praise of the Mugabes, and then they publicly denigrated them a week later. The sycophant narrative becomes difficult to deny.

Appropriate Ways to Show Honor

Having considered the cultural factors behind the act of kneeling and the possible meanings associated with it, I will conclude with recommendations of culturally appropriate ways that Zimbabweans can show honor, especially in the public arena today. Changing the way people are socialized cannot be legislated, however the process of interacting with other cultures drives change, and a natural process is already happening. Many Zimbabweans no longer kneel in their homes as was done in the past. The practice may slowly be dropped as a natural process through interacting with other cultures and their alternative meanings of the behavior. It will however, continue in some homes and where parents choose to continue it, they must instill the value of true respect that lies behind the form.

Public ways of showing honor must truly serve and respect the leaders towards whom the public action is performed. What kneeling in public does to the image of the leader towards whom a person kneels should be considered. Is the act achieving the intention that should be at the heart of preforming the action? That is both showing respect and honor to the recipient and making them respectable and honorable in the process? If the leader accepts this kind of public acclamation, the reciprocation should be to lovingly serve and honor those who humble themselves. It becomes a big podium, which is perhaps too big for a mere mortal human to climb.

The metaphor of leader as "father" and/or "mother" is likely not going to change much within the Zimbabwean leadership psyche. The question should therefore be, if leaders are like "fathers" and "mothers," how can they be best honored in that role?

Kelley's followership theory[22] identifies five possible followership styles. The ideal follower is what he describes as the effective follower, who is loyal but holds leaders accountable to agreed vision and ideals. There are four other less ideal, yet possible ways to follow:

- Passive followers who uncritically do whatever the leader says.
- Conformists who are overly loyal to the point of sycophancy, pampering to the whims of the leader and culture.
- Alienated followers who were once loyal, but because of some conflict have become offended and cynical. They may still follow, but not wholeheartedly, perhaps even forming their own factions within the system.
- Pragmatic survivors are more concerned about personal interests than the vision. They do whatever is necessary and expedient for their own interests.

Kelley's model makes the vision and shared ideals of the leadership effort the final determinant of appropriate follower behavior. So, in the instance of holders of public office, the shared vision, which is the prosperity of Zimbabwe, should be the goal towards which all involved aspire. In the Church, the concern should be how the behavior brings glory to God and helps advance the Kingdom vision. Honor is an attitude that does not necessarily need the physical display of kneeling to be communicated. It can be shown in the following ways:

1. To loyally and consistently put in the best effort possible towards the success of the vision.
2. To lovingly and respectfully (even while kneeling if necessary) point out to leaders the dangers of some practices and how they deviate from the expressed vision and ideals.
3. Even within the parent/child leadership relationship, highlight, as a mature child within Zimbabwean culture would, leaders' wrong behavior and point out their error in culturally appropriate ways. It may be necessary to work with mediators as is done within Zimbabwean family structures.
4. Cultural practices must not take precedence over what is good for the family. Where kneeling is counter-productive and rather than bringing honor to leaders invites ridicule diminishing their public standing, it should not be done. If it is more honoring not to kneel in such environments, followers must not dishonor the leaders by kneeling.

The above suggestions would describe effective follower practices in the context of appropriate ways to show honor to those in public leadership, whether in church or society in Zimbabwe. The cultural practice of kneeling will likely fall away eventually and be replaced by Western influenced ways of behavior. To try to introduce or propose a new culture might be a possible solution, but because of the dynamics and ever changing character of culture, it will only be temporary. However, the cultural value of honoring leaders should be preserved, and these ways of showing honor, which are largely attitudinal and can be outwardly expressed in whatever way seems appropriate, should be the purpose or meaning behind the forms adopted. In the light of this discussion, these recommendations will be expanded as the implications are considered.

The Implications of Public Kneeling

Before speaking to public officials in society, the Zimbabwean Church needs to do a self-critique on the appropriate ways to honor elders and leaders in Zimbabwe. Is the practice of kneeling to leaders acceptable conduct especially during a worship service or in the general conduct of church life? The Bible generally has a negative view of people kneeling before humans, and even angels would not accept humans kneeling before them. Kneeling is linked to worship, and God is the only one worthy of such honor.

Religion has a very important role in shaping culture. Beliefs play a very important role in influencing practice, and any change of cultural practice should be informed by evaluating the intended meanings associated with the practice, as well as assessing whether the practice is still serving its original purpose. Morals for the Christian, that is, the understanding of what is good or bad, right or wrong, should ultimately come from what God says is right or wrong, good or bad. This makes the Zimbabwean Church central to giving guidance and shaping culture in this matter. The choice that the Church has made to accept people kneeling to leaders, especially in public worship sends a big message to the larger culture approving of the practice. If the church maintains this position, then she cannot do anything else but silently watch as society follows with the behavior.

If public kneeling in society in general continues, it places the society in a bad position when considered from the biblical perspective. The acceptance of this kind of conduct exalts leaders to a demi-god status and puts a heavy load on them because they are human beings, with shortcomings like every-one else. Stress comes because they know that the image they portray in public is far different from the reality of their human frailties, which they often know all too well. The feelings of superiority or being other, different, and exalted above everyone else, specially chosen and belonging to the realm of the gods can easily creep into the psyche. The more this happens, the higher the pedestal they are put on, and the inevitable fall from grace is just a matter of time.

Missiologically this practice should be understood as people dabbling in areas that biblically do not belong in the realm of mere mortal humans with all of their frailties. The Church should critique this culture and this requires maturity and self-theologizing. The Zimbabwean Church should seek to come up with relevant contextual theologies to give guidance to the nation in this area of kneeling before public figures.

Conclusion

This paper has analyzed the leadership implications of the practice of kneeling in Zimbabwean culture. The contexts of public leadership spheres and worship in the church were specifically analyzed. Kneeling to leaders and elders is a deeply ingrained part of Zimbabwean culture with the intention of honoring and showing respect to leaders. While the practice will probably not quickly cease in private practice, especially in the home, it is likely that even in private, it will become less prevalent due to influences from other cultures. Respect can be shown in many ways, and the paper has demonstrated that the outward practice of kneeling is not necessarily indicative of an inner attitude of respect.

After analyzing the issue, the following recommendations about the cultural practice of kneeling are suggested:

1. The Zimbabwean Church needs to lead the way in critiquing this cultural practice. As a mature Church, it should self-theologize and contextualize to address this issue and guide the society in biblically appropriate ways of showing honor.

2. The private practice of kneeling will probably not stop, but will gradually change, with more and more people no longer kneeling because of interaction with other cultures. The private practice should be left to the discretion of individuals.

3. The public practice of kneeling in church worship services or church-related activities should be stopped. The biblical precedent is that kneeling is reserved only for God. It is therefore inappropriate for people to kneel to church leaders and they should teach this and then refuse it, at least during public worship or church-related activities. Private practice of kneeling should be discouraged for the same reasons, but cultural sensitivity is needed in some environments. The discretion of the leader should be guided by the possible misunderstandings that this paper presents.

4. The practice of kneeling in public by high-ranking officials should be stopped. Though the intention may be right, and both the person who is doing it along with the recipient may have the same understanding of the form and meaning; the ideals of the cultural construct in which they are operating can be considered at risk due to their public behavior. How can a person who is so subservient hold the leader accountable, remain impartial, ask tough questions and

ensure justice is done? That kind of conduct belongs to a traditional or monarchical form of governance. It also puts stress on the leaders who are placed on a pedestal too high for human beings. Once on that pedestal, the eventual fall from grace is inevitable.

5. The hierarchical stratifications that go with showing respect need to be critiqued and a more egalitarian society should be the goal. Issues like gender roles, distribution of wealth, and the tendency to see a group of people like those with prominent leadership positions as better than others, need to be critiqued.

6. If Zimbabweans insist on maintaining traditional practices like showing respect through submission, avoidance, handclapping, kneeling or sitting at the appropriate times,[23] then it may be necessary to consider another form of governance that is more suited to the culture. The adoption of colonial systems of governance was inherited, but may not fit well with the culture in which it is being practiced. A new method of governance would need to be developed. This would be Ph.D. thesis level kind of work and is beyond the scope of this paper.

7. Finally, it may be necessary to train public officials so that they desist from kneeling in public as they might instinctively want to follow this practice. The training should primarily be based on biblical teaching and/or the *emic/etic* approaches and understandings of the concept of form, function, and meaning in cultural studies.

End Notes

[1] Farai Machamire, "The Kneeling Brigade's Swelling Numbers," *DailyNews Live*, October 2, 2017, https://www.dailynews.co.zw/articles/2017/10/02/the-kneeling-brigade-s-swelling-numbers.

[2] Machamire.

[3] Ezra Chitando, Masiiwa Ragies Gunda, and Joachim Kügler, *Prophets, Profits and the Bible in Zimbabwe: Festschrift for Aynos Masotcha Moyo* (University of Bamberg Press, 2014), 22.

[4] J C Nicholson, "African Background: The Traditional Culture of the Shona-Speaking People," *International Review of Mission* 55, no. 220 (October 1966): 509.

[5] Michael Gelfand, *Shona Religion* (Cape Town: Juta, 1962); M. F. C. Bourdillon, *The Shona Peoples: An Ethnography of the Contemporary Shona, with Special Reference to Their Religion*, Revised Edition, Shona Heritage Series, v. 1 (Gweru, Zimbabwe: Mambo Press, 1998).

[6] Bourdillon, *The Shona Peoples*, 209. This ceremony is designed to officially bring the spirit of the deceased person back home.

[7] Fani-Kayode Omoregie, "Language and Communication in the Kurova Guva Ceremony in Zimbabwe," *Marang: Journal of Language and Literature* 17, no. 1 (September 7, 2007): 62, https://doi.org/10.4314/marang.v17i1.39310.

[8] Paul G. Hiebert, "Critical Contextualization," *International Bulletin of Missionary Research* 11, no. 3 (July 1, 1987): 104, https://doi.org/10.1177/239693938701100302.

[9] Natasha Booty, "Why Mugabe Still Commands Respect," November 19, 2017, sec. Africa, https://www.bbc.com/news/world-africa-42024658.

[10] The Herald, "'We Are Targeting the Criminals around the President,'" *The Herald*, accessed November 21, 2018, https://www.herald.co.zw/we-are-targeting-the-criminals-around-the-president/.

[11] Craig Ott and Harold A. Netland, eds., *Globalizing Theology: Belief and Practice in an Era of World Christianity* (Grand Rapids, Mich: Baker Academic, 2006).

[12] Ott and Netland, 307.

[13] Richard H. Robbins, *Cengage Advantage Books: Cultural Anthropology: A Problem-Based Approach*, 6 edition (Australia ; Belmont, CA: Cengage Learning, 2012), 217–303.

[14] Robbins, 220.

[15] Robbins, 222.

[16] Robbins, 223.

[17] Newsday, "I Am Already President: Grace," *NewsDay Zimbabwe* (blog), November 21, 2016, https://www.newsday.co.zw/2016/11/already-president-grace/.

[18] L.L. Langness, *The Study of Culture* (Novato, California: Chandler & Sharp Publishers, Inc., 1987), 133.

[19] Newsday, "'Mugabe Is My Father,'" *NewsDay Zimbabwe*, accessed August 4, 2015, https://www.newsday.co.zw/2011/11/11/2011-11-11-mugabe-is-my-father/.

[20] Robert Strauss, "Form, Function, and Meaning Across Cultures – Global Perspectives Consulting," accessed December 1, 2018, http://www.gpccolorado.com/form-function-meaning-cultures/.

[21] Ed Stoddard, "Zimbabwe's State Mouthpiece Captures Fall of First Lady Grace," *Reuters*, November 21, 2017, https://www.reuters.com/article/us-zimbabwe-politics-grace-idUSKBN1DL1F3.

[22] Robert E. Kelley, *Power of Followership, The*, 1 edition (New York: Doubleday Business, 1992).

[23] Nicholson, "African Background," 4.

Works Cited

Booty, Natasha
    2017   "Why Mugabe Still Commands Respect," November 19, 2017, BBC News, section: Africa. https://www.bbc.com/news/world-africa-42024658.

Bourdillon, M. F. C.
    1998   *The Shona Peoples: An Ethnography of the Contemporary Shona, with Special Reference to Their Religion*. Revised Edition. Shona Heritage Series, v. 1. Gweru, Zimbabwe: Mambo Press.

Chitando, Ezra, Masiiwa Ragies Gunda, and Joachim Kügler
    2014   *Prophets, Profits and the Bible in Zimbabwe: Festschrift for Aynos Masotcha Moyo*. Bamberg, Germany: University of Bamberg Press.

Gelfand, Michael
    1962   *Shona Religion*. Cape Town, South Africa: Juta.

Herald, The
    2018   "'We Are Targeting the Criminals around the President.'" *The Herald*. Accessed November 21, 2018. https://www.herald.co.zw/we-are-targeting-the-criminals-around-the-president/.

Hiebert, Paul G.
    1987   "Critical Contextualization." *International Bulletin of Missionary Research* 11(3):104-12 (July): 104–12. https://doi.org/10.1177/239693938701100302.

Kelley, Robert E.
    1992   *The Power of Followership*. 1st edition. New York, NY: Doubleday Business.

Langness, L. L.
1987   *The Study of Culture*. Novato, CA: Chandler & Sharp
        Publishers, Inc.

Machamire, Farai
2017   "The Kneeling Brigade's Swelling Numbers."
        DailyNews Live. October 2, 2017.
        https://www.dailynews.co.zw/articles/2017/10/02/the-
        kneeling-brigade-s-swelling-numbers.

NewsDay
2016   "I Am Already President: Grace." *NewsDay Zimbabwe*
        (blog), November 21, 2016. https://www.newsday.
        co.zw/2016/11/already-president-grace/.

2011   "'Mugabe Is My Father.'" *NewsDay Zimbabwe*.
        Accessed August 4, 2015. https://www.newsday.co.
        zw/2011/11/11/2011-11-11-mugabe-is-my-father/.

Nicholson, J C.
1966   "African Background: The Traditional Culture of the
        Shona-Speaking People." *International Review of
        Mission* 55 (220): 508-10 (October).

Omoregie, Fani-Kayode
2007   "Language and Communication in the Kurova Guva
        Ceremony in Zimbabwe." *Marang: Journal of Language
        and Literature* 17 (1): (September 7, 2007). https://doi.
        org/10.4314/marang.v17i1.39310.

Ott, Craig, and Harold A. Netland, eds.
2006   *Globalizing Theology: Belief and Practice in an Era of
        World Christianity*. Grand Rapids, MI: Baker Academic.

Robbins, Richard H.
2012   *Cengage Advantage Books: Cultural Anthropology: A
        Problem-Based Approach*. 6th edition. Australia;
        Belmont, CA: Cengage Learning.

Stoddard, Ed
2017   "Zimbabwe's State Mouthpiece Captures Fall of First
        Lady Grace." *Reuters*, November 21, 2017.
        https://www.reuters.com/article/us-zimbabwe-politics-
        grace-idUSKBN1DL1F3.

Strauss, Robert
2018   "Form, Function, and Meaning Across Cultures –
        Global Perspectives Consulting." Accessed December
        1, 2018. http://www.gpccolorado.com/form-function-
        meaning-cultures/.

The Asbury Journal 75/1: 127-150
© 2020 Asbury Theological Seminary
DOI: 10.7252/Journal.01.2020S.08

Yohan Hong
Powerlessness and A Social Imaginary in the Philippines: A Case Study on Bahala na

Abstract:

This paper calls attention to the sense of powerlessness of everyday people in the Philippines, and to the missional agency of US-based Filipino Protestants for the transformation of the Philippines. This research has been a journey to discover what kind of power is in play, how the fallen powers can be named and made visible, and then ultimately the ways through which power should be restored. In this process, I referred to the voices, perceptions, stories, and insights of US-based Filipino Protestants in Texas, in order to explore the causes of powerlessness. This paper focuses on how *Bahala na* as a Filipino cultural value, functions at some mythic level in relation to a social imaginary in such a way to cause and perpetuate a sense of powerlessness.

Furthermore, the missional agency of Filipino American Protestants has been seldom investigated in the academia of Diaspora Missiology and Intercultural Studies. This paper concludes that Filipino American Protestants have re-interpreted *Bahala na* in transforming ways through the power of their spiritual discipline and Protestant faith so that this paper shines light on the potentiality for them to be change agents who can help bring about the transformation in the Philippines.

Keywords: Powerlessness, Social Imaginary, *Bahala na,* Filipino American Protestants, Diaspora Missiology

Yohan Hong is a graduate from Ph.D. in Intercultural Studies at Asbury Theological Seminary and senior pastor of Oxford First United Methodist Church in the North Alabama Annual Conference of the United Methodist Church.

Introduction

The issue of powerlessness is too complicated to be defined by one factor. I argue that a sense of powerlessness functions in relation to its underlying social imaginaries in the Philippines. This paper unveils powerlessness by investigating the social imaginary embedded in *Bahala na* in which a sense of powerlessness could be implicit. To explore whether a sense of powerlessness functions as a social imaginary, I will first introduce definitions of social imaginary by several sociologists and then present how *Bahala na* functions as social imaginary causing and perpetuating a sense of powerlessness in the Philippines.

What Is A Social Imaginary?

The social imaginary has been widely discussed in recent years by scholars like Charles Taylor, Benedict Anderson, Arjun Appadurai, and Cornelius Castoriadis.[1] The topic of social imaginaries ranges "from the capitalist imaginary to the democratic imaginary, from the ecological imaginary to the global imaginary."[2] It is Charles Taylor who is usually credited with the definition of social imaginary. In *Modern Social Imaginaries,* Taylor defines social imaginary as "the ways people imagine their social existence, how they fit together with others, how things go on between them and their fellows, the expectations that are normally met, and the deeper normative notions and images that underlie these expectations."[3] Moreover, social imaginary "incorporates a sense of the normal expectations we have of each other, the kind of common understanding that enables us to carry out the collective practices that make up our social life."[4] In other words, this means a way that everyday people imagine their social surroundings. In a social imaginary people perceive the common understanding, conduct the common practices, and discern a sense of legitimacy. It is through the social imaginary that people have "a sense of how things usually go, of what missteps would invalidate the practices."[5]

A social imaginary is distinguished from a social theory in that "a social imaginary is carried in images, stories and legends rather than theoretical formulations."[6] For this reason, a social imaginary refers to "a culture's wide-angle and deep background of understanding that makes possible common practices, unarticulated understandings and relevant sense-giving features."[7] In this regard, it is appropriate to explore Filipino cultural values in order to unveil social imaginaries.

There are some other definitions of a social imaginary. According to Alberta Arthurs, the social imaginary is "the common understanding that makes social practices both possible and legitimate, which provides the backgrounds that makes sense of any given act in daily life."[8] For Manfred Steger, a social imaginary is a "deep-seated mode of understanding that provides the most general parameters within which people imagine their communal existence," so that it creates "an implicit background that makes possible communal practices and a widely shared sense of their legitimacy."[9] Simply put, a social imaginary provides a platform on which everyday people perceive the common understanding, conduct the common practices, and discern a sense of legitimacy. In what follows, I investigate a sense of powerlessness embedded in cultural values as a form of social imaginary.

Social Imaginaries and Powerlessness

In the circle of development studies, no one seems to be using the term *social imaginary* in relation to the concept of power. Instead, some scholars mention several different terminologies that designate "mentality and attitude" as one of the main factors that bring about development. Lawrence Harrison in *Underdevelopment Is a State of Mind* uses the term "the creative capacity to imagine and solve the problems"[10] to underscore the role of mentality and attitude in development. According to Harrison, despite the existing structural cracks in a system of society hindering human progress, human beings have achieved tremendous progress throughout history because of creative capacity. In a broad concept, I would say that a social imaginary is partially equivalent to mentality and attitude. Moreover, the term "creative capacity" represents another ramification of power-to, meaning the capability to decide actions and carry them out.[11] Here I see the interrelatedness between social imaginaries and power or powerlessness.

Some similar concepts to social imaginaries are found in the circle of sociology. Max Weber in *Protestant Ethic and the Spirit of Capitalism* stresses that at the root of achievement is a set of values and attitudes that are associated with Protestant ethic: hard work, thrift, honesty, rationality, and austerity–in sum, "asceticism."[12] Weber points out values and attitudes as a determinant to overcoming a sense of powerlessness and bringing about achievement. In *The Sacred Canopy* Peter Berger presents that the religious beliefs and meanings held by individuals construct "plausibility structures" in which members of society legitimate social practices and orders.[13] The contribution of Berger is to pinpoint a significant role of religion in society to form plausibility structures. In the same sense, social imaginaries are birthed, shaped, and practiced by the influence of religious soil embedded in cultural values. Religion tremendously impacts the formation of social imaginaries and then consequently the mentality and attitude of everyday people, including a sense of powerlessness, because it often uses symbols and other means that tap into the power of imagination. For what follows, I will introduce one cultural practice that connects the psycho-social powerlessness as embedded in Filipino social imaginaries.

Powerlessness and *Bahala na* Mentality

Rolando M. Gripaldo states that *Bahala na* has become "a philosophy of life, a cultural trait that has strongly developed into a significant core of Filipino attitude."[14] Then, the first question is likely to be, "What does *Bahala na* mean? And how do people use this expression in everyday life?" To answer these questions, I need to start with a quote from Teodoro A. Agoncillo's article:

> Can you go through that wall of fire? Bahala na. This is the last morsel we have; where do we get tomorrow's food? Bahala na. Don't gamble your last money: you might go home with pockets inside out. Bahala na. Such fatalism has bred in the Filipino a sense of resignation. He appears indifferent in the face of graft and corruption. He appears impassive in the face of personal misfortune. Yet this "Bahala na" attitude prevents him from being a crackpot.[15]

As the quote above suggests, *Bahala na* is literally translated as "Leave it up to God," "Come what may," "What will be will be," and "I don't care." *Bahala na* is one of the phrases that Filipinos use most often. As a matter of fact, this phrase appears to have "a nationwide linguistic acceptance from more than 80 major languages."[16] Thus, *Bahala na* is widely shared by large groups of people and seems to be the kind of common understanding and normal expectation in which everyday people carry out the collective practices that make up their social life. This fact qualifies *Bahala na* to be a social imaginary.

Despite its popularity, *Bahala na* is an idea that defies definition or explanation because it can be applied in various situations responsibly or irresponsibly. Nevertheless, many Filipino scholars like Jaime Bulatao,[17]

Rolando M. Gripaldo,[18] Tereso C. Casiño,[19] and José M. De Mesa[20] point out the fatalistic attitude that is deeply embedded in *Bahala na*. In everyday life, Filipinos say *Bahala na* when they are confronted with challenging situations and hardships which they are not able to handle and overcome. For this reason, *Bahala na* tends to be recognized as a fatalistic expression. Some other people argue that it can be also used in positive ways as "the spirit to take risks"[21] and "shock absorber"[22] in the midst of insurmountable situations. According to Casiño, "a Filipino toys with fatalism as a means of easing the pain of his or her circumstances, as well as lessening the burden of his existence. In such a case, *Bahala na* functions as a convenient theodicy for Filipinos."[23] De Mesa points out its positive aspect as well: "*Bahala na* provides Filipinos the capacity to laugh at themselves and the situations they are in. It reflects, in addition, the oriental philosophy to be in harmony with nature. While it may appear passive, it is nevertheless dynamic without being coercive."[24]

No matter what its interpretations are, I would like to give an emphasis on the religious connotation deeply embedded in *Bahala na*. I argue that this is not just a cultural expression but also a religious concept even though many Filipinos are ignorant of this. It is important to recognize its religious origin because religion has tremendous impact upon Filipinos' lives. When it comes to ethnic traits of Filipinos, two major things are usually mentioned: trust in God and family-centeredness.[25] Thus, Filipinos are known as one of the most religious peoples in the world. For this reason, it is critical for Filipinos to correctly understand the meanings of *Bahala na* and discern them in such a way as to overcome a sense of powerlessness.

The Religious Origins of *Bahala na*

Bahala na is rooted in traditional Filipino spirituality in which people believe that "a cosmic force (not necessarily a Supreme Being) controls the flow of the events in the universe."[26] Then, in what kind of religious soil did this expression originate and become rooted in Filipino culture? As some Filipino scholars like Lynn Bostrom and F. Landa Jocano assert, it is believed that "the word *Bahala* was derived from the word *Bathala* in Tagalog that literally means God."[27] In this sense, *Bahala na* reasonably has a religious origin in its usage. Interestingly, Casiño argues that throughout Philippine history, *Bahala na* had been nurtured and established in four different religious soils: animism, Hinduism, Islam, and Catholicism.[28]

The first soil was animism. It may be controversial to state that *Bahala na* originated from animism because there seems to be no strong interrelatedness between animism and *Bahala na*. Ancient Filipinos worshipped celestial beings, nature, and ancestral spirits. Then, how can we relate animism to *Bahala na*? Casiño points out the broad influence of animism manifested even today in the form of Folk Catholicism, and in Philippine society as a whole.[29] In the Filipino psyche, according to him, "the world is a series of karma, an ethical pre-deterministic system of cause-and-effect."[30] Therefore, in this animistic worldview, anything that happens to someone is attributed to a cause, that is, "an impersonal force known as suwerte (luck), tsamba (chance), or kapalaran (destiny)."[31] Casiño tries to explain the ancient spiritual soil for Filipino spirituality. In this sense, the cosmology of Filipinos might function as the essential spiritual soil nurturing the birth of *Bahala na*.

The second religious soil was Hinduism. In the 900s A.D, the religious ideas of Hinduism reached the Philippines through Hindu traders from India. A Filipino anthropologist, F. Landa Jocano, asserts that the word *Bahala* originated from the word *Bathala* literally meaning God, but more specifically *Bathala*, known as the highest deity in the folk religion of the Philippines, is of Hindu origin.[32] According to Casiño, Filipinos were able to have the "risk taking and adventuresome trait" because of their faith in *Bathala* who is known as "a powerful yet benevolent deity," consequently believed to "lend, assist, and help regardless of whatever circumstances they have."[33] This interpretation of *Bathala* has greatly influenced Filipino's religiosity in that they not only take a risk in the midst of adversity, but also tend to be fatalistic in waiting for this powerful and benevolent deity. The ambivalence of *Bahala na*, fatalistic and agential, originated from interpreting the meaning of *Bathala*, a Hindu deity.

However, some people might argue that it is problematic to assert a direct cause-and-result relationship between Hinduism and the fatalistic consciousness of ancient Filipinos regardless of the assumption that Hinduism is originally fatalistic. As I explore Filipino history, however, there are some considerable evidences that early Filipino culture with the fatalistic bent of Filipino's religiosity came under the influence of Hinduism in areas such as languages,[34] folklore, arts, and even literature written during pre-colonial period.[35] In effect, religion does not exist by itself. Rather, it is birthed, formed, practiced and melted in cultures, life style, and worldviews of everyday people. Therefore, based on these evidences, I would say that

Filipino religiosity had been greatly influenced by Hinduism, particularly its fatalistic bent.

The third religious soil was Islamic faith, which first arrived in 1380 A.D. through the visit of a Muslim missionary named Mukdum.[36] The Islamic influence upon the fatalistic mentality of Filipinos looks more obvious because of Islam's pre-deterministic consciousness that allows people to "resign themselves to fate (kismet) according to the will of Allah (Insha'Allah)."[37] Casiño asserts that Bahala na "reinforces the belief that every event and circumstance in the universe emanates from the will of Allah."[38] However, his argument falls into inaccuracy in that he did not distinguish between these two words in Arabic: Tawakkul (توكل) and Tawakul (تواكل). Tawakkul (توكل) means "to rely [sic] on Allah and do your best to reach your goal" while Tawakul (تواكل) signifies "complete dependence on Allah without making any effort, thinking in a fatalistic way."[39] In the latter, Muslims tend to think that if Allah wills, it will happen and there is no need for any effort. I think Muslims are expected to believe in the former, but in reality many of them tend to believe and live in the latter. In effect, it is well-known that the pattern of their saying Insha'Allah or according to the will of Allah has a fatalistic connotation. In this sense, I think that Casiño points to the latter when he explains the fatalistic mentality of Filipinos that might have been caused by the Islamic faith. These two different understandings of the will of Allah have greatly influenced Filipino Christians' perceptions of God's will. In sum, animistic religiosity of ancient Filipinos was cultivated in the spiritual soil of fatalistic Hinduism, and then Filipino folk spirituality became more inclined to fatalism under the pre-deterministic attitude of Islam.

The fourth religious soil was Catholic Christianity in the 1500s. When Spanish Catholic friars arrived in the archipelago, they discovered that "Filipinos already had existing religious representations" so that the friars "simply assimilated Filipinos' folk religious expressions in their missionary works."[40] It resulted in "the baptizing of local deities with Christian names."[41] Casiño asserts, "Folk Catholicism developed by giving local deities equivalent functions and powers with patron saints."[42] However, one question arises: "In what specific ways did Spanish Catholicism affect the fatalistic bent of Bahala na?" Due to the Spanish friars' strategy of religious assimilation, over the centuries folk religious concepts including Bahala na had been accepted without critical objection by Filipino Catholics and then later even many Filipino Protestants.[43] As a result, Bahala na seems to be regarded as the equivalent of "Thy will be done" in the Lord's Prayer.[44] Jaime Bulato asserts that this practice of combining *Bahala na* (fatalistic worldview) with "Thy will be done" (faith worldview) has led to the Filipino experience of "split-level spirituality."[45] This syncretistic tendency posed by Bulato and Casiño needs to be further investigated through the eyes of contemporary Filipino Christians through ethnographic research in the Philippines. Interestingly, my interviews with U.S. based Protestant Filipinos in Texas proved that they rarely use *Bahala na* in a fatalistic way, and do not interpret this expression as the equivalent of "Thy will be done." However, my interviewees hinted at the high possibility that this syncretistic tendency could be true in the case of everyday Christians in the Philippines.

Bahala na as a Product of Filipino Religiosity

On the basis of these four religious soils mentioned above, the *Bahala na* attitude had been birthed, nurtured, and rooted into Filipinos' mindsets and cultures. Then, another question arises. Why and how do Filipinos in the Philippines continue to say *Bahala na?* Casiño has one answer to this:

> *Bahala na* evolves as a religious tool or device in which a Filipino practically copes with the adverse demands and circumstances of life. In order to survive, a Filipino toys with fatalism as a means of erasing the pain of his or her circumstances as well as lessening the burden of his existence. In such case, *Bahala na* functions as a convenient theodicy for Filipinos.[46]

This fascinating interpretation of *Bahala na* in a way pinpoints its religious characteristic. When they say *Bahala na* in adversities and crises, Filipinos tend to be consciously or unconsciously reminded of God or a Supreme Being or a cosmic force or even *suwerte* (luck) or *kapalaran* (destiny), which is believed to "control their lives based on a fixed blueprint."[47] I believe that this religious origin of *Bahala na* enabled it to pass down from generation to generation and take roots in Filipinos' mindsets. Filipinos' religiosity has reinforced this expression to continue to exist and function as a social imaginary. Moreover, as an idea or a story is embedded and passed down in a religious form, a social imaginary is also carried in a similar way to this. Taylor explains this point, that social imaginary "is carried in images, stories, and legends."[48] Thus, *Bahala na* is a religious product of different images, stories, and legends of different spiritual soils throughout Filipino history.

Then, if *Bahala na* functions as a social imaginary in the context of the Philippines, in what way is *Bahala na* related to a sense of powerlessness or powerfulness? This question is important because if it is just fatalistic, it feeds upon powerlessness, but if agential, then it is possible to see it as a resource to gain power over a powerless situation. To answer this question, we need to first investigate how Filipinos interpret and practice *Bahala na* in everyday lives.

Bahala na as a Fatalistic Mentality

The most popular interpretation of *Bahala na* is to see it as a fatalistic mentality. As mentioned above, this fatalism has been influenced by traditional religious soils. Casiño pinpoints that in daily practice, "*Bahala na* is considered undesirable because Filipinos tend to use it as a negative psychological justification for their failure to take up human responsibility and accountability in times of hardships and crises."[49] According to Casiño, "The downside of *Bahala na* lies in its fatalistic bent where a Filipinos leaves everything up to *kapalaran* (destiny)."[50]

This proves true by the empirical data collected from my ethnographic research. Jerico, an interviewee, states this point:

> *Bahala na* is something like "Who cares about tomorrow?" Let's leave it to luck or destiny. But the word *Bahala* comes from the word *Bathala*, which means God. So the good meaning of *Bahala na* is "leaving it to God. And God will take care of it." But the downside of it is just saying *Bahala na*, meaning to say, leave it to God without doing anything, sitting down, and just leaving it to destiny. So that's also the problem of many people who stay in poverty status. That is a mentality that means "Whatever we do is because we are like this already." They created that mentality that "I'm already this and there's nothing that I can do about it."

Jerico interpreted *Bahala na* as a fatalistic mentality and related it to the issue of poverty. He articulated that people in poverty tend to use this expression in a fatalistic way. This statement alludes that the *Bahala na* attitude might contribute to perpetuating poverty by justifying frustrating situations without doing their best to overcome them.

This fatalistic interpretation of *Bahala na* is supported by another tendency of everyday people, with a lower economic status in the Philippines, to blame the rich and the government for their circumstances. Here are the words of Jerico:

> If you will only depend on the government or other people for your needs, your sustainability will be a problem. You will remain in that condition. In the Philippines, we always hear people blaming the rich. They say, "We are like this because of the people who are rich. We are like this because of those politicians who've been corrupt." But, then, my question is, "Have you done something really for yourselves? Aren't you just entertaining that mentality that we are like this and we will remain like this?" I think we have a lot of people in the Philippines who have that kind of mentality.

Thus, *Bahala na* can be used as an expression of the poor people to blame the powerful like the rich and the politicians. As a result, they identify themselves as powerless. *Bahala na* might not represent cosmic fatality, but the fatality of structure. The lack of agency inside people is definitely interrelated to the asymmetric structure of power. Precisely, lack of agency is a by-product of an unjust structure and the structure is reproduced and perpetuated by lack of agency.

In the same alignment, Teresa, an interviewee, explains *Bahala na* in the concept of power-within or personal self-confidence: "*Bahala na* is more of powerlessness. Okay, whatever will be will be. That is when you don't have any power. If you feel like you are powerful, you don't say that. If you are confident, you will do everything that you can do. If you want to give up, you want to say *Bahala na*." To Teresa, those who say *Bahala na* in the midst of challenges and hardships beyond their capability communicate their low power-within or low self-confidence.[51] My ethnographic interviews verify that Protestant Filipinos in the US believe this to be the correct interpretation of *Bahala na*. In other words, only those who recognize agency inside them do not say *Bahala na*. Rather, they take up their responsibility and accountability in times of hardships and crises. In conclusion, *Bahala na* is more used as a fatalistic expression rather than agential, consequently feeding upon the powerlessness of everyday people in the Philippines.

Bahala na as an Optimistic Spirit

One lingering question is whether or not *Bahala na* can be used as agential in a certain way. Pe-Pua and Protacio-Marcelino pose an optimistic spirit of *Bahala na*. According to them, *Bahala na* defies definition or explanation because it can be applied variously depending on how one perceives circumstances, life, power, and even faith in God.[52] As a result, they argue that *Bahala na* is not "fatalism" but "determination and risk-taking."[53] In their point of view, in saying *Bahala na*, Filipinos are "telling themselves that they are ready to face the difficult situation before them, and will do their best to achieve their objectives."[54] In fact, Pe-Pua and Protacio-Marcelino assert that Filipinos are believed to "have probably done their best to prepare for the future situation" even before they have uttered *Bahala na*.[55] This interpretation foregrounds the more agential nature of *Bahala na*, and implies an ongoing process for contemporary· Filipino psychologists to re-interpret and re-construct Filipinos' cultural values and ethnic identities.

US-based Protestant Filipinos in Texas are a case for this. They usually do not utter *Bahala na;* the only time they might say *Bahala na* is when they do their best for the good and then wait for God's guidance. Roland pinpoints this:

> My *Bahala na* is, "I'm going to do something good and whatever happens I'm going to stand for it. That's my *Bahala na*. I will leave it to God because I know that God will not leave me. It's going to go through. He's going to help me. If it will fail, I'm still confident because I will get the help of the Lord, because it was just not His will. I guess it is personality and culture. The common *Bahala na* is negative. I don't believe in that *Bahala na*. I believe in *Bahala na* only when it's positive.

Surprisingly, my interviewees in Texas seem to interpret *Bahala na* differently from what everyday people do in the Philippines. As a matter of fact, almost every interviewee answered in such a way that whereas everyday people in the Philippines tend to utter *Bahala na* as a fatalistic mentality, Filipino Americans in Texas tend to use *Bahala na* only in positive ways.

What brought about this difference in its interpretations? What I found from the interview with Roland is that he as a Filipino American Protestant does not believe in destiny, but rather believes in God's will helping those who help themselves. His case demonstrates how theology or faith in God plays a significant role in its interpretation of *Bahala na*. This is aligned with the assertion of Pe-Pua and Protacio-Marcelino, which says that the definition or explanation of *Bahala na* can be applied variously depending on how one perceives circumstances, life, power, and even faith in God.[56] For Filipino American Protestants in Texas, *Bahala na* seems to be not "fatalism" but more of "determination and risk-taking."[57] Thus, those in Texas repackage the concept of *Bahala na*, mainly because they theologize its meaning.

How can this same expression as a social imaginary be used and interpreted differently depending on perception of situation, life, power, and faith in God? How should we understand the ambivalence of *Bahala na* in its interpretation and application? To explore the answers of these questions, I found out another aspect of a social imaginary, that is, social imaginary's susceptibility to change.

Susceptibility of Social Imaginary to Change

Noticeably, the social imaginary can change. Jeffery Buckles maintains, "Although the social imaginary explains and reproduces human interaction, it is not static, and is susceptible to change as human knowledge changes, meaning that how humans know, interpret and live in the world is not a constant"[58] Since social imaginaries can change, they "enable humankind to make sense of the world in which they live, as current knowledge is used to interpret the domains."[59] In this regard, *Bahala na* is susceptible to change. That is why there is the ambivalence in interpreting *Bahala na*: a fatalistic mentality and an optimistic spirit. Throughout my ethnographic research, many participants stated that everyday people in the Philippines tend to use *Bahala na* as a fatalistic mentality, whereas Filipino American Protestants in Texas do not. As a matter of fact, almost all my participants answered that they do not say *Bahala na* as a fatalistic mentality, and also have rarely heard this expression among Filipino Americans in Texas. As mentioned, I argue that theology or faith in God played a crucial role in making this difference.

Then, what other factors brought about this difference between Filipinos in the Philippines and Filipino American Protestants in Texas? Based on my ethnographic research, the impacting determinants are social location, education, and time focus.

Social Location

First, their social location in Texas seems to affect their religious reading of *Bahala na*. Jerico demonstrates:

> I've never heard the word *Bahala na* among Filipino Americans in Texas. Everything is accessible in the US. Those who are not rich also eat what the rich eat here. But you have to work. You have to do something. So, for the Filipinos who migrated in the US, *Bahala na* system does not work. God will help those who help themselves. Manna will not just drop from the heaven. You can always do something to better your life.

According to Jerico, Filipino Americans in Texas seem to not stay in a sense of fatalism. Rather, they appear to believe in God who helps those who help themselves. To them, relying on God does not mean just waiting for God's help without doing anything. Trusting in God requires their responsible actions accordingly. Although theology is still guiding their actions, I would assert that a shift in social location precipitates a shift in theological distinctive.

Nevertheless, I do not believe that all Filipinos in poverty in the Philippines say *Bahala na* in fatalistic ways. I do not also believe that all Filipinos in Texas interpret *Bahala na* with an optimistic spirit. In the words of Buckles, as Filipinos interpret their domains (the Philippines and Texas) in different ways, the interpretation of *Bahala na* changes.[60] On one hand, everyday people under the asymmetric structure of power in the Philippines tend to perceive their frustrating realities in fatalistic ways. On the other hand, Filipinos in Texas believe that they can overcome their circumstances and everything is possible as long as they work hard in the USA where socio-political-economic structures of power appear to be more supportive to the well-being of everyday people. Thus, the interpretation of *Bahala na* is susceptible to change depending on its social location.

Education

Second, education plays a crucial role in forming, legitimating, and perpetuating social imaginary by enabling the development of persons. Through education, persons develop a form of consciousness, for "to be conscious of things requires some set of concepts through which experience is ordered and made sense of and through this ability to make sense of the world."[61]

The participants in my research evidenced that many of them overcame poverty and a sense of powerlessness through education. The interviewees stated that their continuous education even under the disempowering structures of the Philippines made them self-confident and finally enabled their dreams to come true in the States. Here is one example for this case from my interviewee, Patria:

> When it comes to low socio-economic status, they just accept that we are poor, and cannot go to school. For me, it is all about my self-goal and self-motivation. My husband and I came from a poor family, not an elite one. My parents were teachers. So they had a little money. But my parents taught us that education is your best tool to improve yourself. We were not trained to depend on the wealth that our parents might have. Not depend on our family. They taught us that you have to desire to be somebody someday. They taught us that we had to study hard, and study well. They told us that once you study hard, you would know how to reach your goal. So it was an individual choice instead of depending on the government or assistance. My husband and I had our goals.

Some people assert that the power structure is the most crucial factor that determines whether people become powerful or powerless. As a matter of fact, many of my interviewees stated that the poor people in the Philippines tend to be fatalistic because of the disempowering structures. However, other people like Patria assert that education motivated her to be successful and organized in her life so that, in the words of Richard Pring,[62] she has been able to develop a form of consciousness. Patria delivered some insights on how people overcome situations and are also overwhelmed by situations. It is dependent upon the mentality of people. In her words, it is an individual choice, and an individual's self-motivation, not structural evil. This connotes how she made a difference by exercising her self-confidence or power-within under the asymmetric power structure where power-over dominates. In the words of Harrison, she maximized her "creative capacity"[63] to imagine a better future, and solve problems she faced. It turned out that the poverty and lack of resources around her life paradoxically reinforced her to keep on seeking self-confidence to improve her life by education. In this sense, it is noticeable that education plays a significant role in awakening people's agency and developing the creative capacity of human beings for progress.

In addition, her story also demonstrates how her power-to or self-confidence was wielded to make a decision for her own destiny instead of remaining in powerlessness. In the words of Harrison, power-within and power-to of Patria conquered "a paralyzing and self-defeating mythology"[64] deeply embedded in people's mindsets where powerlessness might take root. The case of Patria illustrates how education can affect the change of a social imaginary by the intricate interplay between agency and structure.

Time Focus

Third, time focus appears to affect the interpretation of *Bahala na* between Filipinos in the Philippines and Filipino Americans in Texas. Time focus has been one of the significant issues in development studies. Harrison maintains that the worldview's time focus like past, present, or future is of crucial importance for development. He states:

> If a society's major focus is on the past–on the glory of earlier times or in reverence of ancestors–or if it is absorbed with today's problems of survival, the planning, organizing, saving, and investment that are the warp and woof of development are not likely to be encouraged. Orientation toward the future implies the possibility of change and progress.[65]

Harrison points out that more potential for development lies in orientation toward the future, not the past, and today. His assertion hints at why everyday people in the Philippines are more focused on today and tend to interpret *Bahala na* as a fatalistic mentality. June, an interviewee, pinpoints that Filipinos in the Philippines are more focused on present survival.

> They are more focused on surviving on a day-to-day basis. You know, they focus on themselves like "we need to survive." They say, "We need to find a way to get food in our mouth today. I don't care much about what's going on in the local community or in a bigger picture." I think a lot of people in the Philippines are focused on "We need to get through one day at a time." You know, people here in the US have more of the vision for the future. They say, "I can see tomorrow what I want to happen."

In June's view, everyday people in the Philippines might be apt to remain powerless and delay development in their lives because their time focus is on the present. That is the reason why they do not plan for the future. Here the new alignment is presented between time focus and plan. The challenges and hardships in their lives might cause people to say *Bahala na* which hinders them from dreaming of and planning a better future. This demonstrates how everyday people with a lower socio-political-economic status could become fatalistic.

In the same vein, several interviewees in Texas mentioned the phrase "plan for the future" when they were asked to explain *Bahala na*. It seemed that time and *Bahala na* are interrelated in some ways. Here are the words of Luz: "*Bahala na* is not a good attitude. When you say this, it is because you do not plan ahead of time. If you do not plan, you will fail." Ruth, an interviewee, also states: "People who are not more into planning use this expression. I am more of a planner. You would rarely hear that word from me. I would draft a plan. I am more of an organized person." Patria, an interviewee, asserts: "*Bahala na* is like whatever comes. No! I don't like whatever comes. I would like to have a plan. I would like to have steps. I write down if I have two things to decide. I write what is good of this and what is bad of that. Then I've never been down to *Bahala na*. I plan my life." Interestingly, those in Texas who are focused on planning their future do not say *Bahala na* with a fatalistic mentality. In summation, the different perceptions on time focus of everyday people demonstrates why *Bahala na* as a social imaginary is susceptible to change and why the interpretation of this social imaginary ended up being ambivalent between fatalism and optimism.

Bahala na and Split-level Christianity

As discussed above, *Bahala na* has a multi-layered background from different religious traditions. From these religious soils, Filipinos in contemporary Philippine society confront two frameworks for understanding God's will: "either a God who predetermines one's destiny or a God who is interested in and cares for everyday people."[66] In the former, Filipinos "leave themselves to fate" and "simply wait passively on their fortunes or misfortunes."[67] In the latter, Filipinos "live a life of faith, guided in a personal relationship with God."[68] Moreover, Spanish Christianity in the Philippines did not transform the traditional fatalistic concept of *Bahala na* to a Christian way of understanding God's will.[69] For this reason, according to Casiño, many contemporary Filipino Christians have tended to "combine faith with fate," and to equate "Thy will be done" and *Bahala na* "without critical reflection and theological objection," which results in a syncretistic form of spirituality.[70]

In my ethnographic research with US-based Protestant Filipinos, almost every participant replied that they neither believe in nor use *Bahala na* in a fatalistic way. As described earlier, the causes for this difference come from various factors such as social location, education, and time focus. Nevertheless, I would like to underscore their faith in interpreting God's will as the major cause of that difference. In the interviews, they communicated an awareness of the agency inside them, which is based on interpreting God's will in such a way that God helps those who help themselves. Their understanding of God's will does not exclude a sense of personal responsibility and of trust in Divine Providence. They show a good example of how to overcome the syncretistic form of *Bahala na*.

Conclusion

In this paper, I investigated one major Filipino cultural value, that is, *Bahala na*, which produce negative social imaginaries that generate and perpetuate a sense of powerlessness in the Philippines. My interviewees and some scholarly writings show that this cultural value functions at some mythic level in relation to social imaginaries in the Philippines, and that there seems to be strong interrelationships between this social imaginary and a sense of powerlessness. Furthermore, a sense of powerlessness results from a lack of agency inside people, and this agency is also strongly affected by social imaginaries in a society. In addition, these social imaginaries are birthed, nurtured, fortified, and practiced under the influence of the social system. For this reason, a sense of powerlessness is not only a matter of social structure, but also of social imaginary. Such cultural values should be explored as the main causes for a sense of powerlessness.

My interviews discovered that *Bahala na*, on one hand, tends to be recognized as a fatalistic expression rather than agential. When people are confronted with challenging situations and hardship that are beyond their control, they utter this expression and consequently feed upon powerlessness of everyday people in the Philippines. This paper explored the fatalistic religious background embedded in *Bahala na*, which had birthed, nurtured, and established *Bahala na*: animism, Hinduism, Islam, and Catholicism. On the other hand, some people argue that *Bahala na* can be also used in positive ways as a "shock absorber" in which people are willing to face their hardships and do their best to achieve their own goals. My interviews found that Filipino American Protestants in Texas do not utter *Bahala na* and they do not believe in destiny or fatalism. Rather, they view God as the One who helps those who help themselves. Two factors made this difference: their perspective in interpreting God's will and the awareness of agency in themselves.

End Notes:

[1] Please refer to these authors and their books: Appadurai, Arjun. *Modernity at Large.* University of Minnesota Press, 1996; Anderson, Benedict. *Imagined Communities.* Verso, 1991; Castoriadis, Cornelius. *The Imaginary Institution of Society.* MIT University Press, 1987; Taylor, Charles. *Modern Social Imaginaries.* Duke University Press, 2004.

[2] Adams et al., "Social Imaginaries in Debate," *Social Imaginaries* 1.1 (2015), 15.

[3] Charles Taylor, *Modern Social Imaginaries* (Durham and London: Duke University Press, 2004), 23.

[4] Ibid., 24.

[5] Ibid.

[6] Ibid., 23.

[7] Charles Taylor, *A Secular Age* (MA: The Belknap Press of Harvard University Press, 2007), 171-2.

[8] Alberta Arthurs, "Social Imaginaries and Global Realities," *Public Culture,* Fall 2003, 15 (3), 579.

[9] Manfred B. Steger, *The Rise of the Global Imaginary* (Oxford: Oxford University Press, 2009), 6.

[10] Lawrence E. Harrison, *Underdevelopment is a State of Mind,* (Lanham, MD: 2000), 2.

[11] Duncan Green, *From Poverty to Power* (UK: Oxfam International, 2012), 25.

[12] Max Weber, *Protestant Ethic and the Spirit of Capitalism* (NY: Routledge, 1992), 79.

[13] Peter Berger, *The Sacred Canopy* (NY: Doubleday & Company, Inc., 1967), 48.

[14] Rolando M. Gripaldo, "Bahala na: A Philosophical Analysis," in *Filipino Cultural Traits: Claro R. Ceniza Lectures. Council for Research in Values an Philosophy (2005),* 194.

[15] Teodoro A. Agoncillo, "Filipino Traits and Custom," from the website called ONLI IN DA PILIPINS. (http://web.archive.org/web/20060419070300/www.rogersantos.org/filtraits.html). Accessed on 08/31/16.

[16] Tereso C. Casiño, "Mission in the Context of Filipino Folk Spirituality: *Bahala na* as a Case in Point," *Seoul Consultation, Study Commission IX*, 83.

[17] Jaime Bulatao, "Split-Level Christianity," *Philippines Sociological Review 13* (1965), 119-121.

[18] Rolando M. Gripaldo, "Bahala na: A Philosophical Analysis," in *Filipino Cultural Traits: Claro R. Ceniza Lectures. Council for Research in Values and Philosophy (2005)*. 194-211.

[19] Tereso C. Casiño, "Mission in the Context of Filipino Folk Spirituality: *Bahala na* as a Case in Point," in *Seoul Consultation, Study Commission IX*.

[20] José M. de Mesa, *And God Said, "Bahala na!": The Theme of Providence in the Lowland Filipino Context,* Quezon City, the Philippines: Publishers' Printing Press, 1979.

[21] Leonardo N. Mercado, *Elements of Filipino Philosophy.* Tacloban City, Philippines: Divine Word University Publications, 1976.

[22] Tereso C. Casiño, *Seoul Consultation, Study Commission IX,* 86.

[23] Ibid.

[24] Jose M. De Mesa, *In Solidarity With Culture: Studies in Theological Re-Rooting.* Maryhill Studies 4. (Quezon city, The Philippines: Maryhill School of Theology, 1987), 162.

[25] Vitaliano R. Gorospe, "Understanding the Filipino Value System," *Values in Philippine Culture and Education,* (Washington D.C.: The Council for Research in Values and Philosophy, 1994), 65.

[26] Tereso C. Casiño, *Seoul Consultation, Study Commission IX,* 85.

[27] Lynn C. Bostrom, "Filipino *Bahala na* and American fatalism," in *Silliman Journal 15 (1968),* 401; F. Landa Jocano, *Folk Christianity: A Preliminary Study of Conversion and Patterning of Christian Experience in the Philippines* (Quezon City, the Philippines: Trinity Research Institute, 1981), 5.

[28] Casiño, 83.

[29] Casiño, *Seoul Consultation, Study Commission IX,* 84.

[30] Ibid.

[31] Ibid., 86.

[32] F. Landa Jocano, *Folk Christianity: A Preliminary Study of Conversion and Patterning of Christian Experience in the Philippines* (Quezon City, the Philippines: Trinity Research Institute, 1981), 5.

[33] Casiño, 84.

[34] About 25% of the words in many Philippine languages are from Sanskrit and Tamil, which are all of Hindu origin. Refer to Postma, Antoon. (1992), "The Laguna Copper-Plate Inscription: Text and Commentary," *Philippine Studies*, 40(2): 183-203.

[35] Maria Halili, *Philippine History* (Quezon City, the Philippines: Rex Book Store, Inc., 2010), 46-47.

[36] Tereso C. Casiño, *Seoul Consultation, Study Commission IX,* 84.

[37] Ibid.

[38] Ibid.

[39] https://www.quora.com/Is-the-use-of-'Inshallah'-a-fatalist-culture-Does-it-mean-that-you-don't-have-to-make-an-effort-to-do-anything/

[40] Tereso C. Casiño, *Seoul Consultation, Study Commission IX,* 84.

[41] Ibid.

[42] Ibid.

[43] Casiño, 84.

[44] Ibid.

[45] Jaime Bulatao, "Split-Level Christianity," *Philippine Sociological Review 13 (1965),* 119-121.

[46] Casiño, 86.

[47] Casiño, 86.

[48] Charles Taylor, *Modern Social Imaginaries,* (Durham and London: Duke University Press, 2004), 23.

[49] Casiño, 86.

[50] Ibid.

[51] Power-within means personal self-confidence, often linked to culture, religion, or other aspects of collective identity, which influence

what thoughts and actions appear legitimate or acceptable. Refer to Duncan Green, *From Poverty to Power* (UK: Oxfam International, 2012), 25.

[52] Rogelia Pe-Pua and Elizabeth Protacio-Marcelino, "Sikolohiyang Pilipino (Filipino psychology): A Legacy of Virgilio G. Enriquez," *Asian Journal of Social Psychology* (2000) 3: 55.

[53] Ibid.

[54] Ibid.

[55] Ibid.

[56] Pe-Pua and Protacio-Marcelino, *55*.

[57] Ibid.

[58] Jeffrey J. Buckles, "What are the educational implications of developing a new social imaginary, brought about by the challenges to be faced in the 21st century?" a Thesis for Doctor of Education, University of Hull, 2015, 26.

[59] Ibid.

[60] Jeffrey J. Buckles, 26.

[61] Richard Pring, *Personal and Social Education in the Curriculum* (London: Hodder and Stoughton, 1984), 12.

[62] Pring, 12.

[63] Lawrence E. Harrison, *Underdevelopment is a State of Mind* (Lanham, MD: 2000), 2.

[64] Ibid.

[65] Ibid., 6.

[66] Tereso C. Casiño, *Seoul Consultation, Study Commission IX*, 86.

[67] Ibid.

[68] Ibid., 86-87.

[69] Ibid., 86.

[70] Ibid. 86-87.

Works Cited

Adams et al.,
  2015   "Social Imaginaries in Debate," *Social Imaginaries,* 1(1).

Agoncillo, Teodoro A.
  2006   "Filipino Traits and Custom," from the website called
          ONLI IN DA PILIPINS.(http://web.archive.org/web/
          20060419070300/www.rogersantos.org/filtraits.ht ml).
          Accessed on 08/31/16.

Antoon, Postma
  1992   "The Laguna Copper-Plate Inscription: Text and
          Commentary," *Philippine Studies,* 40(2): 183-203.

Arthurs, Alberta
  2003   "Social Imaginaries and Global Realities," *Public
          Culture,* 15(3): 579-586.

Berger, Peter
  1967   *The Sacred Canopy.* NY: Doubleday & Company, Inc.

Bostrom, Lynn C.
  1968   "Filipino *Bahala na* and American fatalism," *Silliman
          Journal,* 15(3): 399-413.

Buckles, Jeffrey J.
  2015   "What are the educational implications of developing
          a new social imaginary, brought about by the challenges
          to be faced in the 21st century?" a Thesis for Doctor of
          Education, University of Hull.

Bulatao, Jaime
  1965   "Split-Level Christianity," *Philippines Sociological
          Review,* 13(2): 119-121.

Casiño, Tereso C.
  2009   "Mission in the Context of Filipino Folk Spirituality:
          Bahala na as a Case in Point," *Seoul Consultation, Study
          Commission IX,* 83-96.

De Mesa, José M.
  1979   *And God Said, "Bahala na!": The Theme of Providence
          in the Lowland Filipino Context,* Quezon City,
          Philippines: Publishers' Printing Press.

  1987   *In Solidarity With Culture: Studies in Theological Re-
          Rooting.* Maryhill Studies 4. Quezon city,
          The Philippines: Maryhill School of Theology.

Gorospe, Vitaliano R.
    1994   "Understanding the Filipino Value System." In *Values in Philippine Culture and Education*, ed. By M.B. Dy, 66-70. Washington D.C.: The Council for Research in Values and Philosophy.

Green, Duncan
    2012   *From Poverty to Power.* UK: Oxfam International.

Gripaldo, Rolando M.
    2005   "Bahala na: A Philosophical Analysis." In *Filipino Cultural Traits: Claro R. Ceniza Lectures*, 203-220. Council for Research in Values and Philosophy.

Halili, Maria
    2010   *Philippine History.* Quezon City, the Philippines: Rex Book Store, Inc.

Harrison, Lawrence E.
    2000   *Underdevelopment is a State of Mind.* Lanham, MD.

Jocano, F. Landa
    1981   *Folk Christianity: A Preliminary Study of Conversion and Patterning of Christian Experience in the Philippines.* Quezon City, the Philippines: Trinity Research Institute.

Mercado, Leonardo N.
    1976   *Elements of Filipino Philosophy.* Tacloban City, Philippines: Divine Word University Publications.

Pe-Pua, Rogelia and Protacio-Marcelino, Elizabeth
    2000   "Sikolohiyang Pilipino (Filipino psychology): A Legacy of Virgilio G. Enriquez," *Asian Journal of Social Psychology,* 3: 49-71.

Pring, Richard
    1984   *Personal and Social Education in the Curriculum.* London: Hodder and Stoughton.

Steger, Manfred B.
    2009   *The Rise of the Global Imaginary.* Oxford: Oxford University Press.

Taylor, Charles
    2007   *A Secular Age.* MA: The Belknap Press of Harvard University Press.

    2004   *Modern Social Imaginaries.* Durham and London: Duke University Press.

Weber, Max
      1992   *Protestant Ethic and the Spirit of Capitalism.* NY: Routledge.

The Asbury Journal 75/1: 151-160
© 2020 Asbury Theological Seminary
DOI: 10.7252/Journal.01.2020S.09

From the Archives: John Haywood Paul and Iva Durham Vennard- Holiness in Education

John Haywood Paul (1877-1967) was a gifted preacher and writer, but he was also an educator and administrator.[1] He taught at Meridian College in Mississippi (1909-1914), Asbury College in Kentucky (1916-1922) and served as a vice-president of Asbury College and then president of Taylor University in Indiana from 1922 to 1931. He went on to become the president of John Fletcher College in Iowa (1933-1936) and then returned to teach at Asbury Theological Seminary (1941-1946). He served on the Seminary's Board of Trustees from 1941 to 1962. He also worked as an editor with Dr. H.C. Morrison on *The Pentecostal Herald*, and then became the associate editor of *The Herald* for 25 years, until his death at 90 years of age. But in looking at his papers in the archives, the correspondence that stands out the most is with Iva Durham Vennard (1871-1945). This remarkable holiness evangelist would become the founder of the Chicago Evangelistic Institute, later Vennard College, which she led from 1910 until her death. The correspondence reveals a close friendship and respect between these two educators, who each influenced higher education in the Holiness Movement in different, but equally important ways.

Iva Durham Vennard became a Methodist at a young age at a revival, and while still a teenager experienced entire sanctification. She attended Wellesley College and then Swarthmore College, but did not complete a degree due to a call to be an evangelist. As an evangelist she sang and preached at revivals, but when she heard about the emerging deaconess movement, which opened many doors for women in Christian service, she trained as a deaconess in the Deaconess Home in Buffalo, New York. She continued on with her work as a deaconess evangelist for a number of years, when in 1902 she founded the Epworth Evangelistic Institute in St. Louis, Missouri to train deaconesses in evangelism.[2] While fervent in her holiness and evangelism, Vennard also emphasized humanitarianism. Her deaconesses were trained in nursing and education. They had practical experience working in jails, juvenile courts, individual homes, and in the red-light district of St. Louis. In 1910, Vennard resigned as the principal of Epworth, because the Methodist leaders in St. Louis would no longer permit her to maintain a focus on entire sanctification and holiness in her deaconess work, and wanted the social action part of the work to take precedence.[3]

John H. Paul (second from the left), with Dr. H.C. Morrison (on his left) and Dr. Andrew Johnson (on his right) with another unidentified man. This picture was taken circa 1920, when Dr. Paul was a young professor at Asbury College. (Image courtesy of Asbury Theological Seminary Archives and Special Collections.)

In one of the earliest letters in the correspondence from the Asbury Theological Seminary Archives and Special Collections, Vennard writes to Paul, then the vice president of Asbury College with concerns about her lack of a degree. She writes, "Dear Friend and Brother: At the considerable risk of consuming a considerable amount of your time I am writing this morning for your advice. I wish to call your attention to the fact that I have no degree, having never completed my college work for a B.A." She goes on to outline her work at Illinois State Normal University, Wellesley, and Swarthmore. She then writes, "It was at this juncture that the Lord called a radical halt. My supreme renunciation struck the depths when I yielded all my plans for higher education. I do not regret my choice for I think I see the providence of it...I might have lost my spiritual vision. But at the time my consecration was so thorough that I put the thought of finishing up and taking my degree entirely out of all my plans and launched whole-heartedly into Evangelism." After detailing her work since that point she concludes the letter, "I shall greatly appreciate any counsel you can give me in regard to this matter, for I begin to see that as the Principal of this Institution a Degree might help us in getting recognition and standing for the work here." Dr. Paul responds positively, suggesting the option that if she wanted to try getting a graduate degree, "I am in a position to write you a letter which would get you a rating as one whose education is equivalent to the A.B. degree."

As Vennard continues this correspondence, she is interested in the possibility Dr. Paul suggests, but she is concerned because such a letter would work at Chicago University, but "I would hesitate to have my name associated with the Divinity Department of Chicago University." She also notes, "I do not wish to take it to Northwestern for the Methodists have opposed me so many years, and the Faculty at Garrett are so prejudiced against our Institute work that it would only be giving them another opportunity to humiliate me by refusing." While the correspondence does not reveal the results of this discussion on her own educational degree, Vennard is frequently referred to as Dr. Vennard and is credited with having a doctor of divinity by Dr. Paul in his obituary.

In 1922, Vennard writes a long letter to Dr. Paul detailing a number of concerns she has for the Chicago Evangelistic Institute and also the vision for a seminary. She closes the letter by commenting, "let me urge again what you and I have both talked of before, and that is that if God wants an orthodox seminary in America at this stage of the Kingdom interests, then Chicago is the logical location for that seminary, and as I see it at present, Bro. Paul, I do not feel that I could possibly undertake this unless you were coming to be its President. If you feel free to assume that responsibility you can count on me for team work to my limit." Paul's response is rather vague, but notes, "I have some data and facts which I am sure you will both be willing and competent to consider at the right time." This might be in reference to his taking the position of president of Taylor University in 1922, or to the formation of Asbury Theological Seminary in 1923. Whatever the case, Vennard is full-heartedly behind his work in Taylor in a letter from 1923, "I am standing by Taylor in every way I can," Vennard wrote, "My opportunities this summer have been in the way of recommending it to students."

The confidence between the two educators continued in 1924, when Dr. Paul wrote Vennard for help in possibly hiring Robert Stewart, who had resigned as the vice-president of Asbury College. He wrote, "A few weeks ago Dr. Morrison wrote me a long letter giving a systematic list of my faults, some of which were very grievous. I think about all of them originated in his imagination and that I could prove an alibi in every case. Among the number was a conspiracy with you to move the seminary to Chicago. I thanked him for his frankness and wrote an explanation after each item, undertaking to disabuse his mind." While she could not help him in that particular moment, she later wrote in 1926, "As I have gone through the years I have been studying people and institutions, and have come to the conclusion that both individuals and institutions that are really vital meet a supreme crisis somewhere along the line. It looks to me that this is one of those times of challenge, both for you and for Taylor. But God will surely see you through. I would like to repreach to you the sermon you preached to us, based on the Lord's message to the Philadelphian Church. It was a great comfort to me and my soul has been feeding on it ever since: 'Because thou hast kept my word and hast not denied my name, I will keep you.' I am claiming it both for C.E.I. and for Taylor."

Dr. John H. Paul taken in 1966 at Asbury Theological Seminary. Dr. Paul served on the Board of Trustees of Asbury Theological Seminary from 1941 to 1962.

Dr. Paul apparently revealed his plans to leave Taylor in 1930 to Vennard before almost anyone else. He wrote, "I am exceedingly tired of administrative duties and would almost any day lay them on the rested shoulders of Dr. Stuart and turn myself into a channel where I could exercise my spiritual gifts if providence should open the way." Vennard replied, "I thoroughly respect Dr. Robert Stuart, and I have no doubt he will make a very fine president, but I cannot refrain from saying that I am happy my own son has had his years at Taylor under your administration. From his early boyhood you have been his ideal in many ways, and he will remember

Taylor with you at the head. I shall keep your confidence and no one will get the information from me first hand."

In 1931, John H. Paul wrote an appeal to Mr. Jamison who he served with on the Board of Trustees of the Chicago Evangelistic Institute. He wrote, "I am writing you with regard to a matter which has been upon the heart of some of us for several weeks... As you know, Sister Vennard has given the prime of her life to this kind of work for only a nominal allowance; just enough, I may say, to cover her living and current personal expense. After some years of broken health, and with no earning power, Brother Vennard is dead. Their little farm has virtually no value for her support and she is rapidly going over the hill in her physical strength. I am wondering if you could agree with me in the suggestion that the Board vote a life-time allowance of one hundred dollars per month to Mrs. Vennard..."

In a letter from Vennard in 1933, when she is congratulating Dr. Paul on becoming the President of John Fletcher College, it becomes clear that he and his family had been renting an apartment at the Chicago Evangelistic Institute and living there since his time at Taylor. The two had become close colleagues in terms of discussing holiness education and the issues of their various institutions. Paul was also on the Board of Trustees of the Chicago Evangelistic Institute. In a hand written note on her official congratulatory letter, Vennard adds in her own handwriting, "We must keep in touch so that we can continue to compare our 'sore thumbs.'" In a draft for a response to another letter to Vennard in 1933, Dr. Paul, wrote, "And may I say that the perfect fellowship and trusted friendship that has marked our way in life is of more value then all the professional interests combined."

The tone of the letters becomes more personal over time. In 1940, Vennard writes to Paul speaking of the death of her longtime secretary, Miss Swartz, when she writes, "Am lost without her, but am trying to pick up the threads and have my work in hand by the time school opens. How many of them I have laid away. Sometimes I feel like a lone tree standing where once a forest had been. And Whittier's lines come back to me again and again, 'How strange it seems with so much gone of life and love, to still live on.'" Her final note to Dr. Paul before her death came in 1943 and was handwritten, she writes,

Dear Brother Paul,
Miss Hibbard brought me your gift and greeting. Thank you so much. The gift was most generous and I shall use it for an extra as you suggested. But much as I appreciate the money and shall enjoy what it brings, the words of loyal friendship meant even more to me.

As the years slip away the old friends tried and true become fewer and more precious.

I feel Brother Paul that I am pulling back to life from the gates of death, but I am encouraged to believe that I am going to be well again and perhaps may have several years more.

They tell me how much everybody enjoyed and was profited by your message at the Convocation. I am so glad. But now, good-bye for now. God bless you and yours,

Faithfully, Iva Durham Vennard

Iva Durham Vennard was a pioneering holiness educator, and Vennard College in Iowa was the continuation of her work at the Chicago Evangelistic Institute, until the school closed in 2008.

John H. Paul responded with a final obituary for his friend and fellow educator published in 1945,

A beautiful young deaconess with a winsome full-gospel message preached for a mission conference in the far South when I was a 'boy preacher.' Ever since, I along with many mutual friends, have had the privilege to observe her career.

Later I came to Louisville to make my headquarters, and a certain architect named Vennard was in charge of the construction of what was then to be the South's greatest hotel, the Seelbach. I never learned the details of how an eminent spiritual builder became acquainted with a prominent material builder, but the news reached me that my favorite lady preacher was now Mrs. Iva D. Vennard.

I began to watch the career of the two and to admire the self-effacing manner in which the talented Mr. Vennard strengthened the hands of his wife in the educational program to which the Lord had called her, and finally in deep sorrow I shared in laying this man in the grave. That I was out of reach when Sister Vennard was called Home is a regret to me; but the fact that I had one last session with her not many weeks before, in which we shared our memories and hopes, is a sweet recollection.

So far as I know, Mrs. Vennard was the first woman in the United States to be a doctor of divinity. Among this nation's Christian education leaders, none has made a better record in business integrity, in administering consecrated finance entrusted to her, in featuring Christ as an uttermost Saviour, avoiding all tangents and training talent for all fields in kingdom service.[4]

Iva Durham Vennard, besides being an educator and holiness evangelist, was also part of one of the most moving and unusual love stories of her time. She married Thomas Vennard in 1904. They had met in 1901 as Iva Durham was planning the opening of the deaconess school in St. Louis. She did not feel she could give up her call to evangelism, but others wanted her to be solely focused on the school, feeling marriage would get in the way. Thomas Vennard assured her that he would wait for her. Pope-Levison wrote that her interest in Vennard stemmed from this relationship,

I was further hooked when I discovered the love story of her courtship with Thomas Vennard, who wrote a letter in the early 1900s in which he pledge to be her "background of support" if she would marry him. The hook dug even deeper when I read his words, "I may be the janitor of an institution of which you are principal founder and controlling head." His comment turned out to be prophetic. True to his word, Thomas sacrificed his successful architectural career in the Chicago Loop in order to oversee, at minimal cost, building renovations at her school, the Chicago Evangelistic Institute.[5]

Thus, Iva Durham Vennard was able to continue in ministry with a supportive husband who played a constant background role in the relationship, which was highly exceptional for the time. When Vennard had to resign from the Epworth Evangelistic Institute, Thomas encouraged her to not give up and reaffirmed his desire to stand behind her and support her work.[6]

During the time she was beginning to organize the Chicago Evangelistic Institute, Vennard was also involved in creating the National Holiness Missionary Society as a part of the National Holiness Association. But in 1910, Vennard launched her life's work, the Chicago Evangelistic Institute, a co-educational school focused on evangelism with a solid core rooted in the doctrines of entire sanctification and holiness. Vennard would die on September 12, 1945, leaving behind a solid holiness educational institution, despite the usual types of conflicts and concerns over finances and maintaining support. In 1951 the Chicago Evangelistic Institute moved from Chicago to University Park, Iowa and it was renamed Vennard College in 1959. In November of 2008 the school closed due to declining enrollment and financial difficulties. Yet, Vennard's passion for holiness and the doctrine of entire sanctification clearly stand out in her contributions to education and evangelism.

The archives of the B.L. Fisher library are open to researchers and works to promote research in the history of Methodism and the Wesleyan-Holiness movement. Images, such as these, provide one vital way to bring history to life. Preservation of such material is often time consuming and costly, but are essential to helping fulfill Asbury Theological Seminary's mission. If you are interested in donating items of historic significance to the archives of the B.L. Fisher Library, or in donating funds to help purchase or process significant collections, please contact the archivist at archives@asburyseminary.edu.

End Notes

[1] All images used courtesy of the Archives of the B.L Fisher Library of Asbury Theological Seminary who own all copyrights to these digital images, unless otherwise noted. Please contact them directly if interested in obtaining permission to reuse these images.

[2] For more on the life and ministry of Iva Durham Vennard, cf. "Iva Durham Vennard" in *Turn the Pulpit Loose: Two Centuries of American Women Evangelists*, Priscilla Pope-Levison, Palgrave Macmillan: New York, NY 2004: 178-185.

[3] *Alabaster and Spikenard: The Life of Iva Durham Vennard, D.D., Founder of Chicago Evangelistic Institute*, Mary Ella Bowie, Chicago Evangelistic Institute: Chicago, IL 1947:152-153.

[4] Bowie: 109.

[5] *Building the Old Time Religion: Women Evangelists in the Progressive Era*, Priscilla Pope-Levison, New York University Press: New York, NY 2014: 174.

[6] "A Career with a Climax." *Heart and Life Magazine: Memorial Number.* Vol. 32, no. 2 (November 1945): 25.

The Asbury Journal 75/1: 161-178
© 2020 Asbury Theological Seminary
DOI: 10.7252/Journal.01.2020S.10

Book Reviews

Ecologies of Faith in a Digital Age: Spiritual Growth Through Online Education
Stephen D. Lowe and Mary E. Lowe
Downer's Grove, IL: InterVarsity Press
2018, 250 pp., paper, $25.00
ISBN: 978-0-8308-5205-5

Reviewed by Matthew Haugen

With the increased prevalence of online education, Stephen and Mary Lowe beg the question as to its viability in Christian higher education. Although seminaries are increasingly *capable* of facilitating online mediums of education, *should* they offer education in this medium? Lowe and Lowe utilize sociology, biblical, theological, and educational studies to explore spiritual growth through online education.

Ecologies of Faith in a Digital Age is organized into three sections and thirteen chapters. Lowe and Lowe argue that 1) there are overlapping and interacting ecologies, 2) online education is one among many other ecologies, and 3) the online medium facilitates a space for seminarians to grow spiritually with one another through the power and presence of the Holy Spirit. Section one shows the ecological dimensions found in scripture. In these varying ecosystems are interconnected and interactive ecologies. Lowe and Lowe see these ecologies through the entirety of scripture, but more specifically in Genesis, Jesus' parables, and Paul's theology of the Body of Christ.

Section two extends the conversation of ecologies to online education. Online platforms of all varieties allow for social networks. Social networks entail individuals and groups of people participating in reciprocal interactions. Although education does not necessitate disembodied learning, I am suspicious of their overly optimistic approach to an online medium of education *and* formation. In short, there was little to no defense on how digital mediums are neutral tools. For instance, Sherry Turkle describes many of the drawbacks of digital social networks on *de-forming people* in subtle but important ways.[1]

Lowe and Lowe's defense of digital mediums being *capable* of formation after the likeness of Christ, however, is well defended in section three. Although the learning is not disembodied because it is online, intentionality of students and professors alike allow for environments conducive for mutual spiritual growth between students. They do admit that embodied realities (i.e., local churches) facilitate the most spiritual growth for students while online education facilitates the greatest construction of knowledge.

Lowe and Lowe's unique contribution in *Ecologies of Faith in a Digital Age* are their concepts of overlapping and interacting ecologies in the fields of education and formation. The primary critique that I have for this work is the overly optimistic portrayal of online mediums. I admit, however, that Lowe and Lowe provide ample examples and counter-examples to provide a more satisfying defense for the *capacity of online mediums for educating seminarians*. This book contributes to the field of online education studies from a Christian perspective. I recommend this book to online Christian educators, Christian higher education administrators, and to those interested in the cross-section of Christian formation and online education.

[1] Sherry Turkle. *Reclaiming Conversation: The Power of Talk in a Digital Age*. (New York, NY: Penguin Press, 2015).

Ever Ancient, Ever New: The Allure of Liturgy for a New Generation
Winfield Bevins
Grand Rapids, MI: Zondervan
2019, 208 pp., paper, $16.99
ISBN: 978-0-310-56613-7

Reviewed by Michael Whitcomb-Tavey

In this book, Winfield Bevins argues for the implementation of a more robust liturgical existence within the walls of the Church. Titled *Ever Ancient Ever New*, he argues that the tried and tested measures of established Church liturgical exercises and practices throughout the centuries is more effective at growing the Church both numerically and spiritually than any other means currently practiced. These forms are sometimes referred to as "ancient," for the majority of them were established many centuries ago, with some of them established millennia ago. This premise essentially stands as an implicit critique on current Church models and practices, which he often refers to as "Church entertainment." His overall concern is that higher forms and uses of liturgy are of more value to the Christian than neglecting them. Throughout his book, he references three traditions that stand as paragons of ancient worship expression: Eastern Orthodoxy, Catholicism, and Anglicanism.

The book is more than argument, however. It is no surprise that there is a growing movement toward older forms of worship amongst younger generations. Many books have been devoted toward analyzing this trend. Those books tend to approach this phenomenon through statistics and objectivity. Winfield stands out in that he approaches this trend from a more subjective perspective, providing multiple case studies and personal examples of people moving toward ancient forms of worship. His book is more reporting than scientific analyzing, in that he cites the reasons many people have personally given him for moving toward a more robust liturgical experience. In fact, he quite often quotes the people he has interviewed. From these interviews, he infers persuasive positions that are both logical and convincing.

His book is separated into three sections. The first section, titled, *Foundations*, argues for the use of liturgy within the Church. This section explores the many reasons why younger generations are shifting toward these ancient forms of worship, and how those forms have inherent power, by the grace of God, to strengthen the faith and Christian identity of both the individual and the community. Although it may be surprising to some, younger generations are not seeking entertainment, but rather robust liturgy. This section naturally leads into the second section, *Journeys*, where he discusses two essential components that drive younger generations toward these forms of worship, and how they are implemented in new and fresh ways in our modern age. This section also introduces the reader to the many interviews he has conducted with people that explain the allure of liturgy. The first component is the allure of Eastern Orthodoxy, Catholicism, and Anglicanism. More specifically, it analyzes the allure of the worship expressions of these three traditions. The second component examines the appeal of community, and how these traditions help foster it. The next two chapters detail how these components are being implemented throughout the spectrum of Christian branches and denominations, including Charismatic congregations. The final section explores liturgy from a more individualistic perspective, and how these forms of ancient worship can also be implemented in one's personal life, as well as for the family home. This section is both insightful and practical. Not only does he argue for the use of liturgy within the home, but also provides examples of how it can be implemented. The book concludes with a short epilogue encouraging the reader to embrace ancient forms of worship.

Winfield's book will provide teachers, students, pastors, non-pastors, and others with a challenging call toward liturgy. This is especially true for Church leaders, where they have the power to make worship changes within their services.

Old Testament Ethics: A Guided Tour
John Goldingay
Downer's Grove, IL: InterVarsity Press
2019, 250 pp., paper, $28.00
ISBN: 978-0-8308-5224-6

Reviewed by Theresa Lieblang

What is ethics? John Goldingay answers this question, based on principles founded upon the Old Testament, in his newly released book, *Old Testament Ethics: A Guided Tour*. He divides ethics of the Old Testament into four broad topics for the basis of his discussion which are: what sort of people we are; how we think; what sort of things we do; what sort of things we do not do. Within these four broad topics Goldingay creates five main parts for the discussion of ethics: Qualities, Aspects of Life, Relationships, Texts, and People. These five main parts comprise a total of forty-three short chapters that can be read in any order with no accumulating argument.

Within each chapter Goldingay incorporates biblical text from his own translation that he elaborates for the sake of discussion. Each chapter ends with a few insightful "Reflection and Discussion" questions that is geared for personal or group study. In the conclusion he compels the reader to reread the Old Testament to better understand the ethical lives of the many biblical characters involved and how God revealed himself through each situation. Goldingay ends with a postscript that gives a brief explanation to the ethics behind the Israelites slaughtering the Canaanites. This explanation briefly elaborates on the historical realities and beliefs of these two nations for the reader who may not be familiar with the pagan worship of the Canaanites and the disobedience of the Israelites.

In his introduction, Goldingay illustrates a few references from the New Testament where Jesus or a disciple is questioned regarding certain ethical issues. The answers to these types of questions always refer back to the Torah or the Prophets. One example is when the Pharisees ask Jesus about divorce and he responds with, "What does it say in the Torah?" In order to better understand Old Testament ethics Goldingay uses three guidelines from Jesus: ask how the implications of the Old Testament's teaching need to be spelled out; ask how its teaching expresses love for God or love for neighbor; ask how far it is laying down creation ideals and how far it is making allowance for our hard-heartedness.

It is within these three guidelines that forty-three succinct chapters are developed to cover the qualities that comprise a community that also entail work ethics and legal issues. He expounds on relationship issues from the broad perspective of nations to the more narrow perspective that addresses the ethics of family members and the household. Goldingay elaborates on the ethical matters found in essential chapters like Genesis 1 and 2, Leviticus 19 and 25, Deuteronomy 15 and 20, Ruth, Psalm 72 and the Song of Songs. He shifts to discuss the lives of some biblical characters to help answer ethical questions which include: Abraham, Sarah and Hagar, Joseph, Shiphrah and Puah, Samson, David, Nehemiah, Vashti, Esther, and Mordecai.

This book is an excellent resource to have for a quick guide on any subject of Old Testament ethics.

The Lost World of the Flood: Mythology, Theology and the Deluge Debate
Tremper Longman III and John H. Walton
Downer's Grove, IL: InterVarsity Press Academic
2018, 192 pp., paper, $20.00
ISBN: 978-0-8308-5200-0

Reviewed by Brian Shockey

The Lost World of the Flood is the latest in a series of books written by Walton, either alone or in collaboration with other scholars, aimed at reading the Old Testament within its ancient Near Eastern context. In this volume, Walton enlists the help of Tremper Longman III as well as geologist Stephen O. Moshier, who contributes one chapter. This volume, like others in the series, is built around a series of propositions made by the authors, which are intended to guide the reader to a certain conclusion. The book presents itself as an academic resource designed for a more popular audience, and as such, is very accessible. Although Longman and Walton note at the beginning that they plan to introduce the reader to a variety of interpretations, they do so mainly in the service of their own argument. This is likely, in part, an effort to reduce the complexity of the topic for the more casual reader.

The book itself is well written and the argument clearly articulated. While the authors assume some familiarity with previous books in the series (particularly those discussing Genesis 1-3), the footnotes are sufficient to allow the reader to engage the material without having read the other books. After outlining some of their strategies for biblical interpretation, Longman and Walton proceed to argue that modern readers have missed the rhetorical shaping of the flood narrative. They affirm that a historical event lies beneath the account in Genesis but suggest this event has been written as theological history. As such, we should expect the author to employ rhetorical methods to emphasize the key interpretive elements of the story. Longman and Walton suggest that our inability to reconcile modern scientific data with a literal account of the flood should lead us to consider whether we have accurately understood ancient concepts of genre and style. They argue that the global flood and description of the ark are hyperbolic in nature, a fact that would have been plain to the original audience. It is the theological interpretation of the flood event and how it relates to the broader context of Genesis that is of chief importance. They further suggest that reading the Genesis account beside the other ancient flood accounts helps to clarify the theological emphasis of the biblical text.

The reader should be aware that Longman and Walton assume a degree of continuity among sources in the ancient Near East (of which the Bible is one), which affects the way they use comparative data. Although they are not interested in arguing for direct literary borrowing from one source to another, they do presuppose that the Bible shares in the broad "cultural river" of the ancient Near East. Little attention is given to the specifics of the relationship between the Bible and the ancient Near Eastern sources and issues of chronology and geography are not discussed. The extent to which one agrees with this presupposition will largely determine how well one receives Longman and Walton's argument. In either case, the book is thought provoking and an excellent addition to the *Lost World* series.

Displaced Persons: Theological Reflection on Immigration, Refugees, and Marginalization
Matthew W. Charlton and Timothy S. Moore, eds.
Nashville, TN: General Board of Higher Education and Ministry, the United Methodist Church
2018, 210 pp., paperback, $39.99
ISBN: 978-0-938162-26-1

Reviewed by Zachariah S. Motts

We are in a global situation where it is imperative for people of faith to reflect upon how they are called to respond to immigrants, refugees, and those who are marginalized in our societies. For that reason, I was cheered to see this title in print and hoped that this book would be an addition to the ongoing conversation and an impetus to response for those who read it. At times, *Displaced Persons* rises toward the occasion, but, on the whole, it takes on too many issues at once and ends up being an erratic collection of essays.

Probably the most frustrating and misleading part of this collection is its subtitle. That may seem like an odd complaint, but simply *Displaced Persons* without *Theological Reflection on Immigration, Refugees, and Marginalization* would have been closer to the mark. The subtitle, within our current milieu, quickly brings to mind the images that are flooding the news of scenes at the US-Mexican border, forced migration from Syria, and boats of migrants crossing the Mediterranean. That is an important topic that should be met with theological reflection and action. However, that is not the thread that binds all of these papers together. There are some papers that do reflect on that topic, but, if you are looking for a focused collection of essays on current human migration, this is not that.

So, skip the subtitle and note that this is a United Methodist (UM) book, and the discussions inside come from people involved in UM student ministry on college and university campuses. Already, one can tell that this is a highly contextualized discussion. That, in itself, of course, is not a mark against it. The topics, though, are free-ranging enough that the best replacement subtitle I could think of was *Marginalized People and the United Methodist Church,* but you still almost have to say something about college and university ministers. There are essays on being an American missionary-pastor-immigrant in Germany, perspectives of emerging adults, hospitality to marginalized people on campus, Native American young people's sense of belonging in the UM, homosexuality and the UM *Book of Discipline,* as well as essays on current human migration issues. It is very difficult to pull all of these essays together under one title.

There are times that, from the perspective of someone who is not a United Methodist, the conversations seem like shots fired in an internecine struggle. A case in point is the essay on homosexuality, "Out of Joint: The Dislocation of Our Bodies from the Church's Sexual Ethic" by Timothy S. Moore (119-142). The starting point of this essay is the language UM *Book of Discipline* and the anthropology implied in that language. Moore then strenuously argues philosophically and theologically against that anthropology, but, for someone outside the denominational struggles, this seems like a rather narrowly focused, intramural debate.

So, in the selection of the essays that appear, the collection feels overly broad. At the same time, the UM specificity of many of the essays seems overly narrow for a wider audience. Perhaps all of this could be forgiven if some of the essays stood out as important pieces, but critical quality is generally lacking. There are interesting essays, well-written essays, but nothing really rises to the level of opening new paths for scholarship or advancing the conversation around immigration, refugees, and marginalization.

Fearfully and Wonderfully, the Marvel of Bearing God's Image
Paul Brand and Philip Yancey
Downer's Grove, IL: InterVarsity Press
2019, 272 pp., paper, $25.00
ISBN: 978-0-8308-4570-5

Reviewed by Michael Whitcomb-Tavey

In *Fearfully and Wonderfully, The Marvel of Bearing God's Image,* Philip Yancey and the children of Dr. Paul Brand have updated this edition for those who live in the context of our modern age. Dr. Brand was a renowned medical orthopedic doctor who served leprosy patients in India from 1946 to 1966, and as the Chief of Rehabilitation at the National Hansen's Disease Center in Carville, Louisiana until 1986. Afterward, he taught at the University of Washington as emeritus professor of orthopedics. He is best known for discovering that leprosy was not a disease of the tissue, but a disease of the nervous system, whereby nerves lose the ability to communicate sensations to the brain. He was a pioneer in surgical techniques of the tendons, and specialized in repairing broken and damaged tendons and nerves in the hands of leprosy patients. He also performed many other surgical procedures, including brain surgery.

Over his many years of service in India, he journaled about his experiences. In addition he wrote about his perspectives concerning leprosy and how it relates to the Church. Much of his insights are analogous. He relates how the body of the Church ought to function according to how an ideal human biologically functions. Those insights eventually were compiled together, and with the help of Philip Yancey, he published several books. Two of his most renowned works of publication are *The Gift of Pain,* and *Fearfully and Wonderfully.* Sadly, Dr. Brand passed away in 2003. As a result, this updated version was produced by Yancey and Dr. Brands' children.

In this book, Dr. Brand discusses how the Church can gain insight into how the Church ought to function by viewing how the human body functions. He explains the ways in which the body functions correctly, and then uses those insights to inspire the Church to function correctly. He also explains the dangers the body experiences, as well as the potential threats it faces. Using that knowledge, he instructs the Church of the dangers and threats that the Body of Christ will encounter.

His book is separated into six sections. The first and second sections discuss how each individual within the body of Christ functions like individual cells within the body. When working together in harmony, the Church can accomplish amazingly redemptive tasks. Such knowledge also forces the Church into a place of acceptance and love for all people. The third section explores Skin and Bone. The sense that garners the most sensation is touch, which is communicated through the skin. In relation to the Church, Dr. Brand explains the need for the Body of Christ to expand their care for other people, from a place of mere financial support to a more meaningful and intimate form of caring, whereby the people of God suffer with those in need and actively engage with such people in both relationship and fellowship. In this way, those in need experience the sensation of "Divine touch." Moreover, just like the skin protects vital and fragile organs, the Church has a duty to protect the most vulnerable, which includes the newly converted. In reference to bone, the human skeleton is both extremely durable and flexible. Based on this knowledge, Dr. Brand exhorts Christians to be both strong in Christian conviction, passion, and commandment, and also flexible enough to adapt and change according to the times in which they live. In doing so, the Church will avoid both legalism (a rigidity that can never adapt to changing times) and licentious progressivism (lacking in structure resulting in an inability to stay grounded during times of change).

Section four explains how blood and oxygen work together, and how they are essential to life. Dr. Brand reveals that the Church also needs vital components for its continued sustenance and life. According to him, this sustenance is found in the blood of Christ, which is communicated to the Church in a mysterious way through communion, and also the life of Christian liturgical practice, which is the "oxygen" of the Church. Section four also details the muscular system, and how it works properly within the human body. As an analogy, the Church grows its muscles when we stretch beyond ourselves to help other people.

The last two sections explore the nervous system and the brain. As has been noted, Dr. Brand discovered that leprosy is the disease of the nervous system. This means that nerves become apathetic toward pain, which can result in bodily harm. It may even result in death. This becomes metaphorical for the Church. One of the greatest dangers to the Church is the threat of apathy, and how it causes inaction. The Church functions best when it both listens to the needs of others and is willing to experience the pain of other people. Finally, in relation to the brain, the reader is taught how the brain commands the body, and how it delegates the different functions of the body. In a similar fashion, Jesus Christ is the Church's head. He commands and delegates its functionality. When the Church listens to and obeys Christ, it functions properly.

In conclusion, this book is deeply insightful. The depth of Dr. Brand's wisdom on these matters is both profound and impressive. *Fearfully and Wonderfully* will provide teachers, students, pastors, non-pastors, and others with a challenging reflection on the status of the Church, and how it should properly function as the Body of Christ. This, then, will affect how each one of its members operates individually in relation to the whole of the body, and also how the whole body grows into an incarnational redemptive force within the world.

Cosmology in Theological Perspective: Understanding Our Place in the Universe
Olli-Pekka Vainio
Grand Rapids, MI: Baker Academic
2018, 224pp., paperback, $24.99
ISBN: 978-0-8010-9943-4
Reviewed by Logan Patriquin

Suppose we—the human race and all other potential embodied conscious agents (ECAs)—inhabit an inflationary universe. That is, a universe that perpetually expands and then, theoretically, collapses and then produces new universes. Think, Big Bang —> Big Crunch —> Big Bang, *ad infinitum*. Of all multiverse theories this option has the most empirical grounding to date. Suppose then our current universe's iteration isn't the first or the last. What implications might this have on Christian doctrines like: incarnation, human uniqueness, and creation itself? While each chapter title is a science fiction reference, Dr. Vainio sets out in

Cosmology in Theological Perspective to add his seasoned voice to some contemporary theological debates for which the label "science fiction" is markedly less tenable nowadays.

The reader of, *Cosmology in Theological Perspective*, will observe an informal, two-part structure. The first three chapters serves as a judicious, interdisciplinary introduction to the material, sweeping through ancient - though not solely Christian - cosmological conceptions, enough Patristic philosophical engagement to provide a historical tie to the discussion, and then a quick review of major, broadly cosmological challenges that historic Christian orthodox has already endured. The second section, then, consists of chapters that individually tackle material from budding discussions in contemporary scientific and cosmological circles.

Take this question for example: does the shear enormity of the cosmos warrant a theological crisis for Christianity? Not according to Vainio. The text's fruitful theological engagement with multiverse theory, cosmological peripheral locality, and the vastness of space is tethered together by two theological/philosophical premises:

(a) "Humans were made for the cosmos" (41).
(b) "As the greatest conceivable being, who is good and loves things that are good, God is more likely than not to create good things in abundance" (82).

Premise (a) may sound fairly tame at first but frame it against the popular conception that "the cosmos was created for humans" (x), and a deeper discussion emerges. Vainio does not pit these claims against one another. Rather, he suggests affirming (a) to get to (x), not *vice versa*, in order to have a richer discussion on human uniqueness and value despite our lack of cosmic centricity (41). Premise (b), labeled the *Theistic Principle of Plentitude (TPP)* by the author, deals more with the material end of the discussion. He wagers that Christians shouldn't be surprised or threatened by a great universe, nor the potential of other ECAs. For, it ought not be shocking that a God with infinite resources would create in plenty. Embracing both (a) and (b) gets us to an intellectocentric cosmology rather than an anthropocentric one (69).

Let us see how accepting Vainio's cosmological presuppositions may help Christians dispense with a commonly articulated objection to stereotypical, populist Christian cosmology by atheists:

1. If God exists, he would create a human-sized universe.
2. Our universe is not human-sized.
3. Therefore, God does not exist (112).

What is at stake, biblically, theologically, philosophically, or from a scientific perspective that Christians would need to commit to premise 1? The author is quick to wield (a) to challenge the conception that cosmic centricity is necessary to ascribe value to human beings, thus also dismantling, in turn, the connected claim that our peripheral locality, cosmologically speaking, denotes insignificance for our species and planet. He opts instead to affirm that human value is not rooting in axiological categories like spatial location, size, or distance (115-119). Human value and uniqueness rest instead in the fact that out of the void of space, God chooses to call and pursue us. Human value, therefore, is fixed in God's saving action not cosmological conventions. As such, very few scientific theories about the vastness or multiplicity of our universe offer genuine theological challenge on this particular front.

Additionally, *TPP* (b) is also an excellent counter to premise 1. Why ought Christians believe that an omnipotent, omniscient, and wholly good God would even desire to create a "human-sized' universe? Instead, one ought to expect a universe potentially teaming with beings capable of comprehending it (99). To say that humans bear the image of God doesn't not necessarily entail that nothing else does (102). Jettisoning premise 1 with (a) and (b) undermines the entire argument.

One area where committing to (a) and (b) gets tricky for Vainio is in his discussion on incarnation. *TPP* most naturally lends itself to the conclusion that, "We are not alone; one or more extraterrestrial races [of embodied conscious agents] exist" (158). The author outlines a number of soteriological possibilities for these speculated ECAs but seems to gravitate to his option d—"Ets are fallen, but their nature is assumed by God in an act of incarnation on their worlds" (159 & 161). In short, a commitment to (a) and (b) seems lead one to embrace, at least the possibility, of multiple incarnations.

Classic, Trinitarian, Christian orthodoxy, as expressed in the great creeds, professes belief in the bodily ascension of Jesus Christ, and consequently the assumption of human nature into the Godhead via the hypostatic union of Christ. Vainio appears to believe that the possibility of adding additional wills to the nature of the Son of God, for every presumable race of ETAs, ought not be a notion too quickly dismissed (162). While he spends about a page and a half trying to present Thomas Aquinas as a theological ally in this endeavor, even the author admits that much more constructive work would need to be done on this point (165). I, for one, concur.

Baker Academic's, *Cosmology in Theological Perspective,* is a dense but worthwhile read. In Lewisian fashion, Dr. Olli-Pekka Vainio implores us to engage our imagination in some of these speculative discussions about the nature of the cosmos and humanity's unique, or not so unique, relation to it. He argues in his conclusion, along with Lewis, that:

> It would be foolish, and obviously false, to think that Christian faith has sailed smoothly through history without ever encountering serious objections and challenges. However, it is equally foolish to think that science and new discoveries somehow necessarily, like a tide, force the Sea of Faith to withdraw from these shores. (180)

Readers will be hard-pressed to disagree.

The Mosaic of Christian Belief: Twenty Centuries of Unity and Diversity
Second Edition
Roger E. Olson
Downer's Grove, IL: InterVarsity Press Academic
2016, 396 pp., paper, $37.99
ISBN: 978-0-8308-5125-6

Reviewed by J. Russell Frazier- Nairobi, Kenya

Roger Olson (Ph.D., Rice University) is Foy Valentine Professor of Christian Theology and Ethics at George W. Truett Theological Seminary, Baylor University. He has served as the president of the American Theological Society (Midwest Division) and co-chair of the Evangelical Theology Group of the American Academy of Religion. He is a prolific writer, having authored or co-authored over 20 books and numerous journal articles and other publications. He is well qualified to write a book of this nature. *The Mosaic of Christian Belief: Twenty Centuries of Unity and Diversity* was first published in 2002; the work under review is the second edition of this work. The author describes the word "mosaic" as "a metaphor for this mediating approach that seeks to emphasize both Christian unity and Christian diversity in terms of belief" (12).

Olson sets out the aim for this work in the introduction entitled "The Need for a 'Both-And' Theology." His work is characterized by mediating theology, which attempts to reflect the consensual tradition as reflected in the Roman Catholic, Eastern Orthodox and Protestant branches of the Church. His goal is stated as follows: "to explain to uninitiated readers what that common tradition includes in terms of unity, what it allows in terms of diversity and what it excludes in terms of heresies…" (12). Another characteristic is that Olson's project is intended to express "the best of evangelical Christianity" (13) and by this, he means a gospel which is centered upon the grace of God. His project makes an attempt to be "irenic in spirit and tone" (14). Olson identifies his work as non-speculative; he purposes not to speculate about controversial doctrinal matters but keep the focus on "the rough unity and colorful diversity of Christian belief" (16). The last characteristic is that of simplicity for the novice (17). With these characteristics, Olson attempts to counter the folk theology and to provide a balance between believing and experiencing within a post-modern culture that has leaned to a subjective spirituality. Olson's antidote is to develop a "both-and" theology, which avoids the errors of the pendulum swing effect rather than an "either-or" theology (23). Olson admits of several influences. He is a Baptist in the "broader evangelical free-church tradition" but has been "spiritually and theologically nurtured" by Pentecostals and Pietists (27). Yet, he learned to value "the wider catholic tradition" of the early church fathers and self-identifies as a progressive evangelical and ecumenicist that respects "his own tradition's distinctives" (28).

Chapter one of Olson's work is entitled "Christian Belief: Unity and Diversity" in which he further reveals the agenda for his project. Against the meaninglessness of an indefinite definition, Olson proposes the identification of "the core of essential Christian beliefs that all mature, capable Christians must affirm in order to be considered truly Christian" (30). Yet, Olson wants to avoid an intolerant dogmatism. The criterion for discerning this core of Christian beliefs is expressed in the Vincentian Canon: "What has been believed by everyone (Christians) everywhere at all times" (34). Olson further clarifies that the Great Tradition entails the agreed upon beliefs of the early church fathers as well as the sixteenth-century

Reformers (36). Though recognized as a secondary, relative authority, the Great Tradition "deserves great respect and should be ignored only with fear and trembling" (44). Olson differentiates between the following three categories: 1) dogmas that he considers essential to the Christian faith; 2) doctrines that are distinctive of a particular faith community; and, 3) opinions that tend to be the reflections of Christians about which there is no consensus (45). Having set out his agenda, Olson proceeds in the remaining chapters of the book to articulate the various theological categories of the Christian faith.

In the remaining chapters of the book, Olson presents a polarity in each chapter. The chapter titles reveal the polarity. Chapter 2 is entitled "Sources and Norms of Christian Belief: *One and Many*." He identifies scripture as "the major source and norm" of authority for the Christian faith (51); the many sources include tradition, reason and experience. Chapter Three is entitled "Divine Revelation: *Universal and Particular*." Olson attempts to achieve a balanced view between the two polarities; however, he may be too Barthian for some readers. "Christian Scripture: *Divine Word and Human Words*" is the title of the fourth chapter. Olson attempts to maintain a balance between the polarities of divine word and human words. Along the way, he discusses themes of inerrancy, infallibility, and inspiration. In the fifth chapter, Olson argues for a balanced view between the transcendence and immanence of God. The chapter is entitled: "God: *Great and Good*." Chapter six is entitled: "God: *One and Three*." Therein, Olson argues with classic Christianity as the subtitle suggests that God is one substance and three persons.

Olson in his chapter on "Creation: *Good and Fallen*" endeavors to avoid certain issues within the theological currents of the day: "...our theme [in this chapter] will be that Christian belief about creation has little to do with specific scientific theories about the age of the earth and the natural processes that led to the emergence of life" (158-159). The fallenness of creation is emphasized, while one side of the polarity is not given equal treatment in this chapter. In chapter 8, Oden discusses the doctrine of providence and his polarities are "*Limited and Detailed*." He affirms that God is in charge of nature and history, but raises questions about the extent of the providence, particularly in the light of evil. In the section on the diverse Christian visions of God's providence, he discusses meticulous providence, limited providence, and open theism (193-199). He doesn't consider open theism heterodox as many theologians have (199), but holds that some view of limited providence holds the most promise for the unity of the Christian faith.

Chapter 9 is entitled "Humanity: *Essentially Good and Existentially Estranged.*" Olson attempts in this chapter to balance the Christian idea of the value and dignity of human beings with the fallen nature of humanity. The author attempts to provide a unifying Christian perspective and finds hope in Emil Brunner's distinction between the "formal image" and the "material image;" the former defines the image of God within terms of "responsible freedom," and the latter is humanity's righteousness before God (224-5). The polarities of Christian belief about Jesus Christ are the subject of the next chapter. Olson articulates the Chalcedon faith, that is the union of the two distinct natures – human and divine – in one eternal, hypostatic union.

"The Holy Spirit: *Divine Person and Power*" is the title of chapter 11. The crucial issue here is that most Christians in their practice emphasize either that the Holy Spirit is a divine person or a divine power (251). The disagreements about the doctrine of the Spirit center around either the status of the Holy Spirit within the Trinity, or the operations of the Spirit within the Church today. Olson appeals for the Church to maintain "and even strengthen" its belief in the personhood of the Holy Spirit and the equality of the Holy Spirit with the other two persons of the Trinity (271). He also calls for greater stress upon the activity of the Holy Spirit without falling into fanaticism. The next two chapters, twelve and thirteen, both deal with the doctrine of salvation. Chapter 12 focuses on the objective and subjective aspects of the atoning work of Christ. Olson expresses concerns for views of the atonement that overstress the polarities and asserts, "*No one explanation does justice to all that happened on the cross*" (emphasis of the original retained, 292). The next chapter discusses salvation as gift and task. Olson argues that salvation is both a gift of divine grace and, at the same time, entails human agency.

The Church is the subject of Olson's chapter 14, which is both visible and invisible. Olson employs the four universal marks of the Church as the unifying consensus on the doctrine of the Church; he discusses in this chapter the sacraments of baptism and the Eucharist. The fifteenth chapter is entitled "Life Beyond Death: *Continuity and Discontinuity.*" Olson points the direction in the balance between continuity and discontinuity with the present life and the life to come; however, he acknowledges much work to be done on this doctrine to reaching a consensus (360-1). The last chapter addresses an eschatological theme: "The Kingdom of God: *Already and Not Yet.*" Here Olson attempts to navigate between the extremes of radical realized eschatology and of adventism.

Olson's work represents a solid introduction to consensual theology or a paleo-orthodox theology that places great emphasis on the theology of the first five centuries of the early Church. His work of course differs from paleo-orthodoxy in that he holds in high regard the magisterial Reformers of the Church. *The Mosaic of Christian Belief* provides a good, solid introduction to Christian theology and would serve well as a textbook for a course in the field. Olson doesn't allow his focus on the consensus to cause him to have myopic vision; he recognizes the on-going tensions and disagreements among theologians in the Church. However, he attempts to point the way forward to consensual thought when possible. The issue with developing a consensual theology is that the author has the responsibility of choosing the polarities. When the polarities are ill chosen, the attempt to balance the polarities is ill conceived. However, Olson has done the Church a service in developing a consensual theology that is well balanced. However, one wonders if the consensus would satisfy those of the Roman Catholic and Eastern Orthodox traditions.

The Asbury Journal 75/1: 179-183
© 2020 Asbury Theological Seminary

Books Received

The following books were received by the editor's office since the last issue of *The Asbury Journal*. The editor is seeking people interested in writing book reviews on these or other relevant books for publication in future issues of *The Asbury Journal*. Please contact the editor (Robert. danielson@asburyseminary.edu) if you are interested in reviewing a particular title. Reviews will be assigned on a first come basis.

Ashford, Bruce Riley and Heath A. Thomas
    2019   *The Gospel of Our King: Bible, Worldview, and The Mission of Every Christian.* Grand Rapids, MI: Baker Academic. ISBN: 978-0-8010-4903-3. Price: $22.99

Bevans, Winfield
    2019   *Marks of a Movement.* Grand Rapids, MI: Zondervan Reflective. ISBN: 978-0-310-09835-5. Price: $17.99.

Bouma-Prediger, Steven
    2019   *Earthkeeping and Character: Exploring a Christian Ecological Virtue Ethic.* Grand Rapids, MI: Baker Academic. ISBN: 978-0-8010-9884-0. Price: $24.99.

Brown, Sherri and Francis J. Moloney, SDB
    2019   *Interpreting the New Testament: An Introduction.* Grand Rapids, MI: Wm. B. Eerdmans. ISBN: 978-0-8028-7519-8. Price: $25.00.

Campbell, Douglas A.
    2020   *Pauline Dogmatics: The Triumph of God's Love.* Grand Rapids, MI: Wm. B. Eerdmans. ISBN: 978-0-8028-7564-8. Price: $64.99.

Chatraw, Joshua D. and Karen Swallow Prior
    2019   *Cultural Engagement: A Crash Course in Contemporary Issues.* Grand Rapids, MI: Zondervan Academic. ISBN: 978-0-310-53457-0. Price: $29.99.

Chilcote, Paul W.
    2019   *Active Faith: Resisting Four Dangerous Ideologies with the Wesleyan Way.* Nashville, TN: Abingdon Press. ISBN: 978-1-7910-0172-8. Price: $13.99.

Colyer, Elmer M.
2019   *The Trinitarian Dimension of John Wesley's Theology.*
Nashville, TN: General Board of Higher Education and
Ministry of The United Methodist Church. ISBN: 978-1-
9459-3544-2. Price: $44.99.

Duvall, J. Scott and J. Daniel Hays
2019   *God's Relational Presence: The Cohesive Center of*
Biblical Theology. Grand Rapids, MI: Baker Academic.
ISBN: 978-0-8010-4959-0. Price: $34.99.

Ensminger, Charles D.
2019   *Crafting the Sermon: A Beginner's Guide to Preaching.*
Nashville, TN: Wesley's Foundery Books. ISBN: 978-1-
9459-3560-2. Price: $16.99.

Gehring, Michael J., Andrew D. Kinsey, and Vaughn W. Baker, eds.
2019   *The Logic of Evangelism Revisited.* Eugene, OR: Pickwick
Publications. ISBN: 978-1-5326-0456-0. Price: $23.00.

Georges, Jayson
2019   *Ministering in Patronage Cultures: Biblical Models and*
Missional Implications. Downers Grove, IL: InterVarsity
Press Academic. ISBN: 978-0-8308-5247-5. Price:
$22.00.

Gorman, Michael J.
2019   *Participating in Christ: Explorations in Paul's Theology*
and Spirituality. Grand Rapids, MI: Baker Academic.
ISBN: 978-1-5409-6036-8. Price: $30.00.

Gupta, Nijay K.
2019   *1 & 2 Thessalonians.* Zondervan Critical Introductions to
the New Testament. Grand Rapids, MI: Zondervan
Academic. ISBN: 978-0-310-51871-6. Price: $44.99.

Gupta, Nijay K.
2020   *Paul and the Language of Faith.* Grand Rapids, MI: Wm.
B. Eerdmans. ISBN: 978-0-8028-7343-9. Price: $34.99.

Hardy, H. H., II
2019   *Exegetical Gems from Biblical Hebrew: A Refreshing*
Guide to Grammar and Interpretation. Grand Rapids,
MI: Baker Academic. ISBN: 978-0-8010-9876-5. Price:
$19.99.

Heetland, David L.
2019   *Happy Surprises: Helping Others Discover the Joy of*
Giving. Nashville, TN: Wesley's Foundery Books. ISBN:
978-1-9459-3557-2. Price: $18.99.

Holtzen, Wm. Curtis
2019 *The God Who Trusts: A Relational Theology of Divine Faith, Hope, and Love.* Downers Grove, IL: InterVarsity Press Academic. ISBN: 978-0-8308-5255-0. Price: $28.00.

Johnson, Adam J. and Stanley N. Gundry, eds.
2019 *Five Views on the Extent of the Atonement.* Counterpoints in Bible and Theology Series. Grand Rapids, MI: Zondervan Academic. ISBN: 978-0-310-52771-8. Price: $22.99.

Keener, Craig
2019 *Christobiography: Memories, History, and the Reliability of the Gospels.* Grand Rapids, MI: Wm. B. Eerdmans. ISBN: 978-0-8028-7675-1. Price: $54.99.

King, Roberta R.
2019 *Global Arts and Christian Witness.* Mission in Global Community Series. Grand Rapids, MI: Baker Academic. ISBN: 978-0-8010-9885-7. Price: $26.99.

Kirkham, Donald Henry
2019 *Outside Looking In: Early Methodism as Viewed by its Critics.* Nashville, TN: New Room Books. ISBN: 978-1-9459-3543-5. Price: $49.99.

Kreider, Glenn R. and Michael J. Svigel
2019 *A Practical Primer on Theological Method: Table Manners for Discussing God, his Works, and his Ways.* Grand Rapids, MI: Zondervan Academic. ISBN: 978-0-310-58880-1. Price: $16.99.

Long, D. Stephen
2019 *Truth Telling in a Post-Truth World.* Nashville, TN: Wesley's Foundery Books. ISBN: 978-1-9459-3550-3. Price: $28.99.

McNall, Joshua M.
2019 *The Mosaic of Atonement: An Integrated Approach to Christ's Work.* Grand Rapids, MI: Zondervan Academic. ISBN: 978-0-310-09764-8. Price: $34.99.

Merkle, Benjamin J.
2019 *Exegetical Gems from Biblical Greek: A Refreshing Guide to Grammar and Interpretation.* Grand Rapids, MI: Baker Academic. ISBN: 978-0-8010-9877-2. Price: $19.99.

Ott, Craig
    2019   *The Church on Mission: A Biblical Vision for Transformation Among All People.* Grand Rapids, MI: Baker Academic. ISBN: 978-1-5409-6088-7. Price: $19.99.

Ovey, Michael J.
    2019   *The Feasts of Repentance: From Luke-Acts to Systematic and Pastoral Theology.* New Studies in Biblical Theology Series. Downers Grove, IL: InterVarsity Press Academic. ISBN: 978-0-8308-2662-9. Price: $16.84.

Parker, Margaret Adams and Katherine Sonderegger
    2019   *Praying the Stations of the Cross: Finding Hope in a Weary Land.* Grand Rapids, MI: Wm. B. Eerdmans. ISBN: 978-0-8028-7664-5. Price: $21.99.

Rhodes, Ben and Martin Westerholm, eds.
    2019   *Freedom Under the Word: Karl Barth's Theological Exegesis.* Grand Rapids, MI: Baker Academic. ISBN: 978-0-8010-9881-9. Price: $45.00.

Robert, Dana L.
    2019   *Faithful Friendships: Embracing Diversity in Christian Community.* Grand Rapids, MI: Wm. B. Eerdmans. ISBN: 978-0-8028-2571-1. Price: $19.00.

Sider, Ronald J.
    2019   *If Jesus is Lord: Loving Our Enemies in an Age of Violence.* Grand Rapids, MI: Baker Academic. ISBN: 978-0-8010-3628-6. Price: $24.99.

Treier, Daniel J.
    2019   *Introducing Evangelical Theology.* Grand Rapids, MI: Baker Academic. ISBN: 978-0-8010-9769-0. Price: $29.99.

Tyson, John R.
    2019   *Praying with the Wesleys: Foundations of Methodist Spirituality.* Nashville, TN: Wesley's Foundery Books. ISBN: 978-1-9459-3554-1. Price: $18.99.

Volf, Miroslav
    2019   *Exclusion & Embrace: A Theological Exploration of Identity, Otherness, and Reconciliation.* Revised and Expanded. Nashville, TN: Abingdon Press. ISBN: 978-1-5018-6107-9. Price: $32.99.

W., Jackson (pseudonym)
    2018   *Reading Romans with Eastern Eyes: Honor and Shame in Paul's Message and Mission.* Downers Grove, IL: InterVarsity Press Academic. ISBN: 978-0-8308-5223-9. Price: $20.00.

Walker, Andrew G.
    2015   *Notes from a Wayward Son: A Miscellany.* Eugene, OR: Cascade Books. ISBN: 978-1-62564-161-8. Price: $41.20.

Waltke, Bruce K. and James M. Houston
    2019   *The Psalms as Christian Praise: A Historical Commentary.* Grand Rapids, MI: Wm. B. Eerdmans. ISBN: 978-0-8028-7702-4. Price: $36.00.

Wray Beal, Lissa M.
    2019   *Joshua.* The Story of God Bible Commentary. Grand Rapids, MI: Zondervan Academic. ISBN: 978-0-310-49083-8. Price: $49.99.

Wright, N.T. and Michael F. Bird
    2019   *The New Testament in Its World: An Introduction to the History, Literature, and Theology of the First Christians.* Grand Rapids, MI: Zondervan Academic. ISBN: 978-0-310-49930-5. Price: $59.99.

The Asbury Journal

FALL 2020

VOL.75 • NO.2

The Asbury *Journal*

EDITOR
Robert Danielson

EDITORIAL BOARD
Kenneth J. Collins
Professor of Historical Theology and Wesley Studies
J. Steven O'Malley
Professor of Methodist Holiness History

EDITORIAL ADVISORY PANEL
William Abraham, *Perkins School of Theology*
David Bundy, *New York Theological Seminary*
Ted Campbell, *Perkins School of Theology*
Hyungkeun Choi, *Seoul Theological University*
Richard Heitzenrater, *Duke University Divinity School*
Scott Kisker, *Wesley Theological Seminary*
Sarah Lancaster, *Methodist Theological School of Ohio*
Gareth Lloyd, *University of Manchester*
Randy Maddox, *Duke University Divinity School*
Nantachai Medjuhon, *Muang Thai Church, Bangkok, Thailand*
Stanley Nwoji, *Pastor, Lagos, Nigeria*
Paul Numrich, *Theological Consortium of Greater Columbus*
Dana Robert, *Boston University*
Howard Snyder, *Manchester Wesley Research Centre*
L. Wesley de Souza, *Candler School of Theology*
Leonard Sweet, *Drew University School of Theology*
Amos Yong, *Regent University*
Hwa Yung, *United Methodist Church, Kuala Lampur, Malaysia*

All inquiries regarding subscriptions, back issues, permissions to reprint, manuscripts for submission, and books for review should be addressed to:

The Asbury Journal
Asbury Theological Seminary
204 N. Lexington Avenue, Wilmore, KY 40390
FAX: 859-858-2375
http://place.asburyseminary.edu/asburyjournal/
© Copyright 2020 by Asbury Theological Seminary

ISSN 1090-5642

The Asbury Journal
VOLUME 75:2
Fall 2020

TABLE OF CONTENTS

Features

The Asbury Journal

Timothy C. Tennent
President and Publisher

Douglas Mathews
Provost

The Asbury Journal is a continuation of the Asbury Seminarian (1945-1985, vol. 1-40) and The Asbury Theological Journal (1986-2005, vol. 41-60). Articles in The Asbury Journal are indexed in The Christian Periodical Index and Religion Index One: Periodicals (RIO); book reviews are indexed in Index to Book Reviews in Religion (IBRR). Both RIO and IBRR are published by the American Theological Library Association, 5600 South Woodlawn Avenue, Chicago, IL 60637, and are available online through BRS Information Technologies and DIALOG Information Services. Articles starting with volume 43 are abstracted in Religious and Theological Abstracts and New Testament Abstracts. Volumes in microform of the Asbury Seminarian (vols. 1-40) and the Asbury Theological Journal (vols. 41-60) are available from University Microfilms International, 300 North Zeeb Road, Ann Arbor, Michigan 48106.

The Asbury Journal publishes scholarly essays and book reviews written from a Wesleyan perspective. The Journal's authors and audience reflect the global reality of the Christian church, the holistic nature of Wesleyan thought, and the importance of both theory and practice in addressing the current issues of the day. Authors include Wesleyan scholars, scholars of Wesleyanism/Methodism, and scholars writing on issues of theological and theological education importance.

ISSN 1090-5642

Published in April and October

The Asbury Journal 75/2: 192-193
© 2020 Asbury Theological Seminary
DOI: 10.7252/Journal.02.2020F.01

From the Editor

As is the tradition of *The Asbury Journal*, this issue is devoted to papers presented at the 2019-2020 Advanced Research Programs Interdisciplinary Colloquium, held Friday October 11, 2019 at Asbury Theological Seminary. The theme for this colloquium, "Gospel and Culture: A Biblical Theology of Culture and Socio-Anthropological Perspectives on the Bible and Culture" becomes the theme for this issue of the *Journal*. Understanding how we read and interpret scripture in the light of various cultural contexts is vital, both to the work of missiologists and for biblical scholars. Scripture was written in one context, has been translated and interpreted into numerous other cultural contexts over time, and now must be presented in such a way as to make sense in new and challenging cultural contexts of our own day and age. These articles seek to meet these types of challenges.

Esther D. Jadhav starts this issue examining the cultural context of Christian higher education and how it seeks to expand its theological understanding of the growing cultural concern for diversity. Her interpretation of this issue is seen through the lens of Wesleyan theology as well as her work at Asbury University in Wilmore, Kentucky. Shawn P. Behan adds to this discussion by examining how a holistic way of doing exegesis will include serious reflections on both scripture and culture. He approaches this argument through the lens of the work of Bishop J. E. Lesslie Newbigin, who was a master at applying scripture to cultural context within the world of missiology. Abbie F. Mantor explores the text of Job 3 through a lens of modern psychological trauma studies, as a way to better understand Job's spiritual state and condition. Dain Alexander Smith completes the colloquium papers through examining how Paul in the book of Romans sought to interpret the Gospel message through the lens of the writings in the Old Testament book of Isaiah, especially in terms of his eschatological vision for peace. Much can be gained in understanding the interplay between the Bible and culture by looking at scripture through a cultural lens in Biblical Studies and by looking at culture through a scriptural lens in Missiology and Intercultural Studies. The two fields need more interaction to further a more holistic understanding of the role both play in the work of the kingdom of God.

In addition to the papers from the colloquium, Kelly J. Godoy de Danielson presents an examination of the Old Testament characters of Rahab and Ruth through the lens of an immigrant Latina. Presented in both English and Spanish, this article seeks to examine how the Old Testament allowed for women outside the people of God to become insiders through oaths of allegiance to God and acts of lovingkindness. This presents a model for seeing how immigrants themselves can see their lives through God's eyes as opposed to the often-derogatory eyes of those born within a specific culture. Finally, the From the Archives essay celebrates the 50th anniversary of the founding of the Ichthus music festival in Wilmore, Kentucky. From 1970 to 2012 it served as a real-life example of seeking to apply scripture to the needs and concerns of contemporary youth culture in the United States. The influence and power of this move of the Holy Spirit continues to this day in the lives of those who worked the festival as well as those who came to listen to the music.

The intersection of scripture and culture, when done well, results in transformed lives. These lives in turn can lead to a transformed culture. The overarching problem is that culture is never static- it constantly changes with every generation, and the application of scripture in one form may only last for a generation. It is a constant struggle in ministry to keep applying scripture to new concerns and new issues for each generation. The Student Volunteer Movement in 1888 adopted as its slogan, "the evangelization of the world in this generation." This was an ambitious aim, but it is also almost impossible, because each generation must adapt scripture to fit the culture of each emerging generation in an ongoing cycle. Several Christian writers have adapted Ronald Regan's quote from his 1967 inaugural address as governor to the Christian faith. Regan noted that freedom was "never more than one generation away from extinction." Of course, claiming that Christianity is never more than one generation away from extinction ignores the revival power of the Holy Spirit, but the idea that culture and scripture must come together in new ways each generation is important for the ongoing mission of the Church. If we neglect this truth, we do so at our peril.

Robert Danielson Ph.D.

The Asbury Journal 75/2: 194-209
© 2020 Asbury Theological Seminary
DOI: 10.7252/Journal.02.2020F.02

Esther D. Jadhav
The Place of Theology in Diversity Efforts in Christian Higher Education: A Wesleyan Perspective

Abstract:
Theology is essential to diversity efforts in Christian Higher Education. In current culture there are at least two ways in which theology emerges in this work, as an afterthought and as foundational in some instances. In this article the author provides a discussion around the question: Does theology have a place in the work of diversity efforts in Christian higher education? This paper asserts that theology is a critical and, significant contributor in diversity as it relates to these efforts taking place across Christian Higher Education in North America. A Wesleyan theological perspective is utilized to demonstrate how Wesleyan theology can speak into diversity efforts in Christian higher education.

Keywords: diversity, higher education, Wesleyan theology, Christian education, intercultural studies

Esther D. Jadhav is the Assistant Vice President for Intercultural Affairs at Asbury University in Wilmore, Kentucky. She is also an ordained minister in the United Methodist Church and received her Ph.D. in Intercultural Studies from Asbury Theological Seminary in 2020.

Introduction

Does theology have a place in the work of diversity efforts in Christian higher education? This paper asserts that theology is a critical and significant contributor in diversity as it relates to these efforts taking place across Christian Higher Education in North America. A Wesleyan theological perspective will be utilized to demonstrate how Wesleyan theology can speak into diversity efforts in Christian higher education. Literature indicates that the work of diversity in Christian higher education has gained prominence in the last fifteen or so years; it has gained significant momentum due to the cultural changes we experience in race relations across North America today.

Recent establishments in the CCCU (Consortium for Christian Colleges and Universities) for the support and resourcing of this work have come in the form of the Commission of Diversity and Inclusion, which was formed in 2015. In intercultural Studies, the area of contextualization has highlighted the importance of attending to cultural contexts as they inform the practices and experiences of individuals and communities. For the purposes of this paper, the focus will be placed on diversity as it relates to creating a space for persons of different cultures and ethnicities in our institutions of higher education. While this notion may appear unnecessary because the common understanding is that *all people are welcome here* in essence, while the written understanding of our practices may reflect differently. Noel B. Woodbridge in his article "Living Theologically" writes,

"Living theologically" sounds like a contradiction in terms, rather like constructive criticism or servant-leadership. The question arises: What has theology to do with everyday life? Stevens (1995:4) claims that, in general, people today do not have any idea of what theology has to do with everyday life. Theology is often considered an abstract discipline. It is rational, reducible to propositions and capable of being categorised (liberal, conservative, evangelical, Reformed, liberation). It is not usually thought of as practical. People in business, law, the professions and the trades often regard the study of theology as a process of becoming progressively irrelevant. In the context of contemporary theological education, many educators at universities and seminaries are concerned that today's theological students are leaving theological institutions and entering the ministry with a fragmented theology instead of an integrated theology. At these institutions there is a tendency to deal

> with theology in an abstract and fragmented manner,
> rather than in a way that integrates theology into
> everyday life.[1]

With increasing pluralism, we experience theology being questioned. One must understand that pluralism is the existence of multiple and multiplex cultures, ethnicities, philosophies, ideologies, practices etc. As an individual who grew up as a Wesleyan in a pluralistic cultural context, I come to this work with the understanding that the existence of pluralism does not minimize the place of theology, however it shares the platform with other religions, cultures, ethnicities so on and so forth. As Woodbridge has very plainly explained that people in the fields of business, law, the professions and the trades often regard theology as irrelevant, my observation is that the people who believe in this theology are questioning its relevance as well, as they see theology being questioned and critiqued for being irrelevant to everyday life. Is theology able to speak to the current culture we are experiencing in North America? Woodbridge brings to our attention the concern that many of our institutions tend to deal with theology in an abstract manner rather than in a manner that addresses its relevance in everyday life. Woodbridge concludes in his article, "theology and life are linked in praise (*orthodoxy*), action (*orthopraxy*) and passion (*orthopathy*)." The importance of theology in everyday life must gain our attention otherwise it will truly become progressively irrelevant as Woodbridge claims.

In our North American context pluralism challenges, us in ways that causes us to either defend our beliefs or shut ourselves to the world, so we are able to maintain our beliefs with little to no dialogue with each other amidst deep cultural, religious, philosophical, and ideological differences. John Inazu in his book *Confident Pluralism* claims,

> Our shared existence is not only possible, but also
> necessary. Confident Pluralism offers a political solution
> to the practical problem of our deep differences. Instead
> of the elusive goal of *E pluribus unum*, it suggests a more
> modest possibility—that we can live together in our
> "many-ness." That vision does not entail Pollyannaish
> illusions that we will overcome our differences and live
> happily ever after. We will continue to struggle with
> those whose views we regard as irrational, immoral,
> or even dangerous. We are stuck with the good, the
> bad, the ugly of pluralism. Yet confident pluralism
> remains possible in both law and society. Confident

pluralism takes both confidence and pluralism seriously. Confidence without pluralism misses the reality of politics. It suppresses difference, sometimes violently. Pluralism without confidence misses the reality of people. It ignores or trivializes our stark differences for the sake of feigned agreement and false unity. Confident pluralism allows genuine difference to coexist without suppressing or minimizing our firmly held convictions. We can embrace pluralism precisely because we are confident in our own beliefs, and in the groups and institutions that sustain them.[2]

John Inazu draws an important conclusion, *confidence without pluralism misses the reality of politics, it suppresses difference, sometimes violently. Pluralism without confidence misses the reality of people. It ignores or trivializes our stark differences for the sake of feigned agreement and false unity.* In essence Woodbridge and Inazu help us understand that culture and theology share an important integrated relationship not a fragmented one. An emphasis on one at the exclusion of the other can prove to be dangerous akin to the words found in James 2:14-17 (NRSV), "What good is it, my brothers and sisters, if you say you have faith but do not have works? Can faith save you? If a brother or sister is naked and lacks daily food, and one of you says to them, 'Go in peace; keep warm and eat your fill,' and yet you do not supply their bodily needs, what is the good of that? So, faith by itself, if it has no works, is dead." Theology and culture can work together to benefit the common good. Thus, pluralism is not an elimination of theology from the marketplace but an acknowledgement of the existence of multiple and multiplex cultures, ethnicities, philosophies, ideologies, practices, etc. and an opportunity to become confident in our own beliefs, and in the groups and institutions that sustain them as Inazu states. I am able to confirm such a position due to my experience of growing up in Mumbai. I grew amidst friends from a plethora of religions. This did not minimize or diminish the value of my religious belief, but only enhanced my understanding and embracing of it. When we encounter difference, whether cultural or religious, we are overcome with fear largely due to the unknown nature of the difference we experience. Instead of beginning with fear we should consider taking the first step as understanding the lived reality of the other.

Diversity in Christian Higher Education: A close encounter

With the theoretical framework of near theologizing, this section will discuss a close encounter with diversity in a Christian higher education institution. Near Theologizing derives its origin from the anthropological understandings of experience-near and experience-distant.

Near and Far Theologizing is based on the anthropologist Clifford Geertz's understanding of two primary ways for understanding other cultures--experience-near and experience-distant. Geertz explains,

> "An experience-near concept is, roughly, one that someone—...in our case an informant—might himself naturally and effortlessly use to define what he or his fellows see, feel think, imagine and so on, and which he would readily understand when similarly applied by others. An experience-distant concept is one that specialists of one sort or another–an analyst, an experimenter, an ethnographer, even a priest or an ideologist--employ to forward their scientific, philosophical or practical aims."[3]

When I began my work at Asbury University in 2002 2.7% of the student population reflected cultures and ethnicities other than Caucasian. Now in 2019, 17%[4] of the student population reflects cultures and ethnicities other than Caucasian. In *The Christian Post*, an article titled, "Christian Higher Ed Becoming Less White, More Diverse in Effort to Reflect God's Kingdom"[5] it is said,

> While most Christian colleges in the United States have been predominantly white institutions, there is an ongoing movement within Christian higher education to diversify student and faculty bodies to ensure that the diversity in God's Kingdom is reflected in His schools. More than eight out of 10 students (82.2 percent) who attended schools affiliated with the Council of Christian Colleges and Universities in 1999 were white. But today, the white students on the nearly 140 campuses affiliated with the CCCU in the United States only account for about six out of every 10 students (62.2 percent in 2016).[6]

What does this mean? It means Asbury and other Christian higher education institutions must work to cultivate a climate that is hospitable to its members both from home and around the world. There are needs particular to the intercultural student community. An intercultural student community is comprised of international and U.S. ethnic minority students. International students have particular needs as it relates to moving to another country for education such as housing, employment, etc., while the needs of U.S. ethnic minorities vary in regard to having a sense of belonging at predominantly white institutions. The U.S. ethnic minorities are insiders, but experience life as outsiders to their own home context in North America. In his book, *Neither Jew Nor Gentile*, George Yancey states,

> The relative lack of students of color within these institutions of higher education indicates that these institutions are potentially sites that are not welcoming to [students of color]. If this type of de facto rejection is an accurate reality for these students of color, then they may have fewer educational choices than majority group students. Those who desire a Protestant educational experience in an atmosphere where they perceive racial acceptance have to find a racially diverse Protestant institution, which is relatively difficult.[7]

Often times the lack of a hospitable campus is due to the lack of intentional efforts in creating such a climate for all students. It cannot be assumed that places of Christian higher education are automatically hospitable. Often times it is quite the contrary. In my work in Christian higher education I have discovered nice people does not equate to people who understand cultural and ethnic differences. Not seeing color or the culture of the other does not translate to what we commonly think it does, *we all are valued*, it is quite the contrary, not seeing or recognizing the color or the culture of the other actually means we do not value the other as an integrated individual made up of their culture and ethnicity, rather we view them as fragmented as Woodbridge points out in the case with students who are leaving theological institutions and entering ministry with a fragmented theology. Often this reality is regarded or even understood as being colorblind, but being colorblind does not eradicate racial prejudice. More often than not being colorblind is dangerous and a great threat to our ability to value the other in our midst. We deal with culture and ethnicity in an abstract and fragmented manner rather than recognizing that people are a sum of their cultural contexts.

Miroslav Volf in his book, *A Public Faith* acknowledges the malfunctions of theology when it comes to relating with others from cultures and ethnicities other than our own. He states,

In the course of Christianity's long history-full of remarkable achievements by its saints and thinkers, artists and builders, reformers and ordinary folks—the Christian faith has sometimes failed to live up to its own standards as a prophetic religion. Too often, it neither mends the world nor helps human beings thrive. To the contrary, it seems to shatter things into pieces, to choke up what is new and beautiful before it has a chance to take root, to trample underfoot what is good and true. When this happens, faith is no longer a spring of fresh water helping good life to grow lushly, but a poisoned well, more harmful to those who drink its waters than any single vice could possibly be—as Friedrich Nietzsche, a fierce critic of Christianity, put in his last and angrily prophetic book, *The Anti- Christ*. True, some of faith's damaging effects can be attributed largely to differences of perspectives.[8]

Such a malfunction is quite likely when we have an abstract approach to theology rather than one rooted in lived reality. Approaching people apart from their lived reality does not give us a comprehensive understanding of who they are, instead it allows us to think of them from our perspective rather than theirs. Theology has valuable contributions to make in diversity efforts in Christian higher education. The place of theology in diversity efforts in Christian higher education becomes more important as theology can serve as a corrective to cultural malfunction and vice versa, a corrective to theological malfunction we experience in our world today. Over the years I have witnessed several instances that indicate the lack of cultural awareness and understanding. Adel S. Abadeer in his article, "Seeking Redemptive Diversity in Christian Institutions of Higher Education: Challenges and Hopes from Within" claims,

> Christian institutions should apply the biblical redeemed foundations of implementing diversity: diversity that welcomes and celebrates with the redeemed spheres in other cultures. They should be proactive in reforming their cultures and engaging with other worldly cultures, since the world itself belongs to God (Plantinga, 2002). They should implement diversity that is transforming, leading by example in response to their new creation as collective units of faithful servants and active agents of renewal. Such diversity should be integrated in their mission statements, curriculum, education, training, employment, leadership, membership, and community services, in addition to concerts, exhibits, galleries, choirs, public lectures, and conferences, as an ongoing process/ journey that

is associated with a significant learning curve effect, which in turn deepens and enriches the institution's diversity. Furthermore, Christian institutions should revisit and evaluate their existing diversity programs, practices, and progress on a regular basis, to build on their achievements and learn from their short- comings so as to enhance their effectiveness in the future.[9]

Abadeer points out that, *Christian institutions should apply the biblical redeemed foundations of implementing diversity: diversity that welcomes and celebrates with the redeemed spheres in other cultures.* For the most part we could all agree on the non-redeemed spheres in cultures such as slavery, and political and economic corruption to name a few. How do we get to a place where we can welcome and celebrate the redeemed spheres in other cultures? I remain perplexed at the words found in Matthew 22: 36- 40 (NRSV), "Teacher, which commandment in the law is the greatest?" He said to him, "'You shall love the Lord your God with all your heart, and with all your soul, and with all your mind.' This is the greatest and first commandment. And a second is like it: 'You shall love your neighbor as yourself.' [40] On these two commandments hang all the law and the prophets." The emphasis on loving our neighbors as ourselves is second to loving the Lord our God with all our heart, soul, and mind. There is no exception made to loving our neighbors; loving God is followed by loving neighbors. Celebrating the redeemed spheres of other cultures includes celebrating the other in these redeemed spheres of cultures.

As we review the writings of George Marsden in, *The Soul of the American University*, Glanzer, Alleman and Ream's, *Restoring the Soul of the University*, or Karen Longman's edited work, *Diversity Matters* we discover institutions of Christian higher education struggling to discover their moral and ethical compass as they navigate the winds of cultural change, not that theology cannot withstand these winds of cultural change. Our interpretations and applications of the very theology we embody are being challenged by the cultural changes as they relate to race relations. An important question is raised in the work of Glanzer, Alleman and Ream, they state,

> According to the common telling of the history of the university, the early universities in Europe and then in America supposedly always had a singular soul- an identity and story that held them together and gave a coherent unity. In fact, scholars discussing what it would mean for a university to have singular soul usually refer

to the older medieval universities as an example. In this view, God supplied the soul, or more particularly, the study of God –theology—supplied it. In contrast, we argue that the mistake of many Christians is the belief that since universities in Europe and colleges in America began in a dominant Christian era that the early structures of how the soul of theology informed the university were somehow closer to the ideal of what a university should be. We wonder if the recent growth of classical education seems to reflect this assumption. We thus contend that Christians need to think critically about past educational structures and institutions they helped to build and perhaps where they were wrong.[10]

Glanzer, Alleman and Ream identify an important task that needs our attention, *we must think critically about past educational structures and institutions they helped to build and perhaps where they were wrong.* We simply cannot assume that *since universities in Europe and colleges in America began in a dominant Christian era that the early structures of how the soul of theology informed the university were somehow closer to the ideal of what a university should be.* The foundations for diversity initiatives in Christian higher education have their strongest support in theology however, to uncover this support one must be willing to struggle with lived reality (culture) and theology simultaneously. Shirley Hoogstra says, "those working in Christian higher education understand the theological imperative of viewing diversity as a gift to be celebrated through our common commitment to Christ and his kingdom. Though we might come from different denominations and experiences, we share a bold and historic belief that unites us: Christ crucified and resurrected."[11] Did our past educational structures and institutions view diversity as a gift to be celebrated through our common commitment to Christ and his kingdom? Perhaps we did in part, and mission history could demonstrate so? I went to St. Xavier's College a Jesuit institution for undergraduate studies. I remember my experience being a rich one. My education was rich because I got to study authors from all around the world including India, unlike the experience of many students in North America who do not receive exposure to scholars from around the world. A significant majority of the educational experience in North America is Eurocentric, from pedagogy to authors whose books are the primary texts for classes.

A Wesleyan View

Campbell and Burns begin their work, *Wesleyan Essentials* with the following understanding,

> We are challenged "to contend for the faith that was once for all entrusted to the saints" in the context of a multicultural society. It is a daunting challenge. Beliefs we once thought universal, and authorities (like the Bible) to which we once appealed as givens, cannot be taken for granted. It is also an exciting challenge. Christ has called us to "make disciples of all nations, baptizing them in the name of the Father and of the Son and of the Holy Spirit" (Matthew 28:19). This challenge no longer requires a passport or a visa: "the nations are at hand.[12]

Cultural and ethnic diversity in North America is advancing at a rapid pace. We are living in a multicultural society and working alongside individuals from a myriad of cultures and ethnicities. This requires that we learn to engage with the cultural and ethnic differences without compromise on the confident or the pluralism as identified by Jon Inazu; *confidence without pluralism misses the reality of politics. It suppresses difference, sometimes violently. Pluralism without confidence misses the reality of people. It ignores or trivializes our stark differences for the sake of feigned agreement and false unity. Confident pluralism allows genuine difference to coexist without suppressing or minimizing our firmly held convictions. We can embrace pluralism precisely because we are confident in our own beliefs, and in the groups and institutions that sustain them.*

In Wesley's ministry we observe a twofold emphasis, his unrelenting commitment to the Christian faith and Christian living. Randy Maddox in his book, *Rethinking Wesley's Theology for Contemporary Methodism* states,

> The place to begin discerning Wesley's approach to theology is with his conception of its purpose. Wesley understood theology to be intimately related to Christian living and the proclamation of Christian faith. Theology is actualized in authentic living and true proclamation. He had little interest in theology for its own sake. Rather, theology was for the purpose of transforming personal life and social relations. This was his "practical divinity." For Wesley, theology was not so much for the purpose of understanding life as for changing life; theology should help effect the love of God and neighbor.[13]

Does our theology help effect the love of God and neighbor? Sometimes it does and sometimes it doesn't. Culture and Theology are not mutually exclusive but are mutually inclusive. When one becomes a Christian, they do not automatically lose their cultural identity. Over time they discern those parts of their cultural identity and practices that do not align with biblical understanding. I am a fourth generation Christian from India, one of the cultural practices that immediately ceded upon conversion for my great grandparents was idol worship. What continued on was their respect for their parents and elders, which is congruent with scriptures. Exodus 20:12 (NRSV) states, "honor your father and your mother, so that your days may be long in the land that the Lord your God is giving you." While Hebrews 13:17 (NRSV)states, "obey your leaders and submit to them, for they are keeping watch over your souls and will give an account. Let them do this with joy and not with sighing—for that would be harmful to you." We live in a creative tension of upholding both theology and culture however, if we do it right, we will find ourselves honoring both God and neighbor. The wrong will correct itself as long as our interactions with the culturally and ethnically other are genuine and authentic because theology is actualized in authentic living and true proclamation.

Campbell and Burns examine three reasons why they find Wesleyan theology relevant for multicultural society. The reasons include the following:

> Wesleyan understanding of Christian faith involves a rich understanding of God's gifts to the whole world. Wesleyan understanding of the gospel involves the claim that our own culture and society, as well as others, stands under God's judgement. Wesleyan understanding of the gospel makes a clear distinction between what is essential for the Christian faith, and what is nonessential.[14]

Wesley understands God's grace was for all people everywhere. Therefore, a Wesleyan theological approach would call on a careful consideration of other cultural traditions including our own. It would also affirm that all cultures, societies and ethnicities of the world stand under God's judgment including our own. Finally, a Wesleyan theological understanding distinguishes between essentials and nonessentials of the Christian faith. They are identified as, "belief in the in the final authority of scripture, and belief in the Holy Trinity. Particular customs of worship, he held to be "opinions" rather than essentials."[15] Where we miss the mark when it comes to diversity efforts is that we use our cultural and ethnic architype as the cornerstone by which to compare all other cultures and ethnicities.

Conclusion

Christian higher education in North America stands at the crossroads of navigating the relationship between culture and theology as it relates to diversity efforts, specifically as it relates to creating a space for persons of different cultures and ethnicities in our institutions of higher education. While this navigation is challenging work, it can be done. This paper sought to assert that theology is a critical and significant contributor in diversity efforts in Christian higher education. With the use of the theoretical framework, experience-near, and significant contributions of scholars, a discussion on diversity in Christian higher education shed light on the reality that persons of different cultures and ethnicities must be understood in light of their cultural and ethnic backgrounds. Culture and ethnicity cannot be dealt with in an abstract and fragmented manner as it is an integral part of one's identity. Outside the chapel at Asbury University are the famous words of E. Stanley Jones, graduate of the school and missionary to India, "here we enter a fellowship, sometimes we will agree to differ, always we will resolve to love and unite to serve." Diversity may require that we sometimes agree to differ, but not at the expense of dehumazing the other simply because they are culturally and ethnically different. This is where theology is absolutely critical as it beckons us to love our neighbor as ourselves in the midst of our differences.

A few key reminders we can take away towards this end are; the understanding that the Christian faith involves a rich understanding of God's gifts to the whole world. Understanding that the gospel involves the claim that our own culture and society, as well as others, stands under God's judgement. Understanding the essentials and nonessentials of the Christian faith. I was recently at a store in Lexington and came across the *Special Time Edition* magazine, it caught my attention because on the cover page a few of the articles were mentioned. One of the articles mentioned was, *What Makes Us Moral*. Primarily the idea that being good, even altruistic, is something all societies value. As I read through the article, I started to reckon with the discussion that was laid out in it because it dealt with our capacity as human beings to be altruistic as well as atrocious. In one breath we would run into danger to help the other and in another we would turn around and harm or destroy the other. Why is this so? David Buss, a professor of psychology at the University of Texas is quoted in the article as saying, "the stuff that makes us who we are ---our capacity for kindness and generosity, as well as for greed and violence—exists in each of us because these abilities conferred some reproductive advantage on our forebears. Our inherent human nature has adaptations that evolved to be beneficial not from a moral sense, but from a fitness sense"[16] referring to the concept of the survival of the fittest. When we experience danger, we turn to atrocious behaviors in dealing with others, this is compounded when we are dealing with the other, who is culturally and ethnically different from the self. The culturally and ethnically different is seen as the enemy. Scripture has something to say about this, the words in Luke 6: 27-31 (NRSV), "But I say to you that listen, love your enemies, do good to those who hate you, bless those who curse you, pray for those who abuse you. If anyone strikes you on the cheek, offer the other also; and from anyone who takes away your coat do not withhold even your shirt. Give to everyone who begs from you; and if anyone takes away your goods, do not ask for them again. Do to others as you would have them do to you." Theology, our understanding of God and God's word has immeasurable significance in providing a corrective to our atrocious malfunctions.

Scott J. Jones, in his book *John Wesley's Conception and Use of Scripture* highlights the importance of the text speaking to the context and the context speaking to the text. He says, "what a person *says* about scripture is one thing. What that same person does with scripture is a separate matter. It is not enough simply to quote a theologian's words about scripture without asking whether his or her use is congruent with those stated views. The words about scripture are called the 'conception,' and what is actually done with scripture is called its 'use'."[17] Wesley relied on experience in addition to scripture, reason, and tradition in the interpretation and use of scripture however, the way Wesley used experience in scriptural interpretation is helpful for our purposes. Jones states, "Wesley relies on experience to describe the physical world. Second, Wesley occasionally makes a survey of the religious state of the world, third, he appeals to experience to give us knowledge of our own spiritual states."[18] We must not encourage theology to go on as fragmented as though it has no implications on our everyday life. Theology has significant implications for our everyday living if we believe theology is for the purpose of transforming personal life and social relations. Moving forward, theology must include the understanding of the physical world, a survey of the religious state of the world and the knowledge of our own spiritual states. Integrated theology should include a survey of the other as well as a survey of the self. When we engage in integrated theology, we will recognize the valuable insights theology can provide in the diversity efforts in Christian higher education.

End Notes

[1] Noel B. Woodbridge, "Living Theologically."

[2] Jon Inazu, *Confident Pluralism*, 6-7.

[3] Clifford Geertz, *Local Knowledge*, 57.

[4] Asbury University profile, https://www.asbury.edu/about/university-profile/

[5] S. Smith, "Christian Education," https://www.christianpost.com/news/christian-higher-ed-becoming-less-white-more-diverse-effort-reflect-god-kingdom.html

[6] Ibid.

[7] George Yancey, *Neither Jew Nor Gentile*, 4.

[8] Miroslav Volf, *A Public Faith*, 4.

[9] Adel S. Abadeer, "Seeking Redemptive Diversity in Christian Institutions of Higher Education: Challenges and Hopes from Within."

[10] Perry Glanzer, Nathan F. Alleman and Todd C. Ream, *Restoring the Soul of The University*, 7.

[11] Karen Longman, *Diversity Matters*, 5.

[12] Ted Campbell and Michael Burns, *Wesleyan Essentials in a Multicultural Society*, 5.

[13] Randy Maddox, *Rethinking Wesley's Theology for Contemporary Methodism*, 35.

[14] Ted Campbell and Michael Burns, *Wesleyan Essentials in a Multicultural Society*, 11-12.

[15] Ibid.

[16] Markham Heid, "The Roots of Good and Evil." *Time* Special Edition, 18.

[17] Scott J. Jones, *John Wesley's Conception and Use of Scripture,* 14.

[18] Ibid., 176-177.

Works Cited

Asbury University
2019   Asbury University Profile. Retrieved from: https://www.asbury.edu/about/university-profile/

Abadeer, Adel S.
2009   "Seeking Redemptive Diversity in Christian Institutions of Higher Education: Challenges and Hopes from Within." *Christian Higher Education*, 8:187–202. DOI: 10.1080/15363750902782373.

Campbell, Ted A. and Michael T. Burns
2004   *Wesleyan Essentials in a Multicultural Society*. Nashville, TN: Abingdon Press.

Geertz, Clifford
1983   *Local Knowledge: Further Essays in Interpretive Anthropology*. New York, NY: Basic Books, Inc.

Glanzer, Perry L., Nathan F. Alleman, and Todd Ream
2017   *Restoring the Soul of the University; Unifying Christian Higher Education in a Fragmented Age*. Downers Grove, IL: Intervarsity Press.

Heid, Markham
2019   "The Roots of Good and Evil." *Time*, Special Edition, *The Science of Good and Evil*.

Inazu D. John
2016   *Confident Pluralism; Surviving and Thriving through Deep Differences*. Chicago, IL: The University of Chicago Press.

Jones, J. Scott
1995   *John Wesley's Conception and Use of Scripture*. Nashville, TN: Abingdon Press.

Longman, Karen, gen ed.
2017   *Diversity Matters: Race, Ethnicity, & the Future of Christian Higher Education*. Abilene, TX: Abilene Christian University Press.

Maddox, Randy
  1998 *Rethinking Wesley's Theology for Contemporary Methodism*. Kingswood Books, Nashville, TN: Kingswood Books.

Marsden, George M.
  1994 *The Soul of the American University: From Protestant Establishment to Established Nonbelief*. New York, NY: Oxford University Press.

Smith, S.
  2018 "Christian Education becomes Less White, More Diverse in Effort to Reflect God's Kingdom." *Christian Post*. Retrieved from: https://www.christianpost.com/news/christian-higher-ed-becoming-less-white-more-diverse-effort-reflect-god-kingdom.html

Snyder, Howard A.
  2011 *Yes in Christ: Wesleyan Reflections on Gospel, Mission, and Culture*. Canada. Clements Publishing Group Inc.

Volf, Miroslav
  2011 *A Public Faith*. Grand Rapids, MI: Brazos Press.

Woodbridge, N.B.
  2010 "Living theologically – Towards a theology of Christian practice in terms of the theological triad of orthodoxy, orthopraxy and orthopathy as portrayed in Isaiah 6:1–8: A narrative approach." *HTS Teologiese Studies/ Theological Studies* 66(2): 807-813. DOI: 10.4102/hts.v66i2.807

Yancey, George
  2010 *Neither Jew No Gentile; Exploring Issues of Racial Diversity on Protestant College Campuses*. New York, NY: Oxford University Press.

The Asbury Journal 75/2: 210-225
© 2020 Asbury Theological Seminary
DOI: 10.7252/Journal.02.2020F.03

Shawn P. Behan
Exegeting Scripture, Exegeting Culture: Combining Exegesis to Fulfill God's Calling

Abstract:

Seminary has separated biblical exegesis from cultural exegesis, teaching them in different programs and seldom requiring them for those outside of those programs. Yet, to fulfill either of these exegetical processes we need both – they are mutually building and supporting entities that only make sense when combined with the other. As teachers, preachers, and leaders of God's Church, it is essential that we learn how to combine these two exegetical processes in order to faithfully live out our calling in God's kingdom. Thus, we must study both biblical and cultural exegesis and learn how to combine the two; for one without the other is knowledge, but combined they form knowledge with the wisdom of how to apply that knowledge. While this seems like a Herculean task, it has been accomplished by many in the history of the Church, often when they did not even know they were doing so. One such previous leader and teacher in the Church is Bishop J. E. Lesslie Newbigin, who's exegetical life made him a renowned name in his own day and continues to challenge us to "do likewise" in our lives.

Keywords: biblical exegesis, cultural exegesis, anthropology, Lesslie Newbigin

Shawn P. Behan is a PhD Candidate in Intercultural Studies at Asbury Theological Seminary. The focus of his dissertation research is on the missionary ecclesiology of Lesslie Newbigin.

"Indeed, *to* know is a thing that pleaseth talkers and boasters; but *to do* is that which pleaseth God. Not that the heart can be good without knowledge, for without that the heart is naught. There is, therefore, knowledge and knowledge - knowledge that resteth in the bare speculation of things, and knowledge that is accompanied with the grace of faith and love, which puts a man upon doing even the will of God from the heart: the first of these will serve the talker; but without the other, the true Christian is not content. 'Give me understanding, and I will keep thy law; yea, I shall observe it with my whole heart' (Psalm 119:34)."

- John Bunyan, *The Pilgrim's Progress*

Bunyan arrived at this point over three hundred years ago, that knowledge is useless without the wisdom found in the grace and love of God to use it appropriately. This is what has brought all of us to higher education (particularly seminary), to gain both knowledge and wisdom in order to serve God to the fullest of our abilities with the entirety of our lives. God has made all of us seekers of knowledge, but we know intuitively that we will never be satisfied with knowledge unless we also gain the wisdom to use knowledge appropriately in service to God's mission. One of the first lessons we learn in seminary is the fact that we will never learn everything we need to know to fulfill God's calling on our lives; so we break knowledge into compartments and discuss the ones we think are most relevant to the futures we envision. While this is good educational practice, it is not good for gaining knowledge and wisdom for the purpose of serving God's mission. Thus, in this paper I will be discussing two major pieces of seminary education that have spent many generations separated from each other, but in gaining wisdom we come to understand that they actually need each other - biblical exegesis and cultural exegesis.

I propose that it is necessary to combine these two exegetical tasks in order to fulfill God's calling on our lives and live out our pilgrimage with knowledge, wisdom, and a joyful heart for fulfilling God's desire. To do this, I will lay forth two main questions: what is the *telos* of biblical exegesis and why does a Christian need to exegete culture? In answering these questions, I will bring up a third question about the possibility of maintaining both exegetical projects in our ministry of teaching and leading in God's Church. This question will be addressed in the example of Bishop J.E. Lesslie Newbigin.

Exegeting the Gospel

One of the first things taught to aspiring pastors and ministry leaders is the appropriate way to interpret scripture. Often in a class like "Inductive Bible Study" we learn about the process of biblical exegesis, as opposed to eisegetical interpretation. Exegesis is the method by which we discern the meaning of the text through the study of the text itself (and its biblical context), and then apply that meaning to our own contexts. Eisegesis, then, being the reading into the text what we want to get out of it for our context. While exegetical interpretations of 2 Kings 2:23-25 (Elisha cursing the boys who mocked him with a bear mauling) would be much tougher than an eisegetical interoperation of these verses, biblical exegesis has served the church well for centuries. While biblical exegesis may have become second nature to many of us, before we get into the heart of this paper it is necessary to take a quick refresher course in biblical exegesis.

A Basic Outline of Exegetical Method

The history of biblical exegesis is a complicated one, with various forms that reach back centuries, its modern methods are relatively new and recently have received renewed interest (Cahill 2000). Within the more modern phenomenon of exegetical studies many methods have been developed. It may be helpful to think of a tree; with biblical exegesis being the trunk, three main branches, and then many stems and leaves sprouting from each of those branches. With this being an overview of exegetical method, we will only identify those branches and briefly discuss their relevance to the overall concept of merging biblical and cultural exegesis.

Biblical exegesis, according to Michael J. Gorman, can be broken down into three main branches or approaches - synchronic, diachronic, and existential (Gorman 2009: 13). The synchronic approach tends to look most explicitly at the text, with some cultural scope of the original writer's culture factored into its analysis; utilizing methods of literacy criticism, narrative criticism, rhetorical criticism, lexical/grammatical/syntactical analysis, semantic or discourse analysis, and socio-scientific criticism (Ibid.: 13-14). This approach tends towards a more literary focus of interpreting scripture within its own historical context. Then there is a diachronic approach, which tends towards more analysis of the development of the biblical text over time, as well as the development of its interpretation and includes: textual criticism, historical linguistics, form criticism, tradition criticism, source criticism, redaction criticism, and historical criticism (together this approach is often referred to as the historical-critical method) (Ibid: 15-16). Lastly there is the existential approach, which focuses on reading scripture "as something to be engaged" for the purposes of some end - often an encounter with the reality beyond the text itself - and includes the methods of: theological exegesis/missional interpretation/spiritual reading, canonical criticism, embodiment, and ideological criticism/ advocacy criticism/liberationist exegesis (Ibid: 18-19). This approach is often used in less formal settings than the classroom or the pulpit. Each one of these approaches can be used to teach the Gospel to a culture, but the exegetical approach alone does not necessarily mean that the Gospel will be understood by the receiving culture.

No matter which approach you prefer, the reality of the necessity for biblical exegesis does not escape us as we search to fulfill our calling as teachers of the Word of God. While these approaches give us the modes for which to approach scripture, exegesis as a whole provides the foundation to our approaching of scripture for the goal of teaching scripture. Thus, it is necessary to also look at biblical exegesis as a whole, not just its methodological parts, in order to start to gain the needed wisdom to appropriately apply the various exegetical methods.

The Foundation of Our Biblical Study & Interpretation

In its most basic form, "[E]xegesis may be defined as the careful historical, literary, and theological analysis of a text," particularly a specific text of Christian scripture (Gorman 2009: 10). This definition seems simple enough, but those with experience in biblical exegesis will tell you that it is much more complicated when you actually approach the exegetical task. There are many methods and approaches to biblical exegesis (as seen above) that complicate the learning and application of this interpretive process. As Christians, we also cannot deny the spiritual reality of biblical exegesis as well. Matthew Levering discusses biblical exegesis (in the historical-critical method) "as an ongoing participation in God's active providence, both metaphysically and Christologically-pneumatologically" (Levering 2008: 1). Which means that while we engage with humanly created methods of interpreting scripture both within the biblical context and for our context, we are also engaging a spiritual act of participating in Christ. This raises the question of the *telos* of such a spiritual act. While discipleship and greater spiritual intimacy with the Lord is a tremendous result of spiritually participating in the interpretation of scripture, if that were the only reason then we would never have to relay what we have learned from the exegetical process - it would only be for our spiritual edification. Yet, exegesis is an eminently other-focused activity, even while both the physical and spiritual activity of exegesis are edifying to the individual, exegesis is meant for the community. This brings us back to the question of what is the ultimate end of biblical exegesis? But before we venture to answer that question, we must also look at the second portion of this article, cultural exegesis.

Exegeting Culture

The second component of this discussion is the exegesis of culture. Often cordoned off in missiology or intercultural studies programs within the teaching of anthropology or sociology, exegesis of culture is a necessity in relating the Gospel to those who have never heard the Good News of salvation through faith in Jesus Christ. Typically, missionaries use elements of anthropology and sociology[1] in order to study culture and find culturally appropriate ways to deliver the Gospel to non-Christians. Undergirding this was the idea that the West was already Christian and therefore their culture was already molded around the Gospel, thus the location for missions was in non-Western cultures. The validity of this assumption can be debated, but it was this assumption that pushed the study of culture into the realm of missions. So let us take a quick look at the role of exegeting culture within its traditional discipline of missiology.

The Role of Anthropology/Sociology

As the academic study of missiology grew in the Twentieth Century, anthropology was closely linked to it, with several prominent missiologists of the mid-century acquiring anthropology degrees.[2] Anthropology, or more specifically cultural anthropology, strives "to look beyond the world of everyday experiences to discover the patterns and meanings that lie behind the world" (Robbins 2009: 2). As a discipline of the social sciences, anthropology has provided the theories and methods by which missionaries have studied culture in order to properly contextualize the Gospel so that different societies could understand the message of the Good News. This study, often utilizing qualitative methods, has provided insights to missionaries in order for them to minister to local communities.

For example, the use of linguistic anthropology in the translation of scriptures, whereby linguistics is used to understand culture, then in turn the missionaries utilize both linguistics and anthropology to craft the translation of scripture. While this is not the only example of anthropology being used in the field, it is the easiest to identify. Now we are in a place in the history of missions where the overwhelming majority of a macro-level culture has been investigated and the Gospel preached, thus we need to move toward more micro-level investigations, and investigations into responses to contextualization. Robert Montgomery concludes, "... what is needed most now in missiology is not the study of mission efforts, as important as these have been and are, but a serious study of the *reasons for the wide variations in response* to the Christian gospel from the peoples of the world" (Montgomery 2012: 289). Such studies must engage both the qualitative methods of anthropology and the quantitative methods of sociology in order to gain a better understanding the variations of micro-cultures and the differences of responses to the gospel in various cultures.[3] But no matter which methods are chosen, the use of the social sciences is essential for the present and future of missiology and the spreading of the Gospel around the globe.

While we have discussed the role of anthropology and sociology within missiology, there remains an underlying question that we have not addressed, why does a Christian need to exegete culture anyway? It is this question, and the question of the goal of exegeting scripture posed above, that we will turn to next.

Combining Biblical & Cultural Exegesis

In each of the above sections we have uncovered some very important questions. What is the end of biblical exegesis? Why would a Christian need to focus on cultural exegesis? The answer to both of these questions lies is in the combining of these two exegeses in order to serve God's calling to bear witness to the Gospel and disciple others to do the same. The concept of *missio Dei* points to the reality that as teachers, preachers, and leaders in God's Church it is our responsibility to bear witness to God's salvific actions throughout the world. "The mission can be nothing else than the continuation of the saving activity of God though the publication of the deeds of salvation" (Vicedom 1965: 9). Thus, by combing biblical exegesis with cultural exegesis we can fulfill this commission to bear witness to salvation in Jesus Christ through biblically sound and culturally relevant publications (in word and deed) of the salvific activities of God.

We have already seen the absolute necessity of biblical exegesis for all Christian communities. For the most effective use of anthropology/ sociology within missiology we look towards contextualization. Contextualization has had a unique history, filled with starts and stops of usage and effectiveness in missions (Hiebert 1987), yet it still remains the most effect tool of the missionary to reach people with the Gospel. For Gospel contextualization to be effective and true to scripture, we must heed the advice of Paul Hiebert and engage in a process of critical contextualization. Hiebert's critical contextualization utilizes three key steps: first is the exegesis of culture (gathering evidence about local customs and beliefs). It is important to note that exegeting of culture comes first only so we know what questions we wish to investigate within scripture. No one exegetes scripture blind, but they are influenced by their cultural perspectives and questions. Knowing the questions that culture is asking about the world or the assumption that a culture is operating within allows us the chance to ask "what does scripture say about that" and begin proper exegesis to discover the answer. But we have to make sure that our exegesis of culture does not pre-determine the answers we seek in scripture – this would be sliding into eisegesis and leads to syncretism.

The second step is an exegetical look at scripture and utilization of the hermeneutical bridge – this includes engagement with the global and historical hermeneutical community. This hermeneutical community includes the local church, the local Christian community, and then widens out in ever increasing circles to incorporate the entire global community. This means that we must be in fellowship with the global Church and ask this global community for evaluation and feedback of our hermeneutical outcomes. As well, we must investigate historical hermeneutics in order to determine whether our interpretations align with historical orthodoxy. Combined, these elements of local, global, and historical communities make up the hermeneutical bridge. Within this hermeneutical bridge, Hiebert points out that the leader must be cross-culturally nimble and able to translate between the biblical and congregational culture to the new culture so that those who hear the Gospel can grasp a clear understanding of it (Hiebert 1987: 109-110).

Lastly in Hiebert's model is the critical response of believers, both old and new, to reflect upon "their own past customs in the light of their new biblical understandings, and to make decisions regarding their response to their new-found truths" (Ibid.: 110). Thus, it is essential that this process happen within and by the full local congregation, and that the leaders of each local congregation properly teach its members how to do this type of critical contextualization both individually and as a community. Thus, even in the old Christian heartlands of Western Culture, we must engage with critical contextualization as culture has changed and so have we. What is most remarkable about Hiebert's model of critical contextualization is that it can be used around the globe, in any culture, at any level, so that any teacher of the Gospel, missionary or not, can lead their community through this process; and its reliance on biblical exegesis to make sense of the cultural exegesis that pushes Hiebert's model to scriptural fidelity.

Contextualization is not a wholly new topic either. New Testament scholar Dean Flemming in 2005 investigated the New Testament to identify and develop the patterns of contextualization that already exist within scripture. The most prominent (but definitely not the only) example of New Testament contextualization is Paul's time in Athens in Acts 17:16-24. In this passage Paul spends time learning the city, seeing the religious culture that abounds, and approaches the culture of Athens in their traditional way - teaching on the Areopagus. Flemming would also point to Jesus as the true and original model of contextualization that we should follow, as Christ contextualized himself in the Incarnation and then within the rituals of the Jewish culture of his day (Flemming 2005: 20-23). It is this model that we see repeated, in different versions, throughout the New Testament, to which Flemming would call the local church to enter into. This is because culture changes, as well as the local church. Thus, there must always be a cycle of contextualizing by exegeting the Bible, exegeting culture, then evaluating culture by the light of scripture. The only issue is whether or not we, the leaders of the local church, will facilitate or hinder contextualization. "The question is not *whether* they (the local church) will contextualize, but *how well* they will contextualize" (Moreau 2018: 230). Therefore, it is the responsibility of teachers and leaders in the local church to make sure that this contextualization happens in a thorough, critical, Hiebertian way; teaching their community to continually critically contextualize.

By using Hiebert's model we have an approach that necessitates the merging of biblical and cultural exegesis for the purposes of witnessing to the Gospel both within our own culture and to new cultures (both macro- and micro-) that we come into contact with during our pilgrimage of knowledge and wisdom to fulfill God's calling. We have also seen that contextualization is both old and continuous. The only question that remains is whether or not we can actually maintain faithfulness to both biblical exegesis and cultural exegesis while we combine them. To answer that question we will turn to the example of Bishop Lesslie Newbigin.

An Exegetical Life: Lesslie Newbigin

Bishop James Edward Lesslie Newbigin was born in Newcastle-upon-Tyne, England on December 9, 1909, and while he grew up in a Christian home it was through the ministry of the Student Christian Movement at the University of Cambridge that he became a Christian (Weston 2006: 1 and James n.d.). After serving with the SCM at the University of Glasgow (where he met his wife Helen) and returning to Cambridge for theological training at Westminster College, the Newbigins applied for mission service to India with the Church of Scotland (Weston 2006: 2-6).

Lesslie, as he preferred to be called, and his wife Helen enter missionary service in southern India in the fall of 1936 and began language training, which was cut short due to a bus accident that broke Newbigin's leg after unsuccessful treatment in India, required the couple to return to England (Wainwright 2000: 4-5). Newbigin served in an administrative role for the foreign missions committee of the Church of Scotland during his recovery, and three years after they first left, he and Helen (with their baby girl Margaret) finally returned to Kanchipuram, India to begin the missions ministry they were called to there (Ibid.: 5). Early on Newbigin became involved with the movement to unify the churches of South India and during his furlough of 1946-47 this project was completed, with Newbigin being elected as one of the new Church of South India's (CSI) founding bishops over the diocese of Madurai and Ramnad (Ibid.: 6-7).

Newbigin would spend the rest of his days in India serving both as a church leader and as an international defender of the South India scheme for unification, which made him a popular figure in the ecumenical movement of the mid-Twentieth Century. "The 'South India miracle' quickly made Newbigin a prominent figure in the growing international ecumenical scene" (James n.d.). He spend years traveling abroad to ecumenical meetings, both to the International Missionary Council (IMC) and the newly formed World Council of Churches (WCC), as well as many other international gatherings considering ecumenism and church unification. By the end of the 1950's, with an agreed upon merging of the IMC and WCC, the IMC asked Newbigin to lead their merger with the WCC and then become the first head of the WCC's Division of World

Mission and Evangelism (CWME) after the planned 1961 merger at the New Delhi consultation (Weston 2006: 9-10). Though reluctant to leave India, the CSI granted his release for five years to oversee this integration project (Ibid.: 9). Giving himself to the task of tackling the integration of these two organizations, Newbigin traveled the world and wrote extensively on issues related to this integration and set up the early movements of the CWME as its first director (Newbigin 1993: 158-201).

Newbigin returned to India in 1965, this time being elected as Bishop of Madras, a major city within the CSI, which effectively elevated him in responsibility and status to the top levels of the ecclesial hierarchy of the CSI, as well as his selection to top level leadership (Ibid.: 202-225). Here Newbigin tackled the needs of a large city and a large diocese, engaging in "fairly extensive social work in the slums of the city" as a means of obedience to Christ to meet human need and towards bringing about the conversion of those being served (Wainwright 2000: 145).

In 1974, at the retirement age of 65 and desiring to open a bishop-level position for the elevation of an Indian leader, Newbigin retired from the CSI and returned to Birmingham, England (Weston 2006: 11-12). His retirement did not last long as he took a post teaching missiology and ecumenism at the Selly Oak College in Birmingham for the next five years (James n.d.). After Newbigin had decided to retire for a second time, he argued for and eventually took up the leadership of United Reformed Church in inner-city Birmingham, working as its pastor for seven more years before retiring for a third time (Weston 2006: 12). Throughout the 1980's and 1990's Newbigin became a popular speaker and writer, until his passing on January 30, 1998 (Wainwright 2000: 14-16). It was during these retirement years that many of his most significant texts were written.

Going back to his first retirement, the Newbigins took an overland trip to get from Madras to France before sailing for England; a long desired trek through regions that had once been the heartlands of Christianity (Weston 2006: 11-12). In Cappadocia they were forced to worship on their own because they could not find any other Christians on Sunday morning (Ibid.: 12). It was this episode that would direct much of Newbigin's theological and missiological attention in his retirement years. "This had a profound effect upon Lesslie and helped to energize his later reflections on European culture, for it brought home just how completely a once-strong Christian heritage could all but disappear" (Ibid.: 12). It is these reflections that would come out in some of his most famous works - *The Other Side of 1984, Foolishness to the Greeks, The Gospel in a Pluralist Society,* and *Proper Confidence* (Ibid.: 13).

Newbigin's writings have an enduring legacy, especial those writings that came after his initial retirement from India. But it was a lifetime of reading, writing, and doing that gave his ideas their longevity. "During his lifetime, Newbigin was highly regarded both as an ecumenical and missionary statesman, and as a cross-cultural missiologist of the first order" (Weston 2012: 10). While this accrued reputation gave him latitude in his writings, since he often "lack(ed) the numerous footnotes characteristics of formal academic pieces" it also provided him with the gravitas to voice his critiques and new ideas in his retirement writings (Ibid.: 11). "Newbigin's return to the UK was also the prelude to a period of intense activity, reflection and writing for which he was to become perhaps best known" (Ibid.: 15). It was a lifetime of experiences that gave him the perspective to reflect on Western Christianity and call for a renewal of the Western Church; and this call was so spectacular that it still challenges us today. "The fact that *The Gospel in a Pluralist Society* continues to resonate and reverberate with a wide range of people, twenty-five years on, surely owes a good deal to the provenance offered by that Glasgow classroom" (Shenk 2015: 47).

But this enduring legacy is not just of an excellent theologian and missionary who rang the bells of renewal for the Western Church; it is also a legacy of combining biblical and cultural exegesis. There are dozens of examples that I could look at concerning Newbigin's biblical and cultural exegesis, but in the following sections I turn to one specific example of each of these exegetical practices and then follow with a discussion of Newbigin's exegetical combination.

Practicing Biblical Exegesis

During his time as General Secretary of the International Missionary Council, Newbigin produced a small bible study addressing the issues of Christian unity called *Is Christ Divided?* This small study of four chapters takes on a verse(s) in each chapter and applies biblical exegetical methods to understand that verse and applying it to the issue of church unity. The first chapter uses John 12:32 in a discussion about Christ being lifted up and drawing all humanity to himself (Newbigin 1961: 5). In this chapter he uses an exegetical linguistics approach to break down the words of this verse and determines that in the sight of the risen Lord our divisions are a sinful splintering of the Church (Ibid.: 9-10). The second chapter looks at 1 Cor. 12:13 for an understanding of the unity of all in Christ. "Here you have the dimensions of the Church's being set forth in their barest simplicity. The material - all sorts and conditions of men, Jews or Greeks, slave or free, mankind in all its variety; the form - one body marked off from the world by the act of baptism; the agent - one mighty Spirit, the Spirit of God" (Ibid.: 11). Thus, in the Church all are united together through the Spirit in the Lordship of Christ. Chapter three investigates the reason for this unity, finding in John 17:22-23 Christ's determination that his followers be one as he is one with the Father, for the glory of the Father (Ibid.: 18-19). Chapter four then takes a look at Mark 13:6-10 as a commissioning of the unified Church to glorify God to all the nations, even amidst the changes of the times (Ibid.: 26-41). In this small book Newbigin searches the scriptures for answers to the issues of unity that he and the IMC were facing as they entered this integration process with the WCC. In this, he models a way of exegeting scripture in order to address contemporary problems, but this is not the only exegesis that Newbigin engages in throughout his life.

Modeling Cultural Exegesis

Another small book of Newbigin's, produced in the mid-1950's, was an English translation of the doctrine and catechesis manual he produced for rural Tamil churches, *Sin and Salvation*. This book provides the foundational questions and answers that were needed to catechize converts in the rural Tamil-speaking villages in south India (Newbigin 1956: 7-10). This book was originally produced for the indigenous leaders and teachers who were traveling to these villages and teaching these issues to new converts, thus its original publication in Tamil. Newbigin had studied deeply the Hindu culture of India and used language of contradiction and harmony to begin to depict the ideas of sin and salvation (Ibid.: 11-15). He also focused on the Hindu values of family and social interaction (Toropov and Buckles 1997: 121) in order to discuss the community of Christian faith (Newbigin 1956: 92-114). All of this coming from his deep study and even admiration for the culture in which he was ministering, in order that he may properly contextualize the Gospel for local peoples to hear, understand, and accept the reality of salvation in Jesus Christ. But this cultural exegesis was only possible because simultaneously he was engaged in biblical exegesis.

Combining the Two

Newbigin dedicated his life to ministry and missions, which drew him to simultaneous exegesis of scripture and culture. It is in the combination in Newbigin that we see the *telos* of biblical exegesis and the reasoning of cultural exegesis - to bear witness to the Gospel among all the Nations of the world. His scriptural exegesis garnered him international acclaim and respect as "he was elected chair of the high-powered" Committee of Twenty-Five, which prepared the theological discussions for the 1954 WCC meeting at Evanston[4] (James: n.d.). He exegeted culture as well, both within Tamil-speaking India and on his return to England. It is his understanding of Hindu, and specifically Tamil, culture that gives Newbigin the credibility to later write in his theology of mission that: "A real meeting with a partner of another faith must mean being so open to him or her that the other's way of looking at the world becomes a real possibility for us" (Newbigin 1995: 184). The only thing holding us back from adopting the views of the religious other is our relationship with Jesus Christ, fostered by a deep reading and interpreting of scripture. So Newbigin modeled throughout his life both the necessity and the possibility of combining scriptural and cultural exegesis, all for the purpose of bearing witness to the Gospel.

Newbigin's biblical exegesis allowed him to properly share the Gospel in biblically sound and orthodox ways. His cultural exegesis allowed Newbigin to properly share the Gospel in culturally relevant and understandable ways. Thus, in the life of Lesslie Newbigin we see that it is necessary to combine biblical and cultural exegesis in order to fully practice both.

Like Newbigin, we too must learn how to merge these exegetical processes for the purposes of teaching and ministering the Word in the cultures and places where God has called us. Even if we are not called to places on the other side of the world, learning how to exegete the micro-cultural differences on the other side of town is essential for presenting a properly exegeted scripture.

Conclusion

Biblical exegesis and cultural exegesis, like biblical studies and missiology, have been separated in the academic world in order to adequately teach both. Yet, learning just one of these exegetical processes is like gaining knowledge without gaining the wisdom to know how to apply that knowledge. In particular for those who are called to teach, preach, and lead within God's Church, it is necessary to gain the knowledge of both exegetical processes. Once we have gained that knowledge we can start to merge them together in the ministries of the Word that God has called us into, thus gaining the wisdom of application. For if we are truly pilgrims of the Kingdom of God, living between the current and future realities of God's reign, then we must always be studying culture in order to properly apply the Bible to our context. And it is in this combination of exegetical processes that we enter into the joy of fulfilling God's will to exercise knowledge with wisdom to share the Gospel and further discipleship.

End Notes

[1] The methods and theories of anthropology and sociology are too large for a discussion here, but for most missiological programs a form of ethnographic cultural anthropology is the preferred approach to exegeting culture.

[2] The history of missiology and anthropology is a complicated one, but you can see in the prominence of missiologists like Alan Tippett, Chuck Kraft, Paul Hiebert, Dan Shaw, Bob Priest, Darrell Whiteman, and others who studied anthropology in order to enter the mission field or teach missiology. Though this connection has been debated by the likes of Whiteman, Priest, and others, it is undeniable that there has been a link between missiology and anthropology for decades.

[3] cf. Montgomery 2012: 283.

[4] A committee that included Karl Barth, Emil Brunner, and Reinhold Niebuhr amongst its illustrious members.

Works Cited

Bunyan, John
    2007   *The Pilgrim's Progress: From this World to that Which is to Come, Delivered Under the Similitude of a Dream.* Edited and abridged by Rosalie De Rosset. Chicago, IL: Moody Publishers.

Cahill, Michael
    2000   "The History of Exegesis and Our Theological Future." *Theological Studies* 61(2) (June): 332-347.

Flemming, Dean
    2005   *Contextualization in the New Testament: Patterns for Theology and Mission.* Downers Grove, IL: InterVarsity Press.

Gorman, Michael J.
    2009   *Elements of Biblical Exegesis: A Basic Guide for Students and Ministers*. Revised and Expanded Edition. Grand Rapids, MI: Baker Academic.

Hiebert, Paul G.
    1987   "Critical Contextualization." *International Bulletin of Missionary Research* 12(3) (Fall): 104-112.

James, Christopher B.
    2019   "Newbigin, J(ames) E(dward) Lesslie (1909-1998)." BU School of Theology Biographies. n.d. Accessed Sept. 29, 2019.http://www.bu.edu/missiology/missionary-biography/n-o-p-q/newbigin-james-edward-lesslie-1909-1998/.

Levering, Matthew
    2008   *Particpatory Biblical Exegesis: A Theology of Biblical Interpretation*. Notre Dame, IN: University of Notre Dame Press.

Montgomery, Robert L.
    2012   "Can Missiology Incorporate More of the Social Sciences?" *Missiology: An International Review* 40(3) (July): 281-292.

Moreau, A. Scott
    2018   *Contextualizing the Faith: A Holistic Approach*. Grand Rapids, MI: Baker Academic.

Newbigin, Lesslie
    1956   *Sin and Salvation*. Eugene, OR: Wipf & Stock.

    1961   *Is Christ Divided?* Grand Rapids, MI: Wm. B. Eerdmans Publishing Co.

    1993   *Unfinished Agenda: An Updated Autobiography*. Eugene, OR: Wipf & Stock.

    1995   *The Open Secret: An Introduction to the Theology of Mission*. Revised Edition. Grand Rapids, MI: William B. Eerdmans Publishing Co.

Robbins, Richard H.
    2009   *Cultural Anthropology: A Problem-Based Approach*. Fifth Edition. Belmont, CA: Wadsworth Cengage Learning.

Shenk, Wilbert R.
    2015   "Newbigin in His Time." In *The Gospel and Pluralism Today: Reassessing Lesslie Newbigin in the 21st Century*, edited by Scott W. Sunquist and Amos Yong, pp. 29-47. Downers Grove, IL: IVP Academic.

Toropov, Brandon and Father Luke Buckles, O.P.
    1997   *The Complete Idiot's Guide to The World's Religions.*
        New York, NY: Alpha Books.

Vicedom, Georg F.
    1965   *The Mission of God: An Introduction to a Theology of
        Mission.* Translated by Gilbert A. Thiele and Dennis
        Hilgendorf. St. Louis, MO: Concordia Publishing Group.

Wainwright, Geoffrey
    2000   *Lesslie Newbigin: A Theological Life.* Oxford, UK: Oxford
        University Press.

Weston, Paul
    2006   Compiled & Introduced. *Lesslie Newbigin: Missionary
        Theologian: A Reader.* Grand Rapids, MI: William B.
        Eerdmans Publishing Co.

    2012   "Leslie Newbigin: His Writing in Conext." In *Theology in
        Missionary Perspective: Lesslie Newbigin's Legacy,*
        edited by Mark T.B. Laing and Paul Weston, 10-16.
        Eugene, OR: Pickwick Publications.

The Asbury Journal 75/2: 226-240
© 2020 Asbury Theological Seminary
DOI: 10.7252/Journal.02.2020F.04

Abbie F. Mantor
Caring for the Sufferers Among Us: Job 3 Through the Lens of Classical Rhetorical Theory and Modern Psychological Trauma Studies

Abstract:

A lack of engagement with the theology of evil and suffering leads to immature responses when tragedy strikes our congregations and alienates the sufferers among us. I believe the best path forward is an interdisciplinary approach that is both intellectually honest and spiritually whole. In this article, I explore the first speech of Job through the lens of classical rhetorical studies and modern psychological trauma theories in order to demonstrate how Job's deep lament offers the Church an example of how to give sufferers the space to work through their grief as they walk their path towards healing and hope.

Keywords: trauma studies, rhetorical studies, Job 3, theology of evil, suffering

Abbie F. Mantor is completing her PhD in Biblical Studies at Asbury Theological Seminary where she has been a Hebrew Teaching Adjunct for the last two years. Her research area includes the Book of Job and trauma studies. She resides in Columbia, SC.

Introduction

The presence of evil has been behind the arguments against the existence of a good God since (at least) the Enlightenment. In his *Dialogues Concerning Natural Religion* David Hume argues that evil proved that God is indifferent to his creation and therefore, is not good (Peterson 2016b: 3). Almost 200 years later, evil was the basis of J. L. Mackie's logical argument against theistic belief. He contended that God cannot be both omnipotent and good while evil is present in this world. A good God would not allow evil and an omnipotent God would be powerful enough to eliminate it (Mackie 1955). Since then philosophers and theologians have offered points and counter points for and against theistic belief based on this problem of evil.

Unfortunately, this ongoing debate tends to be an academic endeavor that the average person tries to avoid. This is at least partly due to a Western culture that desperately wants to avoid suffering. N. T. Wright calls this the new problem of evil. We largely pretend that the world is good until evil hits us squarely in the face. Then, because we have no well-formed theology of evil, we are surprised and respond in immature ways (Wright 2014: 24–25). Like the philosophical debate, the theology of evil tends to be an academic pursuit that rarely trickles down to the pews. For example, the Christian faith does not advocate for universal salvation and yet at funerals we almost always hear people say the deceased "is in a better place." Likewise, most Christians do not believe God is distant and aloof, ready to smite humans for poor decisions. Why then do we tell our suffering brothers and sisters that God has allowed their suffering to strengthen them or that their misery is part of God's good plan? Rabbi Harold Kushner, in his book *When Bad Things Happen to Good People*, rightly argues that these shallow explanations may defend God, but they do not comfort the sufferer (Kushner 1981: 23). This line of thinking heaps shame on victims – if they had stronger faith, this would not have happened; if they were good enough, the pain would end. The sufferers among us are isolated and shamed; they have no one to turn to in order to ask difficult questions. Maybe that is why sufferers for centuries have turned to another man who lost everything and had no one to turn to—Job.

I do not believe that Job simply offers us an example of how to suffer well. Like theological bumper stickers, those arguments often heap blame on suffers and allow the Church to dismiss grief. Instead, I believe the book of Job teaches the Church how to interact with trauma and suffering in a way that is both intellectually honest and spiritually whole. Through the lens of classic rhetorical criticism and modern psychological trauma studies, I will look at the first speech of Job in order to demonstrate how Job's deep lament offers the Church an example of how to give sufferers the space to work through their grief as they walk their path towards healing and hope.

Methodology

Classic Rhetorical Criticism

Rhetoric was defined by Aristotle as "the faculty of observing in any given case the available means of persuasion" (Yu 2011: 5). Similarly, George Kennedy, described rhetoric more recently as "that quality in discourse by which a speaker or writer seeks to accomplish his purpose" (Dozeman 1992: 715). Against his contemporary's focus on the literary style of a text, Kennedy developed a method for New Testament studies attuned to the editor's intent and the perception of the audience (Dozeman 1992: 715). Ryan Cook adapted Kennedy's methodology for use in the Old Testament, specifically the Psalms. For Cook (2015: 458), a rhetorical analysis focuses on two primary questions. First, what is the intended effect of the poem? Second, how is that achieved? Similar to Cook's work in Psalms, I believe the poems of the book of Job can also be rhetorically analyzed in order to posit its effect.

Not all poems are so clear-cut, though. Barbara Hernstein Smith (1968: 131-132) rightly posits that an argument can "develop informally and irregularly through analogies, examples, and inferences, and ... be interrupted by digressions or elaboration." Therefore, it is also in the irregularities of Job's first speech that we are able to discern his purposes and greater rhetorical aims – for his own grief process and as an example for the audience.

Modern Psychological[1] Trauma Research

According to modern research, there are typical patterns people follow in reaction to a traumatic event. First, the victim experiences an overwhelming disruption of their mental processes.[2] They are often left in shock or speechless. Second, they experience an inability to express emotion. Third, defense mechanisms leave a victim stuck in a distorted view of the past with no avenue to move forward. Finally, victims experience a decreased ability to trust other people or to trust God (O'Connor 2011: 4).

It takes more than just time to move beyond the traumatic events and one never fully heals. Instead, victims integrate their trauma into their lives by reinterpreting the events to fit into a larger narrative that they can understand (O'Connor 2011: 47). This requires processing the events and accepting the consequences of the trauma. Additionally, victims must reengage their emotions by allowing themselves to grieve. Grief "involves living in the present with knowledge of the self and of the world as they are" (O'Connor 2011: 68). Lack of emotion de-humanizes the world, but grief opens the heart to feel and experience life again.

For a deeply religious person, studies have shown that asking difficult spiritual questions after a trauma experience is more beneficial than glossing over the events with shallow, pious responses. In general, victims who search for deeper answers experience negative results *initially*, but the long-term results are significantly greater. For example, one study showed higher levels of depression, suicidal thoughts, and PTSD symptoms[3] than victims who do not question their spirituality (Wortmann, Park, and Edmondson 2011: 443), but greater success in the long term (Wortmann, Park, and Edmondson 2011: 447). Another study analyzed a process called "meaning-making" (Currier et al. 2015: 29)placing them at risk for burnout and trauma-related problems (e.g., posttraumatic stress disorder [PTSD], where victims find a framework to explain their traumatic experience. The study also found that those who struggle to find a religious framework take longer to report positive moods, but once they do, the moods reported are far more positive than those who never assigned a spiritual framework to their trauma (McCann and Webb 2012: 150). Therefore, these studies wrestling with God and experiencing a full range of emotions is better than bypassing those emotions for quicker, but superficial recovery.

Analysis of Job 3

A careful analysis of the three stanzas of Job 3 through the lens of classical rhetorical studies and modern psychological trauma theories illuminates the depth of Job's trauma and demonstrates the early stages of his integration process.

1 After this Job opened his mouth and he cursed his day.

2 Job answered and he said:

3 *May the day perish [that] I was born into;*
     and the night [that] he said, "a man was
     conceived."

4 *That day may it be darkness;*
     May God not seek it from above;
     May light not shine upon it.

5   *May darkness and deep darkness redeem it;*
     May a cloud settle upon it;
     May the glooms of the day terrify it.

6 *That night, may darkness seize it;*
     May it not rejoice among the days;
     Among the number of months, may it not
     come.

7 *Behold, that night may it be barren;*
     May a cry of joy not enter it;

8   *May the cursers of the day curse it;*
      Those ready to rouse Leviathan.

9   *May the stars of its twilight grow dark;*
     May it hope for light, but there is none;
     May it not see the eyelashes of dawn.

10   *Because it did not shut the doors of*
     my womb;
     And therefore, hide trouble from my
     eyes.

11 *Why is it not from the womb [that] I would die?*
     From the belly had I come forth I could have
     perished.

12 *Why did knees meet me?*
     Why breasts that I could suckle?

13 *Because if I had laid down, I would be at peace;*
     I would have slept, then I would be at rest.

14   *with kings and advisors of the land;*
      Those who rebuild desolate
      places for themselves.

15.   *Or [I would be] with leaders who*
have gold;

Those who fill their houses
with silver.

16   *Or like a hidden miscarriage, I would*
not exist.

Like children who do not
see light, [I would not exist].

17   *There the wicked have ceased agitation;*
There the weary of strength will have rest.

18   *Altogether prisoners sleep;*
They do not hear the voice of an oppressor.

19   *Small and great are there;*
The servant is free from his master.

20   *Why did he give light to the laborer,*
And life to the bitter of soul?

21   *They are waiting for death, but it is not.*
Therefore, they search for it more than hidden
treasures.

22   *They are joyful concerning rejoicing;*
For they shall rejoice when they find the grave.

23   *[Why did he give light] to the man whose path is hidden?*
Therefore, God hedges around him.

24   *For before my bread my groans come;*
My roarings flow like water.

25   *For fear I trembled, and it came to me;*
That which I feared came to me.

26   *I am not at ease. I am not at peace.*
I am not at rest because agitation has come.

After the introductory lines in vv. 1-2, Job begins his curse of the day of his birth and night of his conception in the first stanza. This topic is introduced in v. 3, particularized in vv. 4-9, and explained in v. 10. Beginning with v. 3, we are introduced to an important word pair – יום (day) and לילה (night). While some commentators quibble over the implication of the use of these two words,[4] I believe this is an example of James Kugel's notion that "A is so, and *what's more*, B is so."[5] The day and night are neither individual entities of disdain, nor do they mean the same thing. Instead we hear Job trying to effectively express the deepest agony of his soul. Kugel paraphrases it well, "my whole life is a waste! Blot out the day of my birth, *in fact,* go back to the very night I was conceived and destroy it (Kugel 1998: 9)."

This desire for wholesale destruction of Job's origins, begs a further question, though. Why does Job desire the day of his birth to perish, not the day of his misfortune? Rhetorically, Job is trying to express that he is not merely saddened at the loss of his livelihood and family but is in such deep agony that he wishes he would have never been born at all. This skewed view of reality introduces us to the depth of Job's trauma right from the start.

Verses 4-5 particularize Job's desire to curse the day of his birth. The use of personification of the day heightens Job's lament. For example, v. 4 describes his abstract day as something concrete to be sought and shined upon. In v. 5, Job personifies darkness as a potential redeemer of his wayward day. Furthermore, the darkness is being personified as one who terrifies, and the day is being personified as someone who can be terrorized. The rhetorical effect is that his grief does not just surround him, it lays claim to him and attacks him.

Next, Job turns in vv. 6-9 to the particularization of the curse of the night of his conception. Where Job's day was dark in v. 4, here Job proclaims that his night is worse than dark—it is barren. The extension of darkness to barrenness is a metonymy that highlights the sadness surrounding infertility. Job sees his life as the deepest kind of darkness and wishes not to go back to his old life, but that he had never existed in the first place.

Job continues with vain requests and unfulfilled hopes. He desires the professional cursers[6] of v. 8 to undo his conception. Of course, this is impossible as the events have already happened. In v. 9 he expresses the desire of his night to remain dark without light ever entering it. Clearly, the impossibility of Job being un-conceived is as impossible as preventing daylight from eclipsing each night. Only God could be capable of fulfilling Job's astronomical requests and yet, strangely, that is the one person Job does not reach out to.

Verse 10 finally answers the reader's burning question, "why?" Although we can understand that Job is sad, why does he insist on non-existence rather than just having his pain alleviated? In Job's mind, the only way to find true respite from his condition is to have never been born. In fact, he accuses the day of his birth and the night of his conception of having failed to protect him. This blame of inanimate objects for failing at an impossible task highlights Job's warped view of reality. The trauma he has experienced is so profound that he cannot possibly imagine integrating it into his life narrative.

Furthermore, Job's elevated language in this stanza gives insight into his process of wrestling with God. Joseph Dodson (2008: 41) explores the rhetorical power of figurative language and suggests metaphor is often used to deflect attention away from a difficult topic. Job gives human characteristics and expectations to the day and night, but is there an underlying metaphor at work as well? Is there a something or a someone that has failed to protect Job? Someone who Job wants to blame, but maybe is not ready to address head on? As the speeches continue, we discover that Job does blame God for not protecting him, but here, in the early stages of wrestling with reality, Job is not direct, maybe not yet comfortable to make such a bold accusation.

The second stanza continues to highlight Job's struggle to integrate his trauma into his life. Rather than admit he is hurt or angry, Job fixates his mind on death and the ease he would have experienced had he never been born or had died right after birth. The intimate wording of vv. 11-12 should bring connotations of love and comfort that newborns receive from their parents.[7] Instead, Job has juxtaposed these concepts with death and lament. Rather than being grateful for loving parents, Job cries out, "Why did good things have to happen to me?" This rhetorical reversal dramatically illustrates both the depth of Job's lament and his warped view of reality.

After expressing grief that he was born, Job goes on in vv. 13-19 to idealize the rest he could have found if he had died. In fact, he believes his life is currently so awful that only death upon entry into the world could provide him with real relief. Job goes beyond describing this rest and begins to list the kinds of people he would be with—kings, leaders, the wicked, prisoners, and the like. While many commentators use the word pair קטן and גדול in v. 19 as the lens to read the whole of the section through, I am unconvinced. First, the classification of קטן or גדול is not always straight forward. For example, Alter (1985: 81) posits that the גדול are listed first, but then why is a hidden miscarriage listed between rich leaders and the wicked? Furthermore, why is the servant listed after the word pair? Rather than a categorization, this word pair should be understood as a merism used to idealize death. In short, the kind of rest that death provides is such that all people—no matter their lot in life—will experience it.

Job clearly has an overly romantic view of death in this stanza. In his mind, to have never been born at all is his best possible life and he would rather throw away his many years of happiness than to continue to experience his deep agony. It is worth emphasizing again—Job does not desire death now, but to have never existed. Oddly, although the variety of people listed would find rest in death after their long lives, Job appears to not believe it is possible for himself. Only death immediately following birth could relieve his pain. This warped view of reality and fantasy life Job is playing out in this stanza again illuminate the depths of his agony and reveal his inner process of wrestling—really avoiding—reality. He would rather have never had life than to find a way to integrate this experience into his life narrative.

Job begins to make a shift, though, in the last stanza of the poem. Rather than hiding behind personifications or idealizing death, Job begins to ask real questions about God. This shift is significant for his integration process. First, Job is stepping back into reality. One way we see this shift is in the repetition of the word light (אוֹר) throughout the poem. In v. 9 the personified day hopes for light but finds none. In v. 16 the miscarried children are described as those who do not see the light. In each of these verses light represents life that is not actualized. In v. 20, though, light does not simply represent life but is overtly connected to it by metonymy. Further, in this statement, Job is finally admitting reality. This is a far cry from integrating his trauma into his life narrative, but he has shifted from the world of imagination and fantasy to asking tough questions about the reality he now experiences.

Second, this shift reveals that Job is wrestling with God and conventional wisdom. Proverbs 2 promises that if someone seeks after understanding as if it were a hidden treasure, they will find it. In Job 3:21, though, Job claims that when no relief is found from a bitter life, people will seek after *death* as if it were a hidden treasure. It could be posited that Job is claiming that wisdom matters little for a life filled with misery. These seemingly impious claims are not exclusive to Job, though, as Ecclesiastes has similar themes.[8] This impious talk is shocking on the lips of Job, though, as his previous words were perfectly aligned with conventional wisdom. For example, after Job received the news that everything he had was gone, his response in 1:21 was, "The Lord gives, and the Lord takes. Let the name of the Lord be blessed." Likewise, after being struck with horrible boils, he said in 2:10, "Must we only take good from God and not take the bad?"

Even in his deep laments in the first two stanzas of the poem, Job avoids directly blaming God or questioning his plan. Here, though, Job is finally willing to voice his deepest concerns. Piety is no longer more important that finding the truth. Job is taking a step into the ring to really begin his wrestling match with God.

Verse 24 brings another important shift in Job's integration process. In the first two stanzas the use of first person was only in reference to the past[9] or in a fantasy,[10] but in vv. 24-26 Job openly admits his present reality. He confesses that his complaints spew forth with no real direction, that he is surrounded by fear, and that he can find no peace in the agitation. With no clear recipient, his complaints avoid blaming God, but also leave behind the fantasy world of the second stanza. His last line is significant because it echoes v. 13. There, Job believed that only in non-existence could he find peace (שֶׁקֶט), sleep (שֵׁנָה), and rest (נוּח). Here, Job admits that he is not at ease (שׁלה), not at peace (שֶׁקֶט), and not at rest (נוּח). By admitting where he really is—rather than dreaming about where he wants to be—Job is stepping back into reality, which is essential to integrating his trauma into his life narrative.

This shift is encouraging for the reader. Through honest inner dialogue, Job finds words to begin accepting the reality of his trauma. Hope and integration seem just around the corner for Job – and his example can be a roadmap for the sufferers among us. In fact, in the overarching rhetoric of the book, the honesty of the introduction allows the reader to empathize with Job in a way the friends cannot. We know that Job is innocent and did not deserve his plight. We are invited to sit next to Job with our deepest grief and allow his harrowing lament speak words we are unable to articulate ourselves. The first speech of Job becomes a safe space to process grief and begin the process of integration. Sadly, we know that Job's friends do not create a safe space for Job to continue processing his trauma. But for a moment the eyelashes of dawn appear on the horizon to bring a ray of light to the darkest soul.

Conclusion

Through the lens of rhetoric and trauma studies, I have tried to illuminate key themes and topics in each stanza of Job 3 that can help the modern reader better understand the intended effect of the poem. In the first stanza (vv. 3-9), Job cloaks his mistrust in the personification of the day of his birth and night of his conception. Rhetorically, Job is both attempting to put words to his deep anguish and avoiding facing his reality.

The audience begins to understand how the traumatic events of chapters 1-2 are really affecting Job. Rather than working through his grief, though, Job places unrealistic expectations on inanimate objects and insists that non-existence is his only relief.

Job continues these themes in the second stanza where his desire for non-existence becomes an elaborate fantasy about how wonderful his life would have been had he never been born. Rhetorically, Job is not criticizing those who are well-off in the world, but rather emphasizing that everyone—small or great—finds rest in death. Ironically, Job does not suggest death now would be his relief, but only death at birth. This romanticizing of death and non-existence only heightens the fact that Job is not yet willing to wrestle with his reality.

This changes though, in the final stanza (vv. 20-26). While Job is not yet willing to fully admit his circumstances or integrate them into his life narrative, he makes strides in that direction. First, his probing questions in vv. 20-23 imply an admittance of reality. Like the author of Ecclesiastes, Job admits that the world is not fair and asks why. Against conventional wisdom, Job is willing to wrestle with God. Second, the switch to the first person in vv. 24-26 further reveal Job's shift in mindset. In the beginning of the poem Job distrusted everyone and hid his pain behind the personified day and night, but here, in the last stanza, he begins to look at his reality more directly even if he cannot yet directly blame God for his situation. The tone of the last stanza indicates that his distrust and pessimism towards God are just below the surface and his admission of reality is a step toward direct confrontation with God.

These subtle allegations are not missed by the friends who interrupt Job's lament to bring a full attack in the following chapters on Job's lack of piety. Unfortunately, the friends miss Job's deep emotional plea and are seemingly ill-equipped to help Job process his trauma. They offer intellectual solutions that sound good but fall flat on Job's grief-stricken ears. It is only after his face-to-face meeting with God that his understanding of suffering is realigned and he finds rest for his soul.[11]

Sadly, the Church often follows the path of the friends—a path that leads to frustration, blame, and broken relationships. How would the book of Job been different if the friends had been what modern researchers call "trauma-informed?" (Bath 2008)which has, in turn, led to a focus on the treatment of trauma-related conditions. Much of the recent literature describes different approaches to therapy. However, there are a few consistent propositions arising from the research and clinical literature which suggest that much of the healing from trauma can take place in non-clinical settings. There is some evidence to suggest that trauma-informed living environments in which healing and growth can take place are a necessary precursor to any formal therapy that might be offered to a traumatised child. It stands to reason that the treatment of children exposed to complex trauma will itself be complex and long-lasting. However, there appears to be a remarkable consensus about the key prerequisites for healing--those critical factors or therapeutic pillars that need to be in place if healing is to take place. Although there is debate about the number of critical factors, there are three that are common to most approaches. This article outlines the three pillars of trauma-informed care: (1 What if they had realized that integrating the traumatic event into one's life narrative was essential for moving forward? What if they knew distancing yourself from reality and wrestling with God were helpful steps in that process? Fortunately, the Church has access to this knowledge. Through careful integration of modern trauma research into biblical narratives such as the book of Job, the Church can find a better path—one that offers intellectually honest answers to the problem of evil and spiritually whole responses to the sufferers among us.

End Notes

[1] Most scholars researching the intersection of trauma studies and the Bible work in the world of literary criticism – focusing on the story as created by the author for a specific purpose. While an insightful endeavor, I find this approach misses the nuances of how the individual characters (real or presented) experience and process trauma. Therefore, I will follow the path of psychological trauma research as laid out by Christopher Frechette and Elizabeth Boase in the introduction of *The Bible Through the Lens of Trauma*. They state that "within the field of psychology, the study of trauma focuses on the range of responses evoked by an experience perceived to pose an extreme threat and that overwhelms an individual's ordinary means of coping" (Boase and Frechette 2017: 4). Clearly, these experiences and responses are recorded for us as literary material, but my focus will not be the way trauma is encoded in the text for a specific audience, but in Job, the individual as recorded in the literature.

[2] O'Connor (2011: 3) is not a trauma specialist, but I have found her research to be extensive and in line with other sources I have found. Therefore, I will rely on her general explanations of trauma that are cast in the context of biblical studies.

³ PTSD symptoms include three categories: reexperiencing (nightmares, flashbacks), emotional numbness, and hyperarousal. See Catherall (2004: 264).

⁴ Clines, for example, insists that day be a 24-hour period, but night is just a night (Clines 1989: 17:81), while Hartley explores the magical quality of these two events that both represent his origin (Hartley 1988: 92) Berlin notes the contrast between the definite הלילה and indefinite יום, but I do not think much can be made of this considering there is only one possible day Job was born into (Berlin 1985: 51).

⁵ See Kugel (1998: 8), see also Alter (1985: 78).

⁶ See Longman (2012); Hartley (1988); Clines (1989); and Balentine (2006).

⁷ The knees could either refer to *lap* or be related to blessing (ברך) a newborn child based on Gen 48:12 and 50:23 (Longman 2012: 103). The adoption language is associated with knees and suggests the reference points to acceptance and concern for the newborn child by mother or father (Stade 1886: 143–65).

⁸ See Eccl 4:3 and 7:1.

⁹ See v. 3, 10.

¹⁰ See v. 11, 12, 13, 16.

¹¹ These conclusions are largely based on the work of Matitiahu Tsevat (1966) and Michael Peterson (2016a).

Works Cited

Alter, Robert
    1985   *The Art of Biblical Poetry*. New York, NY: Basic Books.

Balentine, Samuel E.
    2006   *Job*. SHBC. Macon, GA: Smyth & Helwys.

Bath, Howard
    2008   "The Three Pillars of Trauma-Informed Care." *Reclaiming Children and Youth* 17 (3): 17–21.

Berlin, Adele
    1985   *The Dynamics of Biblical Parallelism*. Bloomington, IN: Indiana University Press.

Boase, Elizabeth, and Christopher G. Frechette, eds.
    2017   *Bible through the Lens of Trauma*. Semeia Studies 86. Atlanta, GA: SBL Press.

Catherall, Donald Roy
    2004   *Handbook of Stress, Trauma, and the Family.* Brunner-Routledge Psychosocial Stress Series. New York, NY: Brunner-Routledge.

Clines, D. J. A.
    1989   *Job 1-20.* Vol. 17. WBC. Dallas, TX: Word Books.

Cook, Ryan J.
    2015   "Prayers That Form Us: Rhetoric and Psalms Interpretation." *JSOT* 39 (4): 451–67. https://doi.org/10.1177/0309089215590359.

Currier, Joseph M., Jason M. Holland, Lisseth Rojas-Flores, Sofia Herrera, and David Foy
    2015   "Morally Injurious Experiences and Meaning in Salvadorian Teachers Exposed to Violence." *Psychological Trauma: Theory, Research, Practice, and Policy* 7 (1): 24–33. https://doi.org/10.1037/a0034092.

Dodson, Joseph R.
    2008   *The "Powers" of Personification: Rhetorical Purpose in the Book of Wisdom and the Letter to the Romans.* BZNW 161. New York, NY: Walter de Gruyter.

Dozeman, Thomas
    1992   "OT Rhetoric and Rhetorical Criticism." In *ABD*, edited by David Noel Freedman, 1st ed., 5:712–15. New York, NY: Doubleday.

Hartley, John E.
    1988   *The Book of Job.* NICOT. Grand Rapids, MI: Eerdmans.

Kugel, James L.
    1998   *The Idea of Biblical Poetry: Parallelism and Its History.* Baltimore, MD: Johns Hopkins University Press.

Kushner, Harold S.
    1981   *When Bad Things Happen to Good People.* New York, NY: Schocken Books.

Longman, Tremper
    2012   *Job.* BCOTWP. Grand Rapids, MI: Baker Academic.

Mackie, J. L.
    1955   "Evil and Omnipotence." *Mind* 64 (254): 200–212.

McCann, Russell A., and Marcia Webb
    2012   "Enduring and Struggling with God in Relation to Traumatic Symptoms: The Mediating and Moderating Roles of Cognitive Flexibility." *Psychology of Religion and Spirituality* 4 (2): 143–53. https://doi.org/10.1037/a0026404.

O'Connor, Kathleen M.
 2011 *Jeremiah: Pain and Promise*. Minneapolis, MN: Fortress Press.

Peterson, Michael L., ed.
 2016a "Christian Theism and the Evidential Arguement from Evil." In *The Problem of Evil: Selected Readings*, edited by Michael L. Peterson, 166–92. Notre Dame, IN: University of Notre Dame Press.

 2016b *The Problem of Evil: Selected Readings*. Notre Dame, IN: University of Notre Dame Press.

Smith, Barbara Herrnstein
 1968 "Poetic Closure: A Study of How Poems End." Chicago, IL: University of Chicago Press.

Stade, B.
 1886 "Auf Jemandes Knieen gebaren." *ZAW*, no. 6: 143–56.

Tsevat, Matitiahu
 1966 "The Meaning of the Book of Job." *Hebrew Union College Annual* 37: 73–106.

Wortmann, Jennifer H., Crystal L. Park, and Donald Edmondson
 2011 "Trauma and PTSD Symptoms: Does Spiritual Struggle Mediate the Link?" *Psychological Trauma: Theory, Research, Practice, and Policy* 3 (4): 442–52. https://doi.org/10.1037/a0021413.

Wright, N. T.
 2014 *Evil and the Justice of God*. Westmont: InterVarsity Press.

Yu, Charles
 2011 "To Comfort Job: The Speeches in the Book of Job as Rhetorical Discourse." University of Wisconsin - Madison. 2012-99070-397.

The Asbury Journal 75/2: 241-254
© 2020 Asbury Theological Seminary
DOI: 10.7252/Journal.02.2020F.05

Dain Alexander Smith
Prophetic Peace in the Epistle to the Romans: Intertextuality, Isaianic Discourse, and Romans 14:17

Abstract:
Interpreters of Romans have not recognized the Isaianic character of Paul's description of the kingdom in Rom 14:17. Therefore, in this paper I demonstrate that there is an intertextual relationship between multiple Isaianic texts and Rom 14:17. First, I identify key texts in Isaiah that depict kings or kingdoms and share terms found in Romans: righteousness, peace, joy, good, and spirit. Second, I conclude by rereading Romans 14:17 in dialogue with Isaianic kingdom texts. This reading reveals that Romans presents the kingdom of God—and the church community—as the fulfillment of Isaiah's eschatological hope for peace.

Keywords: Romans, Isaiah, intertextuality, peace, kingdom of God

Dain Alexander Smith is a PhD student in Biblical Studies at Asbury Theological Seminary, Wilmore, KY

Introduction

It is safe to say that Paul's epistle to the Romans is one of the most contested documents in the New Testament, especially since the Protestant reformation. In recent decades, interpreters have investigated the use and influence of scripture in Paul's epistles.[1] Consequently, interest has arisen in the multitude of scriptural citations, allusions, and echoes in Romans.[2] Although citations and allusions pervade the entire letter, interpreters have been drawn to Rom 9–11, likely due to the sheer density of citations.[3] Isaiah has taken a central position in the discussion because it is cited by name five times, quoted numerous times, and Isaianic allusions and echoes permeate Romans.[4] Moreover, multiple scholars have noted that the New Testament's theology concerning the gospel and the kingdom of God is intimately connected to Isaiah's eschatological hope, and this connection between the gospel and Isaiah is often identified in Romans.[5] Lastly, in recent years interpreters of Romans have noticed the prominence of peace language in contrast to the other Pauline Epistles, and this has spurred numerous investigations.[6]

However, interpreters have overlooked the intimate connection between peace and Isaiah in Romans, and interpretations of Rom 14:17 have not recognized the Isaianic character of Paul's description of the kingdom.[7] Therefore, in this paper I demonstrate that there is an intertextual relationship between multiple texts of Isaiah and the description of the kingdom of God in Rom 14:17. Paul's statement, "The kingdom of God is … righteousness, peace, and joy in the holy spirit," is not a uniquely Pauline description, but it is characteristic of multiple Isaianic kingdom discourses.[8] In order to demonstrate this relationship, first, I identify key texts in Isaiah that depict kings or kingdoms, and I indicate that these texts also mention key terms found in Romans: righteousness, peace, joy, good, and the Spirit. Second, I conclude by rereading Romans 14:17 in dialogue with Isaianic kingdom texts. This reading reveals that Romans presents the kingdom of God—and the church community—as the fulfillment of Isaiah's eschatological hope for peace.

Isaiah's Kingdom of Peace and Righteousness

Isaiah is a massive work, and there is no way to cover every text that depicts a king or a kingdom. However, in the following section I demonstrate that peace and righteousness are primary themes in LXX

Isaiah's kingdom discourses. Secondarily, good, joy, hope, and Spirit also appear regularly in kingdom discourses.

Isaiah begins with indictment. The people of God are laden with corruption and iniquity. The prophet writes, "Woe, sinful nation, people weighed down with iniquity, offspring who do evil, children who deal destruction" (Isa 1:4). Later, after the song of the vineyard, Isaiah explains God's disdain for the vineyard; "he hoped for justice, and behold there was bloodshed; he hoped for righteousness, and behold there was a cry!" (Isa 5:7).[9] Clearly, the prophet Isaiah had a problem with the people of God—they were unjust, violent, and corrupt.

Isaiah offers a solution to this quandary in Isa 7, 9, and 11 by envisioning a king who will lead God's people to redemption.[10] Beginning in 7, the prophet explains that a king will be born who does good, not evil; "a virgin will conceive in the womb, and she will birth a son, and you will name him Emmanuel. ... before he knows to prefer evil he will choose *good* (ἀγαθόν). For before the child knows *good* (ἀγαθὸν) or evil, he refuses evil, to choose *good* (ἀγαθόν)" (LXX Isa 7:14–16). Although this prophetic utterance may have been about Hezekiah in its initial telling, the depiction of a royal child becomes more phantasmagorical and eschatological in Isa 9 and 11.

> For a child was born to us, and a son was given to us, whose government was upon his shoulder: and his name is called the Messenger of great counsel: for I myself will bring *peace* (εἰρήνην) upon the rulers (ἄρχοντας), and health to him. His rule (ἀρχὴ) is great, and of his *peace* (εἰρήνης) there is no limit upon the throne of David, and his *kingdom* (βασιλείαν), establish it and support it in *righteousness* (δικαιοσύνῃ) and in judgment, from now and forever. (LXX Isa 9:5–6; emphasis added)

This royal child does not just choose good over evil, but he brings peace to rulers, rules his kingdom in peace, and establishes righteousness forever. Then in Isa 11:1–5 the promised ruler is depicted as Spirit empowered and the paragon of righteousness. Ultimately, the plight of Israel's corruption is prophetically placated by divine intervention. God anoints a new Davidic king with the Spirit, and that ruler will lead God's people to peace, righteousness, and goodness. Ben Witherington concludes, "in Isaiah 7, and even more in Isaiah 9, and finally very clearly in Isaiah 11 our prophet speaks not only of the near horizon but of the more distant one where an ideal or eschatological ruler with divine attributes and even the very character of God will come and set things right once and for all" (2017: 180).

In a similar manner, Isa 32 hopes for a kingdom where there is a righteous king. "For behold, a *righteous king will reign* (βασιλεὺς δίκαιος βασιλεύσει), and rulers will rule with judgment" (LXX Isa 32:1). Yet, for the time being, society is still doomed; "the positive promise for the future leaves no doubt that in the present Judah has a problem" (Goldingay 2012: 180). This is most exemplified in 32:7, "For the counsel of the wicked will deliberate as a lawless counsel, in order to destroy the poor with *unjust* (ἀδίκοις) words and ruin the cause of the poor in judgement." The leaders in Israel show little concern for the poor and the needy, and they govern with injustice rather than justice. Yet, Isaiah is not without hope and the discourse changes. God's people are destined for destruction but there is still hope.

> Daughters listen to my words with *hope* (ἐλπίδι) ... the families have left the rich city; they will abandon the desirable houses; ... until the *Spirit* (πνεῦμα) from upon high shall come upon you all ... and *righteousness* (δικαιοσύνη) will dwell in Carmel, and *the works of righteousness will be peace* (ἔσται τὰ ἔργα τῆς δικαιοσύνης εἰρήνη), and *righteousness* (δικαιοσύνη) will ensure relief, by believing (πεποιθότες) for eternity; and his people will dwell in a city of peace (εἰρήνης), they will dwell by believing (πεποιθώς)." (LXX Isa 32:9, 14–18; emphasis added)

The prophetic hope of Isaiah is a kingdom where the Spirit of God is poured out upon the people, and righteousness (δικαιοσύνη) and peace (εἰρήνη) reign (Goldingay 2012: 182). Interestingly, although Isa 7, 9, and 11 highlight different kingly characteristics, ch. 32 disperses those kingly characteristics throughout the kingdom. Therefore, Isaiah's hope is not just for a righteous and peaceful ruler, it is also for a righteous and peaceful kingdom populated by righteous and peaceful people.

This hope does not disappear, and it arises again in Isa 59–60. The prophet asks in 59:1, "Is the hand of the Lord not strong enough to save? Or has he made his ear heavy, so that he should not hear?" The prophet responds with more indictment, and "focuses on the depth and extent of their depravity" (Harman 2011: 442). "Your sins separated you and God, ... your hands have been defiled with blood and your fingers with sins, and your lips speak lawlessness, and your tongue practices *unrighteousness* (ἀδικίαν). No one speaks *justice* (δίκαια) ... they believe (πεποίθασιν) in emptiness and they speak vanity" (59:2–4). Then in 59:8–9 the prophetic indictment increases, "*they did not know the way of peace* (ὁδὸν εἰρήνης οὐκ οἴδασιν) ... *they did not know peace* (οὐκ οἴδασιν εἰρήνην). Because of this, judgment was withdrawn from them, and *righteousness* (δικαιοσύνη) did not reach them; while they waited for light, darkness came to them, waiting for day break, in darkness they walked." The prophet depicts a bleak reality, one where God's people are waiting for justice, but their own injustices have isolated them from their redeemer. Yet, similar to 32, the text turns positive.

> The deliverer will come for the sake of Zion, and he will turn away the impiety of Jacob. And this is my covenant with them, says the Lord; my *spirit* (πνεῦμα), which is upon you, and the words, which I gave into your mouth, shall not fail your mouth and from the mouths of your descendants, for the Lord has spoken, from now and forever. Shine, shine, O Jerusalem, for your light is present, and the glory of the Lord is risen upon you. Behold, darkness will cover the earth ... but the Lord shall appear upon you, and his glory will be seen upon you. And kings (βασιλεῖς) will live in your light, and nations in your brightness. (Isa 59:20–60:3; emphasis added)

Isaiah envisions a time when God redeems Israel and God's Spirit rests upon them, so much so that foreign kings live in their new found light. The presence of God and the anointing of the Spirit results in a new kingdom full of righteousness and peace from top to bottom.

> I will bestow your rulers (ἄρχοντάς) in *peace* (ἐν εἰρήνῃ) and your overseers (ἐπισκόπους) in *righteousness* (ἐν δικαιοσύνῃ); and they will never again obey unrighteousness (ἀδικία) in your land, nor destruction nor misery in your boarders, but your walls will be called salvation, ... and *all your people are righteous* (ὁ λαός σου πᾶς δίκαιος). (Isa 60:17–18, 21; emphasis added)

Isaiah 59 and 60 depict a kingdom that is helplessly unjust and violent until God intervenes. Kings, rulers, and all the people of Israel are turned peaceful and righteous at the arrival of God and the pouring out of the Spirit.

More passages in Isaiah pair peace and righteousness, but I highlight those above because they demonstrate that Isaiah has a pattern and a vocabulary for discussing kingdoms.[11] Isaiah begins with indictment, then God sends a leader who is empowered by the Spirit, or the Spirit is sent to empower the people. This divine intervention leads to redemption and restoration, not just for unrighteous rulers, but also for unrighteous people. The result of this transformation is radical peace, righteousness, justice, goodness, joy, and renewed hope.

Romans 14:17 in Intertextual Dialogue with Isaiah

The Isaianic texts delineated above indicate that Isaiah has a consistent "socially charged" discourse (Bakhtin 1981: 291)—or a consistent "ideologeme" (Kristeva: 1980: 31)—when discussing a renewed and restored kingdom.[12] Investigating intertextuality is not just about a sharing of signs (lexical similarity), it is also about a sharing of discourses. Therefore, if Romans shares with Isaiah similar topics, patterns, and vocabulary, then the two can be read together intertextually.

The literary structure of Romans begins by stating its author and its dialogue partners. Romans 1:1-2 states, "Paul, a slave of Christ Jesus, called an apostle, set apart for the *gospel of God, which was promised beforehand through the prophets*." Romans begins by placing Paul's discourse in dialogue with, potentially, many prophetic discourses outside of the text. However, the literary structure of Romans offers interpreters clues to which prophetic texts are important for understanding Romans. Isaiah is cited by name five times, and the NA 28 notes an astounding 19 quotations of Isaiah throughout Romans. Thus, Isaiah plays an important role in Romans, and Isaiah is the most pronounced dialogue partner.

Paul's first large block quotation in Rom 3:10-18 pulls from Isaiah. Paul places Ecclesiastes, Psalms, and Isaiah together to explain that "all are under sin" (Rom 3:9). The catena begins with Eccl 7:20, "a righteous/just (δίκαιος) person does not exist, not even one," and then it sandwiches Isa 59:7-8 between two Psalm citations; the words chosen from Isaiah in Rom 3:15-17 are, "their feet are swift to shed blood, destruction and misery are in their ways, and they did not know the way of peace (εἰρήνης)."

The scriptural catena in Rom 3 is paradigmatic for how peace is presented throughout Romans. With the exception of Paul's greeting, every time peace is mentioned righteousness/justice is also mentioned.[13] Romans 2:10 states, "Glory, honor, and peace (εἰρήνη) to all who does good." This statement is in a pericope concerning "God's righteous judgment (δικαιοκρισίας)" (2:5), and it is followed by 2:13, "For the ones who hear the law are not righteous (δίκαιοι) in God's sight, but the ones who do the law will be made righteous (δικαιωθήσονται)." Romans 5:1 states, "Therefore, since we are made righteous by faith (Δικαιωθέντες), we have peace (εἰρήνην) with God through our Lord Jesus Christ." Romans 8:6, "The mind of the Spirit is life and peace (εἰρήνη)." Then 8:10 explains, "the Spirit is life because of righteousness (διὰ δικαιοσύνην)." Rom 12:18–19 exhorts, "live peacefully (εἰρηνεύοντες) with all people. Never procure-retributive-justice (ἐκδικοῦντες) for yourselves, ... for it is written, 'I myself will repay retributive-justice' (ἐκδίκησις) says the Lord." Finally, Romans 14:17 and 19, "The kingdom of God is ... righteousness (δικαιοσύνη), peace (εἰρήνη), and joy in the holy Spirit. ... Therefore then, let us pursue the things of peace (εἰρήνης)."

The appearance of kingdom, righteousness, peace, good, joy, and the Spirit in Isaiah and Romans validates this paper's argument—the two works share a "socially charged" discourse, or "ideologeme." Romans repeatedly pairs peace with righteousness because Isaiah does the same. Moreover, in the contexts where peace is mentioned, goodness, joy, and the Spirit also regularly occur. Therefore, it is necessary to reconsider Rom 14:17 and its surrounding context in dialogue with Isaiah's key kingdom texts.

There is no one kingdom text in Isaiah that perfectly holds all the terms from Rom 14:17, but there are many texts that share the topic and some of the terminology. Interpreters have often noted the similarities between Rom 14:17 and 5:1–5.[14] Interestingly, the NA 28 and Michael J. Gorman note an allusion to Isa 32:17, "the works of righteousness (δικαιοσύνης) will be peace (εἰρήνη)," in Rom 5:1, "since we are made righteous (δικαιωθέντες) by faith we have peace (εἰρήνην) with God" (2013: 234). Multiple reasons indicate that Rom 14:17, like 5:1, is an allusion to Isa 32. First, both texts describe a kingdom (Isa 32:1 and Rom 14:17); second, both pair righteousness and peace (Isa 32:17–18; Rom 14:17); and third, both mention the Spirit (Isa 32:14; Rom 14:17). Furthermore, if one extends beyond 14:17 and into the surrounding context, there is more evidence that Rom 14 alludes to Isa 32. In Isa 32:17 the righteous are described as "believing (πεποιθότες) for eternity/an age," and 32:18 repeats, "they will dwell by believing (πεποιθώς)." Interestingly, in Rom 14:14, Paul uses the same verb (πείθω) in the perfect like Isa 32:17 and 18. "I know and I have been persuaded (πέπεισμαι) by the Lord" (Rom 14:14). Reading Rom 14 and Isa 32 in dialogue reveals that the peaceful, eschatological kingdom that Isaiah hoped for is presented as a reality in Romans. The people of God, in Christ, represent a peaceful kingdom where God's Spirit reigns and the ripples of righteousness and peace permeate the population. Perhaps, Paul understands that he is now participating in this eschatological "believing" (πεποιθότες) community and he has been "persuaded" (πέπεισμαι). The people of the kingdom in Isaiah live in righteousness and peace and believe in the Lord, and Paul does the same.[15]

Isaiah 59–60 is one of the most extensive discourses on the peaceful and righteous kingdom. There is a direct quotation from Isa 59:7–8 in Rom 3:15–17. Therefore, it is also possible that Rom 14:17 and the surrounding context alludes to Isa 59–60 because it has already been cited in Romans. Both texts describe kingdoms (Isa 59:20–60:3; Rom 14:17), and both texts emphasize righteousness, peace, and the Spirit (Isa 59:21; 60:17–18, 21; Rom 14:17). Furthermore, in Isa 59 after mentioning those who "do not know the way of peace," the prophet explains, "in darkness they walked (περιεπάτησαν)" (59:9). "Walk" (περιπατέω) is a rare term in in LXX Isaiah, only appearing in chapters 59 and 8, but "walk" also appears in Rom 14:15. "For if your brother is grieved because of food, then you are not walking (περιπατεῖς) according to love." Additionally, "walk" also appears in 13:12–13, "Therefore, let us put off the works of darkness, and put on the armor of light. As in the day, let us walk (περιπατήσωμεν) honorably." Although "walk" is not a rare word in Pauline literature, the reversal of walking in darkness from Isa 59:9 to walking in the day in Rom 13:13 is striking. Furthermore, in 14:1 Paul writes, "Welcome those who are weak in faith not for the purpose of disputes of opinions (διαλογισμῶν)." This term for "opinion" (διαλογισμός) is only used five times in Pauline literature, and it only occurs in LXX Isaiah in 59:7—but it is used twice.[16] "Their swift feet run to wickedness to shed blood; and their *opinions* are the *opinions* of fools (οἱ διαλογισμοὶ αὐτῶν διαλογισμοὶ ἀφρόνων), destruction and misery are in their ways." Notice, when Paul cites Isaiah in Rom 3:15–17, the phrase "their *opinions* are the *opinions* of fools" is omitted, but Paul uses this emphatically repeated term later in Rom 14:1. Reading Rom 13–14 in dialogue with Isa 59–60 reveals that Paul wanted the Christian community to be the kingdom depicted in Isaiah—where the Spirit of God rested upon God's people, and they knew the ways of righteousness and peace. However, the quarrels over eating certain foods and observing certain days threatened the peace. If the community quarreled over "opinions" (διαλογισμός), they were at risk of turning away from God's light and wandering back into darkness. "It is a real political and social peace that Christ enables and, moreover, demands of those who truly belong to His kingdom. This cannot be a one-sided peace, favouring one group over another" (Campbell 2008: 25). Therefore, when Rom 14 is read in dialogue with Isa 59–60, it becomes a text that is appealing to kingdom ethics —an ethic of peace not violent division.

Conclusion: the Eschatological Kingdom of Peace

Although scholars in recent decades have interpreted Rom 14:17 in terms of Paul's eschatology and his ethics, the connection between peace, righteousness, and Isaiah's kingdom discourses has been overlooked. In this paper I revealed that there is a larger socially charged discourse that explains Paul's articulation of the kingdom. "The kingdom of God ... is righteousness, peace, and joy in the Holy Spirit" because the eschatological hope of Isaiah was a reality in Paul's present. In Paul's believing communities, people are made righteous through the work of Christ and the power of the Spirit. The result of this transformation is a community founded on peace—those who are righteous, or justified, are peacemakers.

Craig Evans has noticed the connection between Jesus's ministry and Isaiah's kingdom, but he has overlooked this in Romans. Moreover, Evans does not recognize the importance of peace to the kingdom in Isaiah. He writes, "The principal elements of Jesus' proclamation of the kingdom are present in Second Isaiah ... the demand for repentance, and the summons to faith are all rooted in the language and vision of Second Isaiah" (1997: 672–73). Evans is correct that repentance and faith are essential to the kingdom, but this study has also demonstrated that peace is essential to Isaiah's kingdom and to the Gospel. Moreover, Evans is quick to conclude that Isa 52:7 is the foundation of Paul's understanding of the gospel, but he overlooks that peace is essential to the gospel in 52:7: "one who proclaims the good news of peace (εὐαγγελιζομένου ἀκοὴν εἰρήνης), ... I shall make your salvation heard, saying, oh Zion, your God will reign (Βασιλεύσει σου ὁ θεός)" (1997: 689–90). In a similar manner, Ross Wagner writes, "Paul finds in Isaiah a fellow preacher of the gospel, the message that reveals God's righteousness for all who believe, for the Jew and also for the Greek" (2002: 356). Although Evans and Wagner are correct that Isaiah is integral to Paul's articulation of the gospel, they overlook the centrality of

Isaiah's kingdom of peace. Wagner even emphasizes righteousness, but he misses the connection of peace and righteousness in Isaiah and Romans.

Isaiah's kingdom discourses explain the union of the kingdom, gospel, righteousness, and peace in Rom 14:17 and many other texts in the NT (Luke 1:79; Acts 10:35–36; 2 Pet 3:13–14; Jas 3:18; Heb 12:13). More work is needed in Luke, Acts, the General Epistles, and Hebrews in order to demonstrate whether it is appropriate to read these texts in dialogue with Isaiah. Yet, at the moment, it seems that Romans is not unique. Peace and righteousness are essential to the gospel and the kingdom of God.

In conclusion, Romans 14 imagines a community where God has replaced division and violence with righteousness and peace through the Holy Spirit. The church then, and today, must not only be made righteous, but it must also be made peaceful. The kingdom of God requires that Christians be peacemakers. "Pursuing the kingdom of peace is a call to work for peace. ... Christians are called to become actively involved in the transformation of the world. They not only wait but also work for that kingdom" (Simmons 1982: 603). This call to work for peace is not passive, it is active. Peace in God's kingdom is creative, productive, and transformative. When Christians pray, "may your kingdom come and will be done," they are praying for peace, and they are praying for the power to make peace.

End Notes

[1] For an overview of the various ways in which NT authors were thought to use scripture see, Richard B. Hays, *Echoes of Scripture in the Letters of Paul* (New Haven: Yale University Press, 1989), 5–14; to see contemporary proposals, Vernon K. Robbins, *Exploring the Texture of Texts: A Guide to Socio-Rhetorical Interpretation* (Valley Forge, PA: Trinity Press International, 1996); Craig A. Evans, and James A. Sanders eds., *Early Christian Interpretation of the Scriptures of Israel: Investigations and Proposals*, JSNTSupp 148 (Sheffield: Sheffield Academic, 1997); Kenneth D. Litwak, "Echoes of Scripture? A Critical Survey of Recent Works on Paul's Use of the Old Testament" *CurBR* (1998): 260–88; Richard B. Hays, *The Conversion of the Imagination: Paul as Interpreter of Israel's Scripture* (Grand Rapids: Eerdmans, 2005); Stanley E. Porter, ed. *Hearing the Old Testament in the New Testament*, McMaster New Testament Studies (Grand Rapids: Eerdmans, 2006); J. Ross Wagner, "Paul and Scripture" in *Blackwell Companion to Paul*, ed. Stephen Westerholm (Blackwell, 2011), 154–71; G. K. Beale, *Handbook on the New Testament Use of the Old Testament: Exegesis and Interpretation* (Grand Rapids: Baker Academic, 2012), 40; B. J. Oropeza, and Steve Moyise, eds., *Exploring Intertextuality: Diverse Strategies for New Testament Interpretation of Texts* (Eugene, OR: Cascade, 2016).

[2] Craig A. Evans, "Paul and the Hermeneutics of 'True Prophecy': A Study of Romans 9–11," *Biblica* 65 (1984): 560–70; "Paul and the Prophets: Prophetic Criticism in the Epistle to the Romans (with Special Reference to Romans 9–11)," in *Romans & The People of God,* eds. Sven K. Soderlund and N. T. Wright (Grand Rapids: Eerdmans, 1999), 115–28; Shiu-Lun Shum, *Paul's Use of Isaiah in Romans: A Comparative Study of Paul's Letter to the Romans and the Sibylline and Qumran Sectarian Texts,* WUNT 156 (Tübingen: Mohr Siebeck, 2002); J. Ross Wagner, *Heralds of the Good News: Isaiah and Paul "In Concert" in the Letter to the Romans,* NovTSup (Leiden: Brill, 2002); "Isaiah in Romans and Galatians," in *Isaiah in the New Testament,* The New Testament and the Scriptures of Israel (London: T&T Clark, 2005), 117–32; Florian Wilk, "Paul as User, Interpreter, and Reader of the Book of Isaiah," in *Reading the Bible Intertextually,* eds. Richard B. Hays, Stefan Alkier, and Leroy A. Huizenga (Waco, TX: Baylor University Press, 2005), 83–100; Christopher R. Bruno, "The Deliverer from Zion: The Source(s) and Function of Paul's Citation in Romans 11:26–27," *TynBul* 59 (2008): 119–34; Mark Forman, "The Politics of Promise: Echoes of Isaiah 54 in Romans 4.19–21," *JSNT* 31 (2009): 301–324; Dane C. Ortlund, "The Insanity of Faith: Paul's Theological Use of Isaiah in Romans 9:33," *TJ* 30 (2009): 269–88; Dietrich-Alex Koch, "The Quotations of Isaiah 8,14 and 28,16 in Romans 9,33 and 1 Peter 2,6.8 as Test Case for Old Testament Quotations in the New Testament," *ZNW* 101 (2010): 223–40; Andrew David Naselli, *From Typology to Doxology: Paul's Use of Isaiah and Job in Romans 11:34–35* (Eugene, OR: Pickwick Publications, 2012); Delio DelRio, *Paul and the Synagogue: Romans and the Isaiah Targum* (Eugene, OR: Pickwick Publications, 2013); Robert C. Olson, *The Gospel as the Revelation of God's Righteousness: Paul's Use of Isaiah in Romans 1:1–3:26,* WUNT 428 (Tübingen: Mohr Siebeck, 2016); J. Edward Walters, "How Beautiful Are My Feet: The Structure and Function of Second Isaiah References in Paul's Letter to the Romans," *Restoration Quarterly* 52 (2019): 29–39.

[3] Evans, "Paul and the Hermeneutics of 'True Prophecy,' " 560–70; Evans, "Paul and the Prophets," 115–28; Wagner, *Heralds of the Good News*; Bruno, "The Deliverer from Zion," 119–34; Ortlund, "The Insanity of Faith," 269–88; Koch, "The Quotations of Isaiah," 223–40; Naselli, *From Typology to Doxology.*

[4] Isaiah is cited by name in Rom 9:27, 29; 10:16, 20; 15:12, and the NA 28 notes quotation from Isaiah in Rom 2:24; 3:15–17; 9:20, 33; 10:11, 15, 21; 11:8, 26, 27, 34: 14:11; 15:21. For a full treatment of the potential allusions and echoes see, Shum (2002: 177–257) and Wagner (2002: 342–43).

[5] Craig A. Evans, "From Gospel to Gospel: The Function of Isaiah in the New Testament," in *Writing and Reading the Scroll of Isaiah: Studies of an Interpretive Tradition,* vol. 2 (Leiden: Brill, 1997): 689–90. Also see, J. F. A. Sawyer, *The Fifth Gospel: Isaiah in the History of Christianity* (Cambridge: Cambridge University Press, 1996), 21–41; Evans, "Paul and the Prophets," 115–28.

⁶ Pieter G. R. De Villers, "Peace in the Pauline Letters: A Perspective on Biblical Spirituality," *Noet* 43 (2009): 1–26; Victor P. Furnish, "War and Peace in the New Testament," *Interpretation* 38 (1984): 363–379; Albin Jr. Huss, "The Voice of Isaiah in Paul's Proclamation of Peace" (PhD diss., Trinity Evangelical Divinity School, 2005); Michael J. Gorman, "The Lord of Peace: Christ Our Peace in Pauline Theology," *Journal for the Study of Paul and His Letters* 3 (2013): 219–53; Edward M. Keazirian, *Peace and Peacemaking in Paul and the Greco-Roman World*, StBibLit (New York: Peter Lang, 2013); Mary Schmitt, "Peace and Wrath in Paul's Epistle to the Romans," *The Conrad Grebel Review* 32 (2014): 67–79; Willard M. Swartley, *Covenant of Peace: The Missing Peace in New Testament Theology and Ethics* (Grand Rapids: Eerdmans, 2006).

⁷ This is not to say that no scholars have recognized the importance of peace in Pauline Literature. Swartley, *Covenant of Peace*, offers a comprehensive treatment of the theology of peace in the NT (2006), and Michael J. Gorman writes, "There are, of course, exceptions, according to Swartley: The New Testament ethics of Wolfgang Schrage, Allen Verhey, and Richard Hays, and J. Christiaan Beker's theology of Paul for example" (2013: 221).

⁸ All New Testament quotations are my own translation.

⁹ Both Isa 1:4 and 5:7 are my translation of the Hebrew text.

¹⁰ Form this point forward, every reference to Isaiah is exclusively referring to LXX Isaiah, and the translation is my own.

¹¹ There are more passages to consider in Isaiah that pair righteousness and peace: Isa 7:14–16; 9:5–6; 11:1–5; 26:1–5, 9–14; 33:5–8; 41:1–3; 48:14–19; 54:10–14; 57:1–2.

¹² Mikhail Bakhtin explains "socially charged discourse" as "each word tastes of the context and contexts in which it has lived its socially charged life; all words and forms are populated by intention. Contextual overtones (generic, tendentious, individualistic) are inevitable in words" (1981: 293). Julia Kristeva, explains ideologeme as "The concept of text as ideologeme determines the very procedure of a semiotics that, by studying the text as intertextuality, considers it as such within (the text of) society and history" (1980: 37).

¹³ The translated terms righteousness, righteous, justice and just are discussed interchangeably in this paper because they represent the Greek word family δίκ- e.g. δίκαιος, δικαιοσύνη, etc.

¹⁴ Colin G. Kruse, *Paul's Letter to the Romans*, The Pillar New Testament Commentary (Grand Rapids: Eerdmans, 2012), 522–23; Gorman, "The Lord of Peace," 234 and 239. Also see, Jack P. Lewis, " 'The Kingdom of God . . . Is Righteousness, Peace, and Joy in the Holy Spirit' (Rom 14:17): A Survey of Interpretation," *Restoration Quarterly* 40 (1998): 53–68.

¹⁵ There may be more intertextual echoes; Isa 32:11 uses πείθω and λυπέω, and Rom 14:15 also uses λυπέω, but space does not permit an explanation of this relationship.

¹⁶ Διαλογισμός: Rom 1:21; 14:1; 1 Cor 3:20; Phil 2:14; 1 Tim 2:8.

Works Cited

Bakhtin, M. M.
    1981   *The Dialogic Imagination: Four Essays.* Edited by Michael Holquist. University of Texas Press Slavic Series 1. Austin, TX: University of Texas Press.

Campbell, William S.
    2008   "Unity and Diversity in the Church: Transformed Identities and the Peace of Christ in Ephesians." *Transformation* 25 (1): 15–31.

Evans, Craig A.
    1997   "From Gospel to Gospel: The Function of Isaiah in the New Testament." In *Writing and Reading the Scroll of Isaiah: Studies of an Interpretive Tradition,* 2:651–91. Leiden, Netherlands: Brill.

Goldingay, John
    2012   *Isaiah.* Grand Rapids, MI: Baker Books.

Gorman, Michael J.
    2013   "The Lord of Peace: Christ Our Peace in Pauline Theology." *Journal for the Study of Paul and His Letters* 3 (2): 219–53.

Harman, Allan M.
    2011   *Isaiah: A Covenant to Be Kept for the Sake of the Church.* Ross-shire, UK: Christian Focus.

Kristeva, Julia.
    1980   *Desire in Language: A Semiotic Approach to Literature and Art.* Edited by Leon S. Roudiez. Translated by Thomas Gora and Leon S. Roudiez. European Perspectives. New York, NY: Columbia University Press.

Shum, Shiu-Lun.
    2002   *Paul's Use of Isaiah in Romans: A Comparative Study of Paul's Letter to the Romans and the Sibylline and Qumran Sectarian Texts.* WUNT 156. Tübingen: Mohr Siebeck.

Simmons, Paul D.
    1982   "The New Testament Basis of Peacemaking." *Review & Expositor* 79 (4): 597–605.

Swartley, Willard M.
   2006   Covenant of Peace: The Missing Peace in New Testament
           Theology and Ethics. Grand Rapids, MI: Eerdmans.

Wagner, J. Ross.
   2002   Heralds of the Good News: Isaiah and Paul "In Concert"
           in the Letter to the Romans. Vol. 101. NovTSup. Leiden,
           Netherlands: Brill.

Witherington, Ben.
   2017   Isaiah Old and New: Exegesis, Intertextuality, and
           Hermeneutics. Minneapolis, MN: Fortress.

The Asbury Journal 75/2: 255-270
© 2020 Asbury Theological Seminary
DOI: 10.7252/Journal.02.2020F.06

Kelly J. Godoy de Danielson
*Women on the Outside Looking In: Rahab and Ruth
as Foreign Converts to the People of God*

Abstract:
How Does an outsider become an insider? This is a question that
emerges from considering both the modern immigrant situation and the
unique situation of non-Israelite women becoming part of the people of
God in the Old Testament. The usual pattern in the Old Testament is to be
born into the people of Israel, but for men there is the possibility to become
part of the covenantal people through the physical act of circumcision. In
this patriarchal society, women usually had no choice but to follow the
decisions of their husbands. But what if there was no husband? The Bible
tends to take a particularly harsh view on Israelite men marrying non-
Israelite women, so even marriage does not seem to be an acceptable
pathway for unmarried or widowed women. But two significant women in
the Old Testament do successfully navigate the transition from outsider to
insider, Rahab and Ruth. This article explores what this means for
understanding conversion within the Old Testament context as well as its
potential theological implication for the immigrant community in today's
world. Understanding the importance of a person's allegiance to YHWH as
well as following up this allegiance through actions of loving-kindness
(*hesed* חֶסֶד) are the key similarities which bind these two women together
and help create a theological bridge for immigrants in our modern context.

Keywords: Ruth, Rahab, women, conversion, immigration, people of God

Kelly J. Danielson is a 2020 graduate of Asbury Theological Seminary with
a Masters in Biblical Studies. She is also a native of El Salvador in Central
America.

Introduction

How does an outsider become an insider? This is a question that frequently confronts me as an immigrant in a foreign country. When your skin color and accent set you apart, you are almost always seen as an outsider, even after living for 20 years in your current context. This question also emerges at times in the Old Testament. The usual pattern is for one to be born into the people of Israel, but for men there is the possibility to become part of the covenantal people through the physical act of circumcision. In this patriarchal society, women usually had no choice but to follow the decisions of their husbands. But what if there was no husband? The Bible tends to take a particularly harsh view on Israelite men marrying non-Israelite women, so even marriage does not seem to be an acceptable pathway for unmarried or widowed women. But there are two significant women in the Old Testament who successfully navigate the transition from outsider to insider, and become not just members of the people of God, but essential parts of the history of God's salvation plan as ancestors of both King David as well as Jesus in the New Testament. The question this raises for me is how does this happen and what is the implication for the immigrant community?

In addition, the issue of conversion is one that has been an important point for evangelical theology for a long time. How does one become a Christian? Most of this is theologically rooted in New Testament scriptures, but is often overlooked in a theological study of the Old Testament. The only real equivalent for looking at the issue of New Testament conversion is to examine this issue of how people outside the people of Israel became part of the people of God. The same stories of Rahab and Ruth, which answer the first question, help us understand the nature of conversion as well as how women without husbands might have been able to transition from outsiders to insiders in the Old Testament context.

Male Circumcision as a Pathway to the People of God

In Genesis 17, God establishes the covenant between God and Abraham and his descendants. Verse seven emphasizes that this will be an "everlasting" covenant for generations. This covenant will include the land of Canaan as well as the act of male circumcision. In verse ten, it is clear that every male must be circumcised to be part of the covenant, and verse twelve makes provision that those bought from foreigners are also to be circumcised. Finally verse fourteen warns that any male who is not circumcised will be cut off from the covenant. Verses 23-27 indicated that Abraham, Ishmael, and all the men in his household, born or bought, were circumcised that very day.

In Exodus 12, the crucial ritual meal of the Passover is established. In this chapter, Moses instructs the people on the future celebration of this meal, and he notes in verse 48, "A foreigner residing among you who wants to celebrate the LORD's Passover must have all the males of his household circumcised; then he may take part like one born in the land." (NIV). This allows for men outside of the Israelite community to become part of the people of God through the physical act of circumcision- aligning themselves and submitting to the covenant of Abraham.

In Joshua, chapter five, Joshua commands the Israelites to be circumcised before the conquest of Canaan. For some reason, the practice seems to have been abandoned in the wilderness, but now the covenant is to be renewed. Joshua often appears in the book as a type of "new Moses" for the people, so the renewal of the covenant at Gilgal (Joshua 5:2-12) should not be surprising. When the covenant is renewed at Mount Ebal in chapter eight, it is clear that foreigners are included among the people of God. Verse 33 notes that, "Both the foreigners living among them and the native-born were there" for the reading of the Book of the Law.

But while foreign men have a way to join the Israelite people through circumcision, such a possibility is denied to women, even through marriage. The prohibitions against Israelite men marrying foreign women is made clear in the story of Dinah in Genesis 34 and Deuteronomy 7:3-4, "Do not intermarry with them. Do not give your daughters to their sons or take their daughters for your sons, for they will turn your children away from following me to serve other gods, and the LORD's anger will burn against you and will quickly destroy you." The same prohibitions are repeated by Joshua in Joshua 23:12-13. Other passages repeat this concern including 1 Kings 11:2 and Ezra 9:14. Nevertheless, two women in scripture do enter the people of God as foreigners during the early period of Israel's history, and they are not insignificant. Nor are these two women unconnected. Matthew 1:5 connects Rahab as the mother of Boaz, who would marry Ruth, the grandmother of King David, and ultimately become ancestors of Jesus.[1]

Rahab: From Foreign Prostitute to One of God's People

The story of Rahab in Joshua chapters two and six is an interesting exception to much of the conquest literature.[2] Rahab is first shown as a prostitute in the city of Jericho, where she encounters the two spies sent by Joshua to study the city for conquest. She successfully hides the two spies and redirects those sent by the King of Jericho in search of the spies. Before letting the spies go, she gives an interesting speech in verses 9-13 of chapter two,

> I know that the LORD has given you this land and that a great fear of you has fallen on us, so that all who live in this country are melting in fear because of you. We have heard how the LORD dried up the water of the Red sea for you when you came out of Egypt, and what you did to Sihon and Og, the two kings of the Amorites east of the Jordan, whom you completely destroyed. When we heard of it our hearts melted in fear and everyone's courage failed because of you, for the LORD your God is God in heaven above and on the earth below.
>
> Now then, please swear to me by the LORD that you will show kindness[2] to my family, because I have shown kindness (*hesed* חֶסֶד) to you. Give me a sure sign that you will spare the lives of my father and mother, my brothers and sisters, and all who belong to them- and that you will save us from death. (NIV)

The spies leave after swearing an oath and telling her to bring everyone into her house and hang a scarlet cord outside the window as a sign, and they would be spared. In Joshua 6:17, 22-23, 25, Rahab and her family are spared, with verse 25 noting, "But Joshua spared Rahab the prostitute, with her family and all who belonged to her, because she hid the men Joshua had sent as spies to Jericho- and she lives among the Israelites to this day." Ruth 4:18-22, which outlines the genealogy of David notes that Salmon, the father of Boaz (who is her husband according to Matthew 1:5⁻ See footnote 1) is an Israelite going back to Perez, one of the sons of Judah. This marriage solidifies Rahab as an insider and one of the people of God.

Moberly (2013: 71) discusses how Rahab is compared with Achan in Joshua. Rahab as the ultimate outsider- a Canaanite woman and a prostitute who becomes an insider, while Achan, an insider with a pedigree becomes the ultimate outsider, as he and his entire family are stoned for disobedience. In the same way, Moberly points out how Rahab shows the quality of *hesed* חֶסֶד (steadfast love or kindness) and because of her words and actions, "she is exempted from *herem* חֵרֶם, despite the lack of exemption clauses in Deuteronomy, and enabled (with her family) to become part of Israel."[3]

Ruth: The Moabite Who Became One of the People of God

In the book of Ruth, we see another exceptional case of a woman who becomes part of the people of God. Naomi and her husband, Elimelek had gone into the land of Moab with their sons, Mahlon and Kilion, and both of them married women of Moab, Orpah and Ruth. When her sons and husband die, Naomi decides to return to her own people. In Ruth 1:8, Naomi releases both Orpah and Ruth from their obligations to her and praises them for their kindness (*hesed* חֶסֶד), but encourages them to go home to their families and remarry. The two young women at first refuse, but Naomi lays out the reality that she will have no more children to provide as husbands. Orpah finally leaves, but Ruth still stays. Naomi again tries to get Ruth to leave her, but Ruth responds in Ruth 1:16-17,

> Don't urge me to leave you or to turn back from you.
> Where you go I will go, and where you stay I will stay.
> Your people will be my people and your God my God.
> Where you die I will die, and there I will be buried. May
> the LORD deal with me, be it ever so severely, if even
> death separates you and me. (NIV)

Ruth continues to show her faithfulness in supporting Naomi while gleaning the fields of Boaz, a close relative of Naomi. Ultimately, Boaz becomes the ideal kinsman-redeemer and redeems the rights to the land of Naomi's family and thus the right to marry Ruth, who becomes the grandmother of the future King David. When Boaz redeems his rights to Ruth, the elders say in Ruth 4:11-12, "We are witnesses. May the LORD make the woman who is coming into your home like Rachel and Leah, who together built up the family of Israel. May you have standing in Ephrathah and be famous in Bethlehem. Through the offspring the LORD gives you by this young woman, may your family be like that of Perez, whom Tamar bore to Judah." Once again, a foreign woman enters the people of God, which is solidified by her marriage to one of the people of God.

While most commentaries focus on the themes of kindness (*hesed* חֶסֶד), loyalty, protecting the weak in society, and the book's support for

Davidic kingship, some point out other possible uses of the book. Fleenor and Ziese (2008: 320) note the possible implications of the book as protest,

> As literature of protest, it is argued that the text contains a message directed to those seeking to narrowly define the "people of God." As such, the text deliberately undermines (or subverts) a so-called "purity position" seeking to expel "good" aliens (like Ruth) from the Jewish community. A variation of this view considers the message of the book to be an encouragement directed toward the gentile wives of Jewish husbands. In this, Ruth is the poster child: a model proselyte for all foreigners to imitate.

Only some writers tend to develop the outsider nature of Ruth in this story, even though the text itself refers to Ruth as the "Moabite" specifically in a number of places (Ruth 1:22, 2:2, 2:21, 4:5, and 4:10), highlighting her status as a stranger or outsider in the community. In this sense, identity also becomes a theme, as Matthews (2004: 207) writes, "Ruth, who has become a liminal or socially undefined figure by her decisions and actions, must establish a new identity within a strange community. In essence, she must 'find her place.' Both physically and socially, in Bethlehem."

The Conversion of Rahab and Ruth
There are a number of similarities in the stories of Rahab and Ruth, although on the surface they are very different kinds of women. Rahab is a prostitute, while Ruth is an unfortunately childless widow. First and foremost, they are women who do not have husbands who will decide their spiritual direction. However, both make oaths tying themselves to the God of Israel. These oaths are closely tied to concepts of kindness and loyalty. Both also exhibit faithful obedience in carrying out these oaths. Finally, because of their faithful obedience, each is permitted to enter the people of God, and this is ultimately sealed through marriage, despite previous prohibitions against this practice.

William Barrick (2000) argues that conversion is modeled in the Old Testament by stories such as Rahab, Ruth, Naaman, and the sailors and Ninevites in Jonah as a way of understanding the concept of the circumcision of the heart (Deuteronomy 10:16 and 30:6) as opposed to physical circumcision as a way to enter the people of God. As such Barrick also sees the covenant and covenant renewal as a "recommitment to the changed life that had been entered at conversion" (Barrick 2000: 23). Barrick sees Rahab as acknowledging a formal relationship to YHWH in her confession of YHWH's ultimate authority in Joshua 2:11. He also points out her changed life by showing *hesed* חֶסֶד (for the first time in the book of Joshua) (Barrick 2000: 28-29). For Ruth as well, Barrick sees her "oath of allegiance" to Naomi as a confession, which is then lived out by a changed life dominated by *hesed* חֶסֶד (Barrick 2000: 29). As Barrick writes,

> Conversion may be summed up in the Hebrew term *sub* (he turns). Repentance and faith are its primary elements. Faith 'achieves *in practice the acknowledgement by the individual of the sole sovereignty of Yahweh.*' Such acknowledgement is inseparable from conversion which includes penitent humility. Confession of the sovereignty of Yahweh is clearly evident in the cases of Rahab, Ruth, Naaman, the sailors, and the Ninevites. (Barrick 2000: 35)

Ultimately in a final chart, Barrick looks at a number of themes and the ones which he sees as in common for Rahab and Ruth are: a confession of faith (Joshua 2:11, and Ruth 1:16-17), and a change or commitment (Joshua 2:12, Ruth 1:8 and Ruth 3:10).

While Ruth is not mentioned in the New Testament except in Matthew 1:5, Rahab is reflected on in two other passages. In Hebrews 11, the famous chapter on the faithful, verse 31 reads, "By faith the prostitute Rahab, because she welcomed the spies, was not killed with those who were disobedient." In James 2, where James discusses the importance of faith and works, the writer compares Rahab with Abraham in verse 25 and 26 he writes, "In the same way, was not even Rahab the prostitute considered righteous for what she did when she gave lodging to the spies and sent them off in a different direction? As the body without the spirit is dead, so faith without deeds is dead." Biddle and Jackson (2017: 232) make a similar distinction in their assessment of the two spies in the story of Rahab, when they write, "Who saves whom in this story, then? In this striking text, Israel learns that a Deuteronomistic-sermon-preaching Canaanite prostitute can deliver them, even as they make plans for her future deliverance. All expectation is upended. There is no longer a distinction between who is savior and who is saved." The faithful righteous Rahab is held up as a model according to Biddle and Jackson, while the "spies" seem to bring back limited intelligence (and if they are "messengers" as mentioned elsewhere they do not seem to deliver any message).

As faithfulness and good works are the characteristics pointed out in Hebrews and James in the New Testament for Rahab, it is possible to see how she reflects on a Christian understanding of living a Christian life following conversion. It seems to come close to Jesus' understanding of the greatest commandment in Matthew 22:37-39, "Jesus replied, '"Love the Lord your God with all your heart, and with all your soul, and with all your mind." This is the first and greatest commandment. And the second is like it: "Love your neighbor as yourself." All the Law and the Prophets hang on these two commandments.'" Rahab and Ruth make a commitment to God through an oath and follow up on this oath through a sacrificial love of others. There is also a close connection between issues of justice, kindness, and humility, As Smit and Fowl (2018: 220) point out,

> In Mic. 6:8 the Israelites are told that all God requires of them is "to do justice, and to love kindness [hesed חֶסֶד], and to walk humbly with your God." This text from Micah raises the prospect that justice, hesed חֶסֶד, and humility before God are connected. This would lead one to think that success in cultivating one of these virtues leads to and may presume some measure of success in cultivating the other two. If justice requires one to give to others what they are due in God, and if humility is based on rightly knowing one's own state relative to God and others, then hesed חֶסֶד would be that grace which recognizes but is not constrained or limited merely by what is due to others and by where one stands relative to others and God. This would seem to fit Ruth quite well. She goes well beyond justice in her dealings with Naomi and acts with both grace and boldness toward Boaz without ever seeking to aggrandize herself.

In this sense, both Ruth and Rahab go beyond the confines of what is just, and both of them act with kindness while simultaneously exhibiting humility before God.

It is interesting that even in Jewish tradition, there is no question that the story of Ruth is an account of conversion. Brady (2013: 135) writes, "While modern scholars debate whether or not Ruth 1:16-17 actually describes Ruth's conversion to the Israelite religion, within Rabbinic tradition there was no question that Ruth is the proselyte par excellence. The first chapter of Ruth provides for the Rabbinic exegete the prototypical framework for conversion, including Naomi's rejection of the would-be proselyte." It is apparently tradition that a would-be Jewish convert should be turned back three times, and if they still persist, it should be permitted (and this is modeled in Naomi's rejection of Ruth three times). The Jewish writers of the Targum Ruth have added to Ruth 1:16-17 to turn it into a dialogue for conversion. Brady (2013: 137) lays it out like this (with the scripture in regular script and the additions in italics),

> Ruth said, "Do not urge me to leave you, to go back from after you, for *I desire to be a proselyte.*"
> Naomi said, *"We are commanded to keep Sabbaths and holy days such that we may not walk more than two thousand cubits."*
> Ruth said, "Wherever you go, I will go."
> Naomi said, *"We are commanded not to lodge with Gentiles."*
> Ruth said, "Where you lodge, I will lodge."
> Naomi said, *"We are commanded to keep six hundred and thirteen commandments."*
> Ruth said, "What your people *keep I will keep as if they were* my people *from before this.*"
> Naomi said, *"We are commanded not to worship foreign gods."*
> Ruth said, "Your god is my god."
> Naomi said, *"We have four death penalties for guilty: stoning with stones, burning with fire, execution by the sword and hanging on a tree."*
> Ruth said, "How you die, I shall die."
> Naomi said, *"We have a cemetery."*
> Ruth said, "And there I will be buried. *And do not say any more.* May the Lord do thus to me and more against me if even death shall separate me from you."

So, even in the Jewish tradition, Ruth is seen as a text dealing with conversion.

Uriah Kim (2011) brings the additional insight of a biblical scholar who is Korean living as an immigrant in the U.S. He examines both Rahab and Ruth alongside the "man from Luz" (Judges 1:22-26) as examples of the *hesed* חֶסֶד relationship based on loyalty to YHWH. However, his reading as a Korean immigrant is a bit different. He argues that Rahab and Ruth might be insiders in one sense, but this sense of belonging is not complete. While Rahab is allowed to live among Israel, she is also sent to live "outside the camp of Israel" in Joshua 6:23, so that she is not recognized as a real Israelite (Kim 2011: 257-258). I can see his point in this interpretation, but I disagree, since her ultimate marriage to an ultimate insider demonstrates a complete inclusion, but such inclusion may take time. His reading on Ruth however is quite interesting. His focus is not on Ruth, who through *hesed* חֶסֶד becomes an insider, but rather on Orpah, who also demonstrates the same type of *hesed* חֶסֶד as Ruth, but "her loyalty to her people disqualifies her from being a part of Israel" (Kim 2011: 260). Ruth becomes a model minority (in the same way as Pocahontas in U.S. myth) because she rejects her own people. Kim ends his article with a powerful conclusion, relevant to the immigrant community today,

> When we practice *hesed* חֶסֶד with others, can we expect God to honor our *hesed* חֶסֶד when the other party does not fulfill their responsibility? We need to remember that Jesus Christ, who is a bicultural being par excellence, fully God and fully human, used *hesed* חֶסֶד to cross the divine-human divide in order to build the relationship between God and humans. Jesus Christ is the assurance that when we practice *hesed* חֶסֶד with others, God will surely honor our *hesed* חֶסֶד. Perhaps home is where *hesed* חֶסֶד is practiced for the sake of human solidarity and for God's kingdom. (Kim 2011: 262)

Rahab and Ruth as Models of Conversion

Rahab was supposed to be subject to the *herem* חֵרֶם announced against Canaan- the idea that the Israelites should "utterly destroy" the Canaanites they found in the conquest. Yet, in the very first battle for the conquest, her family alone is spared because Rahab showed *hesed* חֶסֶד, or kindness to the spies and makes an oath acknowledging the authority of YHWH. In the same way, Ruth shows *hesed* חֶסֶד to Naomi, even after she is freed from her responsibilities, and likewise makes an oath to accept YHWH as her God. Both women end up having their faithfulness to their oaths rewarded by marriage to Israelites for full inclusion into the people of God. In addition, they both become ancestors of King David and Jesus as part of God's model plan of salvation.

Clearly the concept of *hesed* חֶסֶד is vitally important to both accounts and to the process of conversion as seen in the Old Testament. Edward F. Campbell (1990) points out that *hesed* חֶסֶד is used to describe both human relationships and divine action. Basing some of his work off of the book, *The Meanings of Hesed in the Hebrew Bible: A New Inquiry* (1978) by Katherine Doob Sakenfield, Campbell (1990, 67-68) summarizes *hesed* חֶסֶד in five different ways:

- First, *hesed* חֶסֶד is not just a "special favor" but is essential for deliverance from serious danger.

- *Hesed* חֶסֶד is done by a situationally stronger person toward a weaker person.
- The more powerful person has other options and so *hesed* חֶסֶד is not forced.
- A prior relationship is usually involved for *hesed* חֶסֶד to be done, so there is a moral or ethical responsibility to act as opposed to doing nothing.
- The one showing *hesed* חֶסֶד is usually the only one who can preform the action.

So *hesed* חֶסֶד) is more than just a simple act of kindness. It is steadfast kindness, or loving kindness, but it is acting in the same way that God acts with human beings from a position of power to one who is in extreme need. Campbell (1990: 69) writes, "To put it another way, the impact of the book of Ruth is to portray at least Orpah and Ruth, and especially Ruth, acting towards others in the manner in which YHWH acts- living out the imitation of God." Ultimately this act of *hesed* חֶסֶד can be most completely seen in the sacrifice of Jesus Christ on the cross.

Baruch Levine (2013: 6) adds to this understanding by noting that *hesed* חֶסֶד "is an act of kindness and love undertaken without expectation of reward or reciprocity." By acting with *hesed* חֶסֶד toward others, God in turn shows *hesed* חֶסֶד in return.[4] For Rahab and Ruth, the first act of conversion is to act as God would have acted. It is part of their nature to show kindness when it was not necessary to do so for someone who was in a vulnerable position. In the middle of these acts of *hesed* חֶסֶד, both Rahab and Ruth make an oath recognizing the power and authority of the God of Israel over their own lives. Finally, Rahab and Ruth are faithful to their oaths, and in response YHWH shows *hesed* חֶסֶד on them by incorporating them into the people of God, ultimately validating this through marriage. As L. Daniel Hawk (2015: 20) puts it, "Finally, like Rahab, Ruth confesses the God of Israel (Joshua 2:11; Ruth 1:16), displays faithfulness (*hesed* חֶסֶד) to Israelites (Joshua 2:12-14; Ruth 1:8; 3:10) and receives a place for herself and her descendants among the people of God."

Conclusion

So, how does one become a part of the people of God in the Old Testament? It seems to differ in some ways from the New Testament understanding, which tends to place repentance for sins before a confession of faith and finally a changed life.[5] In the case of Rahab and Ruth, there is no repentance of sin.[6] This is especially obvious in the life of Rahab, a prostitute, in which we might expect to see some kind of judgment passed on her profession. In both cases, we see women who have a deep commitment to YHWH and a willingness to recognize YHWH's authority. But this is more than a doctrinal statement of faith. In both cases, this willingness to submit to YHWH is accompanied by concrete actions of *hesed* חֶסֶד. Both Rahab and Ruth act in the way that God would act.

Rahab is not a person with any power in Jericho. Yet, for one brief moment, she is given the power of life and death over the Israelite spies. We do not know what her thoughts may have been at this time, but she could have sought favor with the king of Jericho by turning over the spies, or she could have exacted revenge on the men who she so often had to serve and please in her business. Yet, in that moment, she chose to act with *hesed* חֶסֶד, without any real thought of getting something back for herself, she chose to protect and hide these helpless men. This is compatible with the way God acts towards human beings. However, she does not just do this act of *hesed* חֶסֶד, but she continues to keep the secret- to remain faithful to her promise, even after the spies have left. Because of this, God gives her a second chance at life, along with her family, and gives them a chance to live among the people of God. Ultimately, she will be validated in her actions and marry a descendant of the tribe of Judah, and she will be honored as King David's great-grandmother.

Ruth was also a person without power. She was a widow, and even worse, one without children or land. She shows *hesed* חֶסֶד to Naomi, by refusing to leave her widowed mother-in-law in a difficult situation. Naomi had freed her from her familial responsibilities, and so for perhaps the first time in her life, Ruth was in a position of power. She could choose to go back to her people, to seek a new husband, and build a new family. We can only imagine how dangerous life must have been for Naomi as a widow, alone, with no one to protect her in a foreign land. Ruth's act of *hesed* חֶסֶד probably saved Naomi's life in multiple ways. Not only did she accompany her on what was probably a dangerous journey back to her hometown, but also she gleaned from the fields to feed them both, and cared for the elderly Naomi. Ruth makes an oath to accept YHWH as her God before she really begins her action of *hesed* חֶסֶד. But Ruth is also faithful to her action and carries out ongoing *hesed* חֶסֶד for Naomi. As with

Rahab, she will ultimately be validated for her actions and marry a descendent of the tribe of Judah and become the grandmother of King David. As one thinks about the connection between Rahab and Ruth, one is left wondering if Boaz was open to seeing the positive aspects of Ruth because of the influence of his own mother, Rahab, who had gone through the same process of becoming an insider.

These acts of *hesed* חֶסֶד by Rahab and Ruth are perhaps connected to King David for a reason. He is also a person who is shown as invoking the idea of *hesed* חֶסֶד as well. This can be seen in 2 Samuel 2:6 when he asks God to show *hesed* חֶסֶד to the men of Jabesh Gilead who had buried Saul. It can also be seen earlier in the relationship between David and Jonathan in 1 Samuel 20: 14-15 when they make an oath of *hesed* חֶסֶד between David and Jonathan and his descendants. The faithfulness of this oath is lived out in how David treats Mephibosheth in 2 Samuel 9, after Jonathan and Saul are killed in battle. This entire theme of God showing *hesed* חֶסֶד to those who show *hesed* חֶסֶד may also be reflected in 2 Samuel 7, when God blesses David and says in verses 15-16, "But my love will never be taken away from him, as I took it away from Saul, whom I removed from before you. Your house and your kingdom will endure forever before me: your throne will be established forever." Rahab and Ruth as spiritual ancestors of David are a link to the importance of *hesed* חֶסֶד, and may be a source for David's *hesed* חֶסֶד to others which results in God's favor on his kingship. Jesus Christ in turn fulfills this *hesed* חֶסֶד in the ultimate act of *hesed* חֶסֶד on the cross. Certainly this is part of the spiritual connection we are to draw from the genealogical inclusion of Rahab and Ruth in the family of Jesus presented in the opening of the Gospel of Matthew.

Conversion for Rahab and Ruth speak louder than the physical conversion of male circumcision. Their conversion came from the heart and not just physical identification with the people of God. Their changed lives as women who were a part of the Israelite community was possible because they submitted to YHWH as God and acted on that commitment by living out *hesed* חֶסֶד in their actions with others. Their faithfulness was rewarded as God showed *hesed* חֶסֶד in return by including them into the people of God as insiders. In many ways, the lives of Rahab and Ruth reflect the teaching of Deuteronomy 7:9, "Know therefore that the Lord your God is God; he is the faithful God, keeping his covenant of love to a thousand generations of those who love him and keep his commandments." By recognizing the authority of God and faithfully keeping his commandments by living in *hesed* חֶסֶד, we experience conversion and a changed life, and can rely on God to show us *hesed* חֶסֶד in return.

So, what are the lessons to be learned for the immigrant community, living as outsiders in a different culture? We cannot define our lives based on what the insiders expect, because we may never become accepted as insiders. God sees and knows our allegiance based on our testimony and faith. By living out *hesed* חֶסֶד in our lives and community, we are living as God would have us live, not as the insider society or culture would have us live. God alone decides who are included within the people of God, even if congregations and churches do not extend this inclusion in turn to the outsiders among them. Nevertheless, immigrants should strive to advocate and fight for equal treatment and inclusion within the community. Justice and *hesed* חֶסֶד are connected, along with humility. There seems to be no expectation that Rahab would reject her Canaanite identity or Ruth her Moabite identity as part of the conversion process, except in terms of their allegiance to the God of Israel over their traditional gods. Ruth binds herself to Naomi and her community based on family relationships, but Rahab has no such obligation. In neither case are legal requirements, citizenship, or official recognition required. Being included in the people of God is based on no other requirements than allegiance to God and acting with *hesed* חֶסֶד. This is true for both insiders and outsiders in any community. The focus is no longer on hoping others will allow you into their circle, but rather on trusting that God will include you among God's people if you live a life aligned to God and act accordingly in loving-kindness to others, in spite of how they might treat you in return.

End Notes

[1] There are some issues here, but I will not go into detail due to the scope of this paper. Richard Bauckham (1995) does a good job looking into the questions of the relationship between Rahab and Ruth. The only account that connects Rahab to the father of Boaz is in Matthew, it is not found in the Old Testament. Bauckham indicates that this was probably accepted Jewish tradition at the time Matthew was written, even though the time between Rahab and Ruth should be much greater than one generation. Some rabbinic traditions hold that Rahab married Joshua. Other traditions connect Nahshon (the father of Salmon) as one of the spies Rahab rescued. For purposes of this paper, it is enough that Rahab and Ruth are connected in the passage in Matthew, which shows a theological or spiritual connection, even if a real genealogical connection is impossible or unlikely. Scholars

often connect the stories of Rahab and Ruth, since their similarities are quite striking. See also Hawk (2015: 19-20).

[2] It is such an exception that is seems some scholars try to read more into the story than I think the text validates, such as Nicholas Lunn (2014) who uses the story as an example of "intertextuality" as a parallel for the Exodus. There are definite parallels between Joshua and Moses, but I think reinterpreting the story of Rahab in light of the Exodus is a bit of a stretch.

[3] Rahab can be and has been interpreted in many different ways, some good and some bad. For other interpretations of Rahab see Lockwood (2010).

[4] One could argue that Rahab was expecting her and her family to be saved as a result of her kindness, but keep in mind that she really had no guarantee that the spies would keep their word, or that she and her family would not be killed by others during the attack to come.

[5] This is especially interesting in the case of Rahab, who was both a prostitute and likely a person who worshipped the Canaanite gods. Yet, her oath and acts of *hesed* חֶסֶד seem sufficient for her conversion. This may be because her sinful life was led before she made her oath to YHWH. In the Old Testament the focus on repentance seems to be often aimed at the people of Israel, those who are already insiders.

[6] Although Hawk (2015: 50) does note that the use of the Hebrew work *sub* (turning or returning) is frequently an illusion to repentance or turning back to YHWH, so Ruth as "the one who returned" in 1:22b can carry the idea of repentance.

Works Cited

Barrick, William D.
    2000   "Living a New Life: Old Testament Teaching About
            Conversion." *The Master's Seminary Journal* 11(1)
            (Spring): 19-38.

Baukham, Richard
    1995   "Tamar's Ancestry and Rahab's Marriage: Two Problems
            in the Matthean Genealogy." *Novum Testamentum*
            37(4): 313-329.

Biddle, Mark E. and Melissa A. Jackson
    2017   "Rahab and Her Visitors: Reciprocal Deliverance." *Word
            and World* 37(3) (Summer): 226-233.

Brady, Christian M. M.
    2013   "The Conversion of Ruth in Targum Ruth." *The Review of
            Rabbinic Judaism* 16: 133-146.

Campbell, Edward F.
1990   "Naomi, Boaz, and Ruth: *Hesed* and Change." *Austin Seminary Bulletin* 105(2): 64-74.

Dearman, J. Andrew
2009   "Observation on 'Conversion' and the Old Testament." *Ex Auditu* 25: 22-36.

Fleenor, Rob and Mark S. Ziese
2008   *Judges and Ruth.* College Press NIV Commentary. Joplin, MO: College Press Publishing Company.

Hawk, L. Daniel
2015   *Ruth.* Apollos Old Testament Commentary. Downers Grove, IN: InterVarsity Press.

Kim, Uriah Y.
2011   "Where is the Home for the Man of Luz?" *Interpretation* (July): 250-262.

Levine, Baruch A.
2013   "On the Concept *Hesed* in the Hebrew Bible." *The Living Pulpit* (Fall): 6-8.

Lockwood, Peter F.
2010   "Rahab: Multi-faceted Heroine of the Book of Joshua." *Lutheran Theological Journal* 44(1) (May): 39-50.

Lunn, Nicholas P.
2014   "The Deliverance of Rahab (Joshua 2,6) As The Gentile Exodus." *Tyndale Bulletin* 65(1): 11-19.

Matthews, Victor H.
2004   *Judges and Ruth.* New Cambridge Bible Commentary. Cambridge, UK: Cambridge University Press.

Moberly, R. W. L.
2013   *Old Testament Theology: Reading the Hebrew Bible as Christian Experience.* Grand Rapids, MI: Baker Academic Press.

Sakenfield, Katherine Doob
1978   *The Meanings of Hesed in the Hebrew Bible: A New Inquiry.* Harvard Semitic Monographs no. 17. Missoula, MT: Scholar's Press for the Harvard Semitic Museum.

Smit, Laura A. and Stephen E. Fowl
2018   *Judges and Ruth.* Brazos Theological Commentary on the Bible. Grand Rapids, MI: Brazos Press.

The Asbury Journal 75/2: 271-287
© 2020 Asbury Theological Seminary
DOI: 10.7252/Journal.02.2020F.07

Kelly J. Godoy de Danielson
Mujeres desde Afuera Mirando hacia Adentro: Rahab y Rut como Conversas Extranjeras al Pueblo de Dios

Resumen:
> ¿Cómo se convierte una persona de afuera en una persona de adentro? Esta es una pregunta que surge al considerar tanto la situación moderna del inmigrante moderno como la situación única de las mujeres no israelitas que se convierten en parte del pueblo de Dios en el Antiguo Testamento. El patrón habitual en el Antiguo Testamento es nacer en el pueblo de Israel, pero para los hombres existe la posibilidad de convertirse en parte del pueblo del pacto a través del acto físico de la circuncisión. En esta sociedad patriarcal, las mujeres generalmente no tenían más remedio que seguir las decisiones de sus maridos. ¿Pero, y si no hubiera marido? La Biblia tiende a tener una opinión particularmente dura sobre los hombres israelitas que se casan con mujeres no israelitas, por lo que incluso el matrimonio no parece ser un camino aceptable para las mujeres solteras o viudas. Pero dos mujeres importantes en el Antiguo Testamento navegan con éxito la transición de una persona de afuera a una de adentro, Rahab y Rut. Este artículo explora lo que esto significa para entender la conversión dentro del contexto del Antiguo Testamento, así como su potencial implicación teológica para la comunidad inmigrante en el mundo actual. Comprender la importancia de la lealtad de una persona a YHWH, así como seguir esta lealtad a través de acciones de bondad amorosa (*hesed* חֶסֶד) son las similitudes clave que unen a estas dos mujeres y ayudan a crear un puente teológico para los inmigrantes en nuestro contexto moderno.

Palabras clave: Rut, Rahab, mujeres, conversión, inmigración, pueblo de Dios.

Kelly J. Godoy de Danielson se graduó en 2020 del Seminario Teológico Asbury con una Maestría en Estudios Bíblicos. También es originaria de El Salvador en Centroamérica.

Introducción

¿Cómo se convierte una persona de afuera en una persona de adentro? Esta es una pregunta que con frecuencia me enfrento como inmigrante en un país extranjero. Cuando su color de piel y su acento lo distinguen, casi siempre se le ve como una persona de afuera, incluso después de vivir durante 20 años en su contexto actual. Esta pregunta también surge a veces en el Antiguo Testamento. El patrón habitual es que uno nazca en el pueblo de Israel, pero para los hombres existe la posibilidad de convertirse en parte del pueblo del pacto a través del acto físico de la circuncisión. En esta sociedad patriarcal, las mujeres generalmente no tenían más remedio que seguir las decisiones de sus maridos. ¿Pero, y si no hubiera marido? La Biblia tiende a tener una opinión particularmente dura sobre los hombres israelitas que se casan con mujeres no israelitas, por lo que incluso el matrimonio no parece ser un camino aceptable para las mujeres solteras o viudas. Pero hay dos mujeres importantes en el Antiguo Testamento que navegan con éxito la transición de una persona de afuera a otra de adentro, y se convierten no solo en miembros del pueblo de Dios, sino en partes esenciales de la historia del plan de salvación de Dios como antepasados tanto del Rey David como de Jesús en el Nuevo Testamento. ¡La pregunta que esto me plantea es cómo sucede esto y cuál es la implicación para la comunidad de inmigrantes?

Además, el tema de la conversión ha sido un punto importante para la teología evangélica durante mucho tiempo. ¿Cómo se hace uno cristiano? La mayor parte de esto tiene sus raíces teológicas en las escrituras del Nuevo Testamento, pero a menudo se pasa por alto en un estudio teológico del Antiguo Testamento. El único equivalente real de mirar el tema de la conversión del Nuevo Testamento es para examinar este tema de cómo las personas fuera del pueblo de Israel se convirtieron en parte del pueblo de Dios. Las mismas historias de Rahab y Rut, que responden a la primera pregunta, nos ayudan a comprender la naturaleza de la conversión, así como cómo las mujeres sin maridos podrían haber pasado de ser personas de afuera a personas de adentro en el contexto del Antiguo Testamento.

La Circuncisión Masculina como Camino Para el Pueblo de Dios

En Génesis 17, Dios establece el pacto entre Dios y Abraham y sus descendientes. El versículo siete enfatiza que este será un pacto "eterno" por generaciones. Este pacto incluirá la tierra de Canaán, así como el acto de la circuncisión masculina. En el versículo diez, está claro que todo varón debe ser circuncidado para ser parte del pacto, y el versículo doce establece que los que han sido comprados de extranjeros también deben ser circuncidados. Finalmente, el versículo catorce advierte que cualquier varón que no esté circuncidado será excluido del pacto. Los versículos 23-27 indican que Abraham, Ismael y todos los hombres de su casa, nacidos o comprados, fueron circuncidados ese mismo día.

En Éxodo 12, se establece la comida ritual crucial de la Pascua. En este capítulo, Moisés instruye al pueblo sobre la futura celebración de esta comida, y señala en el versículo 48: "Un extranjero que resida entre ustedes y quiera celebrar la Pascua del Señor debe hacer que todos los varones de su casa sean circuncidados; entonces podrá participar como un nacido en la tierra." Esto permite que los hombres afuera de la comunidad israelita se conviertan en parte del pueblo de Dios a través del acto físico de la circuncisión, alineándose y sometiéndose al pacto de Abraham.

En Josué, capítulo cinco, Josué ordena a los israelitas que se circunciden antes de la conquista de Canaán. Por alguna razón, la práctica parece haber sido abandonada en el desierto, pero ahora el pacto va a ser renovado. Josué aparece a menudo en el libro como un tipo de "nuevo Moisés" para el pueblo, por lo que la renovación del pacto en Gilgal (Josué 5: 2-12) no debería sorprendernos. Cuando se renueva el pacto en el monte Ebal en el capítulo ocho, queda claro que los extranjeros están incluidos entre el pueblo de Dios. El versículo 33 señala que, "tanto los extranjeros que vivían entre ellos como los nativos estaban allí" para la lectura del Libro de la Ley.

Pero mientras que los hombres extranjeros tienen una forma de unirse al pueblo israelita a través de la circuncisión, esa posibilidad se les niega a las mujeres, incluso a través del matrimonio. La prohibición en contra de que los hombres israelitas se casen con mujeres extranjeras se aclara en la historia de Dina en Génesis 34 y Deuteronomio 7: 3-4, "Y no emparentarás con ellas; no darás tu hija a su hijo, ni tomarás a su hija para tu hijo. Porque desviará a tu hijo de en pos de mí, y servirán a dioses ajenos; y el furor de Jehová se encenderá sobre vosotros, y te destruirá pronto." Josué repite las mismas prohibiciones en Josué 23: 12-13. Otros pasajes repiten esta preocupación, incluyendo 1 Reyes 11: 2 y Esdras 9:14. Sin embargo, dos mujeres en las Escrituras ingresan al pueblo de Dios como extranjeras durante el período temprano de la historia de Israel, y ellas

no son insignificantes. Tampoco estas dos mujeres están desconectadas.
Mateo 1: 5 conecta a Rahab como la madre de Booz, quien se casaría con
Rut, la abuela del rey David, y finalmente se convertirían en antepasados
de Jesús.[1]

Rahab: de Prostituta Extranjera a uno más del Pueblo de Dios

La historia de Rahab en los capítulos dos y seis de Josué es
una excepción interesante a gran parte de la literatura sobre la conquista.[2]
Primero se muestra a Rahab como una prostituta en la ciudad de Jericó,
donde se encuentra con los dos espías enviados por Josué para estudiar la
ciudad con el fin de conquistarla. Ella oculta con éxito a los dos espías y
redirige a los enviados por el rey de Jericó en busca de los espías. Antes de
dejar ir a los espías, da un discurso interesante en los versículos 9-13,

> Sé que Jehová os ha dado esta tierra; porque el temor
> de vosotros ha caído sobre nosotros, y todos los
> moradores del país ya han desmayado por causa de
> vosotros. Porque hemos oído que Jehová hizo secar las
> aguas del Mar Rojo delante de vosotros cuando salisteis
> de Egipto, y lo que habéis hecho a los dos reyes de los
> amorreos que estaban al otro lado del Jordán, a Sehón y
> a Og, a los cuales habéis destruido. Oyendo esto, ha
> desmayado nuestro corazón; ni ha quedado más aliento
> en hombre alguno por causa de vosotros, porque Jehová
> vuestro Dios es Dios arriba en los cielos y abajo en la
> tierra. Os ruego pues, ahora, que me juréis por Jehová,
> que como he hecho misericordia (*hesed* חֶסֶד), con
> vosotros, así la haréis vosotros con la casa de mi padre,
> de lo cual me daréis una señal segura; y que salvaréis la
> vida a mi padre y a mi madre, a mis hermanos y
> hermanas, y a todo lo que es suyo; y que libraréis
> nuestras vidas de la muerte.

Los espías se van después de hacer un juramento y decirle que
lleve a todos a su casa y que cuelgue un cordón escarlata afuera de la
ventana como señal, y se salvarán. En Josué 6:17, 22-23, 25, Rahab y su
familia se salvan, y el versículo 25 señala: "Mas Josué salvó la vida a Rahab
la ramera, y a la casa de su padre, y a todo lo que ella tenía; y habitó ella
entre los israelitas hasta hoy, por cuanto escondió a los mensajeros que
Josué había enviado a reconocer a Jericó." Rut 4: 18-22, que describe la
genealogía de David señala que Salmón, el padre de Booz (quien es su
esposo según Mateo 1: 5. Ver nota 1) es un israelita que regresa a Pérez,

uno de los hijos de Judá. Este matrimonio solidifica a Rahab como una persona de adentro y como parte del pueblo de Dios.

Moberly (2013: 71) analiza cómo se compara a Rahab con Acán en Josué. Rahab como la más grande persona de afuera: una mujer cananea y una prostituta que se convierte en una persona de adentro, mientras que Acán, una persona de adentro con un pedigrí se convierte en el más grande persona de afuera, ya que él y toda su familia son lapidados por desobediencia. De la misma manera, Moberly señala cómo Rahab muestra la cualidad de *hesed* חֶסֶד (amor firme o bondad) y debido a sus palabras y acciones, "ella está exenta de *herem* חֵרֶם, a pesar de la falta de cláusulas de exención en Deuteronomio, y habilitada (con su familia) para convertirse en parte de Israel."[3]

Rut: la Moabita que se Convirtió en Uno más del Pueblo de Dios

En el libro de Rut, vemos otro caso excepcional de una mujer que se convierte en parte del pueblo de Dios. Noemí y su esposo, Elimelec, habían ido a la tierra de Moab con sus hijos, Mahlón y Quelión, y ambos se casaron con mujeres de Moab, Orfa y Rut. Cuando mueren sus hijos y su esposo, Noemí decide regresar con su propia gente. En Rut 1: 8, Noemí libera a Orfa y Rut de sus obligaciones para con ella y las elogia por su bondad (*hesed* חֶסֶד), pero las anima a volver a casa con sus familias y volver a casarse. Las dos jóvenes al principio se niegan, pero Noemí expone la realidad de que no tendrá más hijos para dárselos como esposos. Orfa finalmente se va, pero Ruth aún se queda. Noemí nuevamente intenta que Rut la deje, pero Rut responde en Rut 1: 16-17,

> No me ruegues que te deje, y me aparte de ti; porque a dondequiera que tú fueres, iré yo, y dondequiera que vivieres, viviré. Tu pueblo será mi pueblo, y tu Dios mi Dios. Donde tú murieres, moriré yo, y allí seré sepultada; así me haga Jehová, y aun me añada, que sólo la muerte hará separación entre nosotras dos.

Rut continúa mostrando su fidelidad al apoyar a Noemí mientras espiga los campos de Booz, un pariente cercano de Noemí. En última instancia, Booz se convierte en el pariente redentor ideal y redime los derechos a la tierra de la familia de Noemí y, por lo tanto, el derecho a casarse con Rut, que se convierte en la abuela del futuro rey David.

Cuando Booz redime sus derechos sobre Rut, los ancianos dicen en Rut 4:11-12: "Testigos somos. Jehová haga a la mujer que entra en tu casa como a Raquel y a Lea, las cuales edificaron la casa de Israel; y tú seas ilustre en Efrata, y seas de renombre en Belén. Y sea tu casa como la casa de Fares, el que Tamar dio a luz a Judá, por la descendencia que de esa joven te dé Jehová." Una vez más, una mujer extranjera ingresa al pueblo de Dios, que se solidifica con su matrimonio con uno de los del pueblo de Dios.

Si bien la mayoría de los comentarios se centran en los temas de bondad (*hesed* חֶסֶד), lealtad, protección de los débiles en la sociedad y el apoyo del libro a la realeza davídica, algunos señalan otros posibles usos del libro. Fleenor y Ziese (2008: 320) señalan las posibles implicaciones del libro como protesta,

> Como literatura de protesta, se argumenta que el texto contiene un mensaje dirigido a quienes buscan definir estrechamente al "pueblo de Dios". Como tal, el texto deliberadamente socava (o subvierte) una supuesta "posición de pureza" que busca expulsar a los "buenos" extraterrestres (como Rut) de la comunidad judía. Una variación de este punto de vista considera que el mensaje del libro es un estímulo dirigido a las esposas gentiles de esposos judíos. En esto, Ruth es la modelo a seguir: un prosélito modelo para que todos los extranjeros lo imiten.

Solo algunos escritores tienden a desarrollar la naturaleza extranjera de Rut en esta historia, aunque el texto mismo se refiere a Rut como la "moabita" específicamente en varios lugares (Rut 1:22, 2: 2, 2:21, 4: 5 y 4:10), destacando su condición de extranjera o forastera en la comunidad. En este sentido, la identidad también se convierte en un tema, como escribe Matthews (2004: 207), "Rut, que se ha convertido en una figura liminal o socialmente indefinida por sus decisiones y acciones, debe establecer una nueva identidad dentro de una comunidad extraña. En esencia, ella debe 'encontrar su lugar'. Tanto física como socialmente, en Belén."

La Conversión de Rahab y Rut

Hay varias similitudes en las historias de Rahab y Rut, aunque en la superficie son tipos de mujeres muy diferentes. Rahab es una prostituta, mientras que Ruth es una viuda lamentablemente sin hijos.

En primer lugar, son mujeres que no tienen maridos que decidirán su dirección espiritual. Sin embargo, ambos hacen juramentos ligándose al Dios de Israel. Estos juramentos están estrechamente ligados a conceptos de bondad y lealtad. Ambos también muestran una obediencia fiel al llevar a cabo estos juramentos. Finalmente, debido a su fiel obediencia, a cada uno se le permite ingresar al pueblo de Dios, y esto finalmente se sella mediante el matrimonio, a pesar de las prohibiciones anteriores contra esta práctica.

William Barrick (2000) argumenta que la conversión está modelada en el Antiguo Testamento por historias como Rahab, Rut, Naamán y los marineros y ninivitas en Jonás como una forma de entender el concepto de la circuncisión del corazón (Deuteronomio 10:16 y 30: 6) en oposición a la circuncisión física como una forma de entrar en el pueblo de Dios. Como tal, Barrick también ve el pacto y la renovación del pacto como un "nuevo compromiso con la vida cambiada que se había entrado en la conversión" (Barrick 2000: 23). Barrick ve a Rahab como reconociendo una relación formal con YHWH en su confesión de la máxima autoridad de YHWH en Josué 2:11. También señala su cambio de vida al mostrarle *hesed* חֶסֶד (por primera vez en el libro de Joshua) (Barrick 2000: 28-29). Para Ruth también, Barrick ve su "juramento de lealtad" a Noemí como una confesión, que luego es vivida por una vida cambiada dominada por *hesed* חֶסֶד (Barrick 2000: 29). Como escribe Barrick,

> La conversión puede resumirse en el término hebreo sub (se vuelve). El arrepentimiento y la fe son sus elementos principales. La fe "logra en la práctica el reconocimiento por parte del individuo de la soberanía única de Yahvé." Tal reconocimiento es inseparable de la conversión que incluye la humildad penitente. La confesión de la soberanía de Yahvé es claramente evidente en los casos de Rahab, Rut, Naamán, los marineros y los ninivitas. (Barrick 2000: 35)

En última instancia, en un cuadro final, Barrick analiza una serie de temas y los que ve como en común para Rahab y Rut son: una confesión de fe (Josué 2:11 y Rut 1: 16-17) y un cambio o compromiso (Josué 2:12, Rut 1: 8 y Rut 3:10).

Si bien Rut no se menciona en el Nuevo Testamento excepto en Mateo 1: 5, Rahab se refleja en otros dos pasajes. En Hebreos 11, el famoso capítulo sobre los fieles, el versículo 31 dice: " Por la fe Rahab la ramera no pereció juntamente con los desobedientes, habiendo recibido a los espías en paz." En Santiago 2, donde Santiago habla de la importancia de la fe y las obras, el escritor compara a Rahab con Abraham en los versículos 25 y 26 y escribe: "Asimismo también Rahab la ramera, ¿no fue justificada por obras, cuando recibió a los mensajeros y los envió por otro camino? Porque como el cuerpo sin espíritu está muerto, así también la fe sin obras está muerta." Biddle y Jackson (2017: 232) hacen una distinción similar en su evaluación de los dos espías en la historia de Rahab, cuando escriben: "¿Entonces, quién salva a quién en esta historia? En este impactante texto, Israel aprende que una prostituta cananea predicadora de un sermón deuteronomista puede librarlos, incluso mientras hacen planes para su futura liberación. Todas las expectativas se trastocan. Ya no hay distinción entre quién es salvador y quién es salvo." La fiel y justa Rahab es considerada un modelo según Biddle y Jackson, mientras que los "espías" parecen traer de vuelta una inteligencia limitada (y si son "mensajeros" como se mencionó en otra parte, no parecen entregar ningún mensaje).

Como la fidelidad y las buenas obras son las características señaladas en Hebreos y Santiago en el Nuevo Testamento para Rahab, es posible ver cómo ella reflexiona sobre una comprensión cristiana de vivir una vida cristiana después de la conversión. Parece acercarse a la comprensión de Jesús del mayor mandamiento en Mateo 22: 37-39, " Jesús le dijo: Amarás al Señor tu Dios con todo tu corazón, y con toda tu alma, y con toda tu mente Este es el primero y grande mandamiento. Y el segundo es semejante: Amarás a tu prójimo como a ti mismo." Toda la ley y los profetas dependen de estos dos mandamientos.'" Rahab y Rut se comprometen con Dios a través de un juramento y dan seguimiento a este juramento mediante un amor sacrificado por los demás. También existe una estrecha conexión entre cuestiones de justicia, bondad y humildad, como señalan Smit y Fowl (2018: 220),

> En Miqueas 6:8 se les dice a los israelitas que todo lo que Dios requiere de ellos es "que hagan justicia, amen misericordia [*hesed* חֶסֶד] y se humillen ante su Dios". Este texto de Miqueas plantea la perspectiva de que la justicia, el *hesed* חֶסֶד y la humildad ante Dios están conectados. Esto llevaría a uno a pensar que el éxito en el cultivo de una de estas virtudes conduce y puede presumir cierto grado de éxito en el cultivo de las otras dos. Si la justicia requiere que uno dé a los demás lo que se les debe en Dios, y si la humildad se basa en conocer correctamente el propio estado en relación con Dios y los demás, entonces *hesed* חֶסֶד sería esa gracia que

reconoce, pero no está limitado o limitado simplemente por lo que es debido a otros y por donde uno se encuentra en relación con los demás y con Dios. Esto parece encajar bastante bien con Ruth. Va mucho más allá de la justicia en su trato con Noemí y actúa con gracia y audacia hacia Booz sin buscar nunca engrandecerse.

En este sentido, tanto Rut como Rahab van más allá de los confines de lo justo, y ambas actúan con bondad mientras simultáneamente exhiben humildad ante Dios.

Es interesante que incluso en la tradición judía, no hay duda de que la historia de Rut es un relato de conversión. Brady (2013: 135) escribe: "Mientras que los eruditos modernos debaten si Rut 1: 16-17 realmente describe o no la conversión de Rut a la religión israelita, dentro de la tradición rabínica no había duda de que Rut es el prosélito por excelencia. El primer capítulo de Rut proporciona al exégeta rabínico el marco prototípico para la conversión, incluido el rechazo de Noemí al prosélito en potencia." Aparentemente, es tradición que un posible converso judío deba ser rechazado tres veces, y si aún persiste, debe permitírsele (y esto se basa en el rechazo de Noemí a Rut tres veces). Los escritores judíos del Targum Rut han agregado a Rut 1: 16-17 para convertirlo en un diálogo para la conversión. Brady (2013: 137) lo presenta así (con la escritura en escritura regular y las adiciones en cursiva),

> Ruth dijo: "No me instes a que te deje, a que me aleje de ti, *porque deseo ser un prosélito.*"
> *Noemí dijo: "Se nos ha ordenado guardar los sábados y los días santos de manera que no podamos caminar más de dos mil codos."*
> Ruth dijo: "Dondequiera que vayas, yo iré."
> *Noemí dijo: "Se nos ordena no alojarnos con los gentiles."*
> Ruth dijo: "Donde tú te alojes, yo me alojaré."
> *Noemí dijo: "Se nos ha ordenado que guardemos seiscientos trece mandamientos."*
> Ruth dijo: "Lo que tu gente *guarde, lo guardaré como si fuera* mi gente *de antes de esto.*"
> *Noemí dijo: "Se nos ordena no adorar a dioses extranjeros.*"
> Ruth dijo: "Tu dios es mi dios."
> *Noemí dijo: Tenemos cuatro penas de muerte para los culpables: apedrear con piedras, quemar con fuego, ejecutar a espada y colgar de un árbol.*"
> *Ruth dijo: "Cómo mueras, yo moriré."*

Naomi dijo: "Tenemos un cementerio."
Ruth dijo: "Y allí seré enterrada. Y no digas más.
Que el Señor me haga así y más *contra mí*, si hasta la
muerte me separa de ti."

Entonces, incluso en la tradición judía, Rut se ve como un texto que trata sobre la conversión.

Uriah Kim (2011) aporta la perspectiva adicional de un erudito bíblico coreano que vive como inmigrante en los Estados Unidos. Examina tanto a Rahab como a Rut junto con el "hombre de Luz" (Jueces 1: 22-26) como ejemplos de la relación *hesed* חֶסֶד basado en la lealtad a YHWH. Sin embargo, su lectura como inmigrante coreano es un poco diferente. Sostiene que Rahab y Rut podrían ser personas de adentro en un sentido, pero este sentido de pertenencia no es completo. Si bien a Rahab se le permite vivir entre Israel, también se le envía a vivir "fuera del campamento de Israel" en Josué 6:23, de modo que no se le reconoce como una verdadera israelita (Kim 2011: 257-258). Puedo ver su punto en esta interpretación, pero no estoy de acuerdo, ya que su matrimonio definitivo con una persona de adentro demuestra una inclusión completa, pero tal inclusión puede llevar tiempo. Sin embargo, su lectura sobre Rut es bastante interesante. Su enfoque no está en Rut, quien a través de *hesed* חֶסֶד se convierte en una persona de adentro, sino en Orfa, quien también demuestra el mismo tipo de *hesed* חֶסֶד que Rut, pero "su lealtad a su pueblo la descalifica de ser parte de Israel" (Kim 2011: 260). Ruth se convierte en una minoría modelo (del mismo modo que Pocahontas en el mito estadounidense) porque rechaza a su propia gente. Kim termina su artículo con una poderosa conclusión, relevante para la comunidad inmigrante de hoy,

> ¿Cuando practicamos el *hesed* חֶסֶד con otros, podemos esperar que Dios honre nuestra *hesed* חֶסֶד cuando la otra parte no cumple con su responsabilidad? Debemos recordar que Jesucristo, que es un ser bicultural por excelencia, completamente Dios y completamente humano, usó la *hesed* חֶסֶד para cruzar la división divino-humana con el fin de construir la relación entre Dios y los humanos. Jesucristo es la seguridad de que cuando practicamos la *hesed* חֶסֶד con otros, Dios ciertamente honrará nuestra *hesed* חֶסֶד. Quizás el hogar es donde se practica la *hesed* חֶסֶד por el bien de la solidaridad humana y por el reino de Dios. (Kim 2011, 262)

Rahab y Rut como Modelos de Conversión

Se suponía que Rahab estaba sujeto al *herem* חֵרֶם anunciado en contra de Canaán, la idea de que los israelitas debían "destruir por completo" a los cananeos que encontraron en la conquista. Sin embargo, en la primera batalla por la conquista, su sólo familia se salva porque Rahab mostró su bondad o *hesed* חֶסֶד hacia los espías e hizo un juramento reconociendo la autoridad de YHWH. De la misma manera, Rut le muestra *hesed* חֶסֶד a Noemí, incluso después de que ella es liberada de sus responsabilidades, y de la misma manera hace un juramento de aceptar a YHWH como su Dios. Ambas mujeres terminan siendo recompensadas por su fidelidad a sus juramentos mediante el matrimonio con israelitas para su plena inclusión en el pueblo de Dios. Además, ambos se convirtieron en antepasados del rey David y Jesús como parte del plan modelo de salvación de Dios.

Claramente, el concepto de *hesed* חֶסֶד es de vital importancia tanto para los relatos como para el proceso de conversión como se ve en el Antiguo Testamento. Edward F. Campbell (1990) señala que *hesed* חֶסֶד se usa para describir tanto las relaciones humanas como la acción divina. Basando parte de su trabajo en el libro, *The Meanings of* Hesed *in the Hebrew Bible: A New Inquiry* (1978) de Katherine Doob Sakenfield, Campbell (1990, 67-68) resume el *hesed* חֶסֶד de cinco maneras diferentes:

- Primero, *hesed* חֶסֶד no es solo un "favor especial", sino que es esencial para la liberación de un peligro grave.
- *Hesed* חֶסֶד lo hace una persona situacionalmente más fuerte hacia una persona más débil.
- La persona más poderosa tiene otras opciones y, por lo tanto, *hesed* חֶסֶד no se le fuerza.
- Por lo general, se requiere una relación previa para que se haga *hesed* חֶסֶד, por lo que existe una responsabilidad moral o ética de actuar en lugar de no hacer nada.
- El que muestra *hesed* חֶסֶד suele ser el único que puede realizar la acción.

Así que *hesed* חֶסֶד es más que un simple acto de bondad. Es bondad constante, o bondad amorosa, pero es actuar de la misma manera que Dios actúa con los seres humanos desde una posición de poder hacia alguien que está en extrema necesidad. Campbell (1990: 69) escribe: "Para decirlo de otra manera, el impacto del libro de Rut es retratar al menos a Orfa y Rut, y especialmente a Rut, actuando hacia otros de la manera en que YHWH actúa, viviendo la imitación de Dios." En última instancia, este acto de *hesed* חֶסֶד se puede ver más completamente en el sacrificio de Jesucristo en la cruz.

Baruch Levine (2013: 6) se suma a este entendimiento al señalar que *hesed* חֶסֶד "es un acto de bondad y amor realizado sin expectativa de recompensa o reciprocidad." Al actuar con *hesed* חֶסֶד hacia los demás, Dios a su vez muestra *hesed* חֶסֶד a cambio.[4] Para Rahab y Rut, el primer acto de conversión es actuar como Dios hubiera actuado. Es parte de su naturaleza mostrar amabilidad cuando no era necesario hacerlo por alguien que se encontraba en una posición vulnerable. En medio de estos actos de *hesed* חֶסֶד, tanto Rahab como Rut hacen un juramento reconociendo el poder y la autoridad del Dios de Israel sobre sus propias vidas. Finalmente, Rahab y Rut son fieles a sus juramentos, y en respuesta YHWH les muestra *hesed* חֶסֶד incorporándolos al pueblo de Dios, validando finalmente esto a través del matrimonio. Como dice L. Daniel Hawk (2015: 20), "Finalmente, como Rahab, Rut confiesa al Dios de Israel (Josué 2:11; Rut 1:16), muestra fidelidad (*hesed* חֶסֶד) a los israelitas (Josué 2: 12- 14; Rut 1: 8; 3:10) y recibe un lugar para ella y sus descendientes entre el pueblo de Dios."

Conclusión

¿Entonces, cómo se convierte uno en parte del pueblo de Dios en el Antiguo Testamento? Parece diferir en algunos aspectos del entendimiento del Nuevo Testamento, que tiende a anteponer el arrepentimiento de los pecados a una confesión de fe y finalmente a una vida cambiada.[5] En el caso de Rahab y Rut, no hay arrepentimiento del pecado.[6] Esto es especialmente obvio en la vida de Rahab, una prostituta, en la que podríamos esperar ver algún tipo de juicio sobre su profesión. En ambos casos, vemos mujeres que tienen un compromiso profundo con YHWH y la voluntad de reconocer la autoridad de YHWH. Pero esto es más que una declaración doctrinal de fe. En ambos casos, esta voluntad de someterse a YHWH va acompañada de acciones concretas de *hesed* חֶסֶד. Tanto Rahab como Rut actúan de la forma en que Dios actuaría.

Rahab no es una persona con poder en Jericó. Sin embargo, por un breve momento, se le otorga el poder de vida y muerte sobre los espías israelitas. No sabemos cuáles pudieron haber sido sus pensamientos en este momento, pero podría haber buscado el favor del rey de Jericó al entregar a los espías, o podría haber vengado a los hombres a quienes tan a menudo tenía que servir y complacer en su negocio. Sin embargo, en ese momento, eligió actuar con *hesed* חֶסֶד, sin ningún pensamiento real de recuperar algo para ella, eligió proteger y esconder a estos hombres indefensos. Esto es compatible con la forma en que Dios actúa con los seres humanos. Sin embargo, ella no solo hace este acto de *hesed* חֶסֶד, sino que continúa guardando el secreto: permanecer fiel a su promesa, incluso después de que los espías se hayan ido. Debido a esto, Dios le da a ella una segunda oportunidad en la vida, junto con su familia, y les da la oportunidad de vivir entre el pueblo de Dios. En última instancia, será validada en sus acciones y se casará con un descendiente de la tribu de Judá, y será honrada como la bisabuela del rey David.

Rut también era una persona sin poder. Era viuda, y peor aún, sin hijos ni tierra. Ella le muestra *hesed* חֶסֶד a Noemí, negándose a dejar a su suegra viuda en una situación difícil. Noemí la había liberado de sus responsabilidades familiares, por lo que quizás por primera vez en su vida, Rut estaba en una posición de poder. Podía optar por volver con su gente, buscar un nuevo marido y formar una nueva familia. Solo podemos imaginar lo peligrosa que debe haber sido la vida para Noemí como viuda, sola, sin nadie que la protegiera en un país extranjero. El acto de *hesed* חֶסֶד de Rut probablemente salvó la vida de Noemí de muchas maneras. No solo la acompañó en lo que probablemente fue un viaje peligroso de regreso a su ciudad natal, sino que también recogió de los campos para alimentar a ambas y cuidó a la anciana Noemí. Rut hace un juramento de aceptar a YHWH como su Dios antes de que ella realmente comience su acción de *hesed* חֶסֶד. Pero Rut también es fiel a su acción y lleva a cabo una *hesed* חֶסֶד continua por Noemí. Al igual que con Rahab, finalmente será validada por sus acciones y se casará con un descendiente de la tribu de Judá y se convertirá en la abuela del rey David. Cuando uno piensa en la conexión entre Rahab y Rut, uno se pregunta si Booz estaba abierto a ver los aspectos positivos de Rut debido a la influencia de su propia madre, Rahab, que había pasado por el mismo proceso de convertirse en una persona de adentro.

Estos actos de *hesed* חֶסֶד de Rahab y Rut quizás estén relacionados con el rey David por una razón. El es una persona que también se muestra invocando la idea de *hesed* חֶסֶד. Esto se puede ver en 2 Samuel 2: 6 cuando le pide a Dios que muestre *hesed* חֶסֶד a los hombres de Jabes de Galaad que habían enterrado a Saúl. También se puede ver anteriormente en la relación entre David y Jonatán en 1 Samuel 20: 14-15 cuando hacen un juramento de *hesed* חֶסֶד entre David y Jonatán y sus descendientes. La fidelidad de este juramento se vive en la forma en que David trata a Mefiboset en 2 Samuel 9, después de que Jonatán y Saúl murieron en la batalla. Todo este tema de Dios mostrándole *hesed* חֶסֶד a aquellos que muestran *hesed* חֶסֶד también puede reflejarse en 2 Samuel 7, cuando Dios bendice a David y dice en los versículos 15-16: "pero mi misericordia no se apartará de él como la aparté de Saúl, al cual quité de delante de ti. Y será afirmada tu casa y tu reino para siempre delante de tu rostro, y tu trono será estable eternamente." Rahab y Rut como antepasados espirituales de David son un vínculo con la importancia de *hesed* חֶסֶד, y pueden ser una fuente de *hesed* חֶסֶד de David para otros, lo que resulta en el favor de Dios en su reinado. Jesucristo, a su vez, cumple este *hesed* חֶסֶד en el más grande acto de *hesed* חֶסֶד en la cruz. Ciertamente, esto es parte de la conexión espiritual que debemos extraer de la inclusión genealógica de Rahab y Rut en la familia de Jesús presentada en la apertura del Evangelio de Mateo:

La conversión de Rahab y Rut habla más fuerte que la conversión física de la circuncisión masculina. Su conversión vino del corazón y no solo de la identificación física con el pueblo de Dios. Sus vidas cambiadas como mujeres que eran parte de la comunidad israelita fue posible porque se sometieron a YHWH como Dios y actuaron en ese compromiso al vivir *hesed* חֶסֶד en sus acciones con los demás. Su fidelidad fue recompensada cuando Dios mostró *hesed* חֶסֶד en respuesta al incluirlos en el pueblo de Dios como personas de adentro. De muchas maneras, las vidas de Rahab y Rut reflejan la enseñanza de Deuteronomio 7: 9, "Conoce, pues, que Jehová tu Dios es Dios, Dios fiel, que guarda el pacto y la misericordia a los que le aman y guardan sus mandamientos, hasta mil generaciones;" Al reconocer la autoridad de Dios y guardar fielmente sus mandamientos al vivir en *hesed* חֶסֶד, experimentamos la conversión y una vida cambiada, y podemos confiar en Dios para que nos muestre *hesed* חֶסֶד a cambio.

¿Entonces, cuáles son las lecciones que se pueden aprender para la comunidad inmigrante, que vive como personas de afuera en una cultura diferente? No podemos definir nuestras vidas basándonos en lo que esperan los de adentro, porque es posible que nunca seamos aceptados como los de adentro. Dios ve y conoce nuestra lealtad basado en nuestro testimonio y fe. Al vivir *hesed* חֶסֶד en nuestras vidas y en nuestra comunidad, vivimos como Dios quiere que vivamos, no como la sociedad o la cultura de adentro quiere que vivamos. Solo Dios decide quiénes están incluidos dentro del pueblo de Dios, incluso si las congregaciones e iglesias no extienden esta inclusión a su vez a los de afuera entre ellos. Sin embargo, los inmigrantes deben esforzarse por defender y luchar por la igualdad de trato y la inclusión dentro de la comunidad. La justicia y la *hesed* חֶסֶד están conectados, junto con la humildad. No parece haber ninguna expectativa de que Rahab rechazara su identidad cananea o Rut su identidad moabita como parte del proceso de conversión, excepto en términos de su lealtad al Dios de Israel sobre sus dioses tradicionales. Rut se une a Noemí y su comunidad basada en las relaciones familiares, pero Rahab no tiene esa obligación. En ningún caso se requieren requisitos legales, ciudadanía o reconocimiento oficial. Ser incluido en el pueblo de Dios no se basa en otros requisitos que la lealtad a Dios y actuar con *hesed* חֶסֶד. Esto es cierto tanto para los de adentro como para los de afuera en cualquier comunidad. El enfoque ya no está en esperar que otros te permitan entrar en su círculo, sino en confiar en que Dios te incluirá entre el pueblo de Dios si vives una vida alineada con Dios y actúas en consecuencia con bondad amorosa hacia los demás, a pesar de cómo ellos podrían tratarte a cambio.

Notas finales:

[1] Hay algunos problemas aquí, pero no entraré en detalles debido al alcance de este documento. Richard Bauckham (1995) hace un buen trabajo al investigar las preguntas de la relación entre Rahab y Rut. El único relato que conecta a Rahab con el padre de Booz está en Mateo, no se encuentra en el Antiguo Testamento. Bauckham indica que esta probablemente era una tradición judía aceptada en el momento en que se escribió Mateo, aunque el tiempo entre Rahab y Rut debería ser mucho más grande que una generación. Algunas tradiciones rabínicas sostienen que Rahab se casó con Josué. Otras tradiciones conectan a Naasón (el padre de Salmón) como uno de los espías que Rahab rescató. Para los propósitos de este artículo, es suficiente que Rahab y Rut estén conectadas en el pasaje de Mateo, que muestra una conexión teológica o espiritual, incluso si una conexión genealógica real es imposible o improbable. Los eruditos a menudo relacionan las historias de Rahab y Rut, ya que sus similitudes son bastante sorprendentes. Véase también Hawk (2015: 19-20).

[2] Es una excepción tal que parece que algunos eruditos intentan leer más en la historia de lo que creo que el texto valida, como Nicholas Lunn (2014) que usa la historia como un ejemplo de "intertextualidad" como un paralelo del Éxodo. Hay paralelismos definidos entre Josué y Moisés, pero creo que reinterpretar la historia de Rahab a la luz del Éxodo es un poco exagerado.

[3] Rahab puede ser y ha sido interpretada de muchas formas diferentes, algunas buenas y otras malas. Para otras interpretaciones de Rahab, ver Lockwood (2010).

[4] Se podría argumentar que Rahab esperaba que ella y su familia fueran salvados como resultado de su bondad, pero tenga en cuenta que ella realmente no tenía ninguna garantía de que los espías cumplirían su palabra, o que ella y su familia no serían asesinados por otros durante el ataque por venir.

[5] Esto es especialmente interesante en el caso de Rahab, quien era una prostituta y probablemente una persona que adoraba a los dioses cananeos. Sin embargo, su juramento y actos de *hesed* חֶסֶד parecen suficientes para su conversión. Esto puede deberse a que su vida pecaminosa fue llevada antes de hacer su juramento a YHWH. En el Antiguo Testamento, el enfoque en el arrepentimiento parece estar dirigido a menudo al pueblo de Israel, aquellos que ya están adentro.

[6] Aunque Hawk (2015: 50) nota que el uso de la palabra hebrea sub (volverse o regresar) es con frecuencia una ilusión de arrepentimiento o volverse a YHWH, por lo que Rut como "la que regresó" en 1: 22b puede llevar la idea del arrepentimiento.

Trabajos citados

Barrick, William D.
    2000   "Living a New Life: Old Testament Teaching About Conversion." *The Master's Seminary Journal* 11(1) (Spring): 19-38.

Baukham, Richard
    1995   "Tamar's Ancestry and Rahab's Marriage: Two Problems in the Matthean Geneology." *Novum Testamentum* 37(4): 313-329.

Biddle, Mark E. y Melissa A. Jackson
    2017   "Rahab and Her Visitors: Reciprocal Deliverance." *Word and World* 37(3) (Summer): 226-233.

Brady, Christian M. M.
    2013   "The Conversion of Ruth in Targum Ruth." *The Review of Rabbinic Judaism* 16: 133-146.
Campbell, Edward F.
    1990   "Naomi, Boaz, and Ruth: *Hesed* and Change." *Austin Seminary Bulletin* 105(2): 64-74.

Dearman, J. Andrew
    2009   "Observation on 'Conversion' and the Old Testament." *Ex Auditu* 25: 22-36.

Fleenor, Rob y Mark S. Ziese
    2008   *Judges and Ruth*. College Press NIV Commentary. Joplin,
            MO: College Press Publishing Company.

Hawk, L. Daniel
    2015   *Ruth*. Apollos Old Testament Commentary. Downers
            Grove, IN: InterVarsity Press.

Kim, Uriah Y.
    2011   "Where is the Home for the Man of Luz?" *Interpretation*
            (July): 250-262.

Levine, Baruch A.
    2013   "On the Concept *Hesed* in the Hebrew Bible." *The
            Living Pulpit* (Fall): 6-8.

Lockwood, Peter F.
    2010   "Rahab: Multi-faceted Heroine of the Book of Joshua."
            Lutheran Theological Journal 44(1) (May): 39-50.

Lunn, Nicholas P.
    2014   "The Deliverance of Rahab (Joshua 2,6) As The Gentile
            Exodus." *Tyndale Bulletin* 65(1): 11-19.

Matthews, Victor H.
    2004   *Judges and Ruth*. New Cambridge Bible Commentary.
            Cambridge, UK: Cambridge University Press.

Moberly, R. W. L.
    2013   *Old Testament Theology: Reading the Hebrew Bible as
            Christian Experience*. Grand Rapids, MI: Baker
            Academic Press.

Sakenfield, Katherine Doob
    1978   *The Meanings of Hesed in the Hebrew Bible: A New
            Inquiry*. Harvard Semitic Monographs no. 17. Missoula,
            MT: Scholar's Press for the Harvard Semitic Museum.

Smit, Laura A. y Stephen E. Fowl
    2018   *Judges and Ruth*. Brazos Theological Commentary on
            the Bible. Grand Rapids, MI: Brazos Press.

The Asbury Journal 75/2: 288-326
© 2020 Asbury Theological Seminary
DOI: 10.7252/Journal.02.2020F.08

From the Archives: Ichthus Music Festival- The World of Christian Music Comes to Wilmore

It was the "dawning of the Age of Aquarius" as the 1967 musical *Hair* told us.[1] The hippie and New Age Movements were in the ascendancy. The U.S. was in the middle of the Vietnam War. In 1969, it seemed like the counterculture exploded when on August 15-18 the Woodstock Music Festival was held near White Lake, New York. Political and cultural shifts were occurring at a breath-taking pace, and the evangelical church seemed to be desperately trying to figure out how to respond. However, Wilmore remained isolated from much of this cultural change. Yet while cut off from much of what was going on in the U.S. culturally in 1970, an idea emerged, led by students (called the Christian Service Brotherhood) and their faculty advisor, Dr. Bob Lyon of Asbury Theological Seminary, of a Christian music festival as a counterpoint to Woodstock. Using the Wilmore campground, the site of many traditional Holiness camp meetings, the first Ichthus festival was established. It would continue as one of the major Christian music festivals in the U.S. until 2012, for 42 years, and would be called by at least one writer, the "granddaddy" of all Christian music festivals.[2]

Music plays a crucial role in youth culture, and rock and roll has been the defining genre of music used by young people since the 1950s within the context of the United States. While rock and roll partially grew out of gospel music, it took its own secular form of development and so was often actively opposed by many conservative Christians. As the academic study of Christian music has pointed out,

> The dilemma for Christian adolescents then is clear. On the one hand, rock and roll music plays a critical role in establishing identity and defining their social groups, but at the same time it appears to contradict many of

the values they hold as Christians... Standing in the gap between evangelical Christianity on one side and youth culture on the other, contemporary Christian music offers evangelical Christians who cannot identify with what they see on MTV their own set of alter egos. With its angelic waifs, strutting arena rockers, choreographed girl groups, guitar-strumming folkies, flannel encased grunge acts, posturing rappers, and wordy singer-songwriters, contemporary Christian music provides the evangelical audience with the same ethereal voices, the same driving guitars, and the same chunky rhythms that can be found anywhere on the radio dial- but with one important difference: rather than challenging predominant evangelical values, this music affirms them.[3]

The primary goal of the Ichthus music festival in its later years was to reach out and share the gospel message to young people through contemporary Christian music.
(Image courtesy of Asbury Theological Seminary Archives and Special Collections.)

Understanding how the modern contemporary Christian music genre has developed includes understanding how music and the church have interacted for centuries. Some have even argued a direct line from the popular camp meeting tradition to Ichthus to modern festivals such as the Cornerstone Festival that started in 1984, TOMfest (1995), HeavenFest (2008), Lifest (1999), and the Agape Festival (1977).[4] Scholars seem to accept that Larry Norman's 1969 album, *Upon This Rock* (Capitol Records) was the first Christian rock album, occurring contemporaneously with the growth of Jesus Rock in the late 1960s and 1970s from the Jesus Movement, as well as the popular musicals *Jesus Christ Superstar* (1970) and *Godspell* (1971).[5] At the start of this movement, the Ichthus music festival was born with an evangelistic emphasis, according to Bob Lyon, "to use the medium of young people to reach young people."[6] As sociologists Steck and Howard note,

> A key component of the evangelistic rationale of contemporary Christian music is the tradition of music festivals that mark the summer season. With Christian bands for the most part lacking access to the tours and club circuits that support mainstream musicians, the Christian music industry was forced to develop its own resources in order to create opportunities for live performances. And while churches and coffeehouses to some degree replaced the standard clubs and bars, it was the summer music festivals that became the focal point for CCM's (contemporary Christian music) live performances; here is where audiences and performers connect.[7]

The context of Wilmore in 1970 is also important to the development of Ichthus. The cultural turmoil of 1969 had really led to a faith crisis in the evangelical streams of the church, which often functioned as if it was still the 1940s or 1950s. Even while Wilmore seemed remotely isolated from these cultural changes, both Asbury College (now University) and Asbury Theological Seminary were feeling the stresses like the rest of the country and the need for some type of Christian response was increasing. On February 3, the Asbury Revival of 1970 broke out in Hughes Auditorium at Asbury College and began to spread around the nation. This was one important spiritual response focusing on inner spiritual renewal and awakening. Ichthus was an equally spiritual response to the cultural context, but focused instead on an outward cultural engagement and evangelism, even though it was completely separate from the Revival. As

Dr. Steve Seamands, Professor Emeritus of Christian Doctrine at Asbury Theological Seminary and a part of the first Ichthus in 1970 notes,

> Even though Ichthus was not directly connected to the Asbury Revival, years later I began to realize that it probably would have never happened if there hadn't been a revival. The revival created a spirit of openness and boldness. There was a passion for evangelism and outreach, a desire to witness for Christ, that had emerged in the Wilmore community as a result of the revival and that created the impetus for Ichthus.[8]

Those involved with Ichthus at the start note no connection, (and even a bit of skepticism about the Revival) and also point out the divisions between the College (where the Revival occurred) and the Seminary (where Ichthus began) were wide at this time, but it becomes almost impossible to separate these two spiritual moves, which are really two almost simultaneous spiritual responses to the cultural context of 1969. It is highly likely that the Revival triggered enough of a change in the environment of Wilmore itself that allowed for Ichthus to emerge, even when no direct connection existed. Inner renewal by the Holy Spirit was necessary for outward cultural engagement (also a part of the work of the Holy Spirit), and both required a spiritual freedom from the traditional confines of a church caught in outdated cultural patterns. This combination of spiritual renewal and social engagement has become much of the norm in holistic mission today, but in the 1960s and 1970s they remained very separate ideas.

The Ichthus music festival was a groundbreaking effort that helped launch contemporary Christian music and provide a working model for its future growth, while aiming to contextualize the gospel message for a new generation. As Gary Baker, the executive director of Ichthus wrote in 1997,

> This ministry was started out of a response to meet the needs of the youth of this country who were looking for substance in a world in which they had lost faith. In this endeavor, Ichthus Ministries has always been a catalyst for spiritual and social change in youth, as well as a leader in festival ministries. Ichthus is the first and oldest Christian festival in the nation. We find our greatest strength in whose we are and who we are as a festival ministry. As festivals spring up all over the nation, more and more they start out of a mode to entertain rather than to minister the gospel. It is to this mission that Ichthus has always remained loyal, to present Jesus Christ to the

youth who attend the Ichthus festival, that their lives may
be changed for the glory of God.[9]

This was a bold new ministry for its time and fitted to its cultural context.
It challenged traditional ways of doing evangelism and opened doors to
allow the Holy Spirit to work in the lives of young people impacted by the
counterculture of the 1960s and 1970s.

To really understand how the music of the 1960s impacted the
context in Wilmore, it is important to go back a few years before Ichthus.
Ed Kilbourne came as a student to Asbury College in 1962 from a well-
known missionary family in Korea.[10] He had learned how to play the guitar
on the mission field, since it is a portable way to make music and there
wasn't much else for him to do for entertainment. As a result, he was one of
the few people on the campus who could play the guitar, and this novelty
led to groups gathering in the dorms around him and even to informal
singing on Saturday nights in the semi-circle in front of the administration
building on Lexington Avenue. They would sing popular folk songs such
as, "If I had a Hammer," "Michael Row Your Boat Ashore," and "Where
Have All the Flowers Gone," along with popular works by Pete Seeger and
Woody Guthrie. As these sing-alongs became more popular with students
(sometimes even gathering as many as 300 people), Ed was called in to see
President Z.T. Johnson. The Asbury College president felt that Ed was "out
of sympathy with the school" and even told him, "You can't do God's work
with the devil's music." Johnson encouraged Ed to transfer out of Asbury
College, but his mother intervened to prevent that from happening. Ed
continued with his music, even using the Methodist Church in Wilmore to
record music with Rev. David Seamands' permission (he was a friend of Ed's
father, Dr. Ed Kilbourne, former president of Seoul Theological Seminary
and an OMS missionary/leader). Ed's first album, *I Know Where I'm Going*,
was recorded at the Arthur Smith Studios in Charlotte, North Carolina in
1964, while still a student. By the time he graduated from Asbury College,
he was able to hold a small concert in Hughes Auditorium. He went on
to Asbury Theological Seminary, where he took all of Dr. Gilbert James'
classes on the role of the Church in society that he could take. While he
graduated from the Seminary in 1969, a year before Ichthus, most of the
early leaders remember Ed coming back to perform at the first Ichthus. Ed
also recounts leading others at the college in practicing folk music in an
informal group called "The Villagers," who helped him work on developing

the use of a sound system by sneaking onto the Wilmore campgrounds when it was not in use and setting up mock performances on the stage. Ed Kilbourne notes that Asbury had created a famous "bubble" of holiness isolation by keeping out other influences, such as intercollegiate sports, but that it was becoming "harder and harder to hold off the world." He also commented that, "it was the music that broke the bubble." Ed Kilbourne set the stage for the introduction of Ichthus as a formal organization.

It would be easy to dismiss Ed Kilbourne as a typical youthful rebel going against the religious authorities in power in Wilmore, but that would be too simplistic. Influenced by the mission field and yet also influenced by the events of the culture around him, Ed was (and still is) a gifted musician with a progressive theological point of view. Even in the 1960s he was creatively "tweaking" popular folk songs to give them a spiritual bent. A good example is his reworking of Petula Clark's 1965 hit, "My Love," which he recorded as "His Love."

"My Love"
Petula Clark
(Written by Tony Hatch)
1965

My love is warmer than the warmest sunshine,
Softer than a sigh.
My love is deeper than the deepest ocean,
Wider than the sky.
My love is brighter than the brightest star that shines
        every night above,
And there is nothing in this world that can ever change
        my love.

Something happened to my heart the day that I met you.
Something that I never felt before.
You are always in my mind, no matter what I do,
And everyday it seems that I want you more.

(Chorus)

Once I thought that love was meant for anyone else but me.
Once I thought you'd never come my way.
Now it only goes to show how wrong we all can be,
For now I have to tell you every day.

(Chorus)

"His Love"
Ed Kilbourne
(Lyrics modified by Ed Kilbourne)
1965

His love is warmer than the warmest sunshine,
Softer than a sigh.
His love is deeper than the deepest ocean,
Wider than the sky.
His love is brighter than the brightest star that shines
       every night above,
And there is nothing in this world that can ever change
       His love.

Something happened to my heart the day that You walked in.
Something that I never felt before.
And that something is that He has buried all my sins,
And everyday it seems I love Him more.

(Chorus)

Once I thought that this love was meant for anyone else but me.
Once I thought that no one knew the way.
Now it only goes to show how wrong we all can be,
'Cause now I have to tell it every day.

(Chorus)

This type of inventive contextualization, along with his willingness to share his knowledge with others at Asbury College and Asbury Theological Seminary about folk music, sound systems, and even how to play the guitar, was not just foundational- it was crucial to making Ichthus a real possibility, even though Ed was not directly connected to the organizing of Ichthus. It changed the atmosphere in Wilmore just enough to break the "bubble" of isolation and make dramatic change possible. The fact that almost all of the early founders of Ichthus pointed to Ed Kilbourne as an important influence only highlights the significance of how one person can influence and change entire institutions.

The poster and advertising for the very first Ichthus music festival in Wilmore, Kentucky. Held May 9-10, 1970.
(Image courtesy of Asbury Theological Seminary Archives and Special Collections.)

The story of Ichthus as an actual festival begins in the cafeteria of Asbury Theological Seminary one day in mid-March of 1970.[11] A group on campus called the Christian Service Brotherhood was holding an executive meeting with their faculty advisor, Dr. Bob Lyon over breakfast. The Christian Service Brotherhood consisted of a very small minority of the student population who had a genuine concern for social issues, such a racism, the Vietnam War, and poverty. One of them, John Park, had been involved with Dr. Gilbert James' project of taking students to New York City in 1969 to work in ministry in urban areas and become more aware of urban social problems and needs. While Dr. James was not directly involved with Ichthus, his teaching both prior to and after the founding of Ichthus influenced a number of students who would be involved. The Christian Service Brotherhood was really very much on the fringe of the student body at this time. This meeting in the cafeteria included Dave Lewis, the chairman of the Brotherhood, John Park, Peter Emmett, Charlie Paxton, and Larry Minner. While Wilmore was very disconnected from events in the wider culture, reports of Woodstock definitely had disturbed the local community. John Park remembers very clearly when Dr. Lyon said, "You know, there ought to be a Christian alternative to Woodstock- a place for young people to raise the name of Jesus!" Right there at the table, the plan was worked out. John Park even suggested a name for the event. During the summer of 1969 when he had been with Dr. James in Central Harlem, he and a friend had gone into a small shop and bought a fish cross. For him, the cross stood for the original use of the fish symbol in early Christianity as "an announcement, or declaration" of our faith in Christ (the Greek letters being an acronym for "Jesus Christ, Son of God, Savior"). The group accepted the idea and the name Ichthus was attached to the new musical event. Dr. Lyon liked to ask probing questions among his students and stimulated ideas about faith and society in his role as a professor, and as the faculty advisor of the Christian Service Brotherhood he led and supported their work, although indirect support also came from Dr. Gilbert James and Dr. Kenneth Kinghorn, who were all relatively new faculty at the time, coming in 1965-1966.

With only six weeks left to hold the event, and with three of the group planning to graduate that spring, the plans for the event were made quickly and on the spur of the moment. There was no real budget, perhaps $300 (and $100 of that was a gift from Dr. James, and the rest appears to have come from Dr. Lyon and Dr. Kinghorn), but in short order John Park took over the advertising side of things, designing the first poster, printing it off on *The Herald* printing press on campus on the cheapest brown paper stock. Since they didn't know how to publicize the event so quickly, they sent out copies of this advertisement to all the colleges in driving distance of Wilmore, sometimes just addressing them to the student body president, or sending them to friends they knew on the campuses. They had been particularly careful in designing the information to limit the term "rock" and to focus on acoustic folk music of the time avoiding the negative connotations of the psychedelic music of the late 1960s. Dr. Lyon helped arrange the use of the Wilmore campground and provided the leadership while the Christian Service Brotherhood divided much of the work among themselves.

Musicians were almost all local talent, pretty much anyone who could play an instrument and perform. The Christian Service Brotherhood used their contacts to pull together the musical acts. While Ed Kilbourne had graduated, his brother Kent and his younger cousins Ron and Bill Moore had followed in his footsteps and some of them performed at the first Ichthus along with Ed. Bill Moore had not only learned from his cousin, but from 1967-1968 he had traveled to Europe and Asia with an Asbury College group called the New World Singers with Youth for Christ International. As with Ed Kilbourne, this College group sang a mix of secular and religious music in a folk style "sharing their faith through music." They had even produced an album called *Who Will Answer?* with one side containing secular music and the other side sacred. Ron and Bill Moore had also put out their own album in 1969, entitled *Lo and Behold* (it is interesting to note that Ed Kilbourne's influence was so strong that Ron Moore wrote a song "Eddie Was a Pioneer" in honor of their cousin). With their experience and connections, it was possible to pull the music for the first Ichthus together. As John Park relates with a chuckle, the Christian Service Brotherhood had three goals: to see if they could do this, to see how many people would come, and to try not to be run out of town! The first poster and advertisement for the festival reads in part,

> Ours is a musically oriented society. Ichthus 70 moves into that realm with power. Ichthus 70 is a weekend of contemporary expression of the Christian faith through music. Ichthus 70 provides togetherness for hundreds of Christians from colleges across the nation… Ichthus 70 brings you folk and folk rock groups from many schools and areas. Ichthus 70 presents the best in entertainment

with a message. Ichthus 70 offers you two days of music for less than the price of one album. Ichthus 70 is a demonstration of the society of the committed.

The tickets cost $2.50 if you preregistered ($4.50 with housing) and $4.00 at the gate. (By 2010, full event tickets were $99.00 and single day tickets were $47.00 at the gate.) The performers in 1970 included: The Awakening, New World, Rick Bonfin, and Wind Song, while Dr. Bob Lyon was the main teacher.

There definitely was concern on campus and in the town of Wilmore, with even a secret meeting held by business owners worried about the possibility of drugs, communists, and the hippie counterculture coming to Wilmore, but the Christian Service Brotherhood did not find out about this until long after the fact (John Park only learned of this in the 1990s). Also, the Christian Service Brotherhood was not exactly unaware of such different positions on social issues. The shootings at Kent State on May 4, 1970 of four students at an anti-war rally in Ohio a week before the Ichthus festival, led the Christian Service Brotherhood to put up a small table on campus covered with a black cloth, with a sign reading simply "Kent State" and displaying a cross for each of those killed. The opposition was so fierce, they were forced to remove the display by the middle of the day. Nevertheless, the group went forward with their plans, painting a simple banner on painter's canvas and hanging it in the tabernacle on the Wilmore campground. Students from Asbury Theological Seminary, especially the Christian Service Brotherhood, worked that festival and eventually many volunteers would follow, most coming from Asbury College and Asbury Theological Seminary as the festival became more accepted. From those picking up trash and providing stage security to those serving in prayer tents and working concession stands, there were many roles to be filled over the years.

The idea that music is a key part of identity formation among young people is part of what made Ichthus a successful vehicle for communicating the gospel from 1970 to 2012.
(Image courtesy of Asbury Theological Seminary Archives and Special Collections.)

On May 9-10, 1970, the first Ichthus music festival was held at the Wilmore campground in Wilmore, Kentucky. The Wilmore campground was a site for traditional Holiness camp meetings, which continued to be held at the site until 2015 after 125 years of service (currently it is the home of Adventure Serve Ministries). At first there seemed to be little problem with using the campground, since no one knew what Ichthus really was about. Over the next few years increased concern did arise due to the "loud music and long hair" of the counterculture, according to Dr. Seamands, but several voices of older leaders including J. C. McPheeters and Rev. David Seamands, who were on the Wilmore campground board, supported the festival. E. A. Seamands (known as "Tata"), a veteran missionary from India, would attend Ichthus and tell his grandson, "This is not my kind of music, but if it's reaching these kids, why not?" Dr. Bill Moore recalls seeing "Tata" Seamands dancing alongside the stage at one of the early festivals. Steve Moore, the program director from 1973-1976 even remembers "Tata" Seamands speaking from the stage about his time in India. Gradually Ichthus would win over those most concerned with the festival as it brought economic benefits to local merchants, encouraged recruitment for Asbury College, and provided a stable rent income for the Wilmore campground.

John Park also relates how the very first Ichthus drew about 300 to 350 people. Because there was not much contemporary Christian music written at this time, and they did not want to have a simple hymn sing or focus on Southern Gospel music, many of the performers played and sang secular folk music on the first night of the festival. The group had planned a worship service for Sunday morning to help emphasize the Christian nature of the event. One event especially remained strong in John Park's memory. A young lady playing an acoustic guitar and singing in the style of Joan Baez had performed on Saturday night and someone had criticized her for not playing enough "Jesus music," so she asked to sing again on Sunday and performed a beautiful folk version of the hymn "I'd Rather Have Jesus." Park notes that the memory still remains of this young lady singing as one of his most powerful moments of the festival,

> I'd rather have Jesus than silver or gold.
> I'd rather be his than have riches untold.
> I'd rather have Jesus than houses or land.
> Yes, I'd rather be led by his nail pierced hands,
> Than to be the king of a vast domain and be held by sin's dread sway.
> I'd rather have Jesus than anything this world affords today.[12]

Larry Minner, one of the original founders, recalls how some funds were used to buy bread and cold cuts and make sandwiches to feed the crowd. He even laughs as he notes that some of the musicians also helped make egg salad and cold cut sandwiches to pass out to the hungry attendees. Minner notes, "We weren't trying to be different, just have fun with our friends!" Dr. Bill Moore remembers how Seminary wives were involved in preparing food and how his wife had to make ten pounds of potato salad for the event!

This first Ichthus was meant to be a one-time event- a counterprotest to Woodstock. The Christian Service Brotherhood was first and foremost focused on responding to Woodstock, and while Ed Kilbourne and the Asbury Revival of 1970 probably both paved the way for Ichthus in terms of the overall environment in Wilmore, neither was a part of their conscious decision in organizing the event. As the Christian Service Brotherhood gathered at Dr. Lyon's house for a cookout to celebrate the success of their endeavor, Dr. Lyon had hung their canvas banner up at his house. The group was excited about the turnout and how well everything had gone, when someone said, "Why don't we do this again next year?" Until this time no one had really considered this possibility, but at that moment the idea of an annual music festival was born. Minner also added that he thought there was some additional money left over from the success of the first festival and so they thought to spend that the next year. John Park wasn't even sure they broke even.

Dr. Jack Harnish,[13] who was the program chair for 1971 and the general Ichthus chair for 1972 noted that the early years of Ichthus were a bit "haphazard," but soon became organized. The festivals of 1970 and 1971 were rather small in number (with attendance in the 100s to maybe 1,000) and took place in the tabernacle on the Wilmore campground as attendees were housed in the campground dormitories. Musicians were primarily chosen locally or based on "what we could afford" since there was no outside funding except from ticket sales. While the Seminary student body was generally supportive, there was still a lot of concern in the community. Members of the Wilmore campground's board were worried about potential damage to the trees or buildings, local people roped off their lawns to keep people from walking on the grass, and even Asbury College would not extend their curfew to allow students to attend. At the time, the major concerns at Asbury College were "the length of the men's hair and the women's skirts," while at Asbury Theological Seminary there was only a small minority of the student population that protested the Vietnam War and challenged assumptions on campus. Primarily the entire Ichthus event was student led and organized with limited faculty support and encouragement, although Dr. Lyon remains as the primary person behind the idea and was on the board of directors throughout the 1970s.

Part of the poster and advertising for the third Ichthus music festival in Wilmore, Kentucky. Held April 28-29, 1972.
(Image courtesy of Asbury Theological Seminary Archives and Special Collections.)

By the third year in 1972, registrations began to come in and the fledgling festival organizers gave up on the idea of housing the growing numbers, turning to tents and camping instead. Dr. Jim Garlow[14] was the program director for 1972 and he led the idea for the festival to be moved out of the tabernacle into the field behind the Wilmore campground, where a flatbed trailer served as a stage for around 1,200 to 1,400 attendees (Dr. Seamands estimates closer to 2,500). Dr. Harnish suggests that this growth could be traced to Asbury Seminary graduates who brought their youth groups to the festival after graduating. He did the same, bringing his youth groups from the hills of Pennsylvania for a number of years afterward, where Ichthus often became a spiritual highpoint for many of the youth. Dr. Garlow agrees with this assessment calling it a "built-in success factor," as increasing numbers of Seminary graduates returned with youth for an informal home-coming each summer. Ed Kilbourne noted that even Asbury College had to embrace Ichthus, as the festival became "an incredible tool" for publicity, drawing in students for the College who had attended Ichthus as young teens. Such was the influence of the emerging music festival that it helped put Asbury College on the map.

Dr. Jim Garlow, who had some experience in performing with his mother and brother in Kansas before coming to Asbury Theological Seminary, remembers visiting the work of George Dooms and his youth ministry in Evanston, Indiana (which has held an inside concert event called Faith Festival since 1970) to help use his experience with Youth for Christ to find music groups for Ichthus. Dr. Garlow also managed to secure funds from an older businessman in the community to fund a film crew to film some of the 1972 Ichthus concert. This film, titled "One Way, Jesus Way" was about 25 minutes and was sent out to local colleges and churches to promote Ichthus. Dr. Garlow remembers meeting with Seminary President Frank B. Stanger along with Jim Harnish (Dr. Harnish's twin brother) to negotiate some of the tensions and concerns over Ichthus' growing popularity. It was the elderly "Tata" Seamands who came to the festival's defense, stating that it was similar to things done in India on the mission field and was an important missional event. So, as a special honor, Dr. Garlow recalls that they made sure to film "Tata" Seamands standing near the stage clapping along with the music for the final film. Dr. Garlow returned to Ichthus as the Master of Ceremonies for 1973 and 1974. Dr. Garlow also relates the story of how his brother had died in an airplane crash in April of 1974, and then a month later he needed to stand on stage and speak to the crowds throughout Ichthus. He tells how he made it through the entire festival until the very end, when Andraé Crouch and the Disciples ended their performance with "It Won't Be Long." Through his tears, Dr. Garlow told the crowd about the death of his brother and how it had affected him, and Andraé Crouch right then and there, sat down and wrote a song about Jesus coming back for us. The entire event was a powerful moment in his life and also impacted many of those in attendance who heard the testimony.

In 1973 Rev. Travis Hutchison was the General Chair of Ichthus, and with a background in business and experience from working his family's ranch in the Dakotas, he brought more organization to the Ichthus experience. Since he was also eight years older than most of the others and had helped with publicity in an informal way in 1972, he understood some of the unique challenges of the festival. He created multiple teams to oversee different parts of the festival including people in charge of tickets, traffic, the tent city, and a former military member to put in charge of security. While he attended a couple of meetings with Seminary President Frank B. Stanger to convince him that they were not "hippies from Mars," he had good success from having participated earlier in one of Stanger's voluntary groups on healing prayer at the Seminary. He recalls the Wilmore campmeeting board as a bigger challenge. There were concerns about feeding the crowds (there ended up being about 4,800 people present based on ticket sales that year), which he handled by hiring a food service company to set up long tables with sandwiches and McDonalds for Sunday lunch. Another concern he remembered had to do with possible sexual promiscuity on the grounds. Travis laughs when he remembers that John Fitch (of Fitch's IGA) stood up on their behalf and told the board about the former soldier who would be leading security and ended saying, "there won't be any more babies conceived here than in the campmeeting days!" One of Travis' major concerns was to leave enough funds to help support the following year, and because of his work Ichthus in 1973 was able to bring in more well-known groups.

Steve Moore had been a high school senior in 1971 and a part of Jim Garlow's youth group. He was so impressed by the experience he had as a youth at Ichthus that he chose to attend Asbury College as a result. While a college student, Steve became the program director of Ichthus from 1973 to 1976. He notes that his approach to choosing the musicians was "to get the best people you can and turn them loose." Steve worked with Andraé Crouch and the Disciples as well as the Archers, and Earthen Vessel. He remembers when bad weather was threatening to break up the performance early in either 1973 or 1974 that Andraé Crouch turned around on the piano stool while Steve was discussing what to do with Jim Garlow and remarked, "Well, they're going to get wet anyway!" He also reminisced about how Andraé Crouch was following a group singing songs from *Jesus Christ Superstar*, when he addressed the audience with, "Well folks, I gotta tell you, Jesus is more than a superstar to ole' Andraé!" While sometimes criticized for spending too much money, Steve Moore was responsible for setting a pattern of inviting headliners who could help draw a crowd. Yet, it wasn't just about popularity. Steve also remembers in 1976 how the Holy Spirit moved at the invitation given by Bill Glass, the speaker at the time, when the counselors were overwhelmed by the young people who responded. They were "no longer one-on-one but more like one-on-five or six!"

Andraé Crouch, one of the more memorable musicians performing at Ichthus in the early 1970s.
(Image courtesy of Asbury Theological Seminary Archives and Special Collections.)

In reflecting on his involvement with Ichthus, Dr. Harnish noted that his biggest takeaway was "learning as a pastor to think creatively. What if we tried this? - Not being afraid to take a risk." Dr. Garlow noted that it was "impossible to calculate the spiritual impact" of Ichthus. Dr. Bill Moore defined it as a "pivotal spiritual experience" for the young people who attended. Steve Moore agrees that his time with Ichthus was spiritually meaningful and he remembers the musicians as "phenomenal people." Travis Hutchison reflects back on the impact of Ichthus by relating the story of a Jack Daniels whiskey bottle found during the cleanup, which he still treasures as one of his prized possessions. Inside the bottle was a note indicating that the young people who brought the bottle had come to drink and party, but had found the Holy Spirit instead and no longer needed the whiskey they brought. By 1996 the event recorded 14,000 people in attendance and almost 1,000 people who committed their lives to Christ that year alone. There were around 20,000 people present in 2004 before the festival moved to a later date in the year.

Reflecting on how Ichthus was started, it is hard to pin down any one factor. Rather it was a perfect symphony of events led by the Holy Spirit. Ichthus would never have happened without the musical skill, leadership, and cultural challenge brought by Ed Kilbourne to Wilmore. It never would have happened without the earnest concern of Seminary students for reaching out to their generation in a culturally relevant way despite opposition. It never would have happened without the leadership, financial support, and encouragement of young faculty members like Dr. Robert Lyon, Dr. Gilbert James, and Dr. Kenneth Kinghorn at Asbury Theological Seminary. It never would have happened without the support of local businessmen like John Fitch. It never would have happened without key religious leaders such as "Tata" Seamands, David Seamands, and even Frank Stanger being willing to have a vision for something different. And it never would have happened without the Holy Spirit paving the way with both the Asbury Revival and a genuine concern for social needs.

Music, of course, remained the primary draw that brought young people to the Ichthus festival. A wide range of artists were typically chosen, from the more popular contemporary acts to more *avant guarde* and cutting-edge musicians. While a general trend can be seen in moving from folk music styles and gospel music to contemporary Christian rock to Christian rap, punk, grunge, and even Goth and heavy metal, the entire range of Christian music was represented. Steve Moore laughs as he notes, "We just called it Jesus music!" While Ed Kilbourne remains critical of contemporary Christian music for creating a new "bubble" that isolates Christians from the serious social and political concerns of the outside world, which were often addressed by the folk music genre, Ichthus festivals would headline the music of many well-known groups including:

Crimson Bridge (1972)
Andraé Crouch (1973, 1974, 1975, 1976, 1995)
The Imperials (1976, 1988, 1990, 1991)
Ken Medema (1977)
Honeytree (1978)
Andrus, Blackwood, and Company (1978, 1979, 1980, 1984)
Jessy Dixon (1980, 1981)
Joe English Band (1982, 1983)
Petra (1983, 1991, 1996)
Benny Hester (1983)
Phil Keaggy (1984, 1989, 1996)
Larry Norman (1984, 1985, 1993)
Michael Card (1984, 1988)
Altar Boys (1985, 1987, 1988, 1990, 1991, 1993)
Crumbächer (1986)
White Heart (1986, 1988, 1990, 1993, 1994, 1996)
Servant (1986, 1988)
Steven Curtis Chapman (1988, 1989, 1992, 1995)
David and the Giants (1988)
Rich Mullins (1990, 1996)
DC Talk (1990, 1992, 1994)
Newsboys (1990, 1991, 1995, 1997, 1999, 2001, 2004, 2007, 2010)
Michael Peace (1990)
The Choir (1992, 1993, 1996)
Hoi Polloi (1993, 1995, 1996)
Michael W. Smith (1994)
Audio Adrenaline (1994, 1995)
Out of Eden (1996)
MXPX (1996, 2008)
Jars of Clay (1997, 2000, 2007)
Caedmon's Call (1997)

CeCe Winans (1997)
Rebecca St. James (1997)
Third Day (1997, 2004, 2007)
Skillet (1998, 1999, 2000, 2005, 2008, 2009, 2011)
Delirious? (2001, 2003, 2006)
TobyMac (2006, 2010, 2012)
Casting Crowns (2006, 2008)
David Crowder Band (2006, 2007, 2008)
Family Force 5 (2007, 2008)
Superchick (2010, 2011)
Switchfoot (2012)

In 1981 Jessy Dixon headlined the Ichthus Music Festival.
(Image courtesy of Asbury Theological Seminary Archives and Special Collections.)

However, Ichthus organizers also sought to bring in Christian teachers to preach, teach, and evangelize during the course of the festival. Teachers would include: Don Wilkerson (1973), Tom Skinner (1974, 1979), Bill Glass (1976), Josh McDowell (1980, 1989), Steve Camp (1981, 1984), Tony Campolo (1983), Coach Floyd Eby (1986) along with many names of Asbury College and Asbury Theological Seminary professors. Sometime about 1973 when Dr. Lyon went on sabbatical, Dr. John Oswalt was asked to be the faculty representative on the committee. Somewhere about this same time, organizers noticed there were empty spots in the program as the musical groups were changing and setting up. As Dr. Oswalt[15] remembers, "so they asked me if I could do some 3-6 minute talks to fill those spots. Daunting to think of speaking to thousands of milling teenagers! But I said yes, and did four or five of these each year for three years. I always wondered if I was connecting with anyone in all the hubbub. However, there have been a few occasions when someone has reminded me of something I said during one of those times, so apparently there was some connection." Dr. Oswalt also noted that there was a definite concern that entertainment might become the driving force of the festival and so sessions were created to address particular topics, often each having its own tent and being presented a number of times during the festival with seminary students as teachers. Steve Moore definitely recalls Dr. Oswalt and his "incredibly powerful teaching vignettes" as well as his strong support for Ichthus as important moments of his own time with Ichthus.

Dr. John Oswalt of Asbury Theological Seminary teaching from the stage at the Ichthus Music Festival in the 1970's during one of his sessions between performances.
(Image courtesy of Asbury Theological Seminary Archives and Special Collections.)

One of the earlier performers who made a serious impact was Andraé Crouch. While he performed at least five times at Ichthus, primarily in the 1970s, his influence was widespread. Dr. Steve Seamands, who was an associate pastor at a United Methodist Church in New Jersey in 1974, brought his youth group to Ichthus. As he relates,

> Saturday night, during the last few hours of the festival something happened that I'll never (forget). Andraé Crouch and the Disciples were singing and leading the crowd of about 5,000 in worship. Our youth were sitting together as a group on the hillside.
> All of a sudden, many of our youth were crying and hugging each other. I looked at the people sitting around our youth group and they seemed to be unaffected. They were just listening to the music.
> I was somewhat skeptical at first. "Is this just teenage emotionalism brought on by several days of sleep deprivation?" I wondered. I suspect some of that was a part of it, but it didn't take me long to realize that something profoundly real had happened to our group.

It was as if the Holy Spirit, the very presence of God had fallen upon our youth group.

As a result, I took a revival back to New Jersey with me. On the trip back, the youth would spontaneously break into singing on the bus. I especially remember them singing the words from one of Andraé Crouch's songs: "Jesus is the answer to the world today. Above him there's no other. Jesus is the way!"

The following Sunday evening when the youth shared what had happened to them at Ichthus, the presence and power of God was there. Youth who hadn't been able to go to Ichthus were deeply touched. For the next six months incredible things happened in the life of the church. Lives were transformed. Many young adults came to know Christ. What had happened at Ichthus had a leavening effect on the whole church.

Dr. Seamands also notes that several of these youth felt called into ministry and a number continued on to Christian colleges including Asbury College and Asbury Theological Seminary.

Andraé Crouch and the Disciples, often referred to as the "father of modern gospel music," performing at Ichthus in the early 1970s.
(Image courtesy of Asbury Theological Seminary Archives and Special Collections.)

However, the youth in Dr. Seamands' youth group were not isolated in this experience. Tanya Goodman Sykes (of the Happy Goodman Family, a well-known Southern Gospel group) wrote at Andraé Crouch's passing in 2015,

> I can still remember how the rain felt on my skin that day. I was 15 years old, and my friends and I had driven to Wilmore, Kentucky, to attend the Ichthus Festival at Asbury College. We were beyond thrilled because Andraé Crouch and the Disciples were headlining that year. There was a steady drizzle the entire drive up, and just before Andraé took the stage, it gave way to heavy rain, but it didn't dampen my enthusiasm. There was a palpable sense of excitement in the air that day as an entire hillside of dripping wet, mostly teenagers sang along- "Jesus is the answer for the world today..." Truly, I have never experienced anything quite like it before or since. And I certainly have never stood in the pouring rain to hear anyone else.[16]

Travis Hutchison recalls one Saturday evening when Andraé Crouch was preforming and Travis was standing on the stage looking out over the crowd and the "raptured" look on their faces as the Spirit was really working. Suddenly he noticed in different parts of the crowd several groups of 7-15 people who seemed to fall down suddenly to the ground, and into his mind came the thought, "this is the dancing hand of God" and he really understood that God could do anything with his life. Dr. Jack Harnish, also remembered the passing of Andraé Crouch in 2015 writing,

> The highlight of the weekend was a performance by Andraé Crouch and the Disciples. If the whole notion of a folk-rock festival was a bit shocking for the town of Wilmore, the fact that the headliner was an African American was even more controversial. But once he took the stage, no one could question his spirit and his gift... I remember him closing the festival that weekend with, "It won't be long, soon we'll be leavin' here; it won't be long, we'll be goin' home."[17]

By 1998, the Wilmore campground was becoming too small of a venue for this growing musical event, so a 111-acre site, known at the Ichthus Farm (now called Servant Heart Farm) was purchased and became the site of the festival from 1999 till 2012. The space allowed for more stages, bigger venues, and more room for campers. After the move to the new location, the festival had six stages including: The Main Stage, The Deep End, The Edge, two separate Indie Stages, and The Galleria Stage. This reflects both the growth of the festival, but also the diversity that had occurred in contemporary Christian music.

Camping at Ichthus and dealing with the unpredictable weather was part of the Ichthus experience.
(Image courtesy of Asbury Theological Seminary Archives and Special Collections.)

Ichthus was also well known for the amount of rain it seemed to attract. Originally held in early May or late April, (which allowed the festival to make use of a large number of volunteers from Asbury College and Asbury Theological Seminary before the summer break in classes) by 2006 the organizers decided to move the festival to mid-June. Part of this move was due to the weather in 2005. Choosing the rather unfortunate theme of "Let it Rain," did nothing to help matters. As one reviewer noted on the Friday afternoon,

Then, the theme of Ichthus 2005, "Let it Rain," manifested itself. Only it did not just rain, it poured. A tornado warning forced campers to evacuate and take shelter in their vehicles. Cassie and I struggled against the wind and the rain to take down our tent. After the storm blew over, I was very dismayed to hear the rest of the concerts for the evening had been canceled... Saturday, the weather got even stranger. The gravel on the roads helped make them less muddy than last year, but there was still quite a bit of mud. It was also unusually cold... We had hoped to see Day of Fire during the afternoon, but we could not stand the cold. As we were leaving the Extol concert, the unthinkable occurred. It began to snow. I have seen wild weather at Ichthus over the years, but I never expected to see snow.[18]

In 2004, the rain was so bad it shut down the road system on the Ichthus Farm, and as a result paved and gravel roads were added. Another writer noted, "The problem with rain started in 1983, a year that became known as the 'rain year' or 'Mudthus.' However, it rained even harder at the 2002 festival. Last year (2005) set the record for the coldest temperatures."[19]

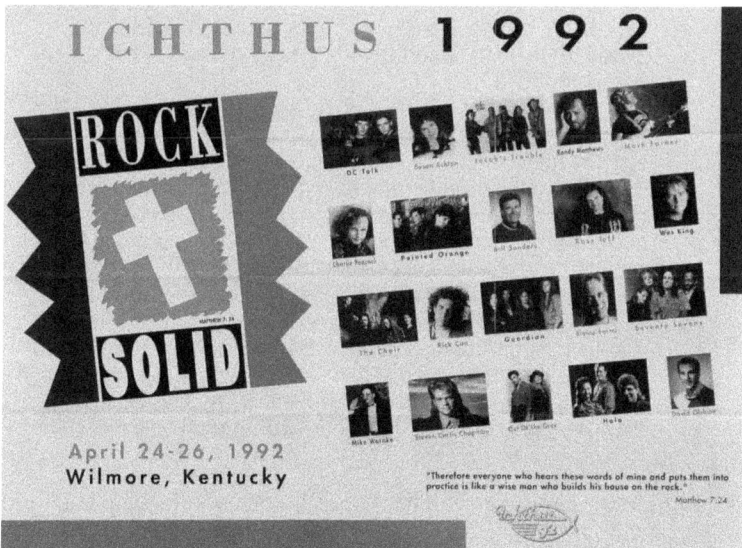

In 1992 DC Talk and Steven Curtis Chapman both performed at the festival with the theme "Rock Solid" demonstrating some of the rapid diversification of contemporary Christian music that was developing.
(Image courtesy of Asbury Theological Seminary Archives and Special Collections.)

Christopher Jackson, a Lutheran pastor from Lexington, attended the 2007, 2008, and 2009 festivals with his youth group. He notes that Ichthus in 2009 attracted around 14,000 people and the festival reported 581 first-time commitments to Christ. He describes the atmosphere and the concert itself,

> The concert area is a huge, fenced in compound on a hill above the campground. Inside the gate you pass two side stages that host bands outside the mainstream of Contemporary Christian Music, bands that either haven't "made it" yet or offer musical styles that are less popular than those on the main stage. Most offer either heavy metal or punk rock. Some bands are more artsy- one stage even featured two violinists- and some defy categorization, like the Psalters, a group of bohemian acoustic musicians who mix such elements as Eastern European melodies, African drumbeats, and the Sanctus into their music.
>
> The side stages also host breakout sessions, when concerts and other activities cease so that festival-goers can hear presenters. In recent years these have included Shaine Claiborne, Matthew Sleeth, M.D., Dr. Devin Brown of Asbury Seminary [*actually Asbury University not Seminary*], and XXX-church, a ministry aimed at preventing and freeing people from the use of pornography.
>
> A little farther in are prayer tents, a Compassion International booth where you can sponsor a needy child, and the merchandise tent with an energy and feel all its own due to the eclectic mix of vendors. Every band sets up a table where they meet fans and hawk CDs, posters and T-shirts. Some vendors sell "Jesus Junk"- buttons, bobble-heads of biblical characters, and apparel. T-shirts reading "It's a relationship, not a religion" are popular...
>
> Past the merchandise tents you finally encounter the main stage, a massive steel and cement structure, with huge speakers and video screens. This is where popular, commercially successful groups play, artists like David Crowder, Skillet, Toby Mac, Grits, and Family Force 5.[20]

While Jackson clearly admired many aspects of the festival, as a traditional Lutheran pastor he also was a bit skeptical about the clothing, tattoos, Mosh pits, and loud music!

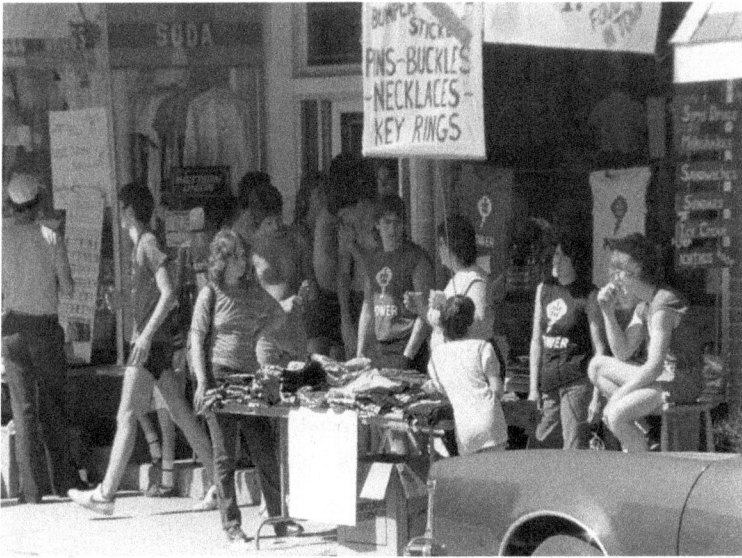

Vendors often sold T-shirts and other faith-related items during the Ichthus festival, like this vendor in front of Sims Drugstore on Main Street Wilmore. (Image courtesy of Asbury Theological Seminary Archives and Special Collections.)

No matter what people thought of the festival itself, Ichthus had a major impact on young people's lives. And some of those lives continue to have an impact. In an article in *Charisma* magazine Leslie Montgomery tells the story of how United States Vice President Mike Pence found Christ. A key part is detailed when she writes,

> A few weeks later, (Mike) Stevens (a fraternity brother from college) invited Pence to attend the annual Ichthus Christian music festival in Wilmore, Kentucky. It was there that Pence's life was transformed.
> "I heard lots of great singing, and I heard lots of wonderful preaching," Pence says, "On Saturday night [while] sitting in a light rain,… my heart really finally broke with a deep realization [that] what had happened on the cross, in some infinitesimal way, had happened for me. And I gave my life and made a personal decision to trust Jesus Christ as my Savior."[21]

The 1978 Ichthus festival at which Vice President Pence committed his life to Christ was held April 28-29, 1978, where much of the teaching was by

Bob Laurent, and the performers included: Honeytree, Andrus, Blackwood and Company, Good News Circle, Pat Terry Group, New Hope, and Selah. In an interview with Rev. Chip DeWitt, who served as the General Chair of the 1978 festival, he shared how as a newlywed senior at the Seminary he and his wife were asked to lead the 1978 festival. Many people advised him against this because of all the work involved and because he was just newly married, but they decided to take on the task. As Chip and his wife, Marge were preparing for the festival, it began raining and they felt concerned that the rain might be a problem, and so the couple walked around the grounds and prayed that God would not let the rain prevent the important work that needed to happen. Little did they know the future Vice President of the United States would be there. At the urging of people in his church, Rev. DeWitt shared the story in a letter with Vice President Pence, and they received not only a personal letter in response, but also a private meeting with the Vice President in Jacksonville, Florida. In the letter from Vice President Pence dated July 10, 2020, he wrote, "I thank God every day for that rainy night in Wilmore. Now I know who else to thank."

With the last Ichthus festival in 2012, it might be useful to think about why the festival ended. Mark Vermillion was called in as a consultant in 2008-2009 and then served as the CEO of Ichthus from 2010-2012.[22] He notes that there were a number of key factors that led to the end of the Ichthus festival. While attendance had dropped from its peak in 1999 and 2000, this was not really the deciding factor. The move of date from April/May to mid-June also had an impact. The later date conflicted with other music festivals and various summer events. As Vermillion notes there was very little going on in April in terms of youth activities like prom, graduation, or even major sports events, but while the move to June was great from a weather perspective, Ichthus suddenly found itself competing with summer camps and other activities. The change in date certainly impacted the number of volunteers Ichthus could count on from Asbury College (University) and Asbury Theological Seminary for working the festival, so that important connection was also minimized. The mortgage on the festival site was also a heavy burden, which Ichthus was not able to get out from under. Although as Vermillion points out, Ichthus was also committed to giving large amounts of money raised to help other ministries and still kept that focus even when they could have used the money for their own costs. In addition to the mortgage on the property, the costs of upkeep and liability continued to create a situation where the festival started each year needing to make a sizeable amount before it could even begin work to break even.

Yet beyond the unique challenges that Ichthus faced, there were other factors that played a larger role. Realities that were true not just for Ichthus, but for all other Christian music festivals and may help account for a decline in the entire genre. The Cornerstone Festival ended in 2012, TOMfest in 2009, HeavenFest in 2016, and the Agape Festival in 2013, so Ichthus was not alone in ending its ministry in this time period. Vermillion points out that changes in youth culture led to a decline in interest in camping or "roughing it" (especially among youth pastors) and an increased interest in luxury camp or hotel experiences. While Ichthus responded to this with single day passes that grouped artists from specific genres on the same day, Vermillion responds, "it was too little, too late." However, it is also interesting to note that the same type of trend was being noticed in secular music festivals as well. Large-scale traditional festivals were aimed at die-hard fans, but crowds, rising prices, the increasing age of those attending (along with an increased desire for comfort over camping and mud), and venue problems led to an increase in smaller, more niche-focused secular festivals during the same time period.[23]

Given the shift away from Christian music festivals in the early 2010s bigger possible factors are changes in the music industry and in music technology. If Steck and Howard were correct, part of the importance of contemporary Christian music festivals was the ability of various Christian musicians to connect with fans outside of occasional performances at churches and coffee houses, since other avenues were closed to them (such as bars and clubs). Music distribution changed drastically with the iTunes Music Store in 2003, Amazon Music in 2007, and Spotify in 2008 bringing the music world into a digital age (this legal use of digital music followed the earlier free exchange of music through Napster and other peer-to-peer networks). This led to an even greater diversification of music into specific niche markets while at the same time leading to a loss in profits for the music recording industry. It so happened that 2012 (the last year of Ichthus) was also the first year digital music sales outpaced physical sales.[24] The greater ease of accessing music by mobile devices and smartphones also changed the way fans interacted with music. Musicians increasingly connected to their fan base through social media and the Internet, and as this happened the importance of the concert experience, and especially the music festival experience became less essential for contemporary Christian music. Mark

Vermillion adds weight to this argument. He notes that digital sales of $0.99 singles through iTunes drastically reduced the sales of albums. This meant that recording artists needed to make up for lost revenue through increased touring schedules. The market became oversaturated and artists sought to charge more for preforming at festivals outside of their touring schedule. All of this led to greater costs at the same time that attendance was slipping. Vermillion also points out that there were very few big headliners in contemporary Christian music and so this led to hiring the same six or seven groups each year and this in turn affected creativity.

Vermillion recalls that he and others were becoming increasingly disappointed in how "'Christian' became a marketing label." He noticed how more "Christian" groups were being formed as a business approach, while genuine people of faith in other genres were excluded. He feels this same disillusionment about the contemporary Christian music industry was also growing among Millennials. Ichthus attempted to solve some of this concern with the Galleria stage, which tended to promote singer-songwriters (often acoustic or unplugged) who had publicly declared their faith, but were part of more secular genres of music. Millennials, like Ed Kilbourne and others involved in the folk music scene of the 1960s, felt that secular music could effectively convey spiritual truth without being specifically labeled as "Christian" and separated out from other musicians. In some ways, Christian music had come full circle at the Ichthus festival. As Mark Vermillion laments, "We couldn't be 'Christian' enough for some, but for others we were too 'Christian.'"

No matter what people may think of the music or the festival itself as a contextualized way to do evangelism, it cannot be denied that Ichthus definitely had an impact on many young people's lives.
(Image courtesy of Asbury Theological Seminary Archives and Special Collections.)

The truth is that album sales, tours, or music festivals no longer drive Christian music. The industry has changed along with the technology that drove the changes. In a 2015 article by James Rickman, Josh Caterer, a Christian musician and worship director is quoted as saying,

> Christian music is driven by a much more tightly controlled industry than secular music is. And it pertains to very specific revenue streams that don't exist in secular music because of CCLI—Christian Copyright Licensing International, which is basically the Christian version of ASCAP or BMI. CCLI keeps track of all the songs that are performed in churches—every church is supposed to pay an annual fee to CCLI. Then CCLI will pay royalties to the songwriters and publishers of that music. So what you have is a situation where, in secular music, it's becoming more difficult to make music because people aren't buying CDs the way they used to, and the music industry is freaking out, but in Christian music, there's this performance revenue stream that comes from churches performing worship songs every week and that is completely unaffected by album sales.

> I happen to know from talking to people in the industry
> that generally they don't care as much about trying to sell
> albums. Making an album is only a way to get people to
> perform these songs in their churches, because if a song
> takes on a life of its own in church world as being a
> popular worship song, that can become a huge revenue
> stream, even if they never sell any records. They could
> give the music away; they just want people to perform it
> in churches.[25]

This insight into the world of contemporary Christian music helps to better understand why contemporary Christian music no longer needs to depend on Christian music festivals to drive album sales among fans. With both revenue from digital music sales and with a special source of revenue through worship song licensing, there is no longer an industry-driven need for musicians to attend music festivals.

Christian music festivals do continue to occur, as is evidenced by the Christian Festival Association, founded in 2006, which currently lists 26 Christian music festivals as their members; although the fact that they also currently list 25 of 28 Christian music festivals as postponed due to the COVID-19 pandemic from 2020 to 2021 may signal some future warning signs.[26] Mark Vermillion made a thought-provoking point when he observed that even if Ichthus had made it to its 50th year in 2020, it would have likely been the last festival anyway due to the current pandemic (or most likely it would have been postponed and then closed due to revenue losses). When asked about the impact of Ichthus, Vermillion concluded the interview by relating a story. After Ichthus ended he was in Memphis at a hotel wearing an old Ichthus T-shirt when a man approached him and asked about his ties to Ichthus. Then the man told him that he had been in the 2012 Ichthus and that festival had radically transformed him from a life of drugs into a life of faith. Vermillion concludes that even when he was feeling down about the end of Ichthus, "God wanted to put an exclamation point on it and say, 'I was at work!'" Even in its closing days, God was still changing lives through Ichthus.

In the same way that Ichthus began with God's perfect timing in a symphony of events and people, Ichthus ended with the same complex mix of factors. Rising costs tied to the purchase of the farm as a festival venue, along with costs for liability and upkeep, hindered the growth of Ichthus at the same time that changes in the youth culture and the changing of the April/May date for the festival reduced the attendance and number of volunteers from Asbury University and Asbury Theological Seminary. But these factors alone are not sufficient to explain the end of the festival. Changes in music technology which spawned radical changes in the music industry all contributed to an environment which was no longer sustainable for a Christian music festival in Wilmore. What is clear is that God did not waste any time or talent. The last Ichthus festival was just as spiritually powerful as the first.

Despite the shift in the Christian music culture over time, it is important to recognize the contextualization of rock and roll, and the adaptation of the music festival setting, has been a major factor in the Christian culture in the United States from 1970 to the present. While the form itself may be in a decline from its peak, events like the Ichthus music festival demonstrated that evangelical Christianity could adapt to the complex youth culture of its time. Spiritually, Ichthus and the Christian music festivals that followed provided a context where young people could come together, drawn by a cultural love of relevant music, be affirmed in their Christian identity, and for many find the relationship with Christ that would grow, guide, and sustain them through adulthood. As with any ministry involved with cultural engagement, it may have been useful for only a moment of time, but for the people who encountered Christ in that moment, it became an eternity.

Special note: **Do you have a special memory of Ichthus? Was your life and walk with Christ changed as a result of the festival? Did you volunteer your time while a student? We would love to hear from you!** Please send us written accounts of your experiences or scans of photographs you may have of the festival. We are hoping to add to the collection of Ichthus materials for future researchers and want to preserve your stories of this incredible ministry. Send your stories or photos to: archives@asburyseminary.edu. We look forward to hearing from you!

The archives of the B.L. Fisher library are open to researchers and works to promote research in the history of Methodism and the Wesleyan-Holiness movement. Images, such as these, provide one vital way to bring history to life. Preservation of such material is often time consuming and costly, but are essential to helping fulfill Asbury Theological Seminary's mission. If you are interested in donating items of historic significance to the archives of the B.L. Fisher Library, or in donating funds to help purchase or process significant collections, please contact the archivist at archives@ asburyseminary.edu.

End Notes

[1] All images used courtesy of the Archives of the B.L Fisher Library of Asbury Theological Seminary who own all copyrights to these digital images, unless otherwise noted. Please contact them directly if interested in obtaining permission to reuse these images.

[2] See Greg Robinson, chapter one, "The Granddaddy of Them All: The Ichthus Festival" in *Christian Rock Festivals*, Rosen Publishing Corporation: New York, NY 2009:7-14.

[3] John M. Steck and Jay R. Howard, *Apostles of Rock: The Splintered World of Contemporary Christian Music*, University of Kentucky Press: Lexington, KY 2004: 5.

[4] Joshua Simon, "Hard Rockers, Holy Rollers." *Life*. Vol. 22 no. 8 (July) 1999: 80.

[5] Steck and Howard, *Apostles of Rock*, 29-30.

[6] Steck and Howard, *Apostles of Rock*, 56.

[7] Steck and Howard, *Apostles of Rock*, 59.

[8] Email correspondence with Dr. Steve Seamands, August 5, 2020.

[9] Gary Baker, *Ichthus Through the Years*. Ichthus Ministries, Inc.: Wilmore, KY 1997: 1. Published privately as a directory of past administrators and brief history of the Ichthus festival. Copy in the Archives and Special Collections of B.L. Fisher Library, Asbury Theological Seminary, Wilmore, KY.

[10] Special thanks to Ed Kilbourne for an in-depth phone interview about music and the context of Wilmore during the 1960s, August 11, 2020.

[11] Special thanks goes to Rev. John Park whose excellent memory and engaging stories provided much of the information in this section through a phone interview, August 5, 2020 (and a follow-up interview on September 3, 2020), as well as Rev. Larry Minner who provided additional and supporting information in a phone interview, August 6, 2020 and Dr. Bill Moore who also provided information about the music in a phone interview, August 14, 2020.

[12] Published in 1922, with words by Rhea F. Miller and music by George Beverly Shea, the lyrics and music copyright are held by The Rodheaver Co. (a division of Word Music, Inc.). The lyrics themselves are in the public domain, being written before 1923, but the use of these lyrics is

also in line with Fair Use for scholarship reasons as advocated by the best practices of the American Musicological Society. The same applies to the use of the publication of the lyrics for "My Love" by Tony Hatch earlier in the article.

[13] Much of my information in this section comes from an in-depth phone interview with Rev. Jack Harnish, August 4, 2020.

[14] Special thanks to Dr. Jim Garlow for a lengthy phone interview, August 11, 2020. Additional phone interviews with Travis Hutchison (August 14, 2020) and Steve Moore (August 26, 2020) were also invaluable sources of information for Ichthus from 1972-1976.

[15] Email correspondence with Dr. John Oswalt, July 31, 2020.

[16] "Remembering Andraé Crouch." April 1, 2015. *Homecoming Magazine* online. Available at: http://www.homecomingmagazine. com/article/remembering-andra-crouch/

[17] Jack Harnish, "'Soon and Very Soon'... He's Gone to Meet the King." *Monday Memo* blog. January 11, 2015. Available at: https://jackharnish.wordpress.com/2015/01/11/soon-and-very-soon-hes-gone-to-meet-the-king/

[18] Laura Nunnery, "Ichthus 2005 'Let it Rain'." May 5, 2005. Jesusfreakhideout.com. Available at: https://www.jesusfreakhideout.com/concerts/ichthus/2005/default.asp

[19] Cassi Haggard, "The Ichthus Experience." *The Times-Tribune*, Corbin, KY. June 14, 2006. Available at: https://www.thetimestribune.com/community/the-ichthus-experience/article_c6db4682-7a76-5203-bd25-3fa4fcb18422.html

[20] Christopher Jackson, "Rock Formation: What I Saw & Heard at the ICHTHUS Christian Music Festival." *Touchstone: A Journal of Mere Christianity*. Vol. 23 no. 5 (Sept./Oct.) 2010: 44-46.

[21] Leslie Montgomery, "The Faith of Mike Pence." *Charisma*. Vol. 44, no. 11 (June/July) 2019: 36. Leslie Montgomery is also the author of *The Faith of Mike Pence*, Whitaker House: New Kensington: PA 2019. Also special thanks to Rev. Chip DeWitt for an in depth telephone interview about his meeting with the Vice President on September 17, 2020, and also for sharing a copy of the personal letter the Vice President sent him on July 10, 2020.

[22] Special thanks to Mark Vermillion for a Zoom interview on August 27, 2020, which confirmed and emphasized the variety of causes that led to the end of the Ichthus music festival.

[23] Eventbrite blog. Career and Lifestyle, "The Rise and Fall of Mega-Music Festivals- And What Comes Next." March 7, 2019. Available at: https://www.eventbrite.com/blog/rise-fall-of-music-festivals-what-comes-next-ds00/

[24] Laurie Segall, "Digital Music Sales Top Physical Sales." CNN Money. January 5, 2012. Available at: https://money.cnn.com/2012/01/05/technology/digital_music_sales/index.htm

[25] James Rickman, "Inside the Sprawling World of Christian Music Festivals." *Paper Magazine*. March 16, 2015. Available at: https://www.papermag.com/inside-the-sprawling-world-of-christian-music-festivals-1427524567.html

[26] https://www.christianfestivalassociation.com/about-us. See also, Aisha Harris, "The Fragile Festival Economy." *The New York Times*. April 21, 2020. Available at: https://www.nytimes.com/2020/04/21/opinion/coronavirus-music-festivals-canceled.html for a more in depth view on how the coronavirus may impact secular festivals and the local economies they support. Similar dynamics are likewise true for Christian music festivals.

The Asbury Journal 75/2: 327-340
© 2020 Asbury Theological Seminary
DOI: 10.7252/Journal.02.2020F.09

Book Reviews

Between the Swastika and the Sickle: The Life, Disappearance, and Execution of Ernst Lohmeyer
James R. Edwards
Grand Rapids, MI: William B. Eerdmans
2019, 368 pp., hardcover, $30.00
ISBN: 978-0-8028-7618-8

Reviewed by Susangeline Patrick

In *Between the Swastika and the Sickle*, James Edwards narrates the remarkable and unique biography of Ernst Lohmeyer, a German New Testament scholar and theologian, who lived through the Nazi years and mysteriously disappeared during the Soviet Communist occupation in 1946, East Germany.

Edwards has offered an in-depth analysis of how the circle of intellectuals responded to Nazism differently. He has also provided extensive contexts, historical background, and theological insights in the life and works of Lohmeyer. Edwards compares and juxtaposes his own scholarship in the New Testament and his own life experiences as an American who has lived in Germany both prior to and post 1990, with Lohmeyer's life and experience. Assigned to investigate how Lohmeyer went missing, Edwards explored primary materials in difficult to access archives, conducted interviews and even made personal connections with Lohmeyer's family members, friends, and witnesses.

Edwards resolved the puzzle of Lohmeyer's disappearance. In the first two chapters, he introduces the reader to why he embarks on the quest of seeking the truth about Lohmeyer's execution. Lohmeyer was accused of war crimes he never committed. The political regime of the time sought to erase Lohmeyer as if he never existed. Thus, Edwards pursued the restoration of the memory of Lohmeyer as a way to resist a historical and political tyranny. Chapters three and four tell of Lohmeyer's upbringing, education, his interests in mathematics and aesthetics that built the foundation of his later critical Biblical scholarship, and his courtship with Melie Seyberth, his later wife. Chapters five through eleven reveal Lohmeyer's academic development, family life, and personal reflections in theologically opposing anti-Semitism in academia and supporting his Jewish colleagues in Breslau. Lohmeyer stood for truth and justice and endured opposition. Chapters twelve through fifteen chronicle Lohmeyer's drafting into the German military, how he navigated through the atrocities of war, the complexity of his return to Greifswald, and his arrest and imprisonment by the NKVD. The last chapters, sixteen and seventeen, turn to the correspondence between Lohmeyer and his wife, Melie Seyberth, and share the essential testimony, "the issue of being a moral human being in a world of violence and chaos" (258). Ultimately, Lohmeyer's memory comes alive to modern readers and presents him as a person of faith and character. His honest confession and self-understanding while in prison set him free and conformed his suffering and death with Christ's. Edwards restores Lohmeyer's honor.

Twenty-first century readers from academia and the church, and students in theology will find Edwards' skillfully crafted biography a remarkable work of research. It compels us to carefully discern our own theological engagements, social consciousness, and personal integrity in the context of politics.

Preaching Isaiah's Message Today
Bill Thompson
Joplin, MO: College Press Pub. Co.
2020, 224 pp., paper, $17.99
ISBN: 978-0-8990-0074-9

Reviewed by Rob Fleenor

In *Preaching Isaiah's Message Today*, Bill Thompson explores how to bring the book of Isaiah from the domain of academic debate to the province of an effective pulpit. Thompson's work offers three goals: to bridge the gap between the Old Testament prophets and preaching, to bridge the gap between mainline and evangelical traditions of North American Christianity, and to provide practical examples of sermons as a culmination of his study. The first section of the book provides an overview of prophets and prophecy itself in relation to preaching: their value in scripture, the nuances of the prophets themselves and the works that bear their names, and the particulars related to the interpretation and exegesis of Isaiah. Chapter two provides a useful conceptual framework for the prophets and the books that bear their names, while chapters three and four narrow the focus to issues related specifically to the book of Isaiah. Chapter three surveys the themes appearing in Isaiah, while chapter four wades through the literary-critical issues, particularly in regard to the question of Isaiah's authorship. While Thompson ultimately finds a canonical approach rooted in a high view of scripture to be the most useful for the task of preaching from Isaiah, he presents a solid and fair overview of the issues involved.

The second section shifts toward homiletic concerns and engages the practical aspects of crafting sermons. Chapter six is a discussion of a straightforward template for effective exegetical study and sermon writing, followed by chapter seven's focus on application. Chapter eight returns to an emphasis on a high view of scripture as the foundation of effective preaching. The prophets were who they were precisely because of their perspective about and connection to God's message.

The third section is a sampling of sermon manuscripts from Isaiah, covering well-known passages such as Isaiah 1, 6, 53, etc. While the preaching style may resonate differently for different readers, the sermons clearly reflect the exegesis and writing framework offered in the second section.

Thompson's writing style is straightforward and organized. The book is highly accessible, bypassing the technical language related to Isaianic studies in favor of a colloquial style that still nimbly discusses the academic issues. Many ministry-themed books are often bogged down by bulky illustrations, but that's not the case here. Illustrations are succinct and illuminating rather than overwrought. The discussion throughout the book is well-documented and provides a strong jumping-off point for a deeper academic study on Isaiah.

The content itself would have benefited from more overt discussion regarding the book's second goal of bridging the gap between evangelical and mainline preaching traditions. Much of the book's accomplishment in this area is implicit, expressed primarily through the scholars and preachers selected and Thompson's even-handed navigation of the issues. The print copy reviewed suffered from some minor pixilation on the fonts and headings, an unfortunate production issue. These are small quibbles that detract little from the book's effectiveness.

Thompson's overview is a strong treatment of prophetic identity and offers good material to mine for audiences not used to processing preaching from the Prophets. The book's treatment of Isaiah is broad enough that students, preachers, and motivated laity would benefit from the summary material.

Thompson's book will prove a useful addition to most preachers' libraries. Preaching students will especially benefit from the exegetical process presented in chapters six and seven, a condensed version of which appears as the second appendix. The first two sections include chapter review questions that should prove helpful, particularly to groups discussing the issues the book raises. Thompson's work will benefit anyone wanting a strong introductory overview of Isaiah and the issues involved in translating his message for contemporary audiences.

Acts of Interpretation: Scripture, Theology, and Culture
S.A. Cummins and Jens Zimmerman, eds.
Grand Rapids, MI: Wm. B. Eerdmans Publishing Co.
2018, 240 pp., paperback, $35.00
ISBN: 978-0-8028-7500-6

Reviewed by Zachariah S. Motts

I had high hopes that this would be a book where some of the leading evangelical interpreters come together to wrestle with the questions our culture is asking today and engage with the urgent voices from the broader world of interpretation. *Act of Interpretation* did not meet my hopes. While most articles are well-written and appropriately scholarly, the authors and their "theological interpretation" do not do much to expand the boundaries of evangelical interpretation. Instead of offering us theology as the queen of the sciences, able to take on the hard questions and deal with new data, there is an atmosphere of almost irenic defensiveness where appeals to canon and church seem to justify an inward turn.

One obvious exception to this was the article by Peter Enns, "The Bible, Evolution, and the Journey of Faith" (63-80). Enns faces squarely the implications and challenges that evolutionary theory brings to biblical interpretation. He deserves credit for his perceptivity and courage, but the fact that this point needs to be argued here in the way that it is also serves as a reminder that evangelicals have delayed and avoided open and honest conversations on this topic for a long time. Enns strongly emphasizes the role of extrabiblical information in interpretation, but the other authors do not reach as far for that information as Enns.

There is an emphasis in multiple essays on looking back into church history and pulling on older sources for the *ressourcement* of theology today. To that end, Hans Boersma offers an exploration of allegorical interpretation by drawing on Melito of Sardis and Origen of Alexandria. He opens with the question that is on the minds of moderns when they read allegorical interpretation: is this just an arbitrary way of reading meaning into a text? When Boersma returns to this question at the end of the essay, he has Melito and Origen perform a monologue where they scoff at our modern suspicions and say that the reading that makes sense in "[the church's] liturgical setting and its confession of faith" is merely exposing the deeper, underlying meaning that is "already there" (174). This is an extremely frustrating ending to an otherwise decent essay and does not take seriously the modern difficulty with accepting these interpretations.

I am not opposed to attempts at *ressourcement*, to interpretations that take seriously the theological, canonical, or liturgical settings, or to giving more weight to the life of the community interpreting the text. My problem is that I do not see in this collection as a whole a way forward for evangelicals to engage the broader world. I do not see applications that take seriously the questions modern people cannot help but ask. Just before I read this book, I finished reading Paul Tillich's *Systematic Theology*. I realize that he is not very popular in evangelical circles, but I was struck by something in his work. No matter what you think of the answers he arrived at, Tillich took very seriously and understood well the questions that modern people could not help but ask. As good as many of these essays are, the collection missed opportunities to open the conversation outward to engage our culture today.

George MacDonald in the Age of Miracles: Incarnation, Doubt, and Reenchantment
Timothy Larsen
Downers Grove, IL: IVP Academic
2018, 150 pp., paper, $18.00
ISBN: 978-0-8303-5373-1

Reviewed by Ginger Stelle

Timothy Larsen's *George MacDonald in the Age of Miracles: Incarnation, Doubt, and Reenchantment* is the compilation of three lectures given as part of the Ken and Jean Hansen Lectureship series at Wheaton College during the 2016-17 academic year. This lecture series features one member of Wheaton's faculty presenting three lectures (with responses from other faculty members) on one of the seven Wade Center authors: C.S. Lewis, J.R.R. Tolkien, Dorothy Sayers, George MacDonald, G.K. Chesterton, Owen Barfield, and Charles Williams. This is the second volume to emerge from this lecture series. In it, Larsen examines the works of George MacDonald in the context of key social and theological developments in the Victorian period.

Chapter one, "George MacDonald in the Age of the Incarnation," begins with a discussion of a general midcentury shift in the Anglican church's theological emphasis from the Atonement to Incarnation (12-13). This shift caused the Victorians to place greater emphasis on Christmas (21). Into this context, he places MacDonald, exploring both MacDonald's explicit discussion of these theological matters and his treatment of the Christmas holiday throughout his fiction. The response from James Edward Beitler III briefly applies Larsen's analysis to MacDonald's fantasy novel *Phantastes*.

Chapter two, "George MacDonald and the Crisis of Doubt," challenges the oft-repeated notion of the Victorian "Crisis of Faith," a widespread loss of faith due to increasing secularization and doubt. In contrast, Larsen suggests that, as "the very notion of 'doubt' presupposes a context where faith is the norm" (50), it is more accurate to call the Victorian period "an Age of Faith." For MacDonald, Larsen argues, honest doubt is often a pathway into a deeper, more mature faith in Christ. Larsen supports this with compelling examples from MacDonald's writings, both fiction and literary criticism. The response from Richard Hughes Gibson moves from

Larsen's analysis to explore MacDonald's belief in poetry as the force best suited to draw humanity nearer to the mind of the Creator.

Finally, Chapter three, "George MacDonald and the Reenchantment of the World," tackles MacDonald's theology of sanctification. Drawing on both biographical and literary sources, Larsen argues that despite MacDonald's claim that he thoroughly rejected the Calvinism of his upbringing, he nonetheless retained a life-long belief in God's providence and the sanctifying power of suffering. The response from Jill Pelaez Baumbaertner digs deeper into MacDonald's views by placing him in context with three poets: John Donne, Martin Luther, and William Blake.

Overall, this is an excellent resource for anyone interested in learning more about George MacDonald. Larsen chooses an unusual path in MacDonald scholarship. Whereas the majority of MacDonald scholarship still focuses on MacDonald's fantasies and/or on his influence on C.S. Lewis and others, Larson presents a more balanced look at MacDonald, pulling many of his examples from MacDonald's non-fantasy work, even including his (rarely-cited) works of literary criticism. He considers MacDonald firmly within his Victorian context, shining an important light on aspects of MacDonald's work that would be easy for a twenty-first century audience to overlook. If the book has a downside, it would be that Larsen does not go into much depth about any individual text, choosing instead to highlight the breadth and consistency of MacDonald's oeuvre. However, this approach also makes the overall work more accessible to a general audience. The end result is a book that opens new ground in MacDonald scholarship and which should appeal to both casual and scholarly readers of George MacDonald alike.

1-2 Thessalonians: Zondervan Critical Introductions to The New Testament
Nijay K. Gupta
Series Editor: Michael F. Bird
Grand Rapids, MI: Zondervan Academic
2019, 320 pp., Hardcover, $44.99
ISBN: 978-0310518716

Reviewed by William B. Bowes

1-2 Thessalonians is the first of the volumes released in Zondervan's *Critical Introduction* series, which aims to provide an extended treatment of details often more sparsely addressed in larger New Testament commentaries. The series concerns itself with a thorough engagement of the issues typically relegated to the introductory section of a commentary, namely matters pertaining to the authorship, composition date, audience, socio-historical context, genre, purpose, literary integrity, literary style, structure, argument and history of interpretation of a biblical text. The content thus bears some similarity to the Sheffield New Testament Guides (produced about twenty years ago) and the more recent T&T Clark Study Guides. The length of this volume (at 320 pages) dwarfs the average length of the Sheffield and T&T Clark volumes, and as a result it has the promise of making a unique contribution in terms of its scope as a reference.

Nijay Gupta has been prolific in his writings on Paul, and this volume is nearly twice as long as his 2016 commentary on 1-2 Thessalonians from the New Covenant series. The book is divided into two sections, one for each of the Thessalonian epistles. Each epistle is assigned four chapters, with the first addressing the text of the epistle, the second addressing the background and situation, the third addressing the themes and various methods of interpretation, and the last addressing the history of interpretation. Each chapter is helpfully broken down into headlines and section divisions, which make them easier to follow and can keep a reader engaged who might otherwise be unaccustomed to a more technical volume. In terms of technicality, the book does presume that the reader has some familiarity with Greek, and if one does not, there are sections that require some skimming. These are relatively minor and most of the Greek is translated, but the book is aimed at an exegete with some language experience or otherwise an educated minister or layperson.

Beginning with the first chapter, Gupta lists the most relevant manuscripts of 1 Thessalonians and examines the most significant textual variants, noting where some are more important than others (21-24). Gupta likewise discusses the integrity of the text and the more significant debates of contemporary scholars, such as the difficult question of interpreting 2:13-16 (25). Date and authorship are then explored, with Gupta also surveying recent scholarship regarding matters of style, influence, and structure (27-37). Chapter five follows this same patter with 2 Thessalonians, surveying text-critical issues and including a particularly helpful breakdown of the structure of the letter, which is not always discussed to a detailed extent in many commentaries (189-190). In each instance where a question of interpretation is raised, Gupta does take a position (with varying levels of certainty). However, he is fair to scholars of different views and is respectful in his treatment of their opinions. Because Gupta does propose a conclusion on each matter, the book can have the feel of a commentary (although it is not labeled as such). Gupta is inclusive of a wide spectrum of viewpoints, and when proposing a conclusive position, his tone is never dogmatic.

The second chapter addresses the background and situation of 1 Thessalonians, with Gupta discussing matters such as the scholarly views surrounding the account of Thessalonica in Acts (53-59), the reasons for which Paul wrote the letter (62), and possibilities regarding the meaning of ambiguous words like ἀτάκτους in 5:14 (64-83). In the sixth chapter, where these same issues are covered for 2 Thessalonians, there is also an extended discussion on the controversial aspect of authorship (197-219). The larger treatment of the issue is exceptionally helpful, since 2 Thessalonians is often placed in the "deutero-Pauline" category. What is especially helpful about this analysis is that Gupta (who does hold to Pauline authorship) takes the time to answer the "why" question, explaining the importance of doing the work of coming to a conclusion about issues like authorship (219).

In the third chapter, Gupta identifies various themes in the letter and how these are identified, with some being more pronounced than others (90-106). Gupta's treatment of the most debated interpretive issues in 1 Thessalonians (in this case 2:7b, 2:13-16, 4:4, 4:11 and 5:3) may be the book's most helpful contribution, in that the reader is provided with the broad spectrum of opinions and an evaluation of the reasoning of each. The discussion of themes in 2 Thessalonians is useful, in that the second epistle has some different emphases than the first (232-233), although the two are related (a connection which Gupta explores carefully). The fourth and eighth chapters begin with the apostolic fathers and look at how the letters have been interpreted from early church history, through the reformation, and into the modern era, which helps to nuance the reader's understanding of the letters and put them into a broader perspective.

Gupta's contribution excels in several areas. First, it holds a balance between academic technicality and readability. Second, Gupta's respect for the scripture comes through, but his respect of other more critical scholars comes through as well, and he is fair in discussing and analyzing varying perspectives. Finally, above all, the book is thorough. In 320 extensive pages, the book completes its aim of a wide-ranging array of helpful tools for any person seeking to develop a deeper understanding of the Thessalonian epistles and their interpretation.

The Rise of Network Christianity: How Independent Leaders Are Changing the Religious Landscape
Global Pentecostal and Charismatic Christianity Series
Brad Christerson and Richard Flory
New York, NY: Oxford University Press
2017, 185 pp., hardcover, $27.61
ISBN: 9780190635671

Reviewed by Matthew C. Maresco

Having begun their research looking into the repercussions of the 1906 Azusa Street Revival in the L.A. area (vii), Christerson and Floy quickly realized that the eruption of Pentecostalism across the globe had created new "roots," as it were, for the movement across the United States and it was these new formations that they would need to study in order to understand the current climate of American Charis/Pentecostalism. In order to organize their presentation, the authors coin the phrase, "'Independent Network Charismatic' Christianity," which they refer by the acronym, "INC" (2). The term, "Charismatic," is utilized as the authors do understand that there is a theological line between Pentecostals and Charismatics in America (7-8); however, both can be referred to as "Charismatic" as they "emphasize miracles and physical manifestations of the Holy Spirit" (1).

Early on, the authors state that they chose to focus on four specific organizations, "Bethel, International House of Prayer (IHOP), Harvest International Ministries (HIM), and the Wagner Leadership Institute," because of how frequently mentioned they were (6). Therefore, these four agencies are presented as exemplars of INC Christianity, with various implications drawn from each to build out what they deduced INC truly is. Having been raised in this world, as my parents helped start IHOPKC and were with Mike's church since the late 80s, I was particularly intrigued to see how the authors would depict INC, as I see wide distinctions between the agencies listed.

My questions were abundantly answered as early as page 8, where the authors refer to C. Peter Wagner as a "highly influential INC leader," and begin to discuss his term, "New Apostolic Reformation," exactly equating his term, NAR, with their own INC. Even though they state that their research spanned from at least "2009 to 2016" (6) and involved "a total of forty-one in-depth interviews," (6) which sounds bizarrely low for such a timeframe, it appears that founding their research upon Wagner's work colored their perceptions of the ministries they subsequently engaged with. As it were, they believed they were walking into a singular ecosystem, whereas I would counter that they have cataloged a list of entirely separate planets in a similar solar system.

Regarding their research itself, I can only strongly speak about their sections on IHOPKC, as my knowledge of Bethel and HIM are only second-degree at best. However, turning to it, I found the work to be lacking considering the effort they claim to have given and the fact that it was published by Oxford Press. An early example can be found in their retelling of the arrival of these ministries, where it is evident that they had an "in-depth interview" with Todd Hunter and never verified his perspective with Mike Bickle or John Arnott (23-26). Where they begin to focus on IHOPKC (37), it is barely the second paragraph that they've already mistaken South Kansas City Fellowship, the church Mike began in 1983, with Metro Christian Fellowship, the church that left the Vineyard movement in October of 1996 (37). Added to which, they mention the attendance of Kansas City Chiefs football players at this church, followed immediately by a statement claiming that Bickle "says during that time he was actively anti-Charismatic," (38) which proves difficult considering the Chiefs players began attending because of a miraculous healing under Mike's ministry.

Regarding one of their assessments of IHOPKC, the authors state, "IHOP employs over 3,000 interns who pay from $1,200 to $4,900 to participate in one of five different internship programs," where they spend, "twenty-four hours a week in training for their internship role." Based on this they state, emphasis theirs, *Most of the work at IHOP is undertaken by people whom IHOP does not directly pay—people who in fact pay IHOP for the privilege of serving the organization. (112)* This is outright false. If they had looked into the internships, they would have learned that the internships are focused on theological training rather than work-related activities, that the more expensive internships provide food and housing for its entire duration, and that not a single person on staff pays to work there. So far, I've selected these three examples to demonstrate how their representation ranges from simple mistakes to outright falsehoods, which brings into question their data on the other agencies.

Another highly problematic area is their utilization of the INC umbrella. For example, the authors take two pages to introduce various methods of intercession, a form of prayer, that they claim are "INC strategies." This is problematic as IHOPKC's teaching on intercession directly, and intentionally, condemns the practices outlined by the authors (94), yet labeling them as "INC strategies" while simultaneously calling IHOPKC part of "INC" implies coherence. Another such example is their statement that INC leaders view modern-day apostolic authority/covering (51-53, 115), a view which IHOPKC rejects. Further, they speak of INC as highly financially successful (105-124), mentioning how an event like "Lou Engle's 'Azusa Now,' would be difficult for a denomination like the Southern Baptist Convention to pull off," (155) which fails to recognize that Lou double-mortgaged his house in order to help pay for the conference. It is in a plethora of ways like these that the authors manage to piece together a coherent whole that simply does not exist.

All of this being said, it is impressive to see that the author's assessments of the strengths and weaknesses of the INC, to use their term, are quite valid. Whereas I would argue that a more accurate book title would be, "The Rise of Ministry Christianity," as every entity is its own ministry, rather than a church, their critique of U.S., non-denominational Charis/Pentecostalism finds firm ground on three out of four fronts: The common over-emphasis on the miraculous (125-131), the lack true community (131-34), and the abundant opportunity for corruption and scandal (140-44). Their fourth, which argues that INC lacks the capacity to create long-term societal reform, seems dubious at best. If one must view non-denominational ministries as a coherent whole, then they must also include the non-profit organizations, religious or otherwise, staffed and/ or founded by non-denominational Christians who may not be actively partnering at a corporate level, but are influenced and interact on the peer-to-peer level.

Lastly, from the strengths that the authors list, they draw out four possible adjustments that the broader spectrum of Protestantism could incorporate, and it is my belief that these are excellent starting points for transformation. It could even be considered ironic that the dissemination of these ideas, "offer[ing] a compelling experience of the supernatural"

(160), "create opportunities for public expression of beliefs and practices" (161-62), "allow followers to lead" (162), and "seek new financial models," (163-65), into Protestantism would join in fulfilling what the authors claim INC seeks: not to form a new movement, but reform the old (26). Due to these conclusions, this book can aid in the pursuit of the Protestant future, learning from the failures and successes found within. However, the data the conclusions are drawn from must be corrected and then reassessed if we are to find a true future.

Can "White" People Be Saved?: Triangulating Race, Theology, and Mission
Missiological Engagement Series
Love L. Sechrest, Johnny Ramírez-Johnson, and Amos Yong, eds.
Downers Grove, IL: IVP Academic.
2018, 240 pp., paper, $30.00
ISBN: 978-0-8308-5104-1

Reviewed by Zachariah S. Motts

I am a Caucasian male and I work for an evangelical missionary organization. In many ways, I am in the target demographic of the discussions in this book. Essay after essay in this collection pulls no punches, and they land some strong blows. Many strong blows. The authors challenge the reader over and over to take a long hard look at the ways race, theology, and mission have interacted in the past, have shaped the conversation today, and what sort of view of the future would be a step in the right direction. This book does not dance around discussing the politics of today or where missionaries have failed in the past. It is a very challenging book, a book that I wholeheartedly welcome and wish there were more conversations like this going on in evangelical circles.

The theme of this collection, as seen in the title, centers on the idea of "whiteness." The vocabulary might be provocative, but it pays to listen closely to how this term is defined. William James Jennings stresses that "no one is born white. There is no white biology, but whiteness is real" (34). The conversation here is larger than white supremacy or white nationalism, and it is not restricted to one racial group or another. Ramírez-Johnson and Sechrest write that the discussion centers around *"privilege* as the critical resource mediated in racist societies... resulting in the privilege for those atop the racial hierarchy and unequal treatment, exclusion from legal protections, exploitation, and violence for those lower on the hierarchy" (11). Unfortunately, the authors assert, this kind of privilege, this whiteness, has been tied into Christian history and the modern mission movement.

The essays explore this from many different angles. They span continents and demographics looking at the ways privilege, colonialism, and racism have shaped the contours of missionary work, church structures, and how we think about God. If you have not worked through these issues before, if privilege has been an unconscious part of your world, there is a lot to be uncomfortable about in these pages. There is much to repent of that is brought to the surface. That is an important part of this, but the authors do not just leave things at criticism. Repentance is a first step on a new path forward with a different vision of how Christian mission can happen. Andrew Draper offers four further steps for White folks to resist whiteness:

> second, learning from theological and cultural resources not our own; third, choosing to locate our lives in places and structures in which we are necessarily guests; fourth, tangible submission to non-White ecclesial leadership; and fifth, hearing and speaking the glory of God in unfamiliar cadences (181).

As someone who has worked in an evangelical mission organization for more than a decade, I have seen many failures to live up to these principles and know the temptation to take advantage of the security and power that whiteness offers. I have benefitted from the privileges of whiteness in the systems I have inherited. There are voices here calling us to face some uncomfortable realities. However, to avoid this discussion or continue to mute these voices would be to perpetuate the twisting of mission into a form that cannot transmit the whole gospel. This is an important book for a missiology or church history student to read, but it is also a book that evangelicals need to read an discuss right now. If we wish to continue to value mission, we will have to face the injustices and anti-Christian stance of whiteness. This book offers an excellent starting point.

The Asbury Journal 75/2: 341-347
© 2020 Asbury Theological Seminary

Books Received

The following books were received by the editor's office since the last issue of *The Asbury Journal*. The editor is seeking people interested in writing book reviews on these or other relevant books for publication in future issues of *The Asbury Journal*. Please contact the editor (Robert.danielson@ asburyseminary.edu) if you are interested in reviewing a particular title. Reviews will be assigned on a first come basis.

Athas, George
  2020   *Ecclesiastes, Song of Songs*. The Story of God Bible Commentary. Grand Rapids, MI: Zondervan Academic. ISBN: 978-0-310-49116-3. Price: $39.99.

Banks, Robert J.
  2020   *Paul's Idea of Community: Spirit and Culture in Early House Churches*. Third edition. Grand Rapids, MI: Baker Academic. ISBN: 978-1-5409-6175-4. Price: $26.99.

Bantu, Vince L.
  2020   *A Multitude of All Peoples: Engaging Ancient Christianity's Global Identity*. Missiological Engagements Series. Downers Grove, IL: InterVarsity Press Academic. ISBN: 978-0-8308-5107-2. Price: $35.00.

Barbeau, Jeffrey W.
  2019   *The Spirit of Methodism: From the Wesleys to a Global Communion*. Downers Grove, IL: InterVarsity Press Academic. ISBN: 978-0-8308-5254-3. Price: $20.00.

Beldman, David J. H.
  2020   *Judges*. The Two Horizons Old Testament Commentary. Grand Rapids, MI: Wm. B. Eerdmans. ISBN: 978-0-8028-2701-2. Price: $34.00.

Burge, Gary M. and Gene L. Green
  2020   *The New Testament in Antiquity: A Survey of the New Testament Within Its Cultural Contexts*. Second edition. Grand Rapids, MI: Zondervan Academic. ISBN: 978-0-310-53132-6. Price: $59.99.

Camp, Lee C.
> 2020   *Scandalous Witness: A Little Political Manifesto for Christians.* Grand Rapids, MI: Wm. B. Eerdmans. ISBN: 978-0-8028-7735-2. Price: $19.99.

Carroll, R., M. Daniel
> 2020   *The Bible and Borders: Hearing God's Word on Immigration.* Grand Rapids, MI: Brazos Press. ISBN: 978-1-58743-445-7. Price: $14.99.

Chilcote, Paul Wesley
> 2020   *Singing the Faith: Soundings of Lyrical Theology in the Methodist Tradition.* Nashville, TN: General Board of Higher Education and Ministry of The United Methodist Church. ISBN: 978-1-9459-3563-3. Price: $32.99.

Challies, Tim
> 2020   *Epic: An Around-the-World Journey Through Christian History.* Grand Rapids, MI: Zondervan Academic. ISBN: 978-0-310-32904-6. Price: $19.99.

Chatraw, Joshua D.
> 2020   *Telling a Better Story: How to Talk About God in a Skeptical Age.* Grand Rapids, MI: Zondervan Reflective. ISBN: 978-0-310-10863-4. Price: $18.99.

Cook, John A. and Robert D. Holmsted
> 2020   *Intermediate Biblical Hebrew: An Illustrated Grammar.* Grand Rapids, MI: Baker Academic. ISBN: 978-0-8010-9762-1. Price: $35.00.

Crowe, Brandon D.
> 2020   *The Hope of Israel: The Resurrection of Christ in the Acts of the Apostles.* Grand Rapids, MI: Baker Academic. ISBN: 978-0-8010-9947-2. Price: $29.99.

Elliott, Mark W.
> 2020   *Providence: A Biblical, Historical, and Theological Account.* Grand Rapids, MI: Baker Academic. ISBN: 978-1-5409-6040-5. Price: $29.99.

Elmer, Muriel I., and Duane H. Elmer
> 2020   *The Learning Cycle: Insights for Faithful Teaching from Neuroscience and the Social Sciences.* Downers Grove, IL: InterVarsity Press Academic. ISBN: 978-0-8308-5383-0. Price: $22.00.

Emerson, Matthew Y.
> 2019   *"He Descended to the Dead": An Evangelical Theology of Holy Saturday.* Downers Grove, IL: InterVarsity Press Academic. ISBN: 978-0-8308-5258-1. Price: $30.00.

Firth, David G.
2019   *Including the Stranger: Foreigners in the Former Prophets.* New Studies in Biblical Theology. Downers Grove, IL: InterVarsity Press Academic. ISBN: 978-0-8308-2919-4. Price: $25.99.

Forrest, Benjamin K., Joshua D. Chatraw, Alister E. McGrath, eds.
2020   *The History of Apologetics: A Biographical and Methodological Introduction.* Grand Rapids, MI: Zondervan Academic. ISBN: 978-0-310-55941-2. Price: $59.99.

García-Johnson, Oscar
2019   *Spirit Outside the Gate: Decolonial Pneumatologies of the American Global South.* Missiological Engagements Series. Downers Grove, IL: InterVarsity Press Academic. ISBN: 978-0-8308-5240-6. Price: $32.00.

Germano, Brian E.
2020   *Christianity, The Wesleyan Way: Principles and Practices for Life and Ministry.* Nashville, TN: General Board of Higher Education and Ministry of The United Methodist Church. ISBN: 978-1-9459-3569-5. Price: $27.95.

Gibbs, Jeremiah
2020   *Find Your Place in God's Mission.* Nashville, TN: General Board of Higher Education and Ministry of The United Methodist Church. ISBN: 978-1-9459-3575-6. Price: $16.99.

Gladd, Benjamin L.
2019   *From Adam and Israel to the Church: A Biblical Theology of the People of God.* Essential Studies in Biblical Theology. Downers Grove, IL: InterVarsity Press Academic. ISBN: 978-0-8308-5543-8. Price: $22.00.

González, Justo L.
2020   *Teach Us To Pray: The Lord's Prayer in the Early Church and Today.* Grand Rapids, MI: Wm. B. Eerdmans. ISBN: 978-0-8028-7796-3. Price: $16.99.

Green, Garrett
2020   *Imagining Theology: Encounters with God in Scripture, Interpretation, and Aesthetics.* Grand Rapids, MI: Baker Academic. ISBN: 978-0-5409-6192-1. Price: $36.00.

Harvey, Barry
2020   *Baptists and the Catholic Tradition: Reimagining the Church's Witness in the Modern World. Second edition.* Grand Rapids, MI: Baker Academic. ISBN: 978-1-5409-6079-5. Price: $27.99.

Howell, Adam J., Benjamin L. Merkle, Robert L. Plummer
    2020   *Hebrew for Life: Strategies for Learning, Retaining, and Reviving Biblical Hebrew.* Grand Rapids, MI: Baker Academic. ISBN: 978-1-5409-6146-4. Price: $22.99.

Huebenthal, Sandra
    2020   *Reading Mark's Gospel as a Text from Collective Memory.* Grand Rapids, MI: Wm. B. Eerdmans. ISBN: 978-0-8028-7540-2. Price: $74.99.

Johnson, Luke Timothy
    2020   *Constructing Paul: The Canonical Paul.* Volume One. Grand Rapids, MI: Wm. B. Eerdmans. ISBN: 978-0-8028-0758-8. Price: $50.00.

Kärkkäinen, Veli-Matti
    2020   *Doing the Work of Comparative Theology.* Grand Rapids, MI: Wm. B. Eerdmans. ISBN: 978-0-8028-7466-5. Price: $35.00.

Kling, David W.
    2020   *A History of Christian Conversion.* New York, NY: Oxford University Press. ISBN: 978-0-1999-1092-2. Price: $150.00.

Kruse, Colin G.
    2020   *The Letters of John.* The Pillar New Testament Commentary. Second edition. Grand Rapids, MI: Wm. B. Eerdmans. ISBN: 978-0-8028-7667-6. Price: $40.00.

Lee, Ahmi
    2019   *Preaching God's Grand Drama: A Biblical-Theological Approach.* Grand Rapids, MI: Baker Academic. ISBN: 978-1-5409-6049-8. Price: $22.99.

Lennox, John C.
    2020   *2084: Artificial Intelligence and the Future of Humanity.* Grand Rapids, MI: Zondervan Reflective. ISBN: 978-0-310-10956-3. Price: $19.99.

Levison, Jack
    2020   *A Boundless God: The Spirit According to the Old Testament.* Grand Rapids, MI: Baker Academic. ISBN: 978-1-5409-6118-1. Price: $21.99.

Longenecker, Bruce W.
    2020   *In Stone and Story: Early Christianity in the Roman World.* Grand Rapids, MI: Baker Academic. ISBN: 978-1-5409-6067-2. Price: $32.99.

Longman, Tremper, III
    2020   *The Bible and the Ballot: Using scripture in Political Decisions.* Grand Rapids, MI: Wm. B. Eerdmans. ISBN: 978-0-8028-7734-5. Price: $24.99.

Mayfield, Tyler D.
2020   *Unto Us a Child is Born: Isaiah, Advent, and Our Jewish Neighbors*. Grand Rapids, MI: Wm. B. Eerdmans. ISBN: 978-0-8028-7398-9. Price: $19.00.

Meilaender, Gilbert
2020   *Thy Will Be Done: The Ten Commandments and the Christian Life*. Grand Rapids, MI: Baker Academic. ISBN: 978-1-5409-6196-9. Price: $21.99.

Okesson, Gregg
2020   *A Public Missiology: How Local Churches Witness to a Complex World*. Grand Rapids, MI: Baker Academic. ISBN: 978-0-8010-9807-9. Price: $24.99.

Park, Hirho Y., and M. Kathryn Armistead
2020   *Nevertheless She Leads: Postcolonial Women's Leadership for the Church*. Nashville, TN: General Board of Higher Education and Ministry of The United Methodist Church. ISBN: 978-1-9459-3566-4. Price: $28.99.

Patton, Matthew H. and Frederic Clarke Putnam
2019   *Basics of Hebrew Discourse: A Guide to Working with Hebrew Prose and Poetry*. Grand Rapids, MI: Zondervan Academic. ISBN: 978-0-310-53576-8. Price: $29.99.

Payne, Don J.
2020   *Already Sanctified: A Theology of the Christian Life in Light of God's Completed Work*. Grand Rapids, MI: Baker Academic. ISBN: 978-1-5409-6130-3. Price: $22.99.

Peacock, Barbara L.
2020   *Soul Care in African American Practice*. Downers Grove, IL: InterVarsity Press. ISBN: 978-0-8308-4671-9. Price: $17.00.

Powell, Mark Allan
2020   *Introducción Al Nuevo Testamento: Un Estudio Histórico, Literario y Teológico*. Grand Rapids, MI: Baker Academic. ISBN: 978-0-8010-9969-4. Price: $44.99.

Rasmus, Juanita Campbell
2020   *Learning To Be: Finding Your Center After the Bottom Falls Out*. Downers Grove, IL: InterVarsity Press. ISBN: 978-0-8308-4587-3. Price: $22.00.

Rice, Richard
2020   *The Future of Open Theism: From Antecedents to Opportunities*. Downers Grove, IL: InterVarsity Press Academic. ISBN: 978-0-8308-5286-4. Price: $26.00.

Romero, Robert Chao
    2020   *Brown Church: Five Centuries of Latina/o Social Justice, Theology and Identity.* Downers Grove, IL: InterVarsity Press Academic. ISBN: 978-0-8308-5285-7. Price: $30.00.

Schnelle, Udo
    2020   *The First One Hundred Years of Christianity: An Introduction to its History, Literature, and Development.* Grand Rapids, MI: Baker Academic. ISBN: 978-1-5409-6015-3. Price: $60.00.

Strahan, Joshua
    2020   *The Basics of Christian Belief: Bible, Theology, and Life's Big Questions.* Grand Rapids, MI: Baker Academic. ISBN: 978-1-5409-6201-0. Price: $24.99.

Strauss, Mark L.
    2020   *Four Portraits, One Jesus: A Survey of Jesus and the Gospels.* Second edition. Grand Rapids, MI: Zondervan Academic. ISBN: 978-0-310-52867-8. Price: $59.99.

Thorsen, Don
    2020   *An Exploration of Christian Theology.* Second edition. Grand Rapids, MI: Baker Academic. ISBN: 978-1-5409-6174-7. Price: $39.99.

Vanhoozer, Kevin J. and Owen Strachan
    2015   *The Pastor as Public Theologian: Reclaiming a Lost Vision.* Grand Rapids, MI: Baker Academic. ISBN: 978-1-5409-6189-1. Price: $19.99.

Webb, William J. and Gordon K. Oeste
    2019   *Bloody, Brutal, and Barbaric?: Wrestling with Troubling War Texts.* Downers Grove, IL: InterVarsity Press Academic. ISBN: 978-0-8308-5249-9. Price: $45.00.

Works, Carla Swafford
    2020   *The Least of These: Paul and the Marginalized.* Grand Rapids, MI: Wm. B. Eerdmans. ISBN: 978-0-8028-7446-7. Price: $24.00.

Wilson, Jim L. and Earl Waggoner
    2020   *A Guide to Theological Reflection: A Fresh Approach for Practical Ministry Courses and Theological Field Education.* Grand Rapids, MI: Zondervan Academic. ISBN: 978-0-310-09393-0. Price: $18.99.

Wright, N.T.
    2020   *Interpreting Jesus: Essays on the Gospels.* Collected Essays of N.T. Wright. Grand Rapids, MI: Zondervan Academic. ISBN: 978-0-310-09864-5. Price: $52.99.

Wright, N.T.
  2020   *Interpreting Paul: Essays on the Apostle and His Letters.*
          Collected Essays of N.T. Wright. Grand Rapids, MI:
          Zondervan Academic. ISBN: 978-0-310-09868-3.
          Price: $44.99.

Wright, N.T.
  2020   *Interpreting Scripture: Essays on the Bible and
          Hermeneutics.* Collected Essays of N.T. Wright. Grand
          Rapids, MI: Zondervan Academic. ISBN: 978-0-310-
          09836-2. Price: $52.99.

Yong, Amos
  2019   *Mission After Pentecost: The Witness of the Spirit from
          Genesis to Revelation.* Mission in Global Community.
          Grand Rapids, MI: Baker Academic. ISBN: 978-1-5409-
          6115-0. Price: $29.99.

www.ingramcontent.com/pod-product-compliance
Lightning Source LLC
LaVergne TN
LVHW051109080426
835510LV00018B/1968